Frederick Saunders

**Evenings with the Sacred Poets**

A Series of Quiet Talks About the Singers and their Songs

Frederick Saunders

**Evenings with the Sacred Poets**
*A Series of Quiet Talks About the Singers and their Songs*

ISBN/EAN: 9783744779371

Printed in Europe, USA, Canada, Australia, Japan

Cover: Foto ©Thomas Meinert / pixelio.de

More available books at **www.hansebooks.com**

WITH THE

# SACRED POETS:

A SERIES OF

QUIET TALKS ABOUT THE SINGERS
AND THEIR SONGS.

BY

THE AUTHOR OF

"FESTIVAL OF SONG," "SALAD FOR THE SOLITARY,"
"MOSAICS," ETC.

"The Poets, who, on earth, have made us heirs
Of truth and pure delight, by heavenly lays."

NEW YORK:
ANSON D. F. RANDOLPH AND COMPANY,
770, BROADWAY.
1870.

Entered, according to Act of Congress, in the year 1869, by
A. D. F. RANDOLPH AND COMPANY,
In the Clerk's Office of the District Court of the United States for the Southern District of New York.

CAMBRIDGE:
PRESS OF JOHN WILSON AND SON.

## THE DESIGN OF THIS VOLUME

Is to present, in the most compact form, the essence of all that is most interesting, in anecdote and historic illustration, referring to the sacred poetry and hymnology of the Christian ages. The notes and incidents relating to poet or poem are also enriched and illuminated with brief yet brilliant inspiration-bursts of holy song. All, therefore, who prefer the Muse of Zion to that of Parnassus, will, it is believed, scarcely fail to be charmed with the exaltation of feeling, religious fervor, and rare spiritual beauty that characterize so rich a cabinet of lyrical gems, whatever estimate may chance to be awarded to their setting. In the preparation of a work like the present, — extending over such wide historic distances, and comprising such an accumulation of facts and citations, — occasionally from obscure times and authorities, — — it is almost too much to expect that it should be wholly free from inaccuracies : should any be found, they must solicit the indulgence of the reader.

It may not be improper to add, that this work was projected, and indeed nearly completed, three years ago ; the manuscript being only recently re-arranged, expanded, and revised for publication. By this delay, however, its department of Hymnology has largely profited; the industrious researches which have recently been devoted to that interesting subject having furnished new and valuable information to these pages.

A word of acknowledgment is certainly demanded on behalf of those eminent Authors whose works have been consulted or quoted in the preparation of this volume. In most instances, references have been indicated at the foot of the page containing the extract; but lest, through accident, any passage should have been appropriated without such acknowledgment, it has been thought best to enumerate here the principal authorities. They are the following: Rev. H. W. Beecher's "Life Thoughts," Rev. S. W. Christophers' "Hymn-writers and their Hymns," Rev. C. Rogers's "Lyra Britannica," Mrs. E. B. Browning's ' Essays on the Greek Christian Poets," Mrs. Charles's "Voice of Christian Life in Song," Rev. G. Macdonald's "England's Antiphon," Professor P. Schaff's "Christ in Song," Miss C. Winkworth's "Lyra Germanica" and "Christian Singers of Germany," Rev. J. Miller's "Our Hymns," Archbishop Trench's "Sacred Latin Poetry," Rev. J. Mason Neale's "Greek Hymns," and the Rev. R. A. Willmott's "Lives of the English Sacred Poets."

FREDERICK SAUNDERS.

NEW YORK, October, 1869.

# CLASSIFICATION.

### FIRST EVENING.
BIBLICAL, GREEK, AND EARLY LATIN . . . . . . . . . . 9

### SECOND EVENING.
MEDIÆVAL LATIN . . . . . . . . . . . . . . . . 41

### THIRD EVENING.
GERMAN-REFORMATION ERA . . . . . . . . . . . 79

### FOURTH EVENING.
GERMAN. — THIRTY YEARS' WAR. . . . . . . . . . 119

### FIFTH EVENING.
SWEDISH, FRENCH, SPANISH, &C. . . . . . . . . . 175

### SIXTH EVENING.
EARLY ENGLISH . . . . . . . . . . . . . . . . 217

### SEVENTH EVENING.
LATER ENGLISH . . . . . . . . . . . . . . . . 269

### EIGHTH EVENING.
LATER ENGLISH (*continued*) . . . . . . . . . . . 331

### NINTH EVENING.
MODERN ENGLISH AND AMERICAN . . . . . . . . 393

### TENTH EVENING.
MODERN ENGLISH AND AMERICAN (*continued*) . . . . 437

INDEX OF NAMES . . . . . . . . . . . . . . . 491

# FIRST EVENING.

## BIBLICAL, GREEK, AND EARLY LATIN.

# FIRST EVENING.

## BIBLICAL, GREEK, AND EARLY LATIN.

THE Divine Oracles are the fountain-source of sacred song. "The golden conception of a Paradise is the poet's guiding thought; the bright idea, which has left its glow among the traditions of Eastern and Western nations in many mythical forms, presents itself in the Mosaic books in the form of substantial history; and the conception, as such, is entirely biblical."* While poetry had thus its birthplace in Palestine, where the aspects of nature are so eminently sublime and suggestive, her earliest priesthood — the patriarchal seers and prophets — were also endowed with a Divine inspiration. Need we wonder, therefore, that the loftiest strains of poesy to which the world has ever listened should be the Hebrew, or that its themes and utterances should immeasurably transcend in grandeur and sublimity the highest achievements of the Attic muse? An eloquent writer † has remarked, that "the Bible is a mass of beautiful figures: its words and thoughts are alike poetical. It has gathered around its central truths all natural beauty and interest: it is a temple with one altar and one God, illuminated by a thousand varied lights and studded ornaments. It has substantially but one dec-

\* Isaac Taylor. † Gilfillan.

laration to make, but it utters it in the voices of creation!" Well might Mrs. Browning ask, "Has not love a deeper mystery than wisdom, and a more ineffable lustre than power?" It is this great burden of the Bible — "God is love" — that renders it, alike, so inestimable a treasure, and so unapproachably glorious. Of the Hebrew lyrics enshrined in the sacred volume, the oldest is the song of Lamech: the next — most imposing, perhaps — is that by the great lawgiver, "chanted on the shores of the Red Sea, with a nation for its chorus;" and that triumphant shout of victory — symbolic of the Divine intervention for the spiritual rescue of humanity — has ever since been reverberating, in sweetest echoes, athwart the ages. No less noteworthy are the songs of Deborah, of Balaam, of Hannah, and of Job. For grandeur of conception, majesty of diction, and force of imagery, where shall we find poetry to equal many passages in the four last chapters of the record of the patriarch of Uz? Throughout the prophetic writings, are there not also to be found marvellous bursts of poetic inspiration, of rare beauty and power? The Proverbs are an illustration of the didactic form of Hebrew poetry; the book of Ruth, of the pastoral; and that of Esther, of the dramatic. The Song of Solomon, so replete with Oriental hyperbole, is amongst the most eminently poetic of the Sacred Scriptures. What glowing beauty and exquisite music mingle in its invocation to Spring:

>  Lo! the winter is past,
>  The rain is over and gone;
>  The flowers appear on the earth;
>  The time of the singing of birds is come,
>  And the voice of the turtle
>  Is heard in our land.

David's lamentation over Jonathan is a beautiful illustration of the rhetoric of grief. Again, what can equal that wonderful description of the decline of life, in Ecclesiastes? —

> When the keepers of the house shall tremble,
> And the strong men shall bow themselves,
> And the grinders shall cease because they are few,
> And those that look out of the windows be darkened.

Of the sublime and grand, the following burst from Isaiah is a beautiful example: —

> Who hath measured the waters
> In the hollow of his hand,
> And meted out heaven with the span,
> And comprehended the dust
> Of the earth in a measure,
> And weighed the mountains in scales,
> And the hills in a balance!

Here is an exquisite passage from Habakkuk: —

> Although the fig-tree shall not blossom,
> Neither shall fruit be in the vines;
> The labor of the olive shall fail,
> And the fields shall yield no meat;
> The flock shall be cut off from the fold,
> And there shall be no herd in the stalls, —
> Yet will I rejoice in the Lord,
> I will joy in the God of my salvation!

How intense, full-souled, and spiritual is the book of Psalms! The divine sentiments embalmed in these deathless songs of the minstrel-monarch of Israel have been ever cherished by the Christian as an invaluable repository of consolation and counsel in all times of affliction, and a divine guide and auxiliary to devout aspirations, in seasons of hope and rejoicing.

Said worthy Dr. Donne, "The Psalms are the manna of the Church. Some are imperial psalms, commanding all affection, and spreading themselves over all occasions, — catholic, universal psalms, — that apply themselves to all necessities." The gifted Edward Irving thus eloquently refers to these matchless inspirations: "Where are there such expressions of the varied conditions into which human nature is cast by the accidents of Providence, — such delineations of deep affliction and inconsolable anguish; and, anon, such joy, such rapture, such revelry of emotion, in the worship of the living God? — such invocations to all nature, animate and inanimate; such summonings of the hidden powers of harmony, and of the breathing instruments of melody? David hath dressed out Religion in such a rich and beautiful garment of divine poesy, as beseemeth her majesty; in which being arrayed, she can stand up before the eyes, even of her enemies, in more royal state, than any personification of love or glory or pleasure, to which highly gifted mortals have devoted their genius." And, still more eloquently, a later and greater son of the church * tells us: "David has left no sweeter psalm than the short Twenty-third. It is but a moment's opening of his soul; yet in it are emitted truths of peace and consolation that will never be absent from the world. It is the nightingale of the Psalms: it is small, of a homely feather, singing slyly out of obscurity; but oh! it has filled the whole world with melodious joy greater than the heart can conceive. It has charmed more griefs to rest than all the philosophy of the world; it has poured balm and consolation into the

* H. W. Beecher.

hearts of the dying. Nor will it fold its wing till the last pilgrim is safe, and time ended; and then it shall fly back to the bosom of God, from whence it issued." It was the Fifty-first Psalm that Rogers, the first martyr of English Protestantism, sang, as he passed from his prison to the stake at Smithfield; and who shall enumerate the multitude of Christian pilgrims who have derived spiritual counsel and comfort from these divine utterances? Listen to this sublime chant of adoration, at the commencement of the One-hundred-and-fourth Psalm:—

> Bless the Lord, O my soul!
> O Lord, my God, Thou art very great:
> Thou art clothed with honor and majesty,
> Who coverest Thyself with light as with a garment,
> Who stretchest out the heavens like a curtain,
> Who layest the beams of Thy chambers in the waters,
> Who makest the clouds Thy chariots,
> Who walkest upon the wings of the wind!

What strength and sublimity, too, in this invocation at the close of the Twenty-ninth Psalm:—

> Lift up your heads, O ye gates;
> And be ye lift up, ye everlasting doors;
> And the King of Glory shall come in!
> Who is this King of Glory?
> The Lord strong and mighty,
> The Lord mighty in battle!
> Lift up your heads, O ye gates;
> Even lift them up, ye everlasting doors;
> And the King of Glory shall come in!
> Who is this King of Glory?—
> The Lord of Hosts,—He is the King of Glory!

And how magnificent a spectacle must it have been to see the glittering throng of Jewish worshippers:

as the mighty procession, with their priests and musicians, moved, in stately measures, onward to the gorgeously appointed Temple, chanting this jubilant anthem of praise to Jehovah! —

> I am glad when they say to me,
> Let us go into the House of Jehovah.
> My feet shall stand within thy gates,
>    O Jerusalem!
> Jerusalem is built a compact city,
> House joins to house within it.
> Thither the Tribes go up, the Tribes of Jehovah,
> To the memorial feast for Israel,
> To praise the majesty of Jehovah.
> There stand the thrones of Judgment,
> The thrones which the King hath established.
> Pray for the peace of Jerusalem,
> They shall prosper that love thee.
> Peace be within thy walls,
> And tranquillity within thy palaces:
> For my brethren and companions' sakes,
> I will say, Peace be within thee;
> Because of the Temple of our God,
> I will seek thy good. *

We learn, from the experience of the centuries, how precious a relic the minstrel-monarch of Israel bequeathed to the Church, in his Psalms. According to Dean Stanley, Sir Patrick Hume beguiled the weary hours of his imprisonment by repeating to himself Buchanan's version of the Psalms, which he had committed to memory. Augustine was consoled, on his conversion, and on his death-bed, by their sweet solace; and Chrysostom, Athanasius, Savonarola, and many others like them, were cheered and sustained thereby amid sore persecution. How many, like Polycarp, and Jerome of Prague, or Jewel and Me-

---
* Herder's paraphrase.

lancthon, expired with the words of a psalm upon their lips? The sixty-eighth Psalm cheered Cromwell's soldiers to victory at Dunbar; and others formed the basis of the brave war-lyrics of the heroic Luther.

David, it has been beautifully said, " has bequeathed us so many psalms in which the waiting, contrite souls, of ages so remote, and races so diverse, as ours from his, find a fuller and fitter expression of their aspirations and their needs, than all the piety and genius of intervening ages have been able to indite. Yes, this untaught shepherd-son of Jesse, this leader in many a sanguinary fight, this man of a thousand faults, knew how to sweep the cords of the human heart, as few or none have ever touched them before or since, — to take that heart, with all its frailty, its error, its sin, and lay it penitently, pleadingly, at the footstool of its Maker and Judge, and teach it by what utterances, in what spirit, to implore forgiveness and help. Other thrones have their successions, dynasties, their races of occupants; but David reigns unchallenged king of Psalmody till time shall be no more." *

" How strange it seems, to fall upon those wonderful lyrics in the Psalms of David, singing to us out of the rude ages of the past, where we naturally expect harshness and severity! How wonderful that our age should go back to this old warrior to learn tenderness! — that the most exquisite views of Divine compassion should spring forth from the world's untrained periods; — from Moses, the shepherd and legislator of the desert; and from David, the sweet

* Horace Greeley.

singer of Israel, whose hand was mightiest among the mighty, whether laid upon the strings of the bow or of the harp." *

The majestic grandeur of the Mosaic record of creation was not unnoticed, even by that noble Greek philosopher, Longinus, who thus curiously cites the passage, in his treatise on the Sublime:—

> And God said — What? Let there be light!
> And there was light!
> Let the earth be!—and the earth was!

Kindred examples of sublimity might be quoted from the New Testament: let one suffice, — the Divine invocation, —

> Lazarus, come forth!

The three Christian songs of primitive times were those of the Virgin, of Zacharias, and of Simeon. These, it has been beautifully said,† formed, "The first triad of Christian hymns, the three matin-songs of Christianity. Ere another was added to the sacred list, the great victory, which had thus been sung, had to be won, — not with songs, but with 'strong crying and tears,' and unutterable anguish, — by one dying, human voice, speaking in darkness from the cross, 'It is finished!'" Yet are these dying-words the fountain-head of every hymn of joy and triumph, which men have ever sung since Eden was closed, or ever will sing throughout eternity.

The sweetest melody that ever echoed from the skies was the ecstatic hymn of the angel-band, on the plains of Bethlehem, announcing the grace of Heaven to our sin-smitten earth:—

---

\* H. W. Beecher.   † Christian Life in Song.

Glory to God in the highest,
On earth peace, good-will toward men!

Jude's closing benediction is a beautiful burst of poetic grandeur: —

Now unto Him that is able to keep you from falling,
And to present you faultless before the presence
Of His glory, with exceeding joy, —
To the only wise God, our Saviour,
Be glory and majesty, dominion and power,
Both now and ever, Amen.

"Its divine Author made the Bible not only an instructive book, but an attractive one: He filled it with marvellous incident and engaging history, — with sunny pictures from Old-World scenery, and affecting anecdotes from the patriarchal times. He replenished it with stately argument and thrilling verse; He made it a book of lofty thoughts and noble images, — a book of heavenly doctrine, but withal of earthly adaptation."\* "As a skilful musician, called to execute alone some masterpiece, puts his lips, by turns, to the mournful flute, the shepherd's-reed, the mirthful pipe, and the war-trumpet; so the Almighty God, to sound in our ears His eternal word, has selected, from of old, the instruments best suited to receive, successively, the breath of His Spirit. Thus we have, in God's great anthem of Revelation, the sublime simplicity of John; the argumentative, elliptical, soul-stirring energy of Paul; the fervor and solemnity of Peter; the poetic grandeur of Isaiah; the lyric moods of David; the ingenuous and majestic narratives of Moses; and the sententious and royal wisdom of Solomon. Yes, it was all this — it was Peter, Isaiah, Matthew, John, or Moses; but it was God." †

In passing from the "goodly fellowship of the prophets," to the "company of the apostles," we come to the wondrous Apocalyptic vision of Patmos. Here metaphor, symbol, and trope revel in richest exuberance and prodigality of beauty and grandeur. In all the realm of Poesy, there are no passages more truly sublime than are to be found in the Apocalypse, the closing book of the sacred canon. An eloquent ecclesiastical historian * compares it, on this account, to the grand altar-window of the great Temple of Truth, or of a cathedral, through which gleams gorgeous imagery of richly variegated hues, diffusing a celestial glory over the earthly sanctuary. May not this beautiful figure be applied, at least in a subordinate sense, to all true sacred poetry; since its themes are, for the most part, those of supernal grandeur, — not limited to the affairs of our present estate of being, but also pertaining to our immortality?

---

How beautiful is genius, when combined
With holiness, — O, how divinely sweet
The tones of earthly harp, whose chords are touched
By the soft hand of Piety, and hung
Upon Religion's shrine ! †

Such noble service has been rendered by multitudes of loving and gifted spirits, whose beautiful melodies, thus consecrated to the sublimest of all themes, and to the highest instincts of our being, are still echoing through the ages, and will ever continue to find a living response in all Christian hearts. Many of those sweet singers belong to the noble army of martyrs and confessors, — men of spiritual might and prowess, — victors

* Mahan. † Wilson.

who have fought valiantly for truth and virtue, in times of darkness and peril. To the ear rightly attuned, some of those grand choral harmonies of the early centuries, as well as the heroic stanzas of the lion-hearted Luther, come laden to us with inexpressible sweetness and power. These minstrelsies are enshrined in the bosom of the Church catholic, as the precious legacy of her departed saints and sages; and all who cherish a hope in the beatitudes of Heaven, will love to linger fondly over these beautiful and expressive utterances. They are the experiences of patient faith in times of sad unrest, — the plaintive "songs in the night" of sorrow, as well as of the alternations of ecstatic bursts of joy. The type of early Christian life which they reveal, is identical, in all its phases, with that of our own time. How can we, then, too highly prize these sacred relics of the past? Yes: the Christian of our own time is stirred by the same antagonisms of flesh and spirit, conscious of the same keen conflict between sin and grace, drawn onward by the same hopes, prompted to action by the same aspirations, and borne aloft by the same impulsive motives. Despite the mental activity and intellectual development of the nineteenth century, we find ourselves on the same platform of faith and hope, and love, with those whose spiritual condition and progress were described centuries ago. The continuous stream of hallowed poesy flows on; age after age lifts up its voice; voice after voice takes up the subject; and it is perpetuated with but a varied rhythm, and in, perhaps, a slightly varied key. The earliest known Christian hymn is that ascribed to Clement, Bishop of Alexandria, who suffered martyrdom A.D. 217. Fragments of still earlier date meet us in the older liturgies; but this Greek hymn is the one complete relic of the worship of the close of the second century. It is remarkable for its quaintly interwoven imagery, under which our Saviour is impersonated. It is also remarkable for its glowing beauty and archaic simplicity. We subjoin some portions of the English rendering by the Rev. Mr. Plumptre: —

> Shepherd of sheep that own
> Their Master on the throne,
> Stir up Thy children meek
> With guileless lips to speak,
> In hymn and song, Thy praise,
> Guide of their infant ways.
> O King of saints, O Lord!
> Mighty, all-conquering Word;
> Son of the highest God,
> Wielding His Wisdom's rod;
> Our stay when cares annoy,
> Giver of endless joy;
> Of all our mortal race
> Saviour of boundless grace, —
>    O Jesus, hear.
>
> . . . .
>
> Lead us, O Shepherd true,
> Thy mystic sheep, we sue:
> Lead us, O holy Lord,
> Who from Thy sons dost ward,
> With all-prevailing charm,
> Peril and curse and harm;
> O Path where Christ hath trod,
> O Way that leads to God,
> O Word abiding aye,
> O endless Light on high,
> Mercy's fresh-springing flood,
> Worker of all things good,
> O glorious Life of all
> That on their Maker call, —
>    Christ Jesus, hear.

Of Clement's personal history scarcely any thing is known, except that he lived in times of terrible persecution; having been himself obliged at length to flee for his life, from Alexandria. The few words following, from one of his homilies, will serve to commend his saintship to our hearty friendship and regard: "Prayer, if I may speak so boldly, is intercourse with God. Even if we do but lisp, even though we silently address God without opening our lips, yet we cry to Him in the inmost recesses of the heart; for God always listens to the sincere direction of the heart to Him." The "Gloria in Excelsis" is probably traceable to an earlier date than that of Clement, — its exact origin not being determined; at all events, it is a precious heirloom in the household of faith; linking, like the divine oracles, the faith and worship of the primitive, with the present age of the Church.

After Clement, we have no account of any other Greek hymnist till Ephræm Syrus, a monk of Mesopotamia, — "that land beyond the flood," in which the "father of the faithful" was called to be a pilgrim. Ephræm is supposed to have died about A.D. 378. The songs of this Syrian saint are regarded, by critics, as among the finest of the Greek Church, being characterized by deep devotional feeling, and force and beauty of imagery. Here are some examples from Daniel's German version of the Syriac: —

>    The heavens in their quiet beauty
>      Praise Thy essential majesty!
>    The heights rejoice, from whence Thou camest,
>      The depths spring up to welcome Thee!
>    The sea exults to feel Thy footsteps,
>      The land Thy tread, Lord, knoweth well;

Our human nature brings thanksgivings
  Because Thy Godhead there doth dwell!
To-day the sun, rejoicing, shineth,
  With happy radiance, tenfold bright,
In homage to that Sun of Glory
  Who brings to all the nations light!
The moon shall shed her fairest lustre,
  O'er all the heavens her softest glow,
Thee, on her radiant heights adoring,
  Who for our sakes hast stooped so low!
And all the starry hosts of heaven,
  In festive robes of light arrayed,
Shall bring their festal hymns, as offerings
  To Him who all so fair hath made.
To-day the forests are rejoicing;
  Each tree its own sweet anthem sings,
Because we wave their leafy branches
  As banners for the King of kings! *

The following funeral hymn by this sweet Syrian singer, formerly sung at the death of children, is replete with touching pathos, and beautifully portrays the strife of Christian faith with natural affection, and the triumph of the former in resignation: —

Child, by God's sweet mercy given to thy mother and to me, —
Entering this world of sorrows, by His grace, — so fair to see:
Fair as some sweet flower in summer, till Death's hand on thee was laid,
Scorched the beauty from my flower, made the tender petals fade.
Yet I dare not weep nor murmur, for I know the King of kings
Leads thee to His marriage-chamber, — to the glorious bridal brings.
Nature fain would leave me weeping, love asserts her mournful right;
But I answer, they have brought thee to the happy world of light!
And I fear that my lamentings, as I speak thy cherished name,
Desecrate the Royal dwelling, — fear to meet deservèd blame,
If I press with tears of anguish into the abode of joy;
Therefore, will I, meekly bowing, offer thee to God, my boy!

* Mrs. Charles's translation.

Yet thy voice, thy childish singing, soundeth ever in my ears;
And I listen, and remember, till mine eyes will gather tears,
Thinking of thy pretty prattlings, and thy childish words of love;
But when I begin to murmur, then my spirit looks above, —
Listens to the songs of spirits; listens, longing, wondering,
To the ceaseless glad hosannas angels at thy bridal sing.*

Gregory, of Nazianzum, ascetic in heart though he was, seems never to have forgotten the genial influences of home, or the inspiring faith of his saintly mother. He lived in troublous times: "The outward attacks of Julian, the apostate, were," as Gregory himself says, "almost a rest, compared with the bitter inward strife of sects and heresies." Through all these perplexities, Gregory Nazianzen, Basil the Great, and Gregory of Nyssa, the three Cappadocian Fathers, had to wend their way; and out of them all, by means of Basil's brother, — Gregory of Nyssa, — has been evolved for us the simple doctrine of the Nicene creed. From amid the tumult of such stirring scenes, such sweetly-syllabled utterances as these come welling up to us from that far-off distance. It is an evening hymn: —

Christ, my Lord, I come to bless Thee, now when day is veiled in night;
Thou, who knowest no beginning, Light of the Eternal Light!
. . . . . . . .
Thou hast set the radiant heavens with Thy many lamps of brightness,
    Filling all the vaults above;
Day and night in turn subjecting to a brotherhood of service,
    And a mutual law of love!

Our last selection from Gregory shall be from his lament over the weakness and desolateness of his old age: —

* Christian Life in Song.

Where are the winged words? Lost in the air.
Where the fresh flower of youth and glory? Gone!
The strength of well-knit limbs? Brought low by care.
Wealth? Plundered: none possess but God alone!
Where those dear parents, who my life first gave, —
And where that holy twain, brother and sister? In the grave!

. . . . . . . .

But Thou, O Christ, my King, art fatherland to me:
Strength, wealth, eternal rest, — yea, all, — I find in Thee!

Here is the opening of one of the hymns or odes of Synesius. The translation is by the author of " The Cathedral."

Come, sweet harp, resounding Teian strains of yore,
With soft airs abounding round the Lesbian shore,
Doric shell, awake thy soft themes no more.
Talk no more of maiden fair with beauty's wiles,
Youth with blessings laden, whom new life beguiles,
Smiling as it flies, flying as it smiles.
Wisdom, which ne'er wrongeth, born of God above,
Toils in birth, and longeth your sweet chords to prove,
And hath bid me flee woes of earthly love.
What is strength or glory, beauty, gold, or fame?
What renown in story, or in kingly name,
To the thoughts of God, — cares which bring not blame?
One o'er steeds is bending, one his bow hath strung,
One his gold is tending; one by youth is sung,
With bright looks, and locks o'er his shoulders flung.
Mine be the low portal, paths in silence trod,
Knowing not things mortal, — knowing things of God;
While still at my side Wisdom holds her rod, —
Wisdom youth adorning, Wisdom cheering age;
Wisdom, wealth's best warning, want's best heritage,
Poverty herself shall with smiles engage.

Synesius of Cyrene, afterwards of Ptolemais, is considered, for his endowments, chief of the poets of the Greek Church: he was, however, too deeply tinctured with the Platonic philosophy to be regarded as a true Christian poet.

St. Anatolius, of Constantinople, who lived in the fifth century of the Christian era, wrote the following terse hymn. The translation is by the lamented J. Mason Neale.

> Fierce was the wild billow, dark was the night,
> Oars labored heavily, foam glimmered white;
> Mariners trembled, peril was nigh:
> Then said the God of God, "Peace, it is I!"
>
> . . . . .
>
> Jesu, Deliverer! come Thou to me;
> Soothe Thou my voyaging over life's sea:
> Thou, when the storm of death roars sweeping by,
> Whisper, O Truth of Truth, "Peace, it is I!"

Andrew, of Crete, who lived in the early part of the seventh century, is the author of the following extracts from "The Great Canon of the Mid-Lent Week." The entire poem extends to over three hundred verses.

> Whence shall my tears begin?
>   What first-fruits shall I bear
> Of earnest sorrow for my sin?
>   Or how my woes declare?
> O Thou, the merciful and gracious One!
> Forgive the foul transgressions I have done.
>
> . . . . .
>
> If Adam's righteous doom,
>   Because he dared transgress
> Thy one decree, lost Eden's bloom
>   And Eden's loveliness,
> What recompense, O Lord! must I expect,
> Who all my life thy quickening laws neglect?

Another eminent ecclesiastical poet of the East, Cosmas, the Hierosolymite, surnamed "the melodist," is the author of the following majestic and glowing stanzas : —

> In days of old, on Sinai the Lord Jehovah came,
> In majesty of terror, in thunder-cloud and flame ! —
> On Tabor, with the glory of sunniest light for rest,
> The excellence of beauty in Jesus was expressed.
> All hours and days inclined there, and did Thee worship meet ;
> The sun himself adored Thee, and bowed him at Thy feet :
> While Moses and Elias upon the Holy Mount
> The coeternal glory of Christ our God recount.
> O holy, wondrous vision ! but what, when this life past,
> The beauty of Mount Tabor shall end in Heaven at last ?
> But what, when all the glory of uncreated light
> Shall be the promised guerdon of them that win the fight ?

Theophanes, who, with the exception of St. Joseph of the Studium, was the most prolific of Oriental hymnographers, furnishes to us a beautiful conceit in the following stanza : —

> O glorious Paradise ! O lovely clime !
> O God-built mansions ! Joy of every saint !
> Happy remembrance to all coming time !
> Whisper, with all thy leaves, in cadence faint,
> One prayer to Him who made them all,
> One prayer for Adam in his fall ! —
> That He, who formed thy gates of yore,
> Would bid those gates unfold once more,
>  That I had closed by sin ;
>  And let me taste that holy tree
>  That giveth immortality
>  To them that dwell therein !
> Or have I fallen so far from grace,
> That mercy hath for me no place ?

The following extract is from an anthem by the same :

> Let our choir new anthems raise ;
>  Wake the morn with gladness :
> God Himself to joy and praise
>  Turns the martyrs' sadness.

This the day that won their crown,
Opened Heaven's bright portal;
As they laid the mortal down,
And put on the immortal!

. . . .

Up, and follow, Christian men!
Press through toil and sorrow!
Spurn the night of fear, and then, —
Oh, the glorious morrow!
Who will venture on the strife?
Blest who first begin it!
Who will grasp the land of life?
Warriors! up, and win it!

Another member of the Studium, Theoclistus, of the ninth century, is the author of these grand lines, translated by Dr. Neale: —

Jesu, — name all names above, — Jesu, best and dearest, —
Jesu, fount of perfect love, — holiest, tenderest, nearest!
Jesu, source of grace completest, — Jesu, purest, Jesu, sweetest,
Jesu, well of power divine, — make me, keep me, seal me, — Thine!
Thou didst call the prodigal, Thou didst pardon Mary:
Thou, whose words can never fail, love can never vary, —
Lord, amidst my lost condition, give — for thou canst give — contrition.
Thou canst pardon all mine ill, — if Thou wilt: oh, say, "I will"!
Woe, that I have turned aside after fleshly pleasure!
Woe, that I have never tried for the heavenly treasure!
Treasure, safe in homes supernal, — incorruptible, eternal!
Treasure, no less price hath won, than the passion of the Son!

John Damascenus, contemporary with the preceding, is the author of these spirit-stirring lines, translated by Mrs. Browning: —

From my lips, in their defilement,
From my heart, in its beguilement,
From my tongue, which speaks not fair,
From my soul, stained everywhere,
O my Jesus, take my prayer!

Spurn me not for all it says, —
Not for words, and not for ways,
Not for shamelessness endured ;
Make me brave to speak my mood,
  O my Jesus, as I would !
Or teach me, which I rather seek,
What to do and what to speak.
I have sinnèd more than she
Who, learning where to meet with thee,
And bringing myrrh, — the highest priced, —
Anointed bravely, from her knee,
Thy blessed feet; accordingly,
My God, my Lord, my Christ !
As Thou saidest not, " Depart,"
To that suppliant from her heart,
Scorn me not, O Word that art
The gentlest one of all words said ;
But give Thy feet to me instead,
That tenderly I may them kiss,
And clasp them close, and never miss,
With over-dropping tears, as free
And precious as that myrrh could be,
T' anoint them bravely from my knee !

Among the magnificent canons, or long hymns, which are the glory of the Eastern Church, we select the celebrated " Hymn of Victory," by St. John of Damascus, sung immediately after midnight on Easter morning, during the symbolical ceremony of lighting the tapers : —

'Tis the day of Resurrection ! earth, tell it all abroad !
The Passover of gladness ! the Passover of God !
From death to life eternal, from earth unto the sky,
Our Christ hath brought us over, with hymns of victory !
Our hearts be pure from evil, that we may see aright
The Lord, in rays eternal of Resurrection light ;
And, listening to His accents, may hear so calm and plain
His own " All Hail ! " and hearing, may raise the victor strain.

Now let the heavens be joyful; let earth her song begin;
Let the round world keep triumph, and all that is therein!
Invisible or visible, their notes let all things blend;
For Christ the Lord hath risen, our joy that hath no end! *

One of the grandest outbursts of sacred song which Dr. M. Neale has rescued from the long-buried past, is the following, by Stephen, of the Monastery of S. Sabbas: —

Art thou weary, art thou languid, art thou sore distrest?
"Come to me," saith One, — and "coming, be at rest!"
Hath He marks to lead me to Him, — if He be my Guide?
In His feet and hands are wound-prints, and His side!
Is there diadem, as monarch, that His brow adorns?
Yea: a crown, in very surety, — but of thorns!
If I find Him, if I follow, what His guerdon here?
Many a sorrow, many a labor, many a tear!
If I still hold closely to Him, what hath He at last?
Sorrow vanquished, labor ended, Jordan past!
If I ask Him to receive me, will He say me nay?
Not till earth, and not till heaven pass away!
Tending, following, keeping, struggling, is He sure to bless?
Angels, martyrs, prophets, pilgrims, answer, Yes!

The last-named singer, with others, continued to prolong the voice of song in the Eastern Church, "whilst the terrible flood was gathering in Arabia, which was so soon to sweep over Christendom, and altogether to desolate and submerge its eastern half. But before that sacred music was silenced, its tone had long begun to ring less clear. Invocations to the 'Mother of God' — 'the All-holy' — crowd thicker and thicker on these later hymns; and if Mohammedanism had not broken all the strings at once, there seems a danger that they would have fallen of themselves into more and more jarring discord. Perhaps the very

* Quarterly Review.

agony of that great desolation tuned many a heart to music it had not known before." * The last singer from the Orient we shall cite, is Phile, who, indeed, is about the last of his order, living at the opening of the fourteenth century. We are indebted for the English version of the following to the accomplished pen of Mrs. Browning: —

> O living Spirit! O falling of God-dew,
> O grace which dost console us, and renew,
> O vital light, O breath of angelhood,
> O generous ministration of things good!
> Creator of the visible, and best
> Upholder of the Great Unmanifest!
> Power infinitely wise, new boon sublime
> Of science and of art, constraining might,
> In whom I breathe, live, speak, rejoice, and write, —
> Be with us in all places, for all time!

In turning to the Western Church, we find the sacred melodies somewhat changed in character; the Latin hymns possessing a rugged grandeur of expression, while they are often deficient in the elegant graces of the Greek, — the language in which Christianity first announced its mission to the world. In the words of an eminent critic,† "The fire of Revelation, in its strong and simple energy, by which, as it were, it rends the rock, and bursts the icy barriers of the human heart, predominates in those oldest pieces of the sacred Latin poesy which are comprised in the Ambrosian hymnology, — a species of song which moves in simplest tones, and seldom uses rhyme."

Of the "Tersanctus," or thrice holy, all we know is, that it has been traced in the earliest known liturgies. The grand anthem "Te Deum Laudamus," according

---

* Christian Life in Song.   † Fortlage.

to tradition, gushed forth in sudden inspiration from the lips of Ambrose, as he baptized Augustine; or other authorities, who reject the legend, believe it to have sprung from an earlier Oriental hymn. If so, might it not possibly have formed part of the worship of the primitive Christians, who, in the time of Pliny, "met before dawn, to sing hymns to Christ, as God?" * That same "Te Deum" has accompanied many a martyr to the stake, in Flanders, Bavaria, Germany, England, and elsewhere. It was the English Bishop Fisher's farewell as he stood beside the block. Once it was lifted up where no lesser hymn would have been fitting, — when Columbus discovered the first gray outline of the New World, and "the crew threw themselves into each other's arms, weeping for joy!" There is an old custom still perpetuated at Magdalen College, Oxford, at the dawn of May-day, when the "Te Deum" is sung in the original Latin, from the tower of the college.† St. Ambrose, born about 340, and probably at Treves, was made bishop of Milan A.D. 374. He died in 397. The hymns that go under his name are very numerous; but only twelve are admitted, by the Benedictine editors, to be from his pen. Ambrose reflected in his poetry, not only the piety, but also the troublous character, of the times in which he lived, — when Christianity was especially militant, being arrayed in direct conflict with heathenism and the Arian heresy.

* "Carmenque Christo, quasi Deo!" — *Pliny*, lib. x.
† An incident in the history of the great Robert Hall serves to set forth the native majesty of the "Te Deum," and its close conformity to the spirit and manner of inspired psalms. He had composed a sermon on a text which had touched his fine sense of grandeur, and had deeply moved his heart. On completing his sermon, he turned to the Concordance to find the text: it was not to be found: it was not in the Bible. It was a sentence from the "Te Deum," — "All the earth doth worship Thee, the Father everlasting."

The practice of responsive chanting, called "Antiphonal," used, it is believed, by Chrysostom, during vigils, in the Eastern Church, was thence introduced into the Western Church.* Contemporary with Ambrose, lived some notable Christian singers, — such as Augustine, Hilary of Poictiers, and Prudentius. In Augustine's "Confessions," which, although written in prose, are eminently poetical, he reveals to us something of the deep spiritual emotion with which he participated in the choral service of his times, where he says, "How did I weep, through the hymns and canticles, touched to the quick by the voices of Thy sweet-attunèd church. The voices sank into mine ears, and the truth distilled into mine heart; whence the affections of my devotions overflowed, — tears ran down, and happy was I therein." The following lines are ascribed to Ambrose, by Augustine : —

Maker of all, the Lord and Ruler of the height!
Who, robing day in light,
Hast poured soft slumbers o'er the night;
That to our limbs the power of toil may be renewed,
And hearts be raised, that sink and cower, and sorrows be subdued.

Augustine presents a beautiful type of character, — the happy union of mental power with childlike humility. He has not left us hymns, but he has embalmed his spirit in noble prose; and he takes rank with the illustrious, in the archives of Christianity. Of the introduction into the church at Milan, of the choral service, he says, — "It was a year, or not much more, that Justina, mother to the emperor Valentinian, then a child, persecuted Thy servant Ambrose, in favor of her heresy, to which she was seduced by the Arians.

---
\* Christopher's Hymn-writers.

The devout people kept watch in the church, ready to die with their bishop, Thy servant. There my mother, Thy handmaid, bearing a chief part in those anxieties and watchings, lived for prayer. We, yet unwarmed by the heat of Thy Spirit, still were stirred up by the sight of the amazed and disquieted city. Then it was instituted (in the church at Milan) that, after the manner of the Eastern churches, hymns and psalms should be sung, lest the people should wax faint through the tediousness of sorrow ; and from that day to this, the custom is retained."

Let us now in imagination listen to the little saintly groups of early morning worshippers, chanting, in the grand sonorous Latin, the following hymn of St. Hilary of Arles : —

  Thou bounteous Giver of the light,
   All-glorious, in whose light serene,
  Now that the night has passed away,
   The day pours back her sunny sheen.
  Thou art the world's true Morning Star !
   Not that which, on the edge of night, —
  Faint herald of a little orb,
   Shines with a dim and narrow light ;
  Far brighter than our earthly sun,
   Thyself at once the Light and Day !
  The inmost chambers of the heart
   Illumining with heavenly ray.

   . . . . .

  Be every evil lust repelled,
   By guard of inward purity,
  That the pure body evermore
   The Spirit's holy shrine may be.
  These are our votive offerings,
   This hope inspires us as we pray,
  That this our holy matin light
   May guide us through the busy day.

Listen to part of an Easter hymn, ascribed to Ambrose: —

> This is the very day of God! —
> Serene with holy light it came, —
> In which the stream of sacred blood
>    Swept over the world's crime and shame.
> Lost souls with faith once more it filled,
>    The darkness from blind eyes dissolved;
> Whose load of fear, too great to yield,
>    Seeing the dying thief absolved!
>
> . . . . .
>
> O admirable Mystery!
> The sins of all are laid on Thee:
> And Thou, to cleanse the world's deep stain,——
> As man, dost bear the sins of men.
> What can be ever more sublime!
> That grace might meet the guilt of time,
> Love doth the bonds of fear undo,
> And death restores our life anew! *

Here is the commencement of another Ambrosian hymn on the Ascension of our Lord: —

> At length, the longed-for joy is given,
>    The sacred day begins to shine,
>    When Christ, our God, our Hope divine,
> Ascends the radiant steep of Heaven!
> Ascending where He used to be,
>    The Lord resumes His ancient throne:
>    The heavenly realms with joys unknown,
> Only-begotten, welcome Thee!
> The mighty victory is wrought,
>    The prince of this world lieth low;
>    The Son of God presenteth now
> The human flesh in which He fought.
> High o'er the clouds He comes to reign,
>    Gives hopes to those who in Him trust:
>    The Paradise which Adam lost,
> He opens wide to man again.*

\* Mrs. Charles's translation.

"Whilst undisguised Paganism still lingered in Christendom, and Bibles were scarce and readers rare, there was a beautiful and practical meaning in linking the passing hours with Heaven, thus making Time himself read aloud the gospel history, and converting the seasons of the year into a kind of pictorial Bible for the poor. For it must always be remembered that the early Latin hymns were no mere recreations of monastic literary retirement, but sacred popular songs, in a language, probably, as little varying from the common speech of the people then, as the book-Italian of to-day from the various spoken dialects of Milan, Genoa, and Venice. They were not merely read by priests out of missals, or chanted by elaborate choirs in cathedrals; but, as St. Ambrose and St. Augustine tell us, were murmured by the people at their work, and in their homes, and sung in grand choruses in the great congregation." *

Let us now recite a portion of a funeral hymn by Prudentius : —

>Ah! hush now your mournful complainings,
>  Nor mothers your sweet babes deplore ;
>This death, we so shrink from, but cometh
>  The ruin of life to restore.
>Who now would the sculptor's rich marble,
>  Or beautiful sepulchres crave ?
>We lay them but here, in their slumber :
>  This earth is a couch, not a grave.
>
>. . . . . .
>
>The seed, which we sow in its weakness,
>  In the spring shall rise green from the earth ;
>And the dead we thus mournfully bury,
>  In God's spring-time again shall shine forth.

* Christian Life in Song.

> Mother Earth, in thy soft bosom cherish
>   Whom we lay to repose in thy dust;
> For precious these relics we yield thee;
>   Be faithful, O Earth! to thy trust.
> The happy and just times are coming,
>   When God every hope shall fulfil;
> And visibly then must thou render
>   What now in thy keeping lies still.

In parting company with the Greek and early Latin hymnists, we cannot, perhaps, better close our first evening's talk, than by quoting a passage from a valuable work, to which we may have often to refer, and which we now take the liberty to commend to the notice of the reader.\* We have thus sought to trace the stream from its fountain source to the fourth Christian century; and thus far it seems to have preserved its purity. These spiritual songs are fragrant with the aroma of that "Name which is above every name." There is in them the healthy, upward tendency of early times. "They seek rather to pierce the heavens to Christ, than to dive into the heart for emotion. One glorious Person shines above and through them all. The Arian controversy, whilst it brought forth a quantity of vain subtleties and bitter words, rang from the true metal a sound clearer than it had yielded before. It brought up from the old mine many a jewel for the crown of Him who is 'King of kings.' It struck from the heart of the true Church many an adoring hymn to her Lord. And in those early Latin hymns is there not a clearer utterance of the great truth of the Cross,—the truth which sustains the heart in life and death,—than even in the early Oriental hymns? The trust in the Lamb of God, smitten for

\* Christian Life in Song.

our transgressions, and bearing away our sins, does, indeed, shine through the Oriental hymns; but is it not more pervading and glowing in the Ambrosian?" Even in the divided stream of the Christian psalmody of these earliest ages of the Church, the music has been very delicious to us, of the latest; and in many a time of sadness and unrest, these sweet hymns of faith and hope will perchance prove to our hearts as heavenly balm.

## SECOND EVENING.

---

## MEDIÆVAL LATIN.

# SECOND EVENING.

## MEDIÆVAL LATIN.

WE now approach the border-land which divides the ancient civilization from the modern,—that long, dark interval of ten centuries, from the sixth to the sixteenth of the Christian era, usually designated the mediæval ages. Notwithstanding the almost universal moral defection which then prevailed, there existed, in strange contrast, an indestructible life, the life of faith, in a succession of noble and heroic Christian men and women, the light of whose self-denying charities illuminated the surrounding darkness with a celestial radiance. It was, indeed, Christianity in the cloister; but it was Christianity based upon love to God and love to man.

It has been well said, "that this border-land had its rich and wild 'border minstrelsy,'—as fertile of wonders to us, as it was barren of rest and comfort to those who lived in it. Mediæval legend takes wing from thence, as from the heroic ages of modern Christendom. Its heroes are canonized saints,—an army counted and memorialized by its tens of thousands." *

* Mrs. Charles.

There are three clerical magnates whose names greet us on the threshold of this epoch, — Gregory the Great, Venantius Fortunatus, and the venerable Bede. Some faint idea of the fearful desolation and distress that then prevailed throughout the civilized world may be gleaned from the following extracts from a sermon by Gregory the Great, then bishop of Rome (A.D. 590) : —

"Those saints," he says, "on whose graves we stand, had hearts exalted enough to despise the world in its bloom. . . . Once the world enchained us by its charms; now, it is so full of misery, that of itself it points us to God. Everywhere do we see mourning, everywhere do we hear sighs. The cities are destroyed, the castles are ruined, the fields are laid waste, the whole land is desolate."

Yes: amidst all this social and political disorder and desolation, caused mainly by Goth and Saracen, there yet beamed forth the light of Christian faith in the heart of many a valiant soldier of the cross, — Christian heroes! men of moral might and spiritual prowess, who stood for the truth unto the death. We are in quest, however, not so much of the story of *their* lives, as of those whose lyric bursts of holy song mark so beautifully the tidal flow of Christian life.

Like Ambrose, Gregory was of a patrician Roman family; and although possessed of an ample fortune, he abandoned all worldly ambition and retired into a monastery. In becoming a monk, however, he does not seem to have fled from the active to the contemplative life, but rather to have entered into a higher sphere of activity. He founded six monasteries, — one in his father's palace at Rome; and of one of these he became Abbot. He earnestly commended to both clergy and laity the study of the sacred Scriptures. He said the sacred words should, by constant intercourse, penetrate into our being. " God does not now answer us by angelic ministrations," he continues, "or special prophetic voices, because the holy Scriptures include all that is necessary to meet individual cases, and are constructed so as to mould the life of later times by the example of the earlier. The answer, ' My grace is sufficient for thee,' was given to Paul, that it need not be particularly repeated to each one of us."

Gregory was a man for the times in which he lived. Shut up in Rome, with savage hordes at the gates, and pestilence, famine, and flood within; with heresy in the provinces, and the care of every department weighing heavily upon him at home; he never "bated jot of heart or hope," but met every demand in turn; . . . in the pulpit, passionately rousing his flock to spiritual life and action; in the cloisters, keeping his monks to their discipline; or in his closet, writing " morals" on the book of Job; or keeping up a wide correspondence with kings and queens, ecclesiastics and scholars. Then, in the choir, reforming the church service, and giving that musical impulse to the Christian world which will be felt as long as the " Gregorian Chant" continues to charm a human soul.*

A fac-simile volume of the manuscript music of the bishop was published at Paris in 1850, from the original, discovered a few years ago at the Benedictine Monastery at St. Gall, a copy of which is in the Astor Library.

* Christophers' Hymn-writers.

When elected to the Papal chair, Gregory selected a missionary band of nearly forty monks; and, in the year 596, sent them, with many exhortations and blessings, to the coast of Kent. "England still reaps the fruit of his success; and, it may be, records her early sense of obligation to Gregory in her national legend of 'St. George [or St. Gregory] and the Dragon.' Paganism (the 'Dragon'), in England, fell before the cross; and the ultimate result of Augustine's mission was the establishment of a Saxon church, which, for many generations, exemplified the purity and power of the Christian faith. . . . Many a choral chant and many a grand old Latin hymn floated across the channel from the churches of Italy and Gaul to the Saxon church." *

The celebrated hymn, "Veni, Creator Spiritus,"—the authorship of which is now generally ascribed to Gregory the Great, and not to Charlemagne, as some have supposed,— belongs, therefore, to this epoch of time. The advocates of the claims of the Emperor to its authorship rest their plea on the testimony of his secretary, to the effect that Charlemagne could speak the Latin language almost as easily as his own. And, further, that he addressed a letter to his bishops, entitled "De Gratia Septiformis Spiritus." Whereas those who believe, with the German critic, Moné, that it is the production of St. Gregory, possess, we think, the burden of proof in their favor. Gregory's homilies and other writings, his admitted scholarship and eminent piety, if not conclusive, are strong presumptive evidences that he wrote the hymn. Charlemagne was a soldier, Gregory a monk; what the

* Christophers' Hymn-writers.

sword was to the former, the pen was to the latter. Dryden's beautiful paraphrase of this hymn is familiar to most readers. There is another version no less fine, beginning, —

> Come, Holy Ghost, our souls inspire,
> And lighten with celestial fire!
> Thou the anointing Spirit art,
> Who dost Thy seven-fold gifts impart.

This grand hymn has always been invested with peculiar dignity: not only is it retained in the Episcopal Prayer-book for the ordaining of priests and the consecrating of bishops, but it was, also, in earlier times, habitually used — and the use in great part still survives — on all other occasions of extraordinary solemnity, as at the coronation of kings and the celebration of synods by the Protestant Church; and by the Romish, at the creation of popes, and other great occasions.

Contemporary with Gregory the Great, was Venantius Fortunatus, the writer of some hymns "which have taken root in the heart of Christendom, and have been chanted often, doubtless, with deep and solemn feeling, during many centuries."\* The "Vexilla regis prodeunt," "Pange, lingua, gloriosi," and the "Salve, festa Dies," are pronounced by Dr. Mason Neale as belonging to the first class of mediæval hymns; yet compared with the grand old battle-songs of Ambrose, they have too much of the glitter of the tournament on them; yet are they full of pathos.

Fortunatus was an Italian by birth, yet his life was, for the most part, spent in Gaul. He was born in the year 530, and died A.D. 609. He was appointed to

\* Trench.

preside over a monastic institution at Poictiers, founded by Queen Rhadegunda. His finest poem is considered to be his "De Cruce Christi."

We give a part of Mrs. Charles's fine rendering of the "Pange, lingua, gloriosi:"—

Spread, my tongue, the wondrous story of the glorious battle, far !
What the trophies and the triumphs of the cross of Jesus are,—
How the Victim, immolated, vanquished in that mighty war.
Pitying, did the great Redeemer Adam's fall and ruin see,
Sentenced then to death by tasting fruit of the forbidden tree,
And he marked that wood the weapon of redeeming love to be.
Thus the scheme of our redemption was of old in order laid,
Thus the wily arts were baffled of the foe who man betrayed,
And the armor of redemption from Death's armory was made.

The following is a free rendering from the Latin, of his hymn on the Resurrection,—"Salve, festa Dies." "In this sweet poem," writes Professor Schaff, "all nature, born anew in the spring, and arrayed in the bridal garment of hope and promise, welcomes the risen Saviour, the Prince of spiritual and eternal life."

    Hail, Day of days ! in peals of praise,
        Throughout all ages owned,
    When Christ, our God, hell's empire trod,
        And high o'er heaven was throned.
    This glorious morn the world new-born
        In rising beauty shows ;
    How, with her Lord to life restored,
        Her gifts and graces rose !
    The spring serene, in sparkling sheen,
        The flower-clad earth arrays ;
    Heaven's portal bright, its radiant light,
        In fuller flood displays ;
    From hell's deep gloom, from earth's dark tomb,
        The Lord in triumph soars !

> The forests raise their leafy praise,
> The flowery field adores,
> As, star by star, He mounts afar;
> And hell imprisoned lies.
> Let stars and light, and depth and height,
> In hallelujahs rise!
> Lo! He who died, — the Crucified! —
> God over all, He reigns!
> On Him we call, His servants all,
> Who heaven and earth sustains!

In his famous processional hymn, "Vexilla regis prodeunt," as well as in his hymn already cited, may be seen the worship of the cross, which has so long characterized the Papal Church. We therefore cite only the opening stanza of this processional hymn: —

> The royal banners forward go,
> The Cross shines forth in mystic glow,
> Where He in flesh, our flesh who made,
> Our sentence bore, our ransom paid!

A yet more startling instance of the idolatry of the cross occurs in the famous old Latin chant for Good Friday, entitled "O Crux fidelis!" It illustrates the fact, that from the symbolism of the cross came the grosser superstition, which descended to far lower depths, till the supposed wood of the cross was worshipped; thus transferring the homage due to the crucified One, to the cross itself!

Bede, styled the Venerable, for the sanctity of his character, was born A.D. 672, and died in 735. His remains lie buried near the altar of Durham Cathedral. When only seven years old, he was taken to the monastery of Yarrow. "There he read and wrote and prayed, and sang hymns to his Saxon harp, and recorded the history of his people." The last work of his busy, tranquil life, was a Saxon version of St. John's Gospel; finishing it amidst the sufferings of his last illness, and completing the work just as he closed his eyes in death. The details of his last hours are replete with pathetic interest: "They all wept, chiefly for that he said that in this world they should see his face no more; but they rejoiced in that he said, 'I go to my Creator: I have lived long enough: the time of my departure is at hand; for I long to depart and be with Christ.' Thus did he live on till the evening. Then that scholar said to him, 'Dearest master, there is only one thought left to write.' He answered, 'Write quickly.' Soon that scholar replied, 'Now this thought also is written.' He answered, 'Thou hast well said, It is finished. Raise my head in thy hand; for it will do me good to sit opposite my sanctuary, where I was wont to kneel down to pray, that sitting I may call upon my Father!' So he seated himself on the ground in his cell, and sang the 'Glory to Thee, O God, Father, Son, and Holy Ghost!' and when he, had named the 'Holy Ghost,' he breathed his last breath." Such was the calm of a Christian's death-bed in England, eleven hundred years ago. This worthy Saxon monk reflected the brightest aspect of the ascetic life, in its devout and studious retirement. It looks picturesque at this distance. Here is the translation * of one of his hymns on the "Ascension of our Lord" ("Hymnum canamus gloriæ") : —

> A hymn of glory let us sing:
> New hymns throughout the world shall ring;
> By a new way, none ever trod,
> Christ mounteth to the throne of God,
> . . . .

\* Mrs. Charles.

Calm soaring through the radiant sky,
Mounting its dazzling summits high!

. . . . .

May our affections thither tend,
And thither constantly ascend, —
Where, seated on the Father's throne,
Thee reigning in the heavens we own;
And, as the countless ages flee,
May all our glory be in Thee!

A notable and worthy name now meets us in the order of time, — that of Bernard, Abbot of Clairvaux, a monastery which he, in company with a dozen other monks, founded and built. After many months of laborious toil and self-denial, the new Abbey at length was reared, to the sound of sacred song, on a spot which had been previously the haunt of banditti. Bernard was born, A.D. 1091, at Fontaines, near Dijon, of a knightly family. His early training was attended by his mother, the Lady Aletta; and its influence seems to have accompanied him through life, so that his monastery had much of the nature of a home. After he left his father's vineyards and corn-fields in Burgundy for his monastery, five of his brothers soon followed him; and they thus became a band of six brothers, again under one roof, — that of their monastery. In early youth, he acquired so perfect a knowledge of the Latin, that he could preach extempore in that language with as much ease as his native tongue. Bernard's favorite oratory was a woodland bower, — a quiet vernal retreat in an adjacent valley; and here he composed his hymns, and sang them. He lived not only in great harmony with the little community over which he presided, but his beautiful character attracted the ardent admiration and loving esteem of all who knew him: among whom was "Peter the Venerable," Abbot of the monastery of Clugny, who declared that he "had rather pass his life with Bernard, than enjoy all the kingdoms of the world." His heart seems to have been full of love, and his hands full of good works. His dying counsel to his monks was, "to abound more and more in every good work;" and as they stood lovingly around his couch, unable to restrain their grief, his own eyes filled with tears, as he murmured faintly, 'I am in a strait betwixt two, having a desire to depart and be with Christ, which is far better;' nevertheless, the love of my children urgeth me to remain here below." These were his last words on earth; but his sweet spiritual songs still live in many a Christian heart.

Let us now rehearse some of his sweet lines, translated into our vernacular:—

> Jesus, Thou joy of loving hearts!
>   Thou Fount of life! Thou Light of men!
> From the best bliss that earth imparts,
>   We turn, unfilled, to Thee again.
> Thy truth unchanged hath ever stood;
>   Thou savest those that on Thee call;
> To them that seek Thee, Thou art good;
>   To them that find Thee, all in all!
> We taste Thee, O Thou Living Bread!
>   And long to feast upon Thee still;
> We drink of Thee, the Fountain-head,
>   And thirst our souls from Thee to fill.
> Our restless spirits yearn for Thee,
>   Where'er our changeful lot is cast;
> Glad, when Thy gracious smile we see;
>   Blest, when our faith can hold Thee fast.
> O Jesus, ever with us stay!
>   Make all our moments calm and bright;
> Chase the dark night of sin away,
>   Shed o'er the world Thy holy light.

The above, which is a beautiful translation of parts of Bernard's famous hymn, "Jesus, dulcedo cordium," by Dr. Ray Palmer, of New York, has been frequently copied, and recently it has been incorporated into Sir Roundell Palmer's "Book of Praise."

The great and good Bernard was, however, an ascetic of the severest order. Luther called him "the best monk that ever lived." He was one of the most renowned theologians of his age; having, at the instance of the reigning pontiff, been hailed as "the champion of the orthodoxy of his day," in consequence of his triumph over the rationalistic Abelard, in a discussion at Sens, in 1140. But he is most endeared to us of modern times, by his sacred lyrics, which are yet held in just esteem. We can only give the titles of the most renowned : " Salve Caput cruentatum " (Hail! Thou Head so bruised and wounded); "Jesu, dulcis memoria" (O Jesus! Thy sweet memory); and "Jesu, Rex admirabilis" (O Jesus! King most wonderful). Mrs. Charles has made so excellent a translation of the first-named, that we are tempted to present a portion of the poem to the reader : —

> Hail, Thou Head! so bruised and wounded,
> With the crown of thorns surrounded,
> Smitten with the mocking reed,
> Wounds which may not cease to bleed,
>   Trickling faint and slow.
> Hail! from whose most blessed brow
> None can wipe the blood-drops now;
> All the flower of life has fled,
> Mortal paleness there instead ;
> Thou, before whose presence dread
>   Angels trembling bow!
>       .   .   .   .   .

> Let me true communion know
> With Thee, in Thy sacred woe, —
> Counting all beside but dross,
> Dying with Thee on Thy cross:
>   'Neath it will I die!
> Thanks to Thee with every breath,
> Jesus, for Thy bitter death:
> Grant Thy guilty one this prayer, —
> When my dying hour is near,
>   Gracious God be nigh!

Several instances are on record, of the comfort this hymn has afforded Christians at the time of death. It was especially such an evangel in the case of the missionary Schwartz, whom the native Christians in India solaced, by singing it in their own Tamil, into which language it had been translated. Bernard's other noted "passion-hymn" is entitled "Ad faciem Christi in cruce pendentis;" which has been rendered into German by Gerhardt, and into English by Alexander and others. Bernard died, A.D. 1153, aged sixty-two. His last words were, "For ever with the Lord." His first, or some of his first converts, were his own father, brothers, and personal friends. He closed his father's eyes in peace, and then had to witness his brother Gerard's departure to his rest. His touching lamentation over him is replete with pathos and poetic beauty. "Who could ever have loved me as he did? He was a brother by blood, but far more by religion. . . . God grant, Gerard, I may not have lost thee, but that thou hast preceded me; for of a surety thou hast joined those whom in thy last night below thou didst invite to praise God; when suddenly, to the great surprise of all, thou, with a serene countenance and a cheerful voice, didst commence chanting, 'Praise ye the Lord, from the heaven; praise Him, all ye angels!' At that moment, O my brother! the day dawned on thee, though it was night to us; the night to thee was all brightness. Just as I reached his side, I heard him utter aloud those words of Christ, 'Father, into Thine hands I commend my spirit!' Then repeating the verse over again, and resting on the word 'Father,' he turned to me, and, smiling, said, 'Oh, how gracious of God to be the Father of men, and what an honor for men to be His children.' And then, very distinctly, 'If children, then heirs;' and so he died: and so dying, he well-nigh changed my grief into rejoicing, so completely did the sight of his happiness overpower the recollection of my own misery."

St. Bernard left his mark upon his age: he was its governing spirit; a man who more than once scorned to be archbishop; who dictated to kings, and wrote a manual for the "infallible Head of the Church;" who projected a crusade, and "uttered prophecies," &c. He was a mighty man of learning in his day, and his time outlasted several centuries; for, after his death, "he made a mark on the ages as they passed over his tomb, and the Church long bore the impress of his gigantic spirit." But his grim folios of polemical and dogmatic theology are no longer consulted by the scholars of our time.

Another renowned ecclesiastic of the same name — Bernard, of Cluny — was contemporary with the Abbot of Clairvaux. Cluny Abbey was the greatest in France, and the monk was of yet greater celebrity than the Abbey. His great poem, of three thousand lines, is entitled "De contemptu mundi." This poem, by some critics, has been ascribed to Jacobus de Benedictus; but we leave this question with them to determine. This production was written about the year 1145. It is a severe satire on the vices of the times; but it also is one of the sweetest religious poems of the age in which it was written, or of any age. Many a cloistered monk took up the soul-stirring theme, and sang anew the glory-song of the new Jerusalem. Such winged thoughts visited many a monastic cell; but, among their inmates, none has set them to sweeter music than the saintly monk of Cluny. From Dr. Neale's masterly translation of this poem, we select some of its expressive lines, — lines, perhaps, unparalleled for their energy, fervor, and sublimity: —

That peace, — but who may claim it? The guileless in their way,
Who keep the ranks of battle, who mean the thing they say, —
The peace that is for heaven, and shall be for the earth;
The palace that re-echoes with festal song and mirth;
The garden, breathing spices, — the paradise on high;
Grace beautified to glory, unceasing minstrelsy.
There nothing can be feeble, there none can ever mourn,
There nothing is divided, there nothing can be torn;
'Tis fury, ill, and scandal, 'tis peaceless peace, below:
Peace endless, strifeless, ageless, the halls of Syon know!

. . . . . . .

Strive, man, to win that glory; toil, man, to gain that light;
Send hope before to grasp it, till hope be lost in sight!

. . . . . . .

Brief life is here our portion, brief sorrow, short-lived care:
The life that knows no ending, the tearless life, is there!

. . . . . . .

Thou hast no shore, fair Ocean! thou hast no time, bright Day!
Dear fountain of refreshment to pilgrims far away!
Upon the Rock of Ages they raise thy holy tower;
Thine is the victor's laurel, and thine the golden dower!
Jerusalem the golden, with milk and honey blest,
Beneath thy contemplation sink heart and voice oppressed!

I know not, oh, I know not, what social joys are there!
What radiancy of glory, what light beyond compare!
. . . . . . . .
They stand, those halls of Syon, conjubilant with song,
And bright with many an angel, and all the martyr-throng;
. . . . . . . .
There is the throne of David, and there, from care released,
The song of them that triumph, the shout of them that feast;
And they who, with their Leader, have conquered in the fight,
For ever and for ever are clad in robes of white!
. . . . . . . .
New mansion of new people, whom God's own love and light
Promote, increase, make holy, identify, unite!
Thou city of the angels! thou city of the Lord!
Whose everlasting music is the glorious decachord!
And there the band of prophets united praise ascribes,
And there the twelvefold charms of Israel's ransomed tribes,
The lily-beds of virgins, the roses' martyr-glow,
The cohort of the Fathers, who kept the faith below.
And there the Sole-begotten is Lord in regal state, —
He, Judah's mystic Lion, — He, Lamb Immaculate!
O fields that know no sorrow! O state that fears no strife!
O princely bowers! O land of flowers! O realm and home of life!

A sacred charm seems to pervade these majestic, soul-stirring stanzas, they bring the hallowed beatific vision so vividly before us; while the poem abounds with rich imagery and glowing beauty. It was said of this hymn, that it brought heaven nearer to us; and that the departing spirit has felt its uplifting power, even on the threshold of its home. So it was with the little sufferer mentioned by Dr. Neale in his notes upon Bernard. He says, "Thankful am I that the Cluniac's verses should have soothed the dying hours of many of God's servants. The most striking instance of which I know, is that of the child, who, when suffering agonies which the medical attendants declared to be almost unparalleled, would lie, without a murmur or motion, while the whole four hundred lines (of the translation) were read to him." It was the same pious recluse that wrote these comforting, quickening lines, who was accustomed to walk with his brother-monks in the cloisters, or in the groves, or retreats of his order, who would sometimes stop, and say to them, "Dear brethren, I must go: there is some one waiting for me in my cell." That "some one," it need hardly be stated, was the object of his devout affection, — his Lord and Saviour. "The name of Jesus," says Bernard, "is not only light, but food; it is likewise oil, without which all the food of the soul is dry; it is salt, unseasoned by which, whatever is presented to us is insipid; it is honey in the mouth, melody in the ear, joy in the heart, medicine in the soul; and there are no charms in any discourse in which His name is not heard."

Adam of St. Victor, who was a contemporary of Bernard, has been regarded as the most fertile of the hymnists of mediæval times; a native of Brittany, or, as some critics think, of Britain. Yet from the fact that the great seat of Latin poetry, in the twelfth century, was France, it is fair to infer that Adam, one of the chief of the band of clerical scribes, had his birth among the French. Hildebert, the two Bernards, and Peter the Venerable, were French; and the religious foundation of St. Victor, — then in the suburbs, and afterwards included within the walls of the city, — it was here he lived and died. The year of his death is not ascertained, but is believed to have been between 1173 and 1194. His epitaph, engraven on a plate of copper in the cloister of St. Victor, remained till the general destruction during the French

Revolution. Archbishop Trench remarks, "It is impossible to doubt that Adam of St. Victor partook to the full of the theological culture of the school to which he belonged; for this, indeed, is evident from his hymns, which have oftentimes as great a theological as poetical or even devotional interest; the first, indeed, predominating, sometimes to the injury of the last. . . . He may not have any single poem to vie with the austere grandeur of the 'Dies Iræ,' nor yet with the tearful passion of the 'Stabat Mater;' although, concerning the last point, there might well be a question, — but then it must be remembered these stand alone."

Adam of the "religious house" of St. Victor is believed to have written thirty-six hymns. Here are some specimen-lines of a translation.\* The subject is "Affliction."

> As the harp-strings only render
>   All their treasures of sweet sound, —
>   All their music, glad or tender, —
>     Firmly struck and tightly bound;
> So the hearts of Christians owe
>   Each its deepest, sweetest strain
> To the pressure firm of woe,
>   And the tension tight of pain.
> Spices crushed, their pungence yield,
>   Trodden scents their sweets respire;
> Would you have its strength revealed,
>   Cast the incense in the fire:
> Thus the crushed and broken frame
>   Oft doth sweetest graces yield;
> And, through suffering, toil, and shame,
> From the martyr's keenest flame,
>   Heavenly incense is distilled!

Dr. Neale regards the "Sequence" for the "Exaltation of the Cross" as his masterpiece. It commences:

\* Mrs. Charles's.

Be the Cross our theme and story,
We who in the Cross's glory
   Shall exult for evermore.
By the Cross the warrior rises,
By the Cross the foe despises,
   Till he gains the heavenly shore!

His hymn on St. Stephen's Day commences, —

Yesterday, the happy earth
Pealed her grateful praises forth,
   Keeping Christ's nativity;
Yesterday, the angel-throng
Met the King of heaven with song
   And with high festivity.

. . . .

Noble wrestler! yield to none,
For thy victory must be won;
   Stephen, struggle bravely through!
Those false witnesses refute,
Satan's synagogue confute,
   With thy holy speech, and true.

. . . .

For that crown that cannot wither,
Press through these brief torments hither:
   Triumph shall reward thy strife.
Death is thy nativity;
And thy sufferings' close shall be
   The beginning of thy life!

The following beautiful stanzas are part of a translation of the celebrated hymn, "Jam lucis orto sidere." It was this hymn that was chanted by the priesthood, in full choir, at the death-bed of William the Conqueror, in A.D. 1087. The cathedral-bell, which announced the hour of morning worship, — just as the sun was rising above the horizon, — was the signal for the matin-song. The monarch had passed away from earth before the singers had ceased.

This admirable hymn is still sung in the original, at Whitsuntide, by the scholars of Winchester College, prior to their vacation. The translation is as follows:

> Now that the sun is gleaming bright,
>   Implore we, bending low,
> That He, the uncreated Light,
>   May guide us as we go.
> No sinful word, or deed of wrong,
>   Nor thoughts that idly rove,
> But simple truth be on our tongue,
>   And in our hearts be love.
> And while the hours in order flow,
>   O Christ! securely fence
> Our gates beleaguered by the foe, —
>   The gate of every sense.
> And grant that to Thine honor, Lord,
>   Our daily toil may tend;
> That we begin it at Thy word,
>   And in Thy favor end!

King Robert II. of France, surnamed "the pious," wrote that renowned and touching hymn, regarded by critics as the "most beautiful of its class in the whole range of Latin sacred poetry." We refer to "Veni, Sancte Spiritus." Although a king, and necessarily cumbered with the affairs of state, yet, as it has been beautifully expressed, "his mind was his hermitage, and in its cloistral quiet he dwelt apart, enclosed by sacred spells of melody and song." He died 1031. Here is the English version of his famous hymn: —

> Holy Spirit, come, we pray,
> Come from heaven, and shed the ray
>   Of Thy light divine!
> Come, Thou Father of the poor!
> Giver of a boundless store,
>   Light of hearts, oh shine!

Matchless Comforter in woe,
Sweetest Guest the soul can know,
   Living waters blest.
When we weep, our solace sweet;
Coolest shade in summer-heat;
   In our labor, rest.

Holy and most blessèd Light,
Make our inmost spirits bright
   With Thy radiance mild;
For without Thy sacred powers,
Nothing can we own of ours,
   Nothing undefiled.

What is arid, fresh bedew;
What is sordid, cleanse anew;
   Balm on the wounded pour;
What is rigid, gently bend;
On what is cold, Thy fervor send;
   What has strayed, restore.

To Thine own, in every place,
Give the sacred sevenfold grace, —
   Give Thy faithful this.
Give to virtue its reward,
Safe and peaceful end afford, —
   Give eternal bliss!

King Robert's hymn had scarcely been sung, when the accents of another notable singer burst upon the ear, — Cardinal Damiani, bishop of Ostia, said to have been a zealous reprover of the vices of his time: he died in 1071. The great hymn on the Joys of Paradise, often attributed to Augustine, is his. Here it is: —

In the Fount of life perennial the parchèd heart its thirst would slake,
And the soul, in flesh imprisoned, longs her prison-walls to break, —
Exile, seeking, sighing, yearning, in her fatherland to wake.

Who can utter what the pleasures and the peace unbroken are,
Where arise the pearly mansions, shedding silvery light afar;
Festive seats, and golden roofs, which glitter like the evening-star!

. . . . . . . .

There, the saints like suns are radiant, like the sun at dawn they glow;
Crownèd victors after conflict, all their joys together flow;
And, secure, they count the battles where they fought the prostrate foe.
Putting off their mortal vesture, in their Source their souls they steep;
Truth by actual vision learning, on its form their gaze they keep;
Drinking from the living Fountain draughts of living waters deep.
Time, with all its alternations, enters not those hosts among;
Glorious, wakeful, blest, no shade of chance or change o'er them is flung;
Sickness cannot touch the deathless; nor old age, the ever young!
There, their being is eternal; things that ceased, have ceased to be;
All corruption there has perished; there they flourish, strong and free:
Thus mortality is swallowed up of Life eternally!

. . . . . . . .

Ever filled, and ever seeking, what they have they still desire;
Hunger, there, shall fret them never, nor satiety shall tire;
Still enjoying whilst aspiring, in their joy they still aspire!
There, the new song, new for ever, those melodious voices sing;
Ceaseless streams of fullest music through those blessed regions ring,—
Crownèd victors ever bringing praises worthy of the King!

This twelfth century was the great era of the Crusades; it was also most vocal with these Christian melodies. From many more of the sweet minstrels of the monastery we might entertain the reader's ear with richest music; but our limits necessarily forbid. We can only indicate by name a few of the leaders of the great choir. There was a long poem on the sufferings of our Lord, by Anselm, bishop of Lucca, who died 1086. Here are the opening stanzas of the English version:—

Rise, my soul, from slumber now, leave the bed of sleep;
Languor, torpor, vanity, — all outside must keep;
While the heart, lit up within, with love's torches, glows,
Dwelling on that wondrous work, and the Saviour's woes,
Reason, thought, affections true, gather all together,
Not by trifles led astray, hither roam and thither;
Fancies wild, distracting doubts, busy cares, depart;
While the sacraments of life pass before the heart.

Peter the Venerable, Abbot of Cluny (1092–1156) wrote a celebrated hymn on the Resurrection of our Lord, entitled "Mortis portis fractis, fortis." We quote Mrs. Charles's fine translation: —

Lo! the gates of death are broken, and the strong man armed is spoiled
Of his armor, which he trusted, by the Stronger Arm despoiled!
    Vanquished is the prince of hell,
    Smitten by the Cross, he fell.
. . . . . .
Thus God brought man back to heaven, when he rose from out the grave,
The pure, primal life bestowing, which creating, first He gave.
By the sufferings of his Maker, to His perfect Paradise,
The first dweller thus returneth: wherefore these glad songs arise.

Hildebert, who in 1125 became archbishop of Tours, wrote a notable hymn of over two hundred lines, — an address to "the Trinity;" which, like other productions of the cloister and the stylus, is somewhat metaphysical, yet characterized by harmony, grace, and terseness. Thomas Aquinas — "the angelic doctor," as he has been styled — composed those renowned sacramental lyrics, "Pange lingua gloriosi," and "Lauda Sion Salvatorem:" the last named, it is said, he wrote at the instance of Pope Urban IV.

That pious recluse, Thomas à Kempis (from the

name of his birthplace, — Kempin, in Holland), was the author of a fine Christian lyric on "The joys of Heaven." He was born in 1380, and died in 1471, in his ninety-first year. He is almost universally known as the author of that famous work, "The Imitation of Christ;" a book that is cherished alike by Protestant and Catholic, — has been more frequently reprinted than any other book, perhaps, except the Bible. It has been translated into all Christian, and some heathen languages. It is even stated that a copy of it in Arabic was discovered, by a travelling monk, in the library of a king of Morocco, which his Moorish majesty prized beyond all his other books. Strange to add, in the face of all this popularity, the authorship of this work has been in dispute during nearly four centuries. In France, the learned have attributed the work to John Gerson, chancellor of the University of Paris, who died in 1429. Thomas à Kempis was an excellent copyist: his copy of the Bible, the labor of fifteen years, was thought a masterpiece of calligraphic art; and, as there is an ancient manuscript of the work extant in the library at Valenciennes, it has been inferred that he only copied the work; but later research has discovered a copy in the library at Brussels, which bears the name of Thomas à Kempis, ten years older, which determines the right of authorship to the pious recluse of the fifteenth century, canon of Utrecht and of Mount St. Agnes.

But we digress. In speaking of this worthy ascetic, who had taught us such exemplary lessons in prose, we had well-nigh forgotten his hymn in which he sings to us so sweetly of the glories of the heavenly state : —

High the angel choirs are raising
  Heart and voice in harmony;
The Creator-King still praising,
  Whom, in beauty there they see.
Sweetest strains, from soft harps stealing;
Trumpets, notes of triumph pealing;
Radiant wings, and white stoles gleaming;
Up the steeps of glory streaming:
Where the heavenly bells are ringing
Holy, holy, holy! singing
  To the mighty Trinity!
Holy, holy, holy! crying;
For all earthly care and sighing
  In that city cease to be!
Every voice is there harmonious,
Praising God, in hymns symphonious;
Love each heart with light enfolding,
As they stand, in peace, beholding
  There the Triune Deity!
Whom adore the seraphim,
  Aye with love eternal burning;
Venerate the cherubim,
  To their Fount of honor turning;
Whilst angelic thrones adoring
  Gaze upon His Majesty!

Reverting back again, for a moment, to the subject of preaching, we might remark, that these mediæval preachers were potent speakers. There are many familiar enough to us by name; but, beyond that, we know but little pertaining to their character and public service. Peter the Hermit must have been a persuasive and powerful speaker, to sway such multitudes by his words: so must have been the Bernards; Peter the Venerable; Adam of St. Victor; Peter of Blois, who became archdeacon of London; Guaric of Igniac; Hildebert, archbishop of Tours; Anthony of Padua, — not to increase the list, — whose popularity, like that of Whitefield and the Wesleys, obliged them to preach in the open field or on the hillside, sometimes having for their audience not less than thirty thousand eager listeners! It is also pleasant to think, with Dr. Neale, who has reproduced some of these mediæval sermons, that, in many instances, they were greatly in advance of the prevalent superstitions of those times. It may excite surprise in some to learn, that, in early and mediæval days, homilies or sermons were not unfrequently in verse; yet such seems to have been the case, as far back as the fourth century, by Ephræm the Syrian. Taste has somewhat changed since those days. Specimens of these curious effusions, of the fourteenth century, were reproduced, recently, in Edinburgh, collated from manuscripts in Oxford and Cambridge. We subjoin a brief specimen of one of these literary curiosities: it is in the Saxon, as pure as Chaucer.

> Now see ye qui and for quas sake,
> Crist com til us our kind * to take;
> His fust com was bodilye,
> Bot an other est gastilye. †
> That es quen Crist gifes us wille,
> His commandment to fulfille;
> For son quen me haf wil to do,
> Al that the preacheour says us to —
> And feles our hearte in charite,
> In sothe ‡ ful siker may we be.
> That Crist is comen in til our hertes
> Gastli, that us til goodnesse ertes, §
> Of us self haf we noht bot sin,
> Bot quen Crist wirkes us wit in,
> Than at the fust beginne, we
> God cresten men for to be.

* Nature.   † Spiritual.   ‡ In truth.   § Inclines.

"Scarcely have the tones of one hymn died away before another has been grandly swelling upon the ear of Christendom. In the fourteenth century, the music of the Church was becoming faint. Truth was sending out its messages but in undertones. Spiritual religion was keeping up its struggling existence within narrow retreats. But even then, as in every crisis of Christian history, there came awakening voices, such as those of Francis of Assissi, and his friend and biographer, Thomas of Celano, — one, the great father of itinerant preaching friars; the other, that hymnist whose one Judgment hymn roused the slumbering choirs of Europe, and still sends forth its deep and solemn music." *

Earnest and stirring as were those many-voiced melodies, re-echoed back to us from the far-distant past, a yet more stately and majestic chant bursts now upon our ear, with its trumpet-like cadences, — in the "Dies Iræ." This grand outburst is the kingliest of them all. A short but significant silence preceded this great hymn of the Mediæval Church, which seemed to usher it in with the greater solemnity. Its tone is a reflex of the theology of the time, — austere and severe, rather than loving and hopeful. It is a single voice, — low, trembling, and penitential; yet it breaks the stillness, and spreads itself abroad over Christendom, awakening and thrilling multitudes of hearts. This voice was lifted up by one solitary Franciscan monk, — Thomas, of Celano, a Neapolitan village, — early in the thirteenth century. This celebrated lyric forms a part of the Burial Service in the Romish Missal, and is chanted in magnificent style at

* Christophers' Hymn-writers.

the great Sistine Chapel at Rome; while portions of it enter into the worship of a large proportion of those who "profess and call themselves Christians." As a literary composition, such is its wondrous fascination, that it has elicited the admiration of many of the greatest scholars; and it has passed into upwards of two hundred translations. A multitude of English versions have been made; the most approved being those by Archbishop Trench, Dean Alford, Dr. W. R. Williams, of New York, Professor Schaff, General Dix, and Dr. Coles, of Newark, who has given us thirteen various renderings from his own pen. This acknowledged masterpiece of Latin poetry has been pronounced the most sublime of all uninspired hymns. Professor Schaff remarks that the secret of "the irresistible power of the 'Dies Iræ' lies in the awful grandeur of the theme, the intense earnestness and pathos of the poet, the simple majesty and solemn music of the language, the stately metre, the triple rhyme, and the vowel assonances chosen in striking adaptation to the sense,—all combining to produce an overwhelming effect, as if we heard the final crash of the universe, the commotion of the opening graves, the trumpet of the archangel, summoning the quick and the dead; and saw the King of 'tremendous majesty,' seated on the throne of justice and mercy, and ready to dispense everlasting life, or everlasting woe! Goethe describes its effect upon the guilty conscience, in the cathedral scene of 'Faust.'" It is no easy thing to determine the choice from the many fine versions recently executed by scholars; but, as all are good, we shall feel the less scrupulous in our selection, and subjoin that which has already received distinguished notice. We refer to that of General Dix, — "written," as he informs us, "amid the tumult, and as a relief from the asperities of war." We only present the first stanza in the original: —

> Dies Iræ, dies illa!
> Solvet sæclum in favillâ,
> Teste David cum Sibyllâ.

---

> Day of vengeance, without morrow!
> Earth shall end in flame and sorrow,
> As from saint and seer we borrow.
>
> Ah! what terror is impending,
> When the Judge is seen descending,
> And each secret veil is rending!
>
> To the throne, the trumpet sounding,
> Through the sepulchres resounding,
> Summons all, with voice astounding.
>
> Death and Nature, mazed, are quaking,
> When, the grave's long slumber breaking,
> Man to judgment is awaking.
>
> On the written Volume's pages,
> Life is shown in all its stages —
> Judgment-record of past ages!
>
> Sits the Judge, the raised arraigning,
> Darkest mysteries explaining,
> Nothing unavenged remaining.
>
> What shall I then say, unfriended,
> By no advocate attended,
> When the just are scarce defended.
>
> King of Majesty tremendous,
> By Thy saving grace defend us;
> Fount of pity, safety send us!
>
> Holy Jesus! meek, forbearing,
> For my sins the death-crown wearing,
> Save me, in that day, despairing.

Worn and weary, Thou hast sought me;
By Thy cross and passion bought me;—
Spare the hope Thy labors brought me.

Righteous Judge of retribution,
Give, oh, give me absolution
Ere the day of dissolution.

As a guilty culprit groaning,
Flushed my face, my errors owning,
Hear, O God, my spirit's moaning!

Thou to Mary gav'st remission,
Heard'st the dying thief's petition,
Bad'st me hope in my contrition.

In my prayers no grace discerning,
Yet on me Thy favor turning,
Save my soul from endless burning!

Give me, when Thy sheep confiding
Thou art from the goats dividing,
On Thy right a place abiding!

When the wicked are confounded,
And by bitter flames surrounded,
Be my joyful pardon sounded!

Prostrate all my guilt discerning,
Heart as though to ashes turning;
Save, oh, save me from the burning!

Day of weeping, when from ashes
Man shall rise 'mid lightning flashes,
Guilty, trembling with contrition,
Save him, Father, from perdition!

Need we wonder that even the sturdy Dr. Johnson confessed, with Sir Walter Scott, that he could not recite it without tears; or that Mozart, when he made it the basis of his celebrated "Requiem," became so intensely excited by the theme as to hasten his death. In the closing days of his earthly career, even when his great intellect became partially obscured, Sir Walter was heard to murmur to himself his own rendering of this memorable canticle.

As the "Dies Iræ" has been pronounced the greatest, so the "Stabat Mater Dolorosa," composed in the thirteenth century, by Jacobus de Benedictis, is the most pathetic of hymns. Of the latter, we present the opening stanzas of Lord Lyndsay's excellent version: —

> By the cross, sad vigil keeping,
> Stood the mournful mother weeping,
>   While on it the Saviour hung;
> In that hour of deep distress,
> Pierced, the sword of bitterness
>   Through her heart with sorrow wrung.
>
> Oh, how sad, how woe-begone
> Was that ever-blessed one,
>   Mother of the Son of God!
> Oh, what bitter tears she shed
> Whilst before her Jesus bled
>   'Neath the Father's penal rod!

There is a beautiful sequel to the "Dies Iræ," supposed to have been written about the same time, called "Dies illa, dies vitæ." We subjoin a portion of Mrs. Charles's translation: —

> Lo, the Day, — the Day of Life!
>   Day of unimagined light,
> Day when Death itself shall die,
>   And there shall be no more night.
>     .   .   .   .   .
> See the King desired for ages,
>   By the just expected long;
> Long implored, at length He hasteth,
>   Cometh with salvation strong.
> Oh, how past all utterance happy,
>   Sweet, and joyful it will be,

When they who, unseen, have loved Him,
　　Jesus, face to face, shall see!
　　　.　　　.　　　.　　　.

There shall be no sighs or weeping,
　　Not a shade of doubt or fear;
No old age, no want or sorrow,
　　Nothing sick or lacking there.
There the peace will be unbroken,
　　Deep and solemn joy be shed;
Youth in fadeless flower and freshness,
　　And salvation perfected.
What will be the bliss and rapture,
　　None can dream and none can tell,—
There to reign among the angels,
　　In that heavenly home to dwell!
To those realms, just Judge, oh, call me!
　　Deign to open that blest gate,—
Thou, whom, seeking, looking, longing,
　　I, with eager hope, await!

We are again indebted to the able pen of Dr. J. M. Neale for the translation of the following, one of the latest of the notable Latin hymns:—

　　Sing victory, O ye seas and lands!
　　Ye floods and rivers, clap your hands!
　　Break forth in joy, angelic bands!
　　Crown ye the King that 'midst you stands,
　　To whom the heavenly gate expands!
　　Bow before His Name Eternal,
　　　　Things celestial, things terrestrial,
　　　　And infernal!
　　Sing victory, angel-guards that wait!
　　Lift up, lift up the eternal gate,
　　And let the King come in with state!
　　And, as ye meet Him on the way,
　　The mighty triumph greet, and say,
　　Hail, Jesu! glorious Prince, to-day!
　　Who is the King of Glory blest,
　　Effulgent in His purple vest?
　　With garments dyed in Bozrah, He

Ascends in pomp and jubilee.
It is the King, renowned in fight,
Whose hands have shattered Satan's might!
Bow before His Name Eternal!
Things celestial, things terrestrial,
And infernal!

The following beautiful lines are part of a translation by Professor Longfellow, of a Latin hymn, written by the celebrated Francisco Xavier, the friend and companion of Loyola, who, for his zeal in the Eastern missions, was styled the "Apostle of the Indies:"—

O God! my spirit loves but Thee:
Not that in Heaven its home may be,—
Not that the souls who love not Thee
Shall groan in fire eternally;
But Thou, on the accursèd tree,
In mercy hast remembered me.
For me the cruel nails, the spear,
The ignominious scoff, didst bear;
Countless, unutterable woes,—
The bloody sweat, death's pangs and throes,—
These Thou didst bear, all these for me,
A sinner, and estranged from Thee.
And wherefore no affection show,
Jesus, to Thee, that lov'st me so?
Not that in heaven my home may be,
Not lest I die eternally,
Not from the hopes of joys above me;
Not even as Thou Thyself didst love me:
So love I, and ever will love Thee;
Surely because my King art Thou,
My God for evermore as now.

There is another celebrated ode, of very ancient origin, "a voice of all ages," entitled "Cælestis urbs Jerusalem." It has been supposed that the earliest English version of it was made by Dickson, of Edinburgh, in the seventeenth century; but recently Dr. Bonar has discovered another version in a manuscript volume in the British Museum, which he regards as of an earlier date. This fine old hymn, not only possesses great poetic merit, but also a talismanic charm for many a Christian pilgrim. It is richly freighted with touching and beautiful memories and associations. Its plaintive and melodious words have been lisped by multitudes, who, amid the sorrows of earth, longed for the beatitudes of the "better country;" by once breathing lips that have long since ceased to make melody on earth, but whose spirits are now with the choruses of the "upper sanctuary." It was the favorite refrain of the Cameronian martyrs and Covenanters, who sang it in the glens and on the mountains of Scotland; and it has been made the vehicle of devout aspiration, alike by prince and peasant, in the cathedral and the cottage.

This hymn was originally entitled "The New Jerusalem; or, the Soul's Breathing after the Heavenly Country." From Mr. Prime's interesting work on this hymn, we extract some portion of it, the entire poem extending to thirty-one stanzas:—

O mother dear, Jerusalem! when shall I come to thee?
When shall my sorrows have an end, thy joys when shall I see?
O happy harbor of God's saints! O sweet and pleasant soil!
In thee no sorrows can be found, no grief, no care, no toil.

. . . . .

Jerusalem the City is of God our King alone;
The Lamb of God, the light thereof, sits there upon His throne.
Thy turrets and thy pinnacles with carbuncles do shine,
With jasper, pearl, and chrysolite, surpassing pure and fine.

. . . . . . . .

> Thy walls are made of precious stones, thy bulwarks diamonds square;
> Thy gates are made of Orient pearl,—O God, if I were there!

The prison-cells of that storied old "Tower," on the banks of the Thames, are covered with the marks and memorials of many a hapless victim of tyranny and persecution. It was there, probably, towards the close of the reign of Elizabeth, that the long prison-song was written, which now is treasured as a sacred relic in the British Museum. The winged words of this glorious old hymn have, however, long since found their way into thousands of Christian hearts, both in Europe and America; and to many it has become an angelic ministrant of grace. A young Scotchman, who was on his death-bed at New Orleans, says the American biographer of Whitefield, was visited by a Presbyterian minister, but continued for a time to shut himself up against all the good man's efforts to reach his heart. Somewhat discouraged, at last the visitor turned away, and, scarcely knowing why, unless it were for his own comfort, began to sing "Jerusalem, my happy home." That was enough; a tender chord was touched; the young patient's heart was melted; and with tears he said, "My dear mother used to sing that hymn!" He no longer refused the good offices of his clerical friend, but listened to his spiritual counsel; and his consolation ensued.

In closing our second evening's studies, we may remark that we have had to omit many notable and beautiful pieces, on account of the erroneous doctrines they teach; and even of those we have indicated to the reader, our extracts have been necessarily brief, on this account. The worship of the Virgin Mary, the dogma of transubstantiation, intercession of saints, and the superstitious addresses to the material cross, which characterize so generally the service of song in the Mediæval Church, have deprived us of the privilege of more largely quoting from those otherwise masterly productions of the monastic ages. We do not, of course, wish to imply that the middle-age theology was wholly corrupt, and ought to be placed under ban : there was a small streamlet that still was preserved in its pristine purity. For the sake of this, therefore, and the natural desire we all feel to know something of what the Church was doing during her thousand years' eclipse, we have made our citations as freely as we might. "In Romanism, we have the residuum of the Middle-age Church and theology, — the lees, after all, or well-nigh all : the wine was drained away. But, in the Mediæval Church, we have the wine and the lees together, the truth and the error; the false observance, and yet, at the same time, the divine truth, which should one day be fatal to it, side by side."\* The ever-living Church of Christ, whether in the Catacombs or among the Swiss Alps, is one with ours : —

"Their song to us descendeth :
The Spirit, who in them did sing, to us His music lendeth.
His song, in them, in us, is one ;
We raise it high, we send it on, —
The song that never endeth !"

Could we bridge over the distance of time, and penetrate through the disguise of cowl and cloister, we should, doubtless, discover that, despite the outward uniformity of convent-life, there existed the same

\* Trench's Sacred Latin Poetry.

internal Christian experience, — of doubt and fear, sorrow and exultation, — that mark the inner Christian life of our own day. The gems of the hymn literature of those remote times we gather from many a hidden mine; and they flash frequently across a chaos of ignorance and darkness. It has been well said, "We need only study the sacred poetry of the Middle Ages, to understand why the Reformation was needed." The idolatry of the Virgin was and still continues to be the great heresy of Latin Christianity : it was born of darkness, and gathered strength from the superstitious weakness of its adherents. As the Bible afforded no authority for the dogma, "tradition" was invoked; and "tradition wove a gorgeous robe for her," while music and painting aided to invest the delusion with their spell.

# THIRD EVENING.

## GERMAN-REFORMATION ERA.

# THIRD EVENING.

## GERMAN-REFORMATION ERA.

THUS far our rapid survey of the sacred poetry of the Latin Church has verified the remark of a great thinker,* that "it is but feebly, and as afar off, that the ancient liturgies (except so far as they merely copied their originals) came up to the majesty and the wide compass of the Hebrew worship, such as it is indicated in Psalm clxviii. Neither Ambrose, nor Gregory, nor the Greeks have reached, or approached this level. As to the powers of sacred poetry, those powers were expanded to the full, and were quite expended too, by the Hebrew bards. What are modern hymns but so many laborious attempts to put in a new form that which, as it was done in the very best manner so many ages ago, can never be well done again, otherwise than in a way of verbal repetition."

As in the hardest winter the roots are still alive in the frozen ground, so in the dim seclusion of monastic life, during some ten centuries, there still lived and germinated the hidden seeds of spiritual life; and many a soul-stirring out-gush of song, which at first

* Isaac Taylor.

resounded amid the solemn stillness of cloistered cell, or echoed along the lofty arches of many a stately cathedral, now reverberated in the homesteads and on the hill-sides of Germany. There is, however, a characteristic freshness and purity, as well as spiritual fervor, in the devotional lyrics which ushered in, and accompanied the Protestant Reformation of Germany. A greater variety in the subjects of these hymns is no less noticeable, as also the peculiar circumstances which called them forth. No longer do these melodies come to us from the cloister of monkish asceticism, devoted mainly to the contemplation of the cross and passion of our Lord, not to refer to the idolatrous character of the majority of them, but they pertain to the daily needs and experiences of active Christian life. They are heart-bursts from the chamber of domestic sorrow, glad orisons of praise from the harvest-field, earnest appeals for Divine succor amidst the terrors of war, — the voices of the inner life of the individual Christian amid the various activities of those stirring times of transition and trial.

Well has it been said by D'Aubigné, that Poetry caught the living flame kindled up by the Reformation. The souls of Luther, and many of his coadjutors, elevated by faith to the loftiest flights of thought, excited to enthusiasm by the conflicts and perils which constantly threatened the infant church, — in a word, inspired by the poetic genius of the Old Testament, and by their faith in the New, — soon poured out their feelings in religious songs, in which poetry and music mingled all the heavenly elements that belonged to either. Thus the sixteenth century witnessed the revival of the psalmody which had consoled the martyrs of the first Christian age. The same year that Luther consecrated his powers of melody and verse to memorialize the martyrs of Brussels, Hans Sachs sang "The Nightingale of Wittenberg." The doctrine, which for four centuries had prevailed in the Church, was as the light of the moon, gleaming upon men wandering in a wilderness. Now the nightingale announced the sun, and rose above the morning clouds, hymning the light of day. But this magnificent harmony, produced by the gospel in the day of its revival, was soon to be disturbed. The songs of the Wittenberg nightingale were interrupted by the whistling of the tempest and the roaring of lions. A mist gathers in a moment over all Germany; and, after a splendid day, there comes a night of the deepest darkness. The struggle between the leaders of the Protestant Reformation, and the Catholicism of the Middle Ages in its decay, forms the principal object of interest of the sixteenth century. The one party was in its decrepitude and decadence; the other, full of the energy of young life.

The invention of the printing-press was gradually affecting a mighty revolution over the world. The Greek and Latin classics, which were till then sealed books, save to the monk, were now free to general perusal. The same, to a certain extent, was being done for the Sacred Scriptures. It was an epoch of wondrous awakening of the nations; it was when Tasso and Ariosto were pouring forth their lays to the ears of kings and princes, celebrating the deliverance of the holy Sepulchre, or the feats of the paladins of Charlemagne. While Portugal was delighted with the strains of a Camoens, and while England gloried in her Shakspeare, and France boasted her Ronsard and her Marot, Germany had, as yet, no poets more eminent than Hans Sachs, who, next to Lope de Vega, has the merit of being the most prolific poet the world has ever known. Germany was mute until the Reformation; then it broke forth into song, for it had something to sing about, — its rescue from spiritual despotism, ignorance, and superstition.

It was fitting that the dawn of the Reformation should be ushered in with the voice of hallowed song; and after the dark night which had brooded so long over the world had receded, a rich choral gush of rejoicing melody did burst forth, like the light, over the liberated land. Since the apostolic times, the most formidable foe the Christian Church has had to oppose, was that system which claimed to be the Church itself. The Council of Trent — as far as worldly influence was concerned, one of the most august and imposing assemblages the world had ever witnessed — provoked, by its action, a cry of surprise, indignation, and grief; but that cry was lost in air.

"Rome inwardly laughed at Christendom around her, while she showed her spell to be of such a nature, that to break it, needed another might than that of emperors, kings, bishops, and doctors, with all the science and all the power of the age and the Church. . . . The philosophers of Alexandria had spoken of a fire wherein men ought to be purified; and now Rome set forth this as a doctrine of the Church; adding, that indulgences could deliver souls from this intermediate state, in which otherwise their sins would detain them. Nothing was omitted that could inspire fire. Man is prompted by his own nature to dread an unknown future; and this dread was worked upon and augmented. Who, then, could withhold the price of a ransom? So the revolting trade went on,—pope after pope finding new methods of increasing it,—till, in the year 1300, Boniface VIII. published a bull, announcing, that, every hundred years, all who presented themselves at Rome should receive a plenary indulgence. From Italy, Sicily, Sardinia, Corsica, France, Germany, Hungary, — from everywhere, the tide set in. In one month, they counted in Rome two hundred thousand pilgrims. All these brought rich offerings, and the Roman treasury was rapidly filled. The next thing was to fix the return of the jubilee at fifty, then at thirty, and lastly at twenty-five years. Then, for the greater convenience of purchasers, and the greater profit of the vendors, both the jubilee and its indulgences were given to every place in Christendom. Thus the clergy had disgraced both religion and themselves. Well might Luther exclaim, 'The ecclesiastical state is opposed to God and his glory. . . . Every man feels disgust when he sees or hears of an ecclesiastic.' The evil had spread through all ranks: corruption of manners kept pace with corruption of faith, and a mystery of iniquity lay like an incubus on the enslaved Church of Christ. The vital doctrines of the Scriptures had nearly disappeared. The strength of the Church had been wasted; and its body lay stretched upon that part of the earth which the Roman empire had occupied, enfeebled, exhausted, and all but lifeless." *

As a set-off for the many knavish tricks and frauds

* D'Aubigné's Reformation.

by which money was extracted, through the terror and credulity of the people, by Tetzel, — a story is told of a Saxon gentleman who outwitted the wily impostor. Having bargained, for thirty crowns, for permission to commit an act of violence, he took out his money's worth upon that functionary himself, for whom he lay in wait, and, having beaten him grievously, carried off the rich chest of indulgence money, which he had helped to fill. On his trial for the audacious act, the "indulgence," which he exhibited, secured his acquittal.

Yet, all along this epoch of spiritual inertia and death, a chain of living witnesses for the truth existed, known as the Waldenses, from the heights of the Piedmont Alps: these ever protested against the superstitions and errors of Rome.

The voice of Protestantism is again lifted up, in England by Wickliffe, and in Bohemia by John Huss, a century before Luther in Saxony. Huss, "the John the Baptist of the Reformation," spread a vast light through the darkness, which was not soon to be extinguished. A pious bishop of Basle, Christopher of Utenheim, caused his name to be written on a picture painted on glass, which is still at Basle,* and encircled it with this device, which he desired to have always before his eyes: "My hope is the cross of Christ: I seek grace, and not works." A poor Carthusian brother, Martin, writes a touching confession, in which he says, "O God, most charitable! I know that I cannot be saved, and satisfy Thy justice, otherwise than through the merit, the very innocent passion, and the death of Thy well-beloved

* D'Aubigné.

Son. Holy Jesus! all my salvation is in Thy hands. Thou canst not turn from me the hands of Thy love, for they have created, formed, and redeemed me!" The piety of the good monk would never have been known to us, had not an old dwelling, which had formed part of the convent in Basle, been taken down, in the year 1776, when this confession of faith was discovered in a wooden box, which his own hands must have placed in the wall of his cell. Let us cherish the hope, that many another cloistered relic of this priceless order, although as yet undiscovered, may have existed, as a memorial that the spirit of truth had not wholly forsaken the haunts of men during these dark ages.

Scarcely had the Councils of Constance and Basle, which condemned Huss and his followers, broken up, when some fearless Christian men arose, like the Old-Testament prophets, and, with voices of thunder, uttered their denunciations against the prevailing vices of the priesthood. These heroic confessors and martyrs went, too, like Huss, to their reward, in a mantle of flame! Savonarola preaches in Florence, in 1497: his thrilling voice and impassioned gesture captivate the hearts of his hearers. "The Church must be renewed!" he exclaims. The Dominican paid the usual penalty of his temerity. Then came John of Wessalia, a scholar of good repute and courage, proclaiming "the Holy Scriptures to be the only source of faith;" and the brave old confessor, with tottering steps, is led to the dungeons of the Inquisition to die.

But John Hilten, a Franciscan monk at Eisenach, in Thuringia, and a great student of prophecy, went farther. When thrown into prison on account of his writings, his advanced age and the filthiness of his dungeon bringing on a dangerous illness, he sent for the friar superintendent, who at once began to rebuke him harshly for his doctrine, and his attacks on the abuses of monastic life. Hilten, forgetting his illness, and fetching a deep sigh, said, "I calmly submit to your injustice, for the love of Christ: but another will come, in the year of the Lord 1516; he will destroy you, and you will not be able to stand against him." Luther was born not long after, a short distance from Hilten's dungeon; commenced his studies in the same town in which the monk was prisoner; and publicly engaged in the Reformation, only a year later than this singular prophecy had indicated.

When Luther was sent to the Franciscan school at Magdeburg, he used to sing in the streets for his bread, as his father was unable to support him. A year after, he removed to a better school at Eisenach, where he had relatives; but they, too, neglected him. And here it was that Ursula, the wife of Conrad Cotta, took compassion on the singing boy, receiving him into her house, where, for some years, he enjoyed one of the most pleasant and profitable periods of his life. In that hospitable home, young Martin greatly extended his knowledge, and laid the foundation for his love of music and song. At the age of eighteen, he entered the University of Erfurt, where he made great attainments; and it was there that he, for the first time, found the Bible, which he read with deep thought, and great wonder and delight. This incident was a controlling one in the life of Luther; he soon after entered the Augustine monastery, at Erfurt, where, after passing through three years of spiritual conflicts, he at length emerged into evangelical rest and peace. The Elector of Saxony, in 1508, invited him to the University of Wittenberg, where he soon was appointed to the Chair of Divinity, and was called to expound the Scriptures daily. Thus gradually and unconsciously was he being prepared for the great work of the Reformation.

Luther was never ashamed to speak of the deep poverty of his youth; when at the height of his greatness, he would recall the fact. Yes: the same voice whose tones had shaken the empire of the world, had once humbly begged a morsel of bread. Then, again, note that obscure antique tome, which, perhaps, had remained unnoticed for centuries, in the library of Erfurt; but it was destined to become, by the Divine Providence, the "Book of Life," not only to a whole nation, but to the world at large; for the seed of the Reformation was contained within it. It was this Latin version of the Scriptures that Luther read and re-read with so much delight; it was the spiritual manna, upon which his hungry soul feasted so often, and which ultimately made him the stalwart champion of the faith.

Light from heaven burst upon the darkened mind of Luther, when the vicar-general Staupitz announced to him for the first time the great foundation truth, that not in works and penance, but in "love toward God, and faith toward the Lord Jesus Christ," true repentance consists. "Seek not conversion in emaciation and suffering, but love Him who first loved thee." Luther listened in rapt attention: his heart was surprised with an unknown joy, his mind with a strange and unknown light. Thus illumined himself, he soon began to scatter abroad those rays of light upon others; while the Bible, which he found chained up in a monastery, in a dead language, he ultimately gave to the common people in their own vernacular. Look again at Luther boldly confronting that august assemblage at the Diet of Worms,— how, noblest of them all, does he stand forth, panoplied in the "whole armor of God."

All eyes are centred upon the marvellous and intrepid monk, albeit slight traces of emotion are observed in his deportment, as he finds himself unsupported in the midst of so much pomp and pageantry of state; but soon he recovers his equanimity, all agitation subsides, and —

> "There he stands in superhuman calm,
> Concentred and sublime! Around him pomp
> And blaze imperial, haughty eyes, and words
> Whose tones breathe tyranny, in vain attempt
> The heaven-born quiet of his soul to move;
> Crowned with the grace of everlasting Truth,
> A more than monarch among kings he stood!"

While his friends thought their cause lost, and rampant enemies were thirsting for his blood, Luther was energetically and prayerfully preparing to give the German nation that Word of God which the Romish priesthood had for centuries hidden from their gaze. "God, who had conducted John to Patmos, *there* to write his *Revelation*, had confined Luther in the Wartburg, *there* to translate His Word."\* Luther well knew the value of the Bible: it was the wellspring of his spiritual life and consolation; and therefore he might well exclaim, "Would that this book

\* D'Aubigné.

were in every language, in every land, before the eyes and in the hearts of all men." This benevolent wish came from the lip of one excommunicated and outlawed by the pretended head of the Church. Among the literary curiosities of the Astor Library, is a copy of the Bull of Pope Leo, against Martin Luther. The title is as follows: "Bulla contra errores Martini Lutheri et sequacium" (Bull against the errors of Martin Luther and his followers).

But, at length, our hero "fought the good fight, and the time of his departure was at hand." He had accomplished the work that had been given him to do; and now he was called to his reward. His death was a beautiful epitome of his life; when speech had failed him for aught beside, he responded to the name of his Saviour. It was fitting, therefore, when the mortal part of this truly great man was being conveyed to its final resting-place, in the Cathedral of Wittenberg, that his sorrowing friends and attendants should chant one of the most touching of the hymns he had composed, while he was yet with them: "Out of the depths I cry to Thee." Here, in the very church, at the doors of which he had first affixed his celebrated "theses," did they now sing those irrepressible heart-utterances that had so stirred all Germany. One of these hymns, or rather psalms, Luther's most characteristic one, "Eine feste Burg ist unser Gott" (God is our refuge in distress), which was often called the Church's Battle-hymn, was written on the occasion of the evangelical princes delivering that *Protest* at the Second Diet of Spires, in 1529, from which we Protestants derive the name; and, in 1530, the Lutherans presented their Confession of Faith, at Augsburg. When Melancthon was at Weimar, he heard a little child sing this hymn, in the street, and confessed how it had comforted him. The first line of this hymn was inscribed upon Luther's tomb. The hymn we shall refer to again.

Martin Luther, it has been said, is regarded by his countrymen as the original of the German mind, — the prototype of all that is most distinctive in German modes of thought and speech. He was no less the representative of the German Protestant Reformation. Others, with Zwinglius, John Huss, and Jerome of Prague, were pioneers in the great crusade; but Luther was the great focal centre of influence that energized and sustained its action, and led it on to a glorious consummation. Luther, therefore, is the parent source, alike of German literature and Christian liberty and civilization for the world.

The critic Gervinus observes, "The language of Luther is of such wondrous purity, and its influence on his immediate contemporaries was so great, that it may be regarded as the basis of our modern high German." His translation of the Scriptures, although not the first German version, was yet the first familiarly read by all classes. It was also the best, and is still regarded as such. Heine says, "He was not only the greatest, but the most German of our history: he was not only the tongue, but the sword of his time."

His biographers portray him, as to his physique, sturdy and stalwart, plebeian in feature, and, to quote Carlyle's words, "a wild amount of passionate energy and appetite! But in his dark eyes were floods of sorrow; and deepest melancholy, sweetness, and mystery were all there. Often did there seem to meet in Luther the very opposite poles in man's character. He, for example, for whom Richter had said his words were half battles, — he, when he first began to preach, suffered unheard-of agony. 'Oh, Dr. Staupitz, Dr. Staupitz,' said he to the vicar-general of his order, 'I cannot do it; I shall die in three months. Indeed, I cannot do it.'

"Dr. Staupitz, a wise and considerate man, said upon this, 'Well, Sir Martin, if you must die, you must; but remember that they need good heads up yonder too. So preach, man, preach, and then live or die as it happens.' So Luther preached and lived, and he became, indeed, one great whirlwind of energy, to work without resting in this world." . . . And then, citing the "Table Talk" for an example of the characteristic tendencies of this true man, — amidst all his denunciations and curses, — Carlyle selects the following passage : —

"We see in it a little bird, having alighted at sunset on the bough of a pear-tree that grew in Luther's garden. Luther looked upon it, and said, ' That little bird, how it covers its head with wings, and will sleep there, so still and fearless, though over it are the infinite starry spaces, and the great blue depths of immensity. Yet it fears not : it is at home. The God that made it, too, is there.' The same gentle spirit of lyrical admiration is in the other passages of his book. Coming home from Leipsic in the autumn season, he breaks forth into loving wonder at the fields of corn. 'How it stands there,' he says, 'erect on its beautiful taper stem, and bending its beautiful golden head with bread in it, — the bread of man sent to him another year.' Such thoughts as these are as little windows through which we gaze into the interior of the depths of Martin Luther's soul, and see visible, across its tempests and clouds, a whole heaven of light and love. He might have painted, he might have sung; could have been beautiful like Raphael, great like Michael Angelo."

Thus have we seen, that, in the great drama of the German Reformation, one colossal figure stands prominently forth, — that of Luther; but the gentle and loving spirit of his friend, Melancthon, did his part to temper the asperity and fiery ardor of his leader; while the great work was in progress in Switzerland, under the guardianship of Zwingli, — a name that ranks second only to that of Luther, and between the two a singular parallel seems to have prevailed, — or rather, we should say, a remarkable contrast was exhibited. Zwingli and Luther were born within a few weeks of each other; the former of wealthy, the latter of poor, parents. The one had a teacher remarkable for learning; the other, one for his cruel severity, — having once whipped a pupil fifteen times in one forenoon. Both these reformers had excellent voices; but one only made his available for his bread. Both became acquainted with the Bible about the same time, 1502; Zwingli at Basle, and Luther at Erfurt. About the year 1505, the first finds a friend, who remains faithful to him through life; the second loses, in a terrible manner, such a one, which makes him turn monk. Both discover the corruptions of the papal system; and, in the year 1517, both obtain peace through faith in Christ. Zwingli attacks fearlessly the mummeries of the

Church; Luther assails the traffic in indulgences, and, without intending it, shakes the papacy to its very foundations.

The great reformers were more strongly contrasted in death than in life. The fiery Luther died peacefully in his bed, at the ripe age of sixty-three; at forty-seven, the gentle Zwingli perished on the battle-field. When the war, which he had vainly tried to prevent, broke out between the Protestant and Papal cantons of Switzerland, the pastor accompanied his brethren in the faith, as field-preacher, to the conflict. In the midst of the action, while bending down to comfort with the words of life a fallen countryman, a stone struck his helmet with such force that he fell to the ground. On his attempting to rise, a hostile spear gave him a fatal stab. He had fallen near a tree. He was leaning on it; his hands were clasped, his lips moved in prayer, while his eyes were directed heavenward. In this state, a party of marauding soldiers found him. "Will you confess? Shall we fetch a priest?" they cry to him. The tongue which had so eloquently combated error is dumb, but a motion of the head signifies a negative. "Then call upon the Mother of God and the blessed saints in your heart," they shout to him. Again he refuses. "Die, then, obstinate heretic," said an officer from Unterwalden, and gave him a deadly blow. Nor did the contrast end here. The remains of Luther were borne to the tomb by a funeral procession of extraordinary pomp; the body of Zwingli was quartered by the common hangman, and the ashes mixed with the ashes of a swine, that it might be impossible for his friends and admirers to identify his remains.

It was not only among princes and in palaces, or in cathedrals and cloisters, that the friends and advocates of the Reformation were to be found; they were yet more numerously scattered among the " common people." Among this worthy class, there was a notable shoemaker, — one Hans Sachs, of Nuremberg; who, after some chequered experiences, tunes his lyre to the service of the Reformed doctrine; and, since the minstrel's song had ceased in the feudal castle, no music had so stirred and aroused the German people as his rude Christian lyrics. Perhaps it would be difficult to decide whether this plebeian poet, or the Elector of Saxony, achieved the most in ushering in the glorious era of the Reformation.

"The recent intellectual discoveries of the age had diffused a multitude of new ideas through every country, with inconceivable rapidity. It seemed as if the minds of men, which had slept for ages, would, by their activity, redeem the time they had lost. Printed speech had taken to itself wings that carried it, as the wind wafts certain seeds, into the remotest regions." \* When Zwingli, "the hope of Switzerland and of the Protestant Church," was suffering from an attack of the plague, and thought to be dying, he gave utterance in German to the following plaintive strain : —

> Death's at my door, walks to my side!
> Hand of all power, in Thee I hide!
> Christ, in alarm I beg for aid;
> Lift Thy pierced arm, break the foe's blade.
> But if, at noon, Thou call'st me home,
> 'Tis not too soon: Jesus, I come!

Meanwhile, the disease seemed to be gaining upon him; and, with the little power remaining to him, he faintly said, —

\* D'Aubigné.

> I'm near my goal, and want Thy cheer!
> Body and soul dissolve with fear;
> Death aims his blow,—my tongue is dumb,
> My senses go, my hour is come!
> The fiend is feeling for his prey;
> He is stealing life away.
> I'll fear no more his voice or eye:
> Jesus, before Thy cross I lie!

But the gentle reformer had not yet finished his work. Life's smouldering spark glowed again. The plague left its prey, and he poured out his heart anew.

> Father, I live! healed of my pain,
> Myself I give to Thee again!
> From all things wrong, oh, keep me free,
> And let my tongue sing only Thee!
> The unknown hour will come at length,
> With darker power to crush my strength.
> But I've no dread; for then I'll rise,
> With lifted head, above the skies.

Zwingli could hardly hold his pen, when, to the indescribable joy of his family, they received the tidings of his recovery in his own handwriting.

In Luther, we see a tendency to hypochondria, in his occasional fits of spiritual and physical depression, which we cannot contemplate without a feeling of awe; but the domestic and social aspects of the reformer complete the picture, and we see him in the ruddy light of his fireside a cheerful, solid, kindly, humorous man. Then, we all know how he loved and valued music; society he valued equally. He was fond of children's prattle; and his sorrow for the death of his little daughter Magdalen is most affecting. His mind was richly stored with classical and biblical lore; and his thoughts were like some of the works of mediæval art, superbly illuminated. He colored his conceptions with the brilliant hues of all objects of physical beauty.

"Music," said Luther, "is one of the most beautiful and noble gifts of God. It is the best solace to a man in sorrow; it quiets, quickens, and refreshes the heart. I give music the next place, and the highest honor, after theology. We see how David, and all the saints, clothed their godly thoughts in verse and song." When afflicted in his conscience, he used to have recourse to this recreative agency. On one of these occasions, when he had shut himself up for two days, some musicians breaking open his door, found him on the floor in a fainting fit, — when they brought him back to consciousness, not so much by medicine or food, as by their concert of sweet sounds. "Luther's Carol for Christmas, written for his own child Hans, is still sung from the dome of the Kreuz-kirche in Dresden, before daybreak on the morning of Christmas-day. It refers to the custom then and long afterwards prevalent in Germany, of making, at Christmas-time, representations of the manger with the infant Jesus. But the most famous of his hymns is his noble version of Psalm xlvi., 'God is my stronghold firm and sure,' which may be called the national hymn of his Protestant countrymen. Luther's hymns are wanting in harmony and correctness of metre, to a degree which often makes them jarring to our modern ears; but they are always full of fire and strength, of clear Christian faith, and brave, joyful trust in God." \*

It was the "Lion-hearted Luther" that so oft solaced himself with sacred song during the stormy encoun-

---

\* C. Winkworth.

ters he had to pass through. Coleridge says, "He did as much for the Reformation by his hymns, as by his translation of the Bible," since his hymns made a bond of union among men who knew little of Creeds and Articles. The common people of Germany sang Luther's strong scriptural words to his own tunes with all their hearts; for, unlike the idle listening to a Latin litany, they were able to comprehend their deep meaning. "The children learned Luther's hymns in the cottage, and martyrs sang them on the scaffold."

In the year 1530, during the Diet of Augsburg, Luther's mental anxiety so overcame his bodily strength, that he fainted; on recovering, he said, "Come, let us defy the devil, and praise God by singing the hymn, 'Out of the depths I cry to Thee.' This hymn has often comforted the sick and dying. It is said to have been the last Protestant hymn sung in Strasburg Cathedral." *

The great Reformation has won from Germany thousands of sacred songs; and the succession have, in the general chorus of other Christian lands, had their respective choirs of singers.

It has been truly said, that the hymns of Germany are her national liturgy. These hymns, ranging through three centuries of time, have been classified into three divisions: representing, severally, the epoch of the Reformation; the great religious struggle of the thirty years' war; and the revival of religion in the days of Franke and Zinzendorf, through the earlier half of the eighteenth century. The ancient church in Bohemia, called the "United Brethren," which

* Miller's Our Hymns, &c.

dates back to the eighth century, was originated by two Greek monks, who first introduced Christianity into that country. In the eleventh century, it separated from the Romish Church: after which, it suffered a series of bitter persecutions, in one of which John Huss was burnt. Amidst all their privations and sufferings, the "Brethren" occupied themselves in printing the Bible; no fewer than three editions having been published in Bohemia before the Reformation.

That event spread great joy among them; and, subsequently, they formed a settlement on the estate of Count Zinzendorf, in Saxony, whence they spread into other countries.

Wetzel, in 1718, estimated the printed German hymns at fifty-five thousand, filling about three hundred volumes. Hans Sachs, who wrote about six thousand of these sacred lyrics, sent forth, from his humble workshop, his brave and earnest songs, while Luther commenced his attack upon the outworks of papal superstition; and, as already said, he thereby accomplished as much in behalf of the great event of the sixteenth century, as did the Elector of Saxony, or Luther by his sermons, and Melancthon by his epistles.

John Huss translated several of the works of Wickliffe into Bohemian. The truths he held dear he caused to be written on the walls of his chapel; and he put hymns into the mouths of the people, which became more terrible weapons than swords and staves. The following is a translation of a martial ode by Trotznou, and sung by the Hussite army:—

Ye champions! who maintain God's everlasting law,
Call on His name again, towards His presence draw;
And soon your steady march your foes shall overawe.
Why should you faint or fear? He shall preserve you still;
Life, love, — all, all that's dear, yield to His holy will;
And He shall steel your hearts, and strengthen against ill.

It was the congregational singing of the Hussite Brethren which, it is said, suggested to Luther the reconstruction of German hymnology. His efforts succeeded in spreading a peculiarity of worship, which has reached as far as the German tongue. By means of a single hymn of Luther, "Nun freut euch liebe Christengemein," many hundreds were brought to the faith, who otherwise would never have heard Luther's name. "His hymns were sung by people of every class, not only in schools and churches, but in dwellings and shops, in markets, streets, and fields." They found entrance even among adversaries. Selnecker relates, that, several of the hymns having been introduced into the chapel-service of the Duke Henry of Wolfenbüttel, a priest made complaint. The duke asked what hymns they were against which he protested. "May it please your highness, they are such as, 'Oh that the Lord would gracious be!'"—"Hold!" replied the duke: "must the Devil, then, be gracious? Whose grace are we to seek, if not that of God only?" The hymns continued to be sung at court. In 1529, a Romish priest preached at Lubeck; and, just as he ended his homily, two boys struck up the hymn of Luther, "O God, from heaven now behold!" when the whole assembly joined as with one voice; and continued to do the same, as often as any preacher inveighed against the evangelical doctrine. At Heidelberg, the Reformation thus made its way by singing. On one occasion, a priest was about to begin the service, standing at the high altar, when a single voice led off the beginning of Paul Speratus's famous hymn, "Es ist das Heil uns kommen her." The vast congregation immediately joined; and the Elector, taking this as a sufficient suffrage of his people, proceeded to introduce the communion in both kinds; for, hitherto, Frederick, from fear of the Emperor, had delayed suppressing the mass. It was Luther's hymns and tunes combined that did the work.

It was in 1467 that the followers of Huss formed themselves into a separate and organized church, known as that of the Bohemian and Moravian Brethren; one of the distinctive peculiarities of which was the free use of hymns and prayers in their mother tongue. "Many such hymns were already in existence, and others were soon written; and, in 1504, they were collected and published by the archbishop, Lucas, — the first example of a hymn-book, consisting of original compositions in the vernacular, to be found in any Western nation which had once owned the supremacy of Rome." *

Goethe was the first to discover that Hans Sachs possessed more than ordinary merit. He managed to make shoes and verses at the same time; was born, in 1494, at Nuremberg, — one of the first cities of Germany to welcome the new doctrine; and soon our poet became vocal in behalf of its claims. During the siege of Nuremberg, in 1561, he wrote a hymn of hope, which has been thus rendered: † —

* Christian Singers of Germany.  † Lyra Germanica.

Why art thou thus cast down, my heart?
Why troubled, why dost mourn apart,
   O'er naught but earthly wealth?
Trust in thy God, be not afraid,
He is thy Friend, who all things made!

Dost think thy prayers He doth not heed?
He knows full well what thou dost need, —
   And heaven and earth are His!
My Father and my God, who still
Is with my soul in every ill.

The rich man in his wealth confides;
But in my God my trust abides.
   Laugh as ye will, I hold
This one thing fast, that He hath taught:
Who trusts in God shall want for naught.

Yes, Lord: Thou art as rich to-day
As thou hast been, and shall be aye:
   I rest on Thee alone;
Thy riches to my soul be given,
And 'tis enough for earth and heaven!

Here are some stanzas of the celebrated German funeral hymn, of Sach: —

Come forth! come on, with solemn song!
The road is short, the rest is long;
The Lord brought here, He calls away!
   Make no delay,
This home was for a passing day.

Here in an inn a stranger dwelt;
Here joy and grief by turns he felt;
Poor dwelling, now we close thy door!
   The task is o'er,
The sojourner returns no more.

Now of a lasting home possessed,
He goes to seek a deeper rest;
Good-night! the day was sultry here,
   In toil and fear;
Good-night! the night is cool and clear.

Chime on, ye bells ! Again begin,
And ring the Sabbath morning in;
The laborer's week-day work is done,
    The rest begun,
Which Christ has for His people won !

Luther's "'Song of praise for the great benefits which God has manifested to us in Christ,' in the original," says Mrs. Charles, "seems to have pressed into it the history of a lifetime, — to be the essence of that 'Commentary on the Galatians,' which contained, as it were, the essence of Luther's life."

Dear Christian people, all rejoice,
    Each soul with joy upspringing;
Pour forth one song, with heart and voice,
    With love and gladness singing.
Give thanks to God, our Lord above,
Thanks for His miracle of love !
Dearly He hath redeemed us !

The devil's captive, bound I lay, —
    Lay in death's chains forlorn;
My sins distressed me night and day,
    The sin within me born;
I could not do the thing I would,
In all my life was nothing good,
    Sin had possessed me wholly.

.    .    .    .    .    .

Then God saw, with deep pity moved,
    My grief that knew no measure;
Pitying, He saw, and freely loved, —
    To save me was His pleasure.
The Father's heart to me was stirred,
He saved me with no sovereign word, —
    His very best it cost Him !

He spoke to His beloved Son,
    With infinite compassion, —
" Go, my Heart's most precious crown,

Be to the lost Salvation!
Death, his relentless tyrant, stay;
And bear him from his sins away
With Thee to live for ever!"

Willing, the Son took that behest;
Born of a maiden mother,
To His own earth He came a guest,
And made Himself my brother.
All secretly He went His way,
Veiled in my mortal flesh He lay,
And thus the foe He vanquished.

We have not given the whole of the verses. A curious use was made of this hymn in the year 1557, when, a number of princes belonging to the reformed religion being convened at Frankfort, they wished to have an evangelical* service in the Church of St. Bartholomew. A large congregation assembled, but the pulpit was occupied by a Roman-Catholic priest, who proceeded to preach according to his own views. After listening for some time in indignant silence, the whole congregation rose, and began to sing this hymn, till they fairly sang the priest out of Church.

Of the score or more of English versions of Luther's great hymn, one of the most recent and best is by Dr. Reynolds, of Chicago. He fitly designates this noble hymn the imperishable pæan of the Reformation. In spite of their rugged, inharmonious measure, Luther's lyrics are full of his characteristic fire and energy. It was this hymn that was chanted over his grave, amid sobs and tears:—

A safe stronghold our God is still, a sure defence and weapon;
He will deliver all from ill that unto us may happen.
    Our old and bitter foe
    Is fain to work us woe;

* i.e. Protestant.

   In strength and cunning, he
   Is armed full fearfully;
   On earth is not his equal.

By strength of ours we naught can do, the strife full soon were ended;
But for us fights the Champion true, by God Himself commended.
   And dost thou ask His name?
   'Tis Jesus Christ! The same
   Whom Lord of Hosts we call,
   God blessed over all,—
   He'll hold the field triumphant.

Though Satan's hosts the earth should fill, all watching to devour us,
We tremble not, we fear no ill, they cannot overpower us.
   This world's false prince may still
   Scowl fiercely, as he will,
   His threatenings are but vain,
   We shall unharmed remain:
   A word shall overthrow him.

God's Word unshaken shall remain, whatever foes invade us!
Christ standeth on the battle-plain, with His own strength to aid us!
   What though they take our life,
   Our goods, fame, children, wife?
   E'en when their worst is done,
   They have but little won:
   The kingdom ours abideth!

Luther's first hymn was, it is believed, called forth by the martyrdom of two young Christian monks, who were burnt alive, at Brussels, by the Sophists:—

Flung to the heedless winds, or on the waters cast,
Their ashes shall be watched, and gathered at the last.
And, from that scattered dust, around us and abroad,
Shall spring a plenteous seed of witnesses for God.
Jesus hath now received their latest living breath,
Yet vain is Satan's boast of victory in their death.
Still, still, though dead, they speak, and, trumpet-tongued, proclaim,
To many a wakening land, the one availing Name!

Hear, now, his beautiful hymn of Faith:—

When the sky is black and lowering, when thy path in life is drear,
Upward lift thy steadfast glances, 'mid the maze of sorrow here.
From the beaming Fount of gladness shall descend a radiance bright;
And the grave shall be a garden, and the hours of darkness, light.
For the Lord will hear and answer when in faith His people pray;
Whatsoe'er He hath appointed shall but work thee good alway.
E'en thy very hairs are numbered, God commands when one shall fall;
And the Lord is with His people, helping each and blessing all.

Then, there is the grand, massive chant, evidently inspired by the "Dies Iræ;" often erroneously ascribed to Luther, which, although worthy of him, was written by Ringwaldt, in 1585:—

  Great God! what do I see and hear!
   The end of things created!
  The Judge of mankind doth appear,
   On clouds of glory seated!
  The trumpet sounds, the graves restore
  The dead which they contained before:
   Prepare my soul to meet Him!

  The dead in Christ shall first arise
   At the last trumpet's sounding,—
  Caught up to meet Him in the skies,
   With joy their Lord surrounding:
  No gloomy fears their souls dismay,
  His presence sheds eternal day
   On those prepared to meet Him.

Here are some admirable lines, from the German, on the "Name that is above every name:"—

To the Name that brings salvation, honor, worship, laud we pay;
That for many a generation hid in God's foreknowledge lay,
Name of gladness, Name of pleasure, by the tongue ineffable;
Name of sweetness, passing measure, to the ear delectable!
'Tis our safeguard and our treasure, 'tis our shield 'gainst sin and hell!

Nicolaus Hermann, who died in the year of our Redemption, 1561, wrote this simple and sweet melody for evening-time : —

> Sunk is the sun's last beam of light,
> And darkness wraps the world in night:
> Christ! light us with Thy heavenly ray,
> Nor let our feet in darkness stray.
> Thanks, Lord, that Thou, throughout the day,
> Hast kept all grief and harm away ;
> That angels tarried round about
> Our coming in and going out.
> Whate'er of wrong we've done or said,
> Let not on us the charge be laid ;
> That, through Thy free forgiveness blest,
> In peaceful slumber we may rest.
> Thy guardian angels round us place,
> All evil from our couch to chase ;
> Both soul and body, while we sleep,
> In safety, gracious Father, keep.

Among these German minstrels we find some eminent women : one was the Princess Louisa Henrietta of Brandenberg, who wrote a beautiful poem on the Resurrection, "Jesus, meine Zuversicht." We quote from the English version of Mrs. Charles : —

> Jesus, my eternal trust and my Saviour, ever liveth !
> This I know; and deep and just is the peace this knowledge giveth,
>     Though death's lingering night may start
>     Many a question in my heart.
> Jesus lives eternally : I shall also live in Him !
> Where my Saviour is, shall be ! What can make this bright hope dim ?
>     Will the Head one member lose,
>     Nor through each its life diffuse ?
> Hope's strong chain around me bound, still shall twine my Saviour grasping;
> And my hand of faith be found, as death left it, Jesus clasping !
>     No assault the foe can make,
>     E'er that deathless clasp shall break !

I am flesh, and therefore, duly dust and ashes must become;
This I know, but know as truly, He will wake me from the tomb!
    That with Him, whate'er betide,
    I may evermore abide!
God Himself, in that blest place, shall a glorious body give me;
I shall see His blissful face; to His heavens He will receive me!
    Then, from this rejoicing heart,
    Every weakness shall depart!

In Professor Schaff's "Christ in Song," we find a translation of a remarkable poem, which Knapp pronounces "the sweetest and most excellent of all German hymns." It is by Dr. P. Nicolai, a Lutheran pastor, at Una, Westphalia. It is still a favorite German hymn, celebrating the spiritual union of Christ and his Church. It was written during a prevailing pestilence in 1597. We give four stanzas of this fine hymn. The translation is Dr. Harbaugh's.

    How lovely shines the Morning Star!
    The nations see and hail afar
        The light in Judah shining.
    Thou David's Son of Jacob's race,
    My Bridegroom, and my King of grace,
        For Thee my heart is pining!
        Lowly, holy, great, and glorious,
        Thou victorious
    Prince of graces,
    Filling all the heavenly places!
    .    .    .    .    .

    Now richly to my waiting heart,
    O Thou, my God, deign to impart
        The grace of love undying.
    In Thy blest Body let me be,—
    E'en as the branch is in the tree,—
        Thy life, my life supplying.
        Sighing, crying for the savor
        Of Thy favor;
    Resting never
    Till I rest in Thee for ever!
    .    .    .    .    .

Wake, wake your harps to sweetest songs!
In praise of Him to whom belongs
  All praise; join hearts and voices.
For evermore, O Christ! in Thee, —
Thee, all in all of love to me, —
  My grateful heart rejoices.
    With joy, employ hymns victorious,
    Glad and glorious;
  E'er be given
  Honor to the King of Heaven!

Oh, joy! to know that Thou, my Friend,
Art Lord, Beginning without end:
  The First and Last — Eternal!
And Thou, at length, O glorious grace!
Wilt take me to that holy place,
  The home of joys supernal!
    Amen, amen!

These charming stanzas are by one of the anonymous German hymnists: —

Smiling, a bright-eyed seraph bent over an infant's dream;
To view his mirrored form he leant, as in the crystal stream.
"Fair infant, come," he whispered low, "and leave the earth with me, —
To a bright and happy world we'll go: this is no home for thee."
Each sparkling pleasure knows alloy, nor cloudless skies are here;
A care there is for every joy, for every smile a tear.
The heart that dances free and light, may soon be chained by sorrow;
The sun that sets in calm to-night, may rise in storm to-morrow!
Alas! to cloud a brow so fair, that griefs and pains should rise!
Alas! that this dark world of care should dim those laughing eyes!
To seek a brighter land with me, infant, thou wilt not fear;
For piteous Heaven the sad decree recalls, that sent thee here!"
It seemed on him the sweet babe smiled, his wings the seraph spread:
They're gone, — the angel and the child. Poor mother! thy son is dead!*

    * Hymns from the Land of Luther.

There is great power in these stanzas, from the German of Langbecker: —

> What shall I be, Lord, when Thy radiant glory,
> As from the grave I rise, encircles me?
> When, brightly pictured in the light before me,
> What eye hath never seen, mine eyes shall see?
> What shall I be? Ah, blessed and sublime
> Is the dim prospect of that glorious time!
> What shall I be, when days of grief are ended?

These impressive lines are from the German of Rosegarten: —

> Through night to light; and though to mortal eyes
>   Creation's face a pall of terror wear,
> Good cheer, good cheer! The gloom of midnight flies,
>   Then shall a sunrise follow, mild and fair.
>
> Through storm to calm; and though his thunder car
>   The rumbling tempest drive through earth and sky,
> Good cheer, good cheer! The elemental war
>   Tells that a blessed healing hour is nigh.
>   .   .   .   .   .   .   .   .
> Through cross to crown; and though thy spirit's life
>   Trials untold assail with giant strength,
> Good cheer, good cheer! Soon ends the bitter strife,
>   And thou shalt reign in peace with Christ at length.
>
> Through death to life; and through this vale of tears,
>   And through this thistle-field of life, ascend
> To the great supper in that world, whose years
>   Of bliss unfading, cloudless, know no end!

From the German of Johann Hofel: * —

> Oh! sweetest words that Jesus could have sought,
> To soothe the mourning widow's heart, — "Weep not!"
> They fall with comfort on my ear,
> When life is dark and trouble near.
>   .   .   .   .   .   .   .

* Hymns from the Land of Luther.

Words that were spoken amid sorrow's strife,
And in the very midst of death and life;
They shall refresh my soul at last,
And strengthen me till life is past.

. . . . . .

Oh! sweetest words that Jesus could have sought,
To cheer His weary, troubled ones, — "Weep not!"
Thrice blessed words! I, listening, stay,
Till grief and sorrow flee away!

Joachim Neander, who was one of the first and the best of the hymn-writers of the "Reformed Church," called his effusions "Bunderslieder" (Songs of the Covenant). In his youth, he was a wild and careless student at Bremen. One day, he and two of his comrades went into St. Martin's Church, with the intention of making a jest of the service: but the sermon touched his conscience so deeply, that he determined to visit the preacher in private; and, from this time, he began to lead a more circumspect life. His love of the chase, however, still clung to him; and, on one occasion, he followed his game on foot so far, that night came on, and he utterly lost his way among rocky and woody hills, where the climbing was difficult even in daylight. He wandered about for sometime, and then suddenly discovered that he was in a most dangerous position, and that one step forward, which he was on the point of taking, would have thrown him over a precipice. A feeling of horror came over him, that almost deprived him of the power of motion: and, in this extremity, he prayed earnestly to God for help; vowing an entire devotion of himself to His service in the future. All at once, his courage returned: he felt as though a hand were leading him, and, following the path thus indicated, he at length reached his home in safety. From this day, he kept his vow; and a complete change took place in his mode of life. In 1674, he was made head-master of the grammar-school at Dusseldorf, belonging to the Reformed Church. It flourished exceedingly under his rule: but he also set on foot private religious meetings, which caused offence; and the elders, one day, deposed him from his mastership, forbade him to preach, and banished him from the town. His pupils would have fought for him; but he forbade them, and quietly submitted to the wrong. It was summer-time, and he wandered out to a deep and beautiful glen near Mettmann, on the Rhine; where, for some months, he lived in a cavern, which is still known by the name of "Neander's Cave." In this retreat, he composed many of his hymns; and among them the following:

> A deep and holy awe
> Put Thou, my God, within my inmost soul,
> While near Thy feet I draw;
> And my heart sings in me, and my voice praises Thee;
> Do Thou all wandering sense and thought control.
>
> . . . . .
>
> O God, the crystal light
> Of Thy most stainless sunshine here is mine;
> It floods my outer sight;
> Ah, let me well discern Thyself where'er I turn,
> And see Thy power through all Thy creatures shine.
>
> . . . . .
>
> Hark! how the air is sweet
> With music from a thousand warbling throats,
> Which echo doth repeat;
> To Thee I also sing, keep me beneath Thy wing;
> Disdain not Thou to list my harsher notes.
>
> Ah, Lord, the universe
> Is bright and laughing, full of pomp and mirth;
> Each summer doth rehearse

A tale for ever new, of wonders Thou canst do
In sunny skies, and on the fruitful earth.
　　Thee all the mountains praise;
　　The rocks and glens are full of song to Thee!
　　They bid me join my lays,
And laud the Almighty Rock, who, safe from every shock,
Beneath Thy shadow here doth shelter me!

In 1679, he was called to be pastor of the very church in Bremen which he had once entered in mockery. But he only preached there one year: he died the next, aged scarcely forty. We are indebted for this interesting glimpse of Neander to Miss Winkworth's "Christian Singers of Germany."

The following, of the plaintive and penitential order, is from his pen: —

　　Behold we here, in grief, draw near,
　　　Pleading at Thy throne, O King!
　　To Thee each tear, each trembling fear,
　　　Jesus, Son of Man, I bring.
　　Let me find Thee, let me find Thee,—
　　　Me, a vile and worthless thing!

　　Look down in love, and from above
　　　With Thy Spirit satisfy;
　　Thou hast sought me, Thou hast bought me,
　　　And Thy purchase, Lord, am I!
　　Let me find Thee, let me find Thee,
　　　Here on earth, and then on high!

　　Hear the broken, scarcely spoken
　　　Utterance of my heart to Thee;
　　All the crying, all the sighing
　　　Of Thy child accepted be;
　　Let me find Thee, let me find Thee,
　　　Thus I pray vehemently!

Here are two beautiful stanzas from the same source, on the glory of God in creation: —

> Lo, heaven and earth, and sea and air,
> Their Maker's glory all declare!
> And thou, my soul, awake and sing, —
> To Him thy praises also bring.
> Through Him, the glorious source of day,
> Can break the clouds of night away;
> The pomp of stars, the moon's soft light,
> Praise Him through all the silent night!

The beautiful penitential hymn just quoted was, we believe, the last he wrote, as it bears date the year preceding his death.

The name of Joachim Neander very naturally reminds us of his great namesake, the church historian, whose full name was Johann August Wilhelm Neander; who was born a century later, at a time when the religious condition of Germany seemed to demand a second Reformation. Although not strictly in the category of German hymnists, yet this second Neander was, Luther-like, a second reformer; and, as such, he forms a connecting link between the Germany of Luther's days and of our own. A brief allusion to him will not, therefore, it is believed, be deemed an unpardonable digression.

This Neander was born in the year 1789, — a year memorable as introducing the fearful drama of the French Revolution, when the moral atmosphere was infected with deadly poisons, and black, thickening clouds were spread over the political and religious horizons. It was then that this remarkable man was given to the world, — a man in whom, more than in any other, was that power which Providence was ordaining should brush away those fuliginous clouds, purge the atmosphere, and throw upon it the reviving rays of the great sun of Christian truth. When only eight years of age, he could learn no more from his private teacher. Just about this time, it is related that a bookseller in Hamburg was struck with the frequent visits to his shop of a bashful, ungainly boy, who used to steal in and seize upon some erudite volume that no one else would touch, and utterly lose himself, for hours together, in study.

About the year 1806, when he was seventeen years old, he was baptized into the Christian Church; and at this period it was that he adopted the name, by which he has since been so well known and loved, "Neander" (literally, "the new man"). He was one of the most laborious of laborious German students. Fifteen lectures a week, at least, he was in the habit of delivering in the university; and never has Berlin had a more exemplary professor, and never perhaps was one more tenderly beloved. His character is described as most symmetrical and beautiful: "open-hearted, and inoffensive as a child, he stood before the world, separated only from every rude contact by the breath of heavenliness which surrounded him." His physique does not seem to have been graceful: on the contrary, his form was thin and bent, and his complexion dark and sallow, indicative of intense study and reflection. He was, however, great, noble, and triumphant as the champion of Christian verity, in a day when its adversaries made their strong attack under the name of their new leader, Strauss. Neander worked earnestly to the last; and, when that day opposed him, he calmly said, to the sorrowing friends who surrounded him, "I am weary: I will now go to sleep;" and, as they conducted him to his bed, the place of his last repose, he whispered, with a voice of mellowing affection, which thrilled through the heart and marrow of all present, "Good-night, good-night." It was his last "good-night" on earth. He slumbered for four hours; and then gently, and almost imperceptibly, "breathed himself into the silent and cold sleep of death." This good man was honored in his death as in his life. The day of his funeral obsequies was observed as a public holiday in Berlin. A vast procession followed the remains to the grave, stretching the length of full two miles. The hearse was surrounded by students carrying lighted candles; in front of the body, Neander's Bible and Greek Testament were carried. The carriages of the King and Princess of Prussia followed in the procession; and, at the grave, a solemn choral was sung by a thousand voices. The benefactions of Dr. Neander can be no longer administered by his own hand; but his name is engraved on an establishment for the reception and instruction of homeless little wanderers, who will long be familiar with "Neander's Haus."

The closing years of the sixteenth, and the opening of the seventeenth century, were not wanting in sacred lyrics, but the singers were of a different order: they were, for the most part, professional writers, rather than from among the people. In the course of a few years, after the peace of Passau, the Reformed religion had spread over more than three-fourths of the country, including all the most populous centres. "The great idea, that every man is personally responsible for his belief and his actions to God Himself, was making itself felt everywhere, breaking up old organizations, and the orderly but rigid routine of mediæval life, prompting to new enterprises, inspiring men with courage to bear imprisonment, exile, or death, for their faith. But it had brought its dangers and difficulties, too, not only in the actual persecutions and wars, which, though on a very limited scale, existed throughout this period, until they culminated in the great struggle of the thirty years' war; but still more in an excessive individualism, which rendered common action almost impossible. For the new mode of thought gave rise to mental conflicts, and doubts and scruples of conscience, for which there was no longer the easy resolution of an authoritative decision of church or priest, and which saddened the lives of many whom we should not now call specially religious persons; and it brought endless disputes on doctrinal questions among the professors of the evangelical faith themselves. Over the temporary compromise between the Romanist and Protestant religions, known as "the Interim;" over every shade of more or less Calvinistic views of the Atonement and the Sacraments,—they quarrelled, not in words only, but in deeds.* Thus divided, and broken up into opposing interests, the States of Protestant Germany were rife with feuds and intestine strifes; while the Jesuits and the House of Hapsburg, on the Romish side of despotism, formed a united and broad phalanx against them. The horoscope of the future might well, indeed, be regarded as ominous of disaster and trouble; and it came in the sanguinary struggle which lasted a lifetime.

* Christian Singers of Germany.

# FOURTH EVENING.

## GERMAN.—THIRTY YEARS' WAR.

# FOURTH EVENING.

## GERMAN.—THIRTY YEARS' WAR.

GREAT men have been compared to fire-pillars, or beacons, to guide us in the great onward progress of the race. They stand forth in colossal grandeur, as the revealed embodiment of the possibilities of even our fallen human nature. And such representative men are given to the world, to do the work of the world's necessity, by the providence of God, at the precise and proper time. Columbus, Newton, Guttenberg, and Luther belong to this category. At the death of Luther, which synchronized with that of Francis I., the Emperor Charles V. entered into a solemn league with the Pontiff Paul III. for the extermination of "heretics," and forthwith took up arms against the Reformed States of Germany: the resistance of the combined States was such, however, that a treaty of peace soon followed. It was on the accession, in 1619, of Ferdinand II., an intolerant bigot, that the great contest of thirty years' duration broke out.

"So far as the human eye can see, the Reformation, except for Gustavus Adolphus, would have been crushed in Germany, and probably in all northern

Europe — with the exception of England — as well." \* He made his appearance at the juncture of danger, when the Protestant princes and free cities of Germany formed themselves, for mutual defence, into what was called the "Protestant Union," to which those on the other side replied by a "Catholic League." "For a while the hidden fires smouldered beneath the surface, or just darted out here and there a tongue of flame to tell of their presence. Not till 1618 did the flames burst openly forth, and then in a remote part of Germany, in Bohemia; but with so much inflammable material everywhere prepared, it was not long before the conflagration spread over all; a fire which should not be extinguished for thirty years, and which, in the end, rather burnt itself out, — all the fuel which could feed it being consumed, — than it can be said to have been extinguished at all."

"This war — the longest, the most terrible, which modern Europe has seen, — in which Germany was tortured, torn to pieces, wrecked, brayed as in a mortar under the iron mace of war, from which, at this day, as many believe, it has only partially recovered — may be conveniently divided into three periods. In the first of these, extending from 1618 to 1630, the arms of the Catholic League and the Emperor were everywhere triumphant, beating down the feeble and half-hearted opposition of the Protestant princes of Germany; scattering the forces of some military adventurers, who, in all ways unequal to the task, would have stood in the gap; and, lastly, compelling Christian the Fourth, King of Denmark, who would fain have meddled in the matter, to withdraw

\* Archbishop Trench.

again, with shame and defeat, to his own land. And now it seemed as though the end had come. All Germany lay prostrate at the feet of the Emperor, and of Wallenstein, his terrible commander." * It was then, at this dire extremity, to which the Protestant cause was reduced by the machinations and subtle artifices of the Jesuits, that the King of Sweden came to its rescue. Responding to the mute appeal of the suffering members of the Reformed faith, he descended upon Germany; in little more than two short years, turned the whole tide of affairs, until, on the plains of Lutzen, he crowned an heroic life with an heroic death. In this brief period was the turning-point of the bloody drama, which for thirty years was enacted on the stage of Germany. The third act of the tragedy commenced with his death. "The cause which he came to support staggered for a season under this blow, yet never entirely lost the superiority which his victories had given it; and when, sixteen years after his death, in 1648, the end at length arrived, then, by the treaty of Westphalia, the entirely equal rights of the two Confessions were recognized; and this has remained the public law of Germany from that day to the present, nor has it at any time since been seriously disturbed." † Gustavus, who had watched the hideous strife for twelve years, not without a presentiment that sooner or later he would be himself drawn into its vortex, might yet very well pause before he committed himself irrevocably to it.

Long delayed by contrary winds, Gustavus at length reached the shores north of the Oder, on midsummerday, 1630, — the centenary of the Augsburg Confes-

* Trench.    † Ibid.

sion. His first act was to lift up an earnest prayer for the Divine aid; and then he went to work. His army was well disciplined and hardy, but ridiculously small compared with that which was to oppose him; yet it took them full eighteen years to get rid of him or them. He was a great general, and knew how to make a small army do the work of a large one.

Unlike his antagonist in the field, Wallenstein, he was not chary of himself; but, at a siege, he would, in the same day, be at once generalissimo, chief engineer, pioneer, and leader of a storming-party to dislodge the foe. At length came the conflict on the field of Lutzen, which proved fatal to the Christian hero. A severe wound, which the king had received in his Polish campaigns, made the wearing of his armor very painful to him. When it was brought to him this morning, he declined to put it on, saying, "God is my armor," and went into the battle without it. Thus unprotected, he was surprised by some Imperial cuirassiers, who were concealed by the heavy mist that prevailed at the time, and shot.

When Gustavus Adolphus was found by his enemies wounded on the field of battle, amid a heap of dying men, it was with a pride only to be equalled in the hour of victory, that he cried out, "I am the King of Sweden, and seal with my blood the liberty and religion of the whole German nation!"

What imperishable interest lingers around those heroic war-hymns of Gustavus Adolphus and Martin Luther; who can read them, and not kindle with deepest sympathy in the spirit-stirring scenes?

The celebrated battle-song of Gustavus Adolphus was so styled, because it was frequently sung by the great and good Swedish monarch and his army, on the field of action; and, for the last time, on the eve of the battle of Lutzen. Its authorship has long been attributed to Altenburg, a pastor in Thuringia; recent researches, however, seem to indicate that he only composed the choral, and that the hymn itself was written down roughly by Gustavus Adolphus, after his victory at Leipzig, and reduced to regular verse by his chaplain, Dr. Fabricius, for the use of the army: —

Fear not, O little flock! the foe who madly seeks your overthrow;
  Dread not his rage and power!
What though your courage sometimes faints, his seeming triumph
    o'er God's saints
  Lasts but a little hour.
Be of good cheer: your cause belongs to Him who can avenge
    your wrongs,
  Leave it to Him, our Lord;
Though hidden yet from all our eyes. He sees the Gideon who shall
    rise
  To save us and His Word.
As true as God's own Word is true, nor earth nor hell with all their
    crew
  Against us shall prevail.
A jest and by-word are they grown: our God is with us, we His
    own, —
  Our victory cannot fail!
Amen, Lord Jesus, grant our prayer: Great Captain, now thine arm
    make bare, —
  Fight for us once again;
So shall Thy saints and martyrs raise a mighty chorus to Thy
    praise,
  World without end, — Amen.

The story of the last battle of the great and good Gustavus is as follows: "The armies of the king and Wallenstein were drawn up till the morning mist dispersed, to commence the attack, when Gustavus commanded Luther's 'Eine feste Burg ist unser Gott,' to be sung; and then that hymn of his own, accompanied by the drums and trumpets of the whole army. Immediately afterwards, the mist broke, and the sunshine burst upon the two armies. For a moment, Gustavus Adolphus knelt beside his horse, in face of his soldiers, and repeated his usual battle-prayer: 'O Lord Jesus Christ! bless our armies and this day's battle, for the glory of Thy holy name!' Then passing along the lines, with a few brief words of encouragement, he gave the battle-cry, 'God with us!' the same with which he had conquered at Leipzig. Thus began the day which laid him low amidst the thickest of the fight, with those three sentences on his dying lips, noble and Christian as any that ever fell from the lips of dying man since the days of the first martyr, 'I seal with my blood the liberty and religion of the German nation.'" This incident adds imperishable interest to the hymn.

What struggles of soul have some of these hymns not witnessed, in what strange and stirring scenes have they not mingled! How has their melody and sweet inspiration brought solace to sorrow, and lent ecstasy to spiritual joy! Like the words of the Holy Book, they linger in the memory; and, in hours of despondency and gloom, how often have they lifted us up from the earthliness of our being, and also imparted even to the sick and dying wondrous consolation!

This war gave birth to great crimes as well as great virtues; but it banished from Germany the arts of industry, and polite studies. Famine and pestilence followed the track of war, destroying even more than fire and sword. All reverence for laws, human or divine, was forgotten; rapine and violence reigned on every side. Schiller informs us that "the soldier was ruler: the commander of an army was a far more important personage in the land than the rightful lord."

All Germany was full of these petty tyrants, and the country suffered equally from its enemies and its defenders. It is computed, that, during this fatal thirty years, Germany lost two-thirds of her population. In Saxony alone, nine hundred thousand human beings perished. Augsburg, from a population of eighty thousand souls, found herself reduced to eighteen thousand; and Munich, Nuremberg, and almost every city of importance shared the same fate. Passing such an ordeal, — so fearful and almost exterminating a war, — it is remarkable that it lived through it; and that, instead of utterly perishing, it should even evince signs of considerable vitality, in the very heart of the crisis which desolated the land.

It was the seed-time of an illustrious band of Christian bards, — Paul Fleming, Paul Gerhardt, Luther, Gellert, Klopstock, and numerous others, many of whom sang and fought at the same time.

Rist, a clergyman in North Germany, who suffered much in his youth from mental conflicts, and in after years from rapine, pestilence, and all the horrors of war, used to say, "The dear Cross hath pressed many songs out of me;" and this seems to have been equally true of many of his contemporaries. It certainly was true of Johann Heermann, the author of some of the most touching hymns for "Passion week," who wrote his sweet songs amidst the perils of war, during which he more than once escaped with his life as by a miracle; so, too, the hymns of Simon Dach speak of the sufferings of the Christian, and his longing to escape from the strife of earth to the peace of heaven. Here are a few stanzas of one of Rist's hymns. The translation is by Catherine Winkworth.

> O living Bread from heaven,
>    How richly hast Thou fed Thy guests!
> The gifts Thou now hast given
>    Have filled my heart with joy and rest.
> O wondrous food of blessing! O cup that heals our woes!
> My heart, this gift possessing, in thankful song o'erflows.
>    For while the life and strength in me
>      Were quickened by this food,
>    My soul hath gazed awhile on Thee,
>      O highest, only Good!
> And Thou hast freely given, what earth could never buy, —
> The Bread of life from heaven, — that now I shall not die!

  .    .    .    .    .    .    .

>    O Love incomprehensible!
>    What wrought in Thee, my Saviour, thus
>      That Thou shouldst have descended
>      From highest heaven to dwell with us!
> Creator! that hath brought Thee to succor such as I,
> Who else had vainly sought Thee! Then grant me now to die
> To sin, and live alone to Thee, that, when this life is o'er,
> Thy face, O Saviour! I may see in heaven for evermore.

  .    .    .    .    .    .    .

> But I, in sinful blindness, am erring every hour,
> Yet boundless is Thy kindness and righteous is Thy power:
> And yet Thou camest, dost not spurn a sinner, Lord, like me!
> Ah, how can I Thy love return? what gift have I for Thee?

Though a great number of Rist's hymns were adopted by many churches, even during his lifetime, he would never suffer them to be sung in his own church; with the exception of a Christmas hymn, which, on one occasion, he allowed the children of the school to practise, and to begin to sing on that festival, "Wenn das Volk aus der Kirche zu gehen beginnt," as the people were beginning to go out of church.

Johann Heermann (1585-1647) was a native of Silesia. Being much tried during the horrors of war, his mind seems to have become the more spiritually enlightened through his bodily sufferings, in the midst of which he wrote the greater number of his hymns. The following beautiful lines are a translation from one of his hymns, by Frances Elizabeth Cox: —

> Such wondrous love would baffle my endeavor
> To find its equal, should I strive for ever:
> How should my works, could I in all obey Thee,
>     Ever repay Thee!
>
> Yet this shall please Thee: if devoutly trying
> To keep Thy laws, mine own wrong will denying,
> I watch my heart, lest sin again ensnare it,
>     And from Thee tear it.
>
> But since I have not strength to flee temptation,
> To crucify each sinful inclination,
> Oh! let Thy Spirit, grace, and strength provide me,
>     And gently guide me.
>
> Then shall I see Thy grace, and duly prize it,
> For Thee renounce the world, for Thee despise it:
> Then, of my life, Thy laws shall be the measure:
>     Thy will, my pleasure!
>
> .   .   .   .   .   .
>
> And when, O Christ! before Thy throne so glorious,
> Upon my head is placed the crown victorious,
> Thy praise I will, while heaven's full chime is ringing,
>     Be ever singing.

Wulffer wrote, in 1648, some impressive stanzas on Eternity, which were the favorite study of Niebuhr.

The greater part of the poem is believed to be of ancient origin.

> Eternity! eternity! how long art thou, eternity!
> And yet to thee time hastes away,
> Like as the war-horse to the fray,
> Or swift as couriers homeward go,
> Or ship to port, or shaft from bow.
> Ponder, O man, eternity!
>
> Eternity! eternity! how long art thou, eternity!
> For even as in a perfect sphere
> End nor beginning can appear,
> Even so, eternity, in thee,
> Entrance nor exit can there be.
> Ponder, O man, eternity!
>
> Eternity! eternity! how long art thou, eternity!
> A circle infinite art thou,
> Thy centre an eternal Now:
> Never we name thy outward bound,
> For never end therein is found.
> Ponder, O man, eternity!
>
> Eternity! eternity! how long art thou, eternity!
> As long as God is God, so long
> Endure the pains of hell and wrong,
> So long the joys of heaven remain:
> O lasting joy! O lasting pain!
> Ponder, O man, eternity!

The hymn of Gottfried Arnold (1667–1704), of which we give two stanzas, was the favorite of Schelling: —

> How blest to all Thy servants, Lord, the road
>   By which Thou lead'st them on, yet oft how strange!
> But Thou in all dost seek our highest good;
>   For truth were true no longer, couldst Thou change.
> Though crooked seem the paths, yet are they straight,
>   By which Thou drawest Thy children up to Thee,
>   And passing wonders by the way they see,
> And learn, at last, to own Thee wise and great!
>     .     .     .     .     .     .

Now seems to us o'er harsh and strict Thy school,
  Now dost Thou greet us mild and tenderly;
Now, when our wilder passions break Thy rule,
  Thy judgments fright us back again to Thee.
With downcast eyes we seek Thy face again;
  Thou kissest us, we promise fair amends;
Once more Thy Spirit rest and pardon sends,
  And curbs our passions with a stronger rein.

Another of the German singers, Baron von Canitz, who lived from 1654 till 1699, wrote some fine melodies. We subjoin his matin song : —

Come, my soul, awake: 'tis morning; day is dawning
  O'er the earth: arise, and pray!
Come to Him who made this splendor: thou must render
  All thy feeble powers can pay.
From the stars, now learn thy duty; see their beauty
  Paling in the golden air:
So God's light thy mists should banish, — thus should vanish
  What to darkened sense seemed fair.

. . . . .

From God's glances shrink thou never, — meet them ever;
  Who submits him to His grace,
Finds that earth no sunshine knoweth, such as gloweth
  O'er his pathway all his days.
Round the gifts He on thee showers, fiery towers
  Will He set: be not afraid;
Thou shalt dwell 'mid angel-legions, in the regions
  Satan's self dares not invade.

Very beautiful is his hymn on the "Name of Jesus:" —

Ah, Jesus, Lord! whose faithfulness in heaven or in earth,
No human lips can celebrate enough to tell Thy worth!
I render thanks to Thee, that Thou in lowly guise wast born,
That Thou didst stoop to pity me, a helpless one forlorn.

Whate'er the anguish of my breast, its fluttering doth cease,
Whene'er Thy name of comfort fills my spirit with Thy peace!
No consolation is so sweet as that Thy name doth give, —
Thy *Jesus*' name! O David's Son, and Lord by whom I live!

Thy name of Jesus is a store of all that heart can need,
Enfolding every precious thing, — fruit, blossom, leaf, and seed!
He spends his time most worthily, who seeks that Name to know:
Its ocean-fulness riseth still as ages onward flow!

Apart from Jesus' precious name, I've nothing to desire;
Of all beside, e'en were it mine, my heart would only tire.
Apart from Him, there's naught of worth, created things are vain:
He is my glory and my wealth, my honor and my gain!

Thy precious name, *Lord Jesus Christ!* is better far to me,
Than all the wealth that can be found in earth, or air, or sea!
Thou art the paradise, set forth by God's own hand of love;
Thy presence is itself the heaven, where I shall dwell above.

. . . . . . . .

All that I ever undertake, I would begin in Thee, —
Thee first, Thee last, Thee midst, O Christ! and evermore to be!

We cite also the following hymn of his, from the "Lyra Germanica:" —

> But, oh, the depth of love beyond comparing,
> That brought Thee down from heaven, our burden bearing!
> I taste all peace and joy that life can offer,
>   Whilst Thou must suffer!
>
> Eternal King, in power and love excelling!
> Fain would my heart and mouth Thy praise be telling;
> But how can man's weak powers at all come nigh Thee,
>   How magnify Thee?
>
> Such wondrous love would baffle my endeavor,
> To find its equal, should I strive for ever;
> How should my works, could I in all obey Thee,
>   Ever repay Thee?
>
> Yet this shall please Thee, if devoutly trying
> To keep Thy laws, my own wrong will denying,
> I watch my heart, lest sin again ensnare it,
>   And from Thee tear it.

John Wesley's translation of the grand "Hymn on the Deity," by Breithaupt, who lived in 1653, has these striking stanzas: —

Thou true and only God, lead'st forth
    The immortal armies of the sky;
Thou laugh'st to scorn the gods of earth;
    Thou thunderest, and amazed they fly!
With downcast eye, the angelic choir
    Appear before Thy awful face;
Trembling, they strike the golden lyre,
    And through heaven's vault resound Thy praise.

.    .    .    .    .    .    .

How sweet the joys, the crown how bright,
    Of those who to Thy love aspire!
All creatures praise the Eternal Name!
    Ye hosts that to His court belong,
Cherubic choirs, seraphic flames,
    Awake the everlasting song!
Thrice holy! Thine the kingdom is,
    The power omnipotent is Thine;
And when created nature dies,
    Thy never-ceasing glories shine!

Fleming, who was born 1609, studied medicine at Leipzig till 1634, when he repaired to try his fortune in the little Duchy of Schleswig-Holstein. He soon afterwards obtained an appointment on the embassy to Peter-the-Great, of Russia. He was deeply impressed with religious feeling, as is evident from the following hymn, written just at the moment of his departure: —

    Only let nothing grieve thee, poor heart, be still!
    Howe'er the Lord bereave thee, bow down, my will!
        Why all this useless sorrow
        For the morrow?
        Will not He
        Who cares for all,
        Whate'er befall,
        Care, too, for thee?
    He rules thy fate: calmly await the Lord's behest;
    Who all things sees, what He decrees must be the best!

He returned from Moscow in 1635, and went subsequently to the Court of Persia. He died at Hamburg in 1640. His hymn, above cited, is still sung in some of the churches of Germany.

These fine lines are from the German of Frederick Arndt: —

Amid life's wild commotion, where nought the heart can cheer,
Who points beyond its ocean to heaven's brighter sphere?
Our feeble footsteps guiding, when from the path we stray,
Who leads to bliss abiding? Christ is our only *Way!*

When doubts and fears distress us, and all around is gloom,
And shame and fear oppress us, who can our souls illume?
Heaven's rays are round us gleaming, and making all things bright,
The Sun of *Truth* is beaming in glory on our sight.

Who fills our hearts with gladness that none can take away?
Who shows us, 'midst our sadness, the distant realms of day?
'Tis Christ! our aid unfailing, the Truth, the Life, the Way.

Weiszel, one of the German hymnologists of the seventeenth century, thus finely introduces a paraphrastic psalm: —

Lift up your heads, ye mighty gates!
Behold the King of Glory waits;
The King of kings is drawing near,
The Saviour of the world is here:
Life and salvation doth He bring.
Wherefore rejoice, and gladly sing
  Praise, O my God, to Thee!
  Creator, wise is Thy decree!

. . . . .

Fling wide the portals of your heart,
Make it a temple set apart
From earthly use for Heaven's employ,
Adorned with prayer and love and joy;
So shall your Sovereign enter in,
And new and nobler life begin.
  Praise, O my God! be Thine,
  For word, and deed, and grace divine.

Here is one of Löwenstern's brave battle-hymns, written amidst the tumult and din of those terrible "thirty years:"—

>Christ, Thou champion of the band who own
>Thy cross, oh, make Thy succor quickly known!
>The schemes of those who long our blood have sought
>    Bring Thou to nought.
>
>Do Thou Thyself for us Thy children fight,
>Withstand the devil, quell his rage and might:
>Whate'er assails Thy members left below,
>    Do Thou o'erthrow.
>
>And give us peace: peace in the church and school,
>Peace to the powers who o'er our country rule,
>Peace to the conscience, peace within the heart,
>    Do Thou impart.
>
>So shall Thy goodness here be still adored,
>Thou guardian of Thy little flock, dear Lord;
>And heaven and earth, through all eternity,
>    Shall worship Thee!

Niebuhr, the church historian, was fond of this hymn of Löwenstern; and might be heard now and then refreshing his own soul, amidst its intense labors and researches, by murmuring the metrical prayer,—

>"And give us peace: peace in the church and school,
>Peace to the powers who o'er our country rule,
>Peace to the conscience, peace within the heart,
>    Do Thou impart!"

Gottfried Arnold, who was born in 1666, in Saxony, of poor parents, published, when thirty years old, a collection of poems and hymns. In 1707, he was appointed pastor of Perleberg, in Brandenburg; and here he spent the last seven years of his life, in unwearied activity, but in peace; for his congregation were of his own way of thinking, and he was protected by the king. In 1713, his health began to fail; and, at Easter, 1714, while he was celebrating the Holy Communion, a Prussian recruiting-party burst into the church, and dragged away a number of young men from the very steps of the altar. This outrage, and his unavailing efforts to save the members of his flock, so affected him, that he took to his bed two days afterwards, and soon after died. Perhaps the best of Arnold's hymns is his deeply thoughtful one, "How blest to all Thy followers, Lord, the road!" But many others are very fine: here are some stanzas, entitled "The Kingdom of God:"—

Anoint us with Thy blessed love, O Wisdom! through and through,
Till Thy sweet impulses remove all dread and fear undue,
And we behold ourselves in Thee a purified humanity,
    And live Thy risen life.
O Perfect Manhood! once again descend Thou in our race,
Be all its lower nature slain, transform us of Thy grace,
Till, pure and holy as Thou art, Thine image shine from every heart,
    And Thou within us live.

Ulrich, Duke of Brunswick, wrote the following touching lines, in 1667:—

Leave all to God, forsaken one, and still thy fears,
For the Highest knows thy fears; thou shalt not wait His help in vain,
    Leave all to God.
Be still, and trust! for His strokes are strokes of love
    Thou must for thy profit bear;
He thy filial fear would move, trust thy Father's loving care,
    Be still and trust!
Know, God is near! Though thou think Him far away,
Though His mercy long have slept, He will come, and not delay,
When His child enough hath wept, for God is near!

The following stanzas form part of a translation
from the German of De Wette, by Whittier: —

World Redeemer! Lord of Glory! as of old to zealous Paul,
Thou didst come in sudden splendor, and from out the clouds didst
    call;
As to Mary in the garden, did Thy risen form appear, —
Come, arrayed in heavenly beauty: come, and speak, and I will
    hear!
    .       .       .       .       .       .

In my heart the voice made answer, "Ask thou not a sign from
    Heaven;
In the Gospel of thy Saviour, Life as well as Light is given.
Ever looking unto Jesus, all His glory thou shalt see:
From thy heart the veil be taken, and the Word made clear to thee.

Love the Lord, and thou shalt see Him; do His will, and thou shalt
    know
How the spirit lights the letter, — how a little child may go,
Where the wise and prudent stumble; how a heavenly glory shines,
In His acts of love and mercy, from the Gospel's simplest lines!"

The following lines, entitled "Going Home," are
from the German of Lange (1650–1727) : —

>    Our beloved have departed,
>    While we tarry, broken-hearted,
>        In the dreary, empty house;
>    They have ended life's brief story,
>    They have reached the home of glory,
>        Over death victorious!
>
>    Whilst with bitter tears we're mourning,
>    Thought to buried loves returning,
>        Time is hasting us along;
>    Downward to the grave's dark dwelling,
>    Upward to the fountain welling
>        With eternal life and song!
>        .   .   .   .   .
>
>    On we haste, to home invited,
>    There with friends to be united

In a surer bond than here;
Meeting soon, and met for ever!
Glorious hope! forsake us never,—
Scatter every doubt and fear!

Here are his lines on the future estate of being:—

What no human eye hath seen, what no mortal ear hath heard,
What on thought hath never been, in its noblest flights, conferred,—
　This hath God prepared in store,
　For His people evermore!

When the shaded pilgrim-land fades before the closing eye,
Then, revealed on either hand, heaven's own scenery shall lie;
　Then the veil of flesh shall fall,
　Now concealing, darkening all.

. . . . . .

When this aching heart shall rest, all its busy pulses o'er,
From her mortal robes undrest, shall my spirit upward soar:
　Then shall unimagined joy
　All my thoughts and powers employ.

Johann Frank, who died at Guben, in Prussia, in 1677, was the author of this,—considered, in the original, one of the richest German communion hymns:—

Deck thyself, my soul, with gladness;
Leave the gloomy haunts of sadness,
Come into the daylight's splendor;
There, with joy, thy praises render
Unto Him whose boundless grace
Grants thee, at His feet, a place;
He whom all the heavens obey
Deigns to dwell in thee to-day!

. . . . .

Sun, who all my life dost brighten,
Light, who dost my soul enlighten,
Joy, the sweetest, man e'er knoweth,
Fount, whence all my being floweth!
Here I fall before Thy feet:
Grant me worthily to eat
Of this blessed heavenly food,
To Thy praise, and to my good.

These brief specimens of German hymnology afford but a very imperfect conception of the rich resources which exist; but these will serve, at least, to illustrate the status of Christian piety during an epoch of almost unparalleled tribulation. These sacred lyrics have comforted and solaced many an afflicted Christian, and were to them, as were also those of the mediæval times, "songs in the night;" and, as such, they speak to us with a peculiar emphasis and force. Listen to this sweet song to the Saviour, by Lindemann, who lived during these troublous times of persecution for the truth : —

> In Thee is gladness amid all sadness,
>    Jesus, Thou sunshine of my heart!
> By Thee are given the gifts of heaven,
>    Thou the true Redeemer art!
> Our souls Thou wakest, our bonds Thou breakest;
> Who trusts Thee surely, hath built securely, —
>    He stands for ever : Hallelujah!
>
> . . . . .
>
> If He is ours, we fear no powers
>    Of earth or Satan, sin or death!
> He sees and blesses in worst distresses,
>    He can change them with a breath!
> Wherefore the story tell of His glory,
> With heart and voices; all heaven rejoices
>    In Him for ever : Hallelujah!

Schmolke (1731) wrote a beautiful hymn, "Himmelan geht unsre Bahn," of which these stanzas form the close : —

> Heavenwards ! faith discerns the prize
>    That is waiting us afar;
> And my heart would swiftly rise,
>    High o'er sun and moon and star,
> To that Light behind the veil,
> Where all earthly splendors pale.

> Heavenward, Death shall lead, at last,
>   To the home where I would be;
> All my sorrows overpast,
>   I shall triumph there with Thee;
> Jesus, who hast gone before,
> That we, too, might heavenward soar!

The sacred poetry of Germany, in the first half of the eighteenth century, was, to some extent, identified with the pietism of that period, — a transition from the state of formalism that preceded it. Schmolke, who then lived, was one who expressed in touching verse much of his personal sufferings and sorrows, his conflicts and consolations. His bereavements in early domestic life, and in his old age his blindness, are evidences that his earthly life was sufficiently checkered with trial; yet he is said to have solaced himself, if not others, with his meditative muse.

"There is one fact most noteworthy, as a sign of the temper in which this great tribulation was met by those who had to drink of its cup of pain deeper, perhaps, than any other, — that very many, among the most glorious compositions in the hymn-book of Protestant Germany, date from the period of the thirty years' war. Many men, as a poet of our own time has said, —

> 'Are cradled into poetry by wrong,
>   And learn in suffering what they teach in song.'

So was it here; and as this was a time full of suffering, and wrath, and wrong, so was it also a time when sacred song, which, since Luther, had shown comparatively little vitality, burst forth in a new luxuriance; and, most noticeable of all, is rich, not so much, as one might have expected, in threnes and lamentations,

*Misereres*, and cries *de profundis* (though these also are not wanting), as in *Te Deums* and *Magnificats*, hymns of high hope and holy joy, rising up from the darkness of this world to the throne of Him 'who giveth songs in the night,' and enables His servants to praise Him even in the fires; some among the chief sufferers, Paul Gerhardt, for instance, and Schirmer (the 'German Job,' as he called himself, with allusion to all that he had gone through), being the chief lyrists as well." \*

Paul Gerhardt ranks next to Luther, whom he in some respects resembles, and from whom he was separated in time by about a century. His hymns happily combine simplicity with depth and force. They are the heart-utterances of one who had a simple but sublime faith in God, and who recognized His fatherly presence in the affairs of life.

A certain impressiveness, a certain sorrowfulness, a certain fervor, were peculiar to him: he was a guest on earth; and everywhere, in his one hundred and twenty-three songs, sun-flowers are sown. This flower ever turns to the sun, so does Gerhardt to a blessed eternity. The love with which the contemporaries of Gerhardt, as far as the bell of an evangelical church was heard, turned to his song, has only one precedent, — the veneration, the devotion, with which Luther's songs were regarded. He was born in Saxony in 1606. When he had attained his twelfth year, the terrible thirty years' war broke out; and his family seem to have suffered much by its ravages. Forced, for a season, to forsake his native land, he was recalled, in 1631, to fill the office of preacher to

\* Archbishop Trench.

the Nicholai Church at Berlin; where he remained for ten years, honored and respected by all who knew him. But his religious sentiments did not wholly coincide with those of the king; and Gerhardt, too conscientious to dissemble, was ordered to resign his appointment and quit the country. Utterly destitute, not knowing where to lay his head or how to provide for his helpless family, Gerhardt left the home where he had spent so many happy years. "But no affliction, however terrible, could shake his confidence in Divine wisdom and mercy. After some consideration, he determined on directing his steps towards his native land, Saxony, where he yet hoped to find friends. The journey, performed on foot, was long and weary. Gerhardt bore up manfully: his heart failed him only when he gazed on his wife and little ones. When night arrived, the travellers sought repose in a little village-inn by the road-side; where Gerhardt's wife, unable to restrain her anguish, gave way to a burst of natural emotion. Her husband, concealing his anxious cares, reminded her of that beautiful verse of Scripture, 'Trust in the Lord; in all thy ways acknowledge Him, and He shall direct thy paths.' The words, uttered to comfort his afflicted partner, impressed his own mind so deeply, that, seating himself in a little arbor in the garden, he composed that hymn which has rendered his name celebrated:"* —

Commit thou all thy griefs and ways into His hands,
To His sure truth and tender care, who earth and heaven commands;
Who points the clouds their course, whom winds and seas obey,—
He shall direct thy wandering feet, He shall prepare thy way.

* De Pontes.

And then listen to the fine closing stanza : —

Give to the winds thy fears, hope, and be undismayed:
God hears thy sighs, and counts thy tears, — God shall lift up thy head.

We are informed, that he composed this beautiful hymn of trust, in the dark hour of his destitution, without pause or effort. It was one of the many German hymns born of sorrow and suffering. "Evening had now deepened, and the pastor and his wife were about to retire to rest, when two gentlemen entered the little parlor in which they were seated. They began to converse with the poet; and soon told him, that they were on their way to Berlin to seek the deposed clergyman, Paul Gerhardt, by order of their lord, Duke Christian of Meresberg. At these words, Madame Gerhardt turned pale, dreading some further calamity. But her husband, calm in his trust in an overruling Providence, at once declared that he was the individual they were in search of, and inquired their errand. Great was the astonishment and delight of both wife and husband, when one of the strangers presented Gerhardt with an autograph letter from the duke himself, informing him that he had settled a considerable pension on him, to atone for the injustice of which he had been the victim. Then the pious and gifted preacher turned towards his wife, and gave her the hymn he had composed during his brief absence, with the words, "See, how God provides! Did I not bid you confide in Him, and all would be well?"* Some years after, Gerhardt was appointed Archdeacon at Lübben, in which office he continued till his death,

---

* In Kelly's biography, this incident concerning Gerhardt's destitution is doubted: it is otherwise regarded by Madame De Pontes in her " Poets and Poetry of Germany."

which took place in 1676, after he had faithfully served in the ministry twenty-five years. This excellent man died, it is related, repeating a verse of his own hymn, which, in our translation, commences, "Wherefore should I grieve and pine?" It was this stanza: —

>  Yea, though death seem close at hand,
>  Calm and quiet should he stand,
>    And his spirit tremble not;
>  Him no death has power to kill,
>  But from many a dreaded ill
>    Bears his spirit safe away;
>  Shuts the door of bitter woes,
>  Opens yon bright path that glows
>    With the light of perfect day!

He stands out the central figure of the second century of the singers of the Reformed Church, as Luther does of the first. One of his hymns, Luther-like, he composed, after a night of weary anguish on the altar-steps of his church at Lübben: and many others of his compositions were born of sorrow and suffering. They penetrated to all ranks of society, and were sung by young and old, even in the streets. Schiller learned Gerhardt's hymns from his mother, his evening-hymn being an especial favorite.

Here are two stanzas from a battle-hymn of Paul Gerhardt, which, we may easily believe, gushed forth from his overcharged heart: —

> Arise, and stem this tide of woe, of heart-ache and of pain;
> Call back Thy flock, and make them know bright days again;
> To peace and wealth the lands restore, wasted with fire, or plague,
>     or sword;
> Come to Thy ruined churches, Lord, and bid them bloom once more.

. . . . . . . .

Give strong and cheerful hearts to stand undaunted in the wars,
That Satan's works, and mighty band, are waging with Thy cause.
    Help us to fight as warriors brave,
        That we may conquer in the field,
        And not one Christian man may yield
            His soul to sin a slave.

Order, according to Thy mind, our life from day to day;
And when this life must be resigned, and Death shall seize his prey,
    When all our days have fleeted by,
        Help us to die with fearless spirit;
        And let us, after death, inherit
            Eternal life on high!

Turn we now to a sweet little lyric of his, on Christmas: —

    All my heart this night rejoices
    As I hear, far and near, sweetest angel-voices;
    "Christ is born!" Their choirs are singing,
    Till the air everywhere now with joy is ringing.
    For it dawns, the promised morrow
    Of His birth, who on earth rescues from her sorrow.
    God, to wear our form, descendeth;
    Of His grace, to our race, here His Son He lendeth.

    .    .    .    .    .    .

    Come, then, let us hasten yonder;
    Let us all, great and small, kneel in awe and wonder.
    Love Him who with love is yearning;
    Hail the star that from afar bright with hope is burning!
    Hither come, ye heavy-hearted,
    Who, for sin, deep within, long and sore have smarted.
    For the poisoned wounds you're feeling
    Help is near, One is here mighty for their healing!

The following translation of another of his fine hymns is from the "Lyra Germanica:" —

        Go forth, my heart, and seek delight
        In all the gifts of God's great might,
            These pleasant summer hours;

Look, how the plains for thee and me
Have decked themselves most fair to see,
   All bright and sweet with flowers.

. . . . . .

The lark soars singing into space,
The dove forsakes her hiding-place,
   And cooes the woods among;
The richly gifted nightingale
Pours forth her voice o'er hill and dale,
   And floods the fields with song.

. . . . . .

I think, art Thou so good to us,
And scatterest joy and beauty thus,
   O'er this poor earth of ours;
What nobler glories shall be given
Hereafter in Thy shining heaven
   Set round with golden towers!

What thrilling joy, when on our sight
Christ's garden beams in cloudless light,
   Where all the air is sweet,
Still laden with the unwearied hymn
From all the thousand seraphim,
   Who God's high praise repeat!

Gerhardt was peculiarly a "son of consolation:" his hymns of charity, hope, and faith, were full of thanksgiving and cheer, just what all Christian utterances ought to be. Whether he sang to the soul's secret needs, or to the loud clarion of battle, the same true-hearted faith inspired his song. Fighting under the standard of Gustavus, no doubts ever crossed his mind about the lawfulness of taking up arms; but he and his comrades felt convinced they were obeying a heaven-sent leader, as truly accredited as Joshua, or Gideon, or David. "Militare est orare" was the motto of their banner.

These beautiful stanzas are from the German of Zehn :—

God liveth ever!
Wherefore, soul, despair thou never!
He who can earth and heaven control,
Who spreads the clouds o'er sea and land,
Whose presence fills the mighty whole,
In each true heart is close at hand.
Love Him, He will surely send
Help and joy that never end.
Soul, remember in thy pains,
God o'er all for ever reigns!

God liveth ever!
Wherefore, soul, despair thou never!
Scarce canst thou bear thy cross? Then fly
To Him where rest is only sweet;
Thy God is great, His mercy nigh,
His strength upholds the tottering feet.
Trust Him, for His grace is sure,
Ever doth His truth endure;
Soul, forget not in thy pains,
God o'er all for ever reigns!

. . . . .

God liveth ever!
Wherefore, soul, despair thou never!
What though thou tread with bleeding feet
A thorny path of grief and gloom,
Thy God will choose the way most meet
To lead thee heavenwards. lead thee home.
For this life's long night of sadness,
He will give thee peace and gladness!
Soul, forget not in thy pains,
God o'er all for ever reigns!

Count Zinzendorf was not one of the least among the sacred brotherhood of song, as he was the founder and champion of the United Moravian Brethren. He was born at Dresden, in the year 1700, and died in

1760. His zeal and self-denying service in behalf of the community he represented, were most exemplary. "In all parts of the world he vindicated the claims of the Moravians, and, when the community was insolvent, he undertook the burden of their debt; and, at his death, he owed more than a quarter of a million of money on that account. He had been elected president of Herrnhut, the estate of the community, in Saxony; and he devoted himself heartily to its spiritual interests."* One of the means employed, according to his biographer,† was singing, to which he attached great importance. "His stock of hymns, which he could at any time recall, was as wonderful as his power of extemporaneous composition. Sometimes he would sing a number of verses taken from various hymns, and interspersed with others composed at the moment, thus producing a kind of lyric discourse, — an echo to the voice of the Hebrew prophets, — which seems to have produced a profound impression." His "Berlin Discourses," a series of daily addresses which he delivered in his own house, passed through many editions, and were translated into several languages. "In 1729, Zinzendorf paid a short visit to St. Thomas; and, 1741, he made a missionary visit to America, where he remained more than a year doing a good work in Pennsylvania, and attempting something for the North-American Indians. One of his celebrated hymns, consisting of thirty-three stanzas, and made familiar to us by Wesley's translation, is, "Jesus, Thy blood and righteousness!"

Here is a compact stanza on Christian Unity, from the German of Count Zinzendorf : —

* Miller's Our Hymns.      † Felix Bovet.

Thou who didst die for all and each, and in that last, sad night,
Didst to Thy flock so sweetly teach Love's all-controlling might;
Still on Thy little band impress, who else may disagree,
Thy last and dying care was this, — Thy members' unity!

The fine hymn, from which the following lines are taken, has been rendered into German, from the Latin, by Count Zinzendorf; or, rather, was poured forth from St. Bernard's heart into his. Here is the English version: —

> Jesus, the very thought of Thee
>   With sweetness fills my breast;
> But sweeter far Thy face to see,
>   And in Thy presence rest.
>
> No voice can sing, nor heart can frame,
>   Nor can the memory find,
> A sweeter sound than Thy blest name,
>   O Saviour of mankind!
>
> O hope of every contrite heart!
>   O joy of all the meek!
> To those who fall, how kind Thou art,
>   How good to those who seek!
>
> But what to those who find? Ah! this
>   Nor tongue nor pen can show;
> The love of Jesus, what it is
>   None but His loved ones know.

Among German hymnists of eminence was Rothe, who was born in Silesia, 1688. and died in 1758. Count Zinzendorf was his friend and patron. He was an excellent pastor, and united in himself ripe scholarship and exemplary piety. The count selected him to fill the office of pastor for his estate of Berthelsdorf, the duties of which he discharged to the admiration of all who knew him. He wrote some hymns, which have been translated, and transferred to our modern collections. One begins, "Lord, at Thy feet we sinners lie;" another, "O Lord, Thy work revive."

A. H. Francke (1691) composed a fine hymn, on his journey to Gotha, after his unjust expulsion from Erfurt, as we are told in the oration delivered at his grave, "in the full experience of the unspeakable consolations of the Holy Spirit." We cite only two specimen stanzas. It is a New-Year's hymn.

Thank God that towards eternity another step is won!
Oh, longing turns my heart to Thee, as time flows slowly on!
  Thou Fountain whence my life is born,
  Whence those rich streams of grace are drawn,
    That through my being run!

. . . . . .

Oh, that I soon might Thee behold! I count the moments o'er;
Ah, come, ere yet my heart grows cold, and cannot call Thee more!
  Come in Thy glory, for Thy Bride
  Hath girt her for the holy-tide,
    And waiteth at the door.

Simon Dach, a professor at Königsberg, where he died in 1659, was remarkable for the contemplative serenity and correct structure of his hymns. The sacred lyrics of Germany, during this epoch, are interfused with the great doctrines of holy Scripture; these, indeed, constitute the warp and woof of their texture; among great diversities of literary and poetic merit, this, their evangelical character, is uniformly maintained. Here is his beautiful homily on self-denial, compacted into two stanzas:—

    Wouldst thou inherit life with Christ on high?
      Then count the cost, and know
      That here on earth below
    Thou needs must suffer with Thy Lord, and die.
    We reach that gain, to which all else is loss,
      But through the Cross!

. . . . . .

Not e'en the sharpest sorrows we can feel,
  Nor keenest pangs, we dare
  With that great bliss compare,
When God His glory shall in us reveal,
That shall endure when our brief woes are o'er
  For evermore!

Listen to his good counsel concerning "Treasure in Heaven:" —

  My soul, let this thy thoughts employ:
    Defer not until death to ponder
    On what shall be the heavenly joy
  Which God's redeemed are promised yonder.

  Thy true wealth lies beyond the skies,
    And there shouldst thou be ever gazing;
    Learn, then, earth's treasures to despise,
  · To heaven your aspirations raising.

There is impressive grandeur about the following poem, translated from the German of Seidl, by C. T. Brooks: —

  "Lord, Thou art great!" I cry, when in the east
    The day is blooming like a rose of fire;
  When, to partake anew of life's rich feast,
    Nature and man awake with fresh desire.
  When art Thou seen more gracious, God of power!
  Than in the morn's great resurrection-hour?

  "Lord, Thou art great!" I cry, when blackness shrouds
    The noon-day heavens, and crinkling lightnings flame,
  And on the tablet of the thunder-clouds
    In fiery letters write Thy dreadful name.
  When art Thou, Lord, more terrible in wrath,
  Than in the mid-day tempest's lowering path?

  "Lord, Thou art great!" I cry, when in the west
    Day, softly-vanquished, shuts his glowing eye;
  When song-feasts ring from every woodland nest,
    And all in melancholy sweetness die.

When giv'st Thou, Lord, our hearts more bless'd repose
Than in the magic of Thy evening shows?

" Lord, Thou art great!" I cry, at dead of night,
    When silence broods alike on land and deep;
When stars go up and down the blue-arched height,
    And on the silver clouds the moonbeams sleep.
When beckonest Thou, O Lord! to loftier heights,
    Than in the silent praise of holy nights?

" Lord, Thou art great!" in nature's every form;
    Greater in none, — simply most great in all;
In tears and terrors, sunshine, smile, and storm,
    And all that stirs the heart, is felt Thy call.
" Lord, Thou art great!" Oh, let me praise Thy name,
    And grow in greatness as I Thine proclaim!

Gleim was born in 1719. Through the good offices of some friends, he obtained an appointment connected with the Cathedral of Halberstadt, whither he removed in 1776, and where he continued to remain several years. Few lives passed away with such uninterrupted tranquillity, as that of Gleim. Overflowing with benevolence, he found, in the exercise of kindness and hospitality, the friendship of Klopstock, and other distinguished men, all the happiness his gentle nature desired. During the seven years' war, when Germany was divided into two hostile camps, it was a stirring and momentous epoch, especially for Prussia. Gleim's devotion to the heroic Prussian hero, Frederick, was kindled into enthusiasm; and he enlisted in the fortunes of his cause. He wrote religious songs, which the soldiers sang on the battle-field. His protracted life was enriched by numerous benefactions conferred upon others; and his memory was sweet, " and blossomed in the dust." There is simple pathos and melody in the following lyric of his : —

For whom hast Thou created, O Lord! this world so bright?
For whom are bud and blossom in the glen and on the height?
For whom the golden cornfield, where our glad footsteps rove?
For whom do yonder sunbeams gild the meadow and the grove?

. . . . . .

The blessings that surround us, should be a call of love,
To raise, with each returning morn, our thoughts to Him above.
Not vainly dost Thou give us this, a heart to feel and love, —
A foretaste of the purer bliss which shall be ours above!

Contemporary with Gleim, was Kleist, who was born in Pomerania, 1715. His poems have procured for him less celebrity than his patriotic devotion to his king and country. The following hymn has long been a favorite with the Prussian soldiers; for the translation, as well as that of the preceding hymn, we are indebted to the pen of Madame De Pontes.

Great is the Lord! The heavens proclaim afar
  His power: they are His seat;
The raging storm is His triumphal car;
  His steed, the lightning fleet.

The hues of morn are a reflection dim
  Of His resplendent might;
The sun itself is but a spark of Him,
  The source of life and light.

. . . . .

Thou foaming ocean, in thy stormy bed,
  Tremble before His frown;
Bend, lofty cedar, bend thy stately head;
  Forests and woods, bow down.

Ye savage monsters, in your rocky den,
  Adore your Maker's power;
Sing Him, ye little warblers of the glen,
  In grove and hill and bower.

Echo, exalt His name! in earth and heaven
  Be that Great Name adored!
And thou, O man! to whom this world is given,
  Worship and bless the Lord!

Kleist bore no inglorious part in several important actions. On one occasion, when the Austrians, with a force of eighty thousand men, surprised the Prussian army, greatly inferior in strength, Kleist, at the head of his battalion, defended a narrow defile, by which their position was commanded, with such resolute valor, that the enemy, after repeated attacks, retired. This gallant deed, in all probability, saved the whole army.

During the calamitous seven years' war, might have been seen in a small room, at Leipzig, a poor scholar surrounded with a heap of books; and, among them, on the table, was a well-used Bible, opened at the second chapter of the book of Job, and the words, underlined, "What! shall we receive good at the hand of God, and shall we not receive evil?" This Christian student was C. F. Gellert, who became one of the most esteemed and honored of the sacred poets of Germany. Princes, and celebrated persons, made pilgrimages to visit him; even Frederic the Great had an interview with him. He was contemporary with Klopstock, Kleist, Schlegel, Lessing, and Goethe. His Muse drew inspiration from the Bible; and his hymns were heart-utterances, and therefore appealed to the heart, — took deep root, and obtained a widespread and enduring popularity. Goethe thus speaks of him as a lecturer: "The reverence and affection which Gellert received from all the young men was extraordinary. His lecture-room was always crowded to the utmost; and Gellert's beautiful soul, purity of will, his admonitions, warnings, and entreaties, delivered in a somewhat hollow and sad voice, produced a deep impression." His hymn on Creation has been thus rendered into our vernacular : —

Creator! when I see Thy might, Thy wisdom, and Thy love,
For ever watching, day and night, o'er all below, above;
 Melted with gratitude and praise,
 I know not how my voice to raise,
  My Father and my God!

Where'er I turn, my dazzled eye beholds Thy wonders still, —
The glorious heavens, the azure sky, adore their Maker's skill!
 Who bids the sun so brightly shine,
 Clothed in his majesty divine,
  Who calls the starry host?

Yet more stirring are some of his stanzas, entitled "The Solace of the Life to come:" —

When these brief trial-days are spent, there dawns a glad eternity!
There, lost in measureless content, our tears and sorrows cease to be;
 Here virtue toils with earnest care:
 Her glorious crown awaits her there!

. . . . . . . .

Here, I must seek: there, I shall find; for there shall virtue all unfold
Before my holier, purer mind, her worth so great, so manifold;
 The God of Love, whom I adore,
 I there shall worship more and more.

There, in that light, shall I discern what here on earth I dimly saw, —
Those deep and wondrous counsels learn, whose mystery filled me here with awe;
 There trace, with gratitude intense,
 The hidden links of Providence.

. . . . . . . .

Perchance, — ah, would that this might be! — will some blest soul in that abode
Cry, "Hail! for thou hast rescued me, and won my heart to heaven and God!"
 Oh, God! what exquisite delight,
 To save a soul from sin and night!

This worthy Christian singer, after a life enriched by very numerous benefactions, and much occasional suffering, endured with exemplary patience and serenity, left the world he had benefited for the "rest that remaineth," in 1769, at the age of fifty-four. "I am weak, and cannot understand much," he said, shortly before he ceased to breathe; "but pronounce the name of my Redeemer, — when I hear that, I feel fresh strength and joy." Gellert's death was regarded as a national calamity. His biographer says, "Perhaps no grave has ever been watered with so many and such sincere tears." Let it be repeated, he was a great Bible reader, and a firm believer in Providence.

Not long ago, there was a pamphlet published in London, entitled "The Adventures of a Hymn," in which are detailed the remarkable results which attended his beautiful hymn, "Ich hab in guten Stunden," written by him under circumstances of great privation and sickness; and, what is still more remarkable, suffering from want of the necessities of life, in consequence of his ultra-generosity to others in distress. But his unfaltering trust in God's promises nerved him to endure in the hour of trial; and when his faith was justified, it uttered itself in fresh songs of thanksgiving. The blessing of many, "who were ready to perish," came upon him like light from heaven.

Here is a beautiful lyric gem from the German of Arndt. The translation is by E. F. Cox.

> Therefore, now, a last good night!
> Sun, and moon, and stars of fire,
> Farewell to your splendor bright!
> Higher now I soar, far higher.
> Where there is such glorious day,
> Ye will vanish quite away.

Weep not, that I bid farewell
To the world and all its errors;
Far from vanity to dwell,
Far from darkness and its terrors;
Weep not, that I take my flight
To the land of endless light!
Weep not, my Redeemer lives,
High above dark earth ascending:
Hope, her heavenly comfort gives;
Faith stands by, her shield extending;
Love eternal whispers near,
" Child of God, no longer fear!"

Schiller, the illustrious friend of Goethe, was born in 1759, and died 1805. He lived in almost monastic seclusion from the world. At sixteen, he published a translation of a part of the "Æneid." He was a great student of Shakspeare; and to this fact, doubtless, we owe his splendid dramas. His Histories of the "Revolt of the Netherlands" and of the "Thirty Years' War" have long been standard authorities. He was by far the greatest tragic poet of Germany, and one of the greatest, also, in modern literature. The moral elevation of his writings place him above most of his German predecessors and successors. His "Song of the Bell" is a wonderful production, and replete with poetic beauties.

The following is an English version of Schiller's "Three Words of Strength," the triple Christian graces: —

There are three lessons I would write,—
Three words, as with a burning pen,
In tracings of eternal light,
Upon the hearts of men.

Have hope! Though clouds environ round,
And gladness hides her face in scorn,
Put thou the shadow from thy brow,
No night but hath its morn.

> Have faith! Where'er thy bark is driven, —
> The calm's disport, the tempest's mirth, —
> Know this: God rules the hosts of heaven,
> The inhabitants of earth.
>
> Have love! Not love alone for one,
> But man, as man, thy brother call,
> And scatter, like the circling sun,
> Thy charities on all.
>
> Thus grave these lessons on thy soul,
> Hope, faith, and love; and thou shalt find
> Strength when life's surges rudest roll,
> Light when thou else wert blind.

This fine spiritual lyric, written in 1713, by Marpurger, has been admirably rendered into our vernacular by Miss Winkworth:—

> Who seeks in weakness an excuse, his sins will vanish never;
> Unless he heart and mind renews, he is deceived for ever.
> The straight and narrow way, that shines to perfect day,
>   He hath not found, hath never trod;
> Little he knows, I ween, what prayer and conflict mean,
>   To one who hath the light of God.
>
> In what the world calls weakness lurks the very strength of evil;
> Full mightily it helps the works of our great foe, the devil.
> Awake, my soul, awake! quickly thy refuge take
>   With Him, the Almighty, who can save;
> One look from Christ, thy Lord, can sever every cord
>   That binds thee now, a wretched slave.
>
> Know, the first step in Christian lore is to depart from sin;
> True faith will leave the world no more a place thy heart within.
> Thy Saviour's Spirit first the heavy bonds must burst,
>   Wherein Death bound thee in thy need;
> Then, the freed spirit knows what strength He gives to those
>   Who, with their Lord, are risen indeed!

Bogatzky, who is not known to us so much by his hymns, of which he wrote about four hundred, as by his "Golden Treasury," was born in 1690, in Hungary. He was early inspired by the faith of the gospel; and, although a person of ample fortune, he devoted himself to visiting the sick, and commending the great truths of Christianity to the poor. His memory is embalmed in the hearts of thousands in every Protestant land, by the hymns, and the "Treasury," he has bequeathed to us. These lines are his:

> Awake, Thou Spirit, who of old
> Didst fire the watchmen of the Church's youth,
> Who faced the foe, unshrinking, bold,
> Who witnessed day and night the eternal truth;
> Whose voices through the world are ringing still,
> And bringing hosts to know and do Thy will!
>
> Oh, that Thy fire were kindled soon,
> That swift from land to land its flame might leap!
> Lord, give us but this priceless boon
> Of faithful servants, fit for Thee to reap
> The harvest of the soul; look down and view
> How great the harvest, yet the laborers few.
>
> . . . . . . .
>
> Oh, haste to help ere we are lost!
> Send forth evangelists, in spirit strong,
> Armed with Thy Word, a dauntless host,
> Bold to attack the rule of ancient wrong;
> And let them all the earth for Thee reclaim,
> To be Thy kingdom, and to know Thy name!

Tersteegen's hymns (1697-1769) possess great poetic beauty, and evince a tranquil and childlike spirit of devotion. His history is a remarkable one. From his childhood, he was delicate in health, thoughtful, and of scrupulous conscience. At Mülheim, he became acquainted with a mystic, — a very religious man, under whose instructions he became converted. His days were busy, but he used to pass whole nights in prayer and fasting. He occupied himself as a weaver; his food was simple, and his frugality enabled him to give to the poor. His peculiar habits of life caused his family, who were worldly, to forsake him; and, even when sick, they never came near him. Notwithstanding his singular devotedness of life, he suffered, for five years, "a state of darkness," having no sense of the love of God; to such an extent, indeed, that he began to doubt whether there was a God at all. It was at this time he sang these sad lines: —

> Lost in darkness, girt with dangers, round me strangers,
>   Through an alien land I roam;
> Outward trials, bitter losses, inward crosses,
> Lord, Thou know'st have sought me home.
> Sin of courage hath bereft me, and hath left me
>   Scarce a spark of faith or hope;
> Bitter tears my heart oft sheddeth, as it dreadeth
>   I am past Thy mercy's scope.
> Peace I cannot find; oh, take me, Lord, and make me
>   From this yoke of evil free;
> Calm this longing never sleeping, still my weeping,
>   Give me hope once more in Thee!

He could obtain no help from outside; but at last, one day, when he was on a journey to a neighboring city, he received such an internal manifestation of the goodness of God, and the sufficiency of the Saviour, that all doubts and troubles vanished in a moment. Henceforth, he had peace and joy, and an intense power of realizing the unseen, which, combined with the experience he had lately gone through, gave him a wonderful faculty of touching and strengthening other hearts. The thirty years of his life, from thirty to sixty years of age, were spent in incessant exertion for the good of others, though his own health was always delicate, and he was subject to frequent attacks of neuralgia. He seems to have possessed a singular power of attracting others, and he used it to the noblest of ends. He was instrumental of great good as a preacher, and as a minister to the sick and destitute. He was a mystic of the purest type; and the fragrant memory of his name is still enshrined in some hearts, although he died just a century ago. Subjoined are two more extracts from his fine hymns: —

> Lord our God, in reverence lowly
> The hosts of heaven call Thee "Holy!"
> From cherubim and seraphim,
> From angel-phalanx far extending,
> In fuller tones, is still ascending
> The "holy, holy," of their hymn.
> . . . . .
> Lord, there are bending now before Thee
> The elders, with their crownèd glory,
> The first-born of the blessèd band;
> There, too, earth's ransomed and forgiven,
> Brought by the Saviour safe to heaven,
> In glad unnumbered myriads stand.
> Loud are the songs of praise
> Their mingled voices raise,
>     Ever, ever!
> We, too, are Thine, and with them sing,
> Thou, Lord, and only Thou art King!
> . . . . .
> They sing, in sweet and sinless numbers,
> The wondrous love that never slumbers,
> And of the wisdom, power, and might,
> The truth and faithfulness abiding,
> And over all Thy works presiding.
> But they can scarcely praise aright;
> For all is never sung,
> Even by seraph's tongue,
>     Never, never!

These are the closing stanzas of his "Pilgrim Song:"—

> Come, gladly let us onward; hand in hand still go,
> Each helping one another through all the way below.
>    One family of love,
> Oh, let no voice of strife be heard,
> No discord, by the angel-guard
>    Who watch us from above!
>
> Oh, brothers! soon is ended the journey we've begun;
> Endure a little longer, the race will soon be won!
>    And in the land of rest,
> In yonder bright, eternal home,
> Where all the Father's loved ones come,
>    We shall be safe and blest!

The following lines are from the German of Uhland, by Mrs. Follen:—

> This is the Sabbath day!
> In the wide field I am alone.
> Hark! now our morning bell's sweet tone:
>    Now it has died away.
>
> Kneeling, I worship Thee:
> Sweet dread doth o'er my spirit steal
> From whispering sounds of those who kneel
>    Unseen, to pray with me.
>
> Around and far away
> So clear and solemn is the sky,
> It seems all opening to my eye:
>    This is the Sabbath day!

Longfellow gives us the following fine poem in his "Hyperion." It is a translation from the German of Uhland.

> Many a year is in its grave
> Since I crossed this restless wave;
> And the evening, fair as ever,
> Shines on ruin, rock, and river.

Then in this same boat, beside,
Sat two comrades old and tried;
One with all a father's truth,
One with all the fire of youth.
One on earth in silence wrought,
And his grave in silence sought;
But the younger, brighter form,
Passed in battle and in storm.
So, where'er I turn my eye
Back upon the days gone by,
Saddening thoughts of friends come o'er me, —
Friends who closed their course before me.
Yet what binds us, friend to friend,
But that soul to soul can blend?
Soul-like were those hours of yore;
Let us walk in soul once more!
Take, O boatman! thrice thy fee;
Take, — I give it willingly;
For, invisible to thee,
Spirits twain have crossed with me.

A yet finer hymn of this distinguished German poet is before us. The translation reads, —

There is a land where beauty will not fade,
  Nor sorrow dim the eye;
Where true hearts will not sink, nor be dismayed,
  And love will never die.
Tell me, — I fain would go, —
For I am burdened with a heavy woe:
The beautiful have left me all alone, —
The true, the tender, from my path have gone,
And I am weak, and fainting with despair;
Where is it, — tell me where?
Friend, thou must trust in Him who trod before
  The desolate path of life;
Must bear in meekness, as He meekly bore,
  Sorrow and toil and strife!
Think how the Son of God
These thorny paths has trod,

Yet tarried out for thee the appointed woe;
Think of His loneliness in places dim,
When no man comforted, or cared for Him;
Think how He prayed, unaided and alone,
In that dread agony, "Thy will be done!"
Friend, do not thou despair:
Christ, in His heaven of heavens, will hear thy prayer.

Rambach (1720) is the writer of the vigorous hymn, of which this is a translation: —

O Mighty Spirit, Source whence all things sprung!
O glorious Majesty of perfect Light!
Hath ever worthy praise to Thee been sung,
Or mortal heart endured to meet Thy sight?
If they who sin have never known,
Must veil their faces at Thy throne,
Oh, how shall I, who am but sin and dust,
Approach untrembling to the Pure and Just?

The voice of conscience in the soul hath shown
Some far-off glimpses of Thy holiness,
And yet more clearly hast Thou made it known
In Thy dear Word that tells us of Thy grace;
But with all-glorious light divine
In His face we behold it shine, —
The Sinless One, who this dark earth has trod,
To win, through sorrow, sinners back to God.

Here is Körner's battle-hymn, written just before he yielded up his young life for the freedom of his country, at the battle of Danneberg, 1791: —

Father, to Thee I cry!
The roaring cannon's vapor shrouds me round,
And flashing lightnings hiss along the ground;
Lord of the fight, I cry to Thee!
O Father, guide Thou me!

Father, be Thou my guide!
In victory's triumph, or in death laid low,
O Lord, unto Thy mighty will I bow!
Even as Thou wilt, so let it be!
God, I acknowledge Thee!

Thy holy presence, Lord,
In the dread thunder of the clashing steel,
As in the rustling autumn-leaves, I feel:
   Fountain of mercies, I acknowledge Thee!
   O Father, bless Thou me!

Thy blessing on me rest!
Into Thy hands, O Father, I resign
The life Thou gavest, and canst take, but mine
   In life or death Thy blessing be!
   Glory and praise to Thee!

Germany's first patriot and poet, Körner, was in the act of reading to a friend his last poem, "The Sword Song," when the signal for the attack was made. He had written it in his pocket-book, in the dawn of the 26th of August, 1813. Körner was among the foremost of those who pressed forward in pursuit of the enemy; and here it was that, in the moment of victory, he met the death which he had so often anticipated, and celebrated with so much enthusiasm. Mrs. Hemans's stirring tribute to his memory has been translated into German, by Körner's father. Her dirge begins: —

A song for the death-day of the brave, —
   A song of pride!
The youth went down to a hero's grave,
   With the sword, his bride!
. . . .
He hath left a voice in his trumpet-lays
   To turn the flight;
And a guiding spirit for after days,
   Like a watchfire's light!

And a name and a fame above the blight
   Of earthly breath;
Beautiful — beautiful and bright —
   In life and death.

Klopstock, "the German Homer," was born in 1724, and died in 1803. At the early age of sixteen, he seems to have projected his epic; and he wrote the first canto of his "Messiah" at Jena. When the first three cantos were published, they attracted much applause. He completed the poem in 1792, at Hamburg. Klopstock seems to have been a very amiable and excellent character. He was twice married, and happy in his unions. Menzel, the German critic, justly remarks: "His poetry as well as his patriotism had its root in that sublime moral and religious faith which his 'Messiah' celebrates;" and he it was who, along with Gellert, lent to modern German poetry that dignified, earnest, and pious character, which it has never lost again.

Here is Klopstock's "Morgenlied" (morning-hymn), translated by Nind:—

When I rise again to life from the tranquil sleep of death,
And, released from earthly strife, breathe that morning's balmy breath,
  I shall wake to other thought:
  The race is run, the fight is fought;
  All the pilgrim's cares are dreams,
  When that dawn of morning gleams!

Help, that no departed day, God of endless life and joy,
To the righteous Judge may say, 'twas profaned by my employ:
  To another morn I wake,
  And to Thee my offering make;
  Oh, may all my days that flee,
  Joys and sorrows, lead to Thee!

Goethe, who has been styled the "Shakspeare of Germany," has written in almost every department and in many of the sciences. His works have exerted a great influence over the national mind of Germany, and indeed of the world at large. He received many distinguished honors from the Emperor of Russia, the great Napoleon, and other notabilities. His famous life closed upon earth in 1832.

Here is a fine paraphrase of Goethe's magnificent "Hymn to the Universe," which forms the prelude to his "Faust:"—

>   Roll on, thou sun, for ever roll,
>     Thou giant, rushing through the heaven!
>   Creation's wonder, nature's soul!
>     Thy golden wheels, by angels driven;
>   The planets die without thy blaze,
>     And cherubim, with star-dropt wing,
>   Float in thy diamond-sparkling rays,
>     Thou brightest emblem of their King!
>
>   Roll, lovely earth! and still roll on,
>     With ocean's azure beauty bound;
>   While one sweet star, the pearly moon,
>     Pursues thee through the blue profound;
>   And angels, with delighted eyes,
>     Behold thy tints of mount and stream,
>   From the high walls of paradise,
>     Swift-wheeling like a glorious dream.
>
>   Roll, planets! on your dazzling road,
>     For ever sweeping round the sun;
>   What eye beheld when first ye glowed!
>     What eye shall see your courses done!
>   Roll in your solemn majesty,
>     Ye deathless splendors of the skies!
>   High altars, from which angels see
>     The incense of creation rise.
>
>   Roll, comets! and ye million stars!
>     Ye that through boundless nature roam;
>   Ye monarchs on your flame-wing cars;
>     Tell us in what more glorious dome,—
>   What orb to which your pomps are dim,
>     What kingdom but by angels trod,—
>   Tell us, where swells the eternal hymn
>     Around His throne, where dwells your God?

These forceful lines are from the same distinguished source : —

>Rest is not quitting the busy career;
>Rest is the fitting of self to its sphere.
>'Tis the brook's motion, clear without strife,
>Fleeting to ocean, after its life.
>'Tis loving and serving the highest and best:
>'Tis onward and upward, and that is true rest.

We are indebted to Professor Porter, of Pennsylvania, for the beautiful translation of one of the most renowned sacred poems of Germany, by Mrs. Meta Hensser Schweizer, who lives at Hirzel, near Zurich. Professor Schaff pronounces the first stanza truly classical in thought and expression: its contrasts are startling and sublime.

>Lamb, the once crucified! Lion, by triumph surrounded!
>Victim all bloody, and Hero, who hell hast confounded!
>>Pain-riven Heart,
>>That from earth's deadliest smart
>O'er all the heavens hast bounded!
>
>Thou in the depths wert to mortals the highest revealing,
>God in humanity veiled, Thy full glory concealing!
>>"Worthy art Thou!"
>>Shouteth eternity now,
>Praise to Thee endlessly pealing.
>
>Heavenly Love, in the language of earth past expression!
>Lord of all worlds, unto whom every tongue owes confession!
>>Didst Thou not go,
>>And, under sentence of woe,
>Rescue the doomed by transgression!
>
>O'er the abyss of the grave, and its horrors infernal,
>Victory's palm Thou art waving in triumph supernal;
>>Who to Thee cling,
>>Circled by hope, shall now bring
>Out of its gulf life eternal!

Among the German poets of the eighteenth century, Novalis was one of the most noted. His brief life-story is remarkable, but we have not space for its recital. Here are two of his hymns : —

> There are dark hours of sadness, dark hours of hopeless pain,
> When thoughts akin to madness flash wildly through the brain;
> When nameless anguish presses the heart beyond control,
> And deepest gloom possesses the faint and trembling soul;
> When every prop seems taken from life's receding shore,
> And the mind, tempest-shaken, obeys the will no more.
> But who, from yonder heaven, pities each earthly woe?
> Who yonder cross hath given for every grief below?
> Thine arms around it twining, to hope and prayer give room,
> For there a flame is shining to light thy path of gloom.
> An angel-form advances, and leads thee to that strand
> Whence thy delighted glances may see the promised land.

### EASTER HYMN.

> I say to all men, far and near, that He is risen again;
> That He is with us now and here, and ever shall remain.
> And what I say, let each, this morn, go tell it to his friend,
> That soon, in every place, shall dawn His kingdom without end.
> Now first to souls who thus awake, seems earth a fatherland;
> A new and endless life they take with rapture from His hand.
> The fear of death and of the grave are whelmed beneath the sea;
> And every heart, now light and brave, may face the things to be.

Spitta's Morning Prayer opens thus beautifully : —

> The golden morn flames up the eastern sky,
> And what dark night had hid from every eye
>   All-piercing daylight summons clear to view;
> And all the forests, vale or plain or hill.
> That slept in mist enshrouded, dark and still,
>   In gladsome light are glittering now anew.
> Shine in my heart, and bring me joy and light,
> Sun of my darkened soul; dispel its night,
>   And shed in it the truthful day abroad;
> And all the many gloomy folds lay bare
> Within this heart, that fain would learn to wear
>   The pure and glorious likeness of its Lord;

Glad with Thy light, and glowing with Thy love,
So let me ever speak and think and move,
　　As fits a soul new-touched with life from heaven,
That seeks but so to order all her course,
As most to show the glory of that Source,
　　By whom alone her strength, her life, are given.

This also is from his pen : —

How weary and how worthless this life at times appears!
What days of heavy musings, what hours of bitter tears!
How dark the storm-clouds gather along the wintry skies!
How desolate and cheerless the path before us lies!
And yet these days of dreariness are sent us from above;
They do not come in anger, but in faithfulness and love:
They come to teach us lessons, which bright ones could not yield;
And to leave us blest and thankful, when their purpose is fulfilled.

　　．　　．　　．　　．　　．　　．　　．

They come to break the fetters which here detain us fast,
And force our long-reluctant hearts to rise to heaven at last;
And brighten every prospect of that eternal home,
Where grief and disappointment and fear can never come!
Then turn not in despondence, poor, weary heart. away,
But meekly journey onwards, through the dark and cloudy day:
Even now the bow of promise is above thee, painted bright;
And soon a joyful morning shall dissipate the night!*

Spitta has portrayed a delightful domestic scene:

O happy house! where two are one in heart,
　　In faith and hope are one;
Whom death only for a while may part,
　　Not end the union here begun;
Who share together one salvation, —
　　Who would be with Thee, Lord, always,
In gladness or in tribulation,
　　In happy or in evil days.

　　．　　．　　．　　．

O happy home! and happy servitude!
　　Where all alike one Master own;
Where daily duty, in Thy strength pursued,
　　Is never hard nor toilsome known;

* Hymns from the Land of Luther.

Where each one serves Thee, meek and lowly,
Whatever Thine appointment be,
Till common tasks seem great and holy,
When they are done as unto Thee!

He has written another sweet lyric, entitled "The Angel of Hope." Here are the opening stanzas: —

A gentle Angel walketh throughout a world of woe,
With messages of mercy to mourning hearts below;
His peaceful smile invites thee to love and to confide:
Oh, follow in His footsteps, keep closely by His side!
So gently will He lead thee through all the cloudy day,
And whisper of glad tidings to cheer the pilgrim-way;
His courage never failing, when thine is almost gone,
He takes thy heavy burden, and helps thee bear it on.

F. Rückert, who died in 1867, "one of the greatest and purest of German poets," wrote a lyric of rare beauty, — "Er ist in Bethlehem geboren." We give two or three of the beautiful stanzas of Professor Porter's translation: —

Where are the seven works of wonder
 The ancient world beheld with pride?
They all have fallen, sinking under
 The splendor of the Crucified!
I saw them, as I wandered spying,
Amid their ruins crumbled, lying:
 None stand in quiet gloria,
 Like Bethlehem and Golgotha.

. . . . .

O Thou who, in a manger lying,
 Wert willing to be born a child,
And on the cross, in anguish dying,
 The world to God hast reconciled!
To pride, how mean Thy lowly manger!
How infamous Thy cross! yet stranger —
 Humility became the law
 At Bethlehem and Golgotha.

. . . . .

With staff and hat, the scallop wearing,
    The far-off East I journeyed through;
And homeward now, a pilgrim bearing
    This message, I have come to you:
Go not, with hat and staff, to wander
Beside God's grave and cradle yonder;
    Look inward, and behold, with awe,
    His Bethlehem and Golgotha.

O heart! what profits all thy kneeling,
    Where once He laid His infant head
To view, with an enraptured feeling,
    His grave, long empty of its dead?
To have Him born in thee with power,
To die to earth and sin each hour,
    And live to Him, — this only, ah!
    Is Bethlehem and Golgotha!

Our last quotation shall be that grand choral, the favorite of Prince Albert, which he set to music, and which was sung at his funeral obsequies : —

I shall not in the grave remain,
    Since Thou death's bonds hast severed;
By hope with Thee to rise again,
    From fear of death delivered.
I'll come to Thee where'er Thou art,
Live with Thee, from Thee never part:
    Therefore to die is rapture!

And so to Jesus Christ I'll go,
    My longing arms extending;
So fall asleep in slumber deep, —
    Slumber that knows no ending, —
Till Jesus Christ, God's only Son,
Open the gates of bliss, — leads on
    To heaven, to life eternal!

Our selections from German hymnology have been necessarily very limited, — scarcely sufficient to afford even an approximate conception of its great wealth.

In dismissing this department of sacred song, we are impressed with one characteristic defect common to most of these compositions; i.e., their prolixity. Yet there is in them much of the true poetic element, which is not to be ignored. These hymns are especially interesting to us, not only as exhibiting pictures of heroic faith under circumstances of peculiar emergency and trial; but also as illustrative of the habits of thought and the mental idiosyncrasies of the people they represent. Germany sang the great pæan of the Reformation, and, during her great baptism of blood, the songs of the conflict and triumph of Light and Liberty over Darkness and Despotism.

# FIFTH EVENING.

## SWEDISH, FRENCH, SPANISH, &c.

# FIFTH EVENING.

## SWEDISH, FRENCH, SPANISH, &c.

BEFORE commencing the researches assigned for our present evening's studious entertainment, the following little legend, concerning a German hymn, claims our attention.

In one of the most obscure streets of Hamburg, some two years after the thirty years' war, lived a poor young man, who obtained a slender and precarious subsistence by means of his violoncello. After a while he fell sick, and he was unable to continue his musical routine. As this was his only means of support, he was, in the emergency, compelled to part with his violin to a Jew, who, with characteristic manœuvring, and much pretended reluctance, at length loaned him a sum much below its value, for two weeks; when, if not redeemed, the instrument was to be forfeited. As he surrendered his violin, he gazed lovingly at it, through his tears; and asked the Jew if he might play one more tune upon it. "You know not how hard it is to part from that violin," he said; "for ten years, it has been my companion and comforter. If I have nothing else, I have had it; at the worst, it spoke to me, and sung back all my courage and hope. Of all the sad hearts that have left your door, there has been none so sad as mine." His voice grew thick; and, pausing for a moment, he seized the instrument, and commenced a tune so exquisitely soft, that even the reluctant Jew listened in spite of himself. A few more strains, and he sang to his own melody two stanzas of his hymn, "Life is weary, — Saviour, take me!" Suddenly the key changed: a few bars, and the melody poured itself out anew, and his face lighted up with a smile, as he sang, "Yet who knows? the Cross is precious!" He laid down the instrument, murmuring, "Ut fiat divina voluntas,"* and rushed from the place.

Going out into the darkness, he stumbled against a person, who seemed to have been listening at the door. "Could you tell me where I could obtain a copy of that song," said he to the musician: "I would willingly give a florin for it." "My good friend, I will cheerfully fulfil your wish without the florin," was the response.

But it is time the parties were introduced to the reader. The name of the musician was George Neumark, and that of his interlocutor John Gutig, who was valet to the Swedish ambassador, Baron von Rosenkranz. Gutig told the baron the story of the hapless musician: his poverty, his musical skill, his beautiful hymns, and his grief at pledging his instrument; he showed the hymn he had given him, also. As the baron was in need of a secretary, he thought so highly of the poor musician, that he forthwith sent for him, and he was at once installed into that office. George Neumark's next step was to reclaim his loved

* As God will, I am still.

violoncello; and, on obtaining it, he called on his landlady, who took a deep sympathy in his tribulations. In a few minutes the room was crowded with friends and neighbors, eager to hear him again play upon his instrument; and he sang to them an excellent sermon, in this wise, his own sweet hymn: "Wer nur den lieben Gott lässt walten."

> Leave God to order all thy ways,
>   And hope in Him, whate'er betide;
> Thou'lt find Him, in the evil days,
>   Thine all-sufficient strength and guide.
> Who trusts in God's unchanging love,
> Builds on the rock that naught can move!

This was his thanksgiving tribute for the good Providence which had rescued him from trial in his great emergency. After two years, the baron procured for him the post of Librarian of the Archives at Weimar, which office he held, with honor, until the close of his life.

This is not a mere monkish legend, but a truthful and instructive incident of real life; for this George Neumark was born at Thuringen in 1621. He studied law at the University of Königsberg, when Simon Dach was president; and, like him, Neumark became both poet and musician. But, being poor and friendless, after enduring much privation in his native place, he removed to Hamburg, in 1650, in hopes of better fortune, and it was here we met with him. Need we point the moral suggested? It is the beauty of a life of persevering integrity, humility, and devout trust in God. For, when asked if he made the hymn himself, he modestly replied: "Well, yes: I am the instrument, but God swept the strings. All I knew was that these words, 'Who trusts in God's unchanging love,' lay like a soft burden on my heart. I went over them again and again, and so they shaped themselves into this song; how, I cannot tell. I began to sing and to pray for joy, and my soul blessed the Lord; and word followed word, like water from a fountain."

Christianity, in Sweden, dates its rise in the ninth century. Anschar, the "Apostle of the North," who waged successful war against the old Scandinavian paganism, died in the year of grace, 835.

"Long after the southern regions of modern Europe emerge into the sober daylight of history, the twilight of legend lingers over the north. The gigantic forms of the old Sagas flit about in the gleam of the northern lights, ages after the chronicles of the south are peopled with a race of solid and ordinary men and women. Four centuries after the times when the people of Milan first sang the hymns of Ambrose; nearly three centuries after Gregory the Great sent Augustine to the English; a hundred years after the Venerable Bede passed his tranquil life in the monastery near Wearmouth, translating the New Testament into Anglo-Saxon, and chronicling his own times, — in Sweden, Christianity was carrying on its first conflict with heathenism." *

It was not, however, until seven centuries later, that its light streamed into those northern regions, and warmed the hearts of that rock-bound people by the recital of the story of the Cross. The Moravian missionaries labored with the Greenlanders in vain, until they rehearsed that all-potent theme. Like the action

* Mrs. Charles.

of the solar rays on the frozen seas, they soon found that the Cross of Calvary has power to melt the heart, although as cold and hard by nature as their own ice-bound coast. The Bible and the German Lutheran hymn-book were translated into the Swedish language; and soon the reception of the gospel awoke the voice of song among them also.

Gustavus Adolphus was a Swede,—nay, more, a self-sacrificing Christian hero; for, if ever a man subordinated self to the interests of a noble cause, it surely was Gustavus, and he it was who really rescued Germany from the yoke of spiritual despotism.

Spegel, Archbishop of Upsala, wrote a paraphrase on part of the Sermon on the Mount, of which the following stanzas form part of an English version, by Mrs. Charles. He was born, A.D. 1645, and died 1714; was contemporary with Paul Gerhardt, and, like him, a great hymn-writer. He accomplished much good for Sweden.

> We Christians should steadfastly ponder
>   What Christ hath so graciously taught;
> For He, who would have us His freemen,
>   Would see us retain in our thought
> How little things earthly are worth,
> Lest those who heap treasures on earth,
>   The heavenly prize leave unsought.
>
> All nature a sermon may preach thee;
>   The birds sing thy murmurs away,—
> The birds, which, nor sowing nor reaping,
>   God fails not to feed day by day;
> And He, who these creatures doth cherish,
> Will He fail thee, and leave thee to perish?
>   Or art thou not better than they?

The lilies, nor toiling nor spinning,
  Their clothing, how gorgeous and fair!
What tints in their tiny robes woven,
  What wondrous devices are there!
All Solomon's stores could not render
One festival robe of such splendor
  As the flowers have for every-day wear.

God gives to each flower its rich raiment,
  And o'er them His treasures flings free,
Which to-day finds so fragrant in beauty,
  And to-morrow all faded shall see.
Thus the lilies smile shame on thy care,
And the happy birds sing it to air:
  Will their God be forgetful of thee?

From the same source,* we derive another beautiful translation from the Swedish of Bishop Franzin, who died A.D. 1818.

  Jesus in thy memory keep,
    Wouldst thou be God's child and friend;
  Jesus in thy heart shrined deep,
    Still thy gaze on Jesus bend.
In thy toiling, in thy resting, look to Him with every breath,
    Look to Jesus' life and death.

  Look to Jesus, till reviving
    Faith and love thy life-springs swell;
  Strength for all things good deriving
    From Him who did all things well;
Work, as He did, in thy season, works which shall not fade away:
    Work while it is called to-day.

  Look to Jesus, prayerful, waking,
    When thy feet on roses tread;
  Follow, worldly pomp forsaking,
    With thy cross, where He hath led;
Look to Jesus in temptation; baffled shall the tempter flee,
    And God's angels come to thee.

* Christian Life in Song.

> Look to Jesus, when dark lowering
>   Perils thy horizon dim,
> By that band in terror cowering,
>   Calm 'midst tempests, look on Him.
> Trust in Him, who still rebuketh wind and billow, fire and flood;
>   Forward, brave by trusting God!

King Oscar, of Sweden, one of the most accomplished monarchs of Europe, was a poet. Mary Howitt's translation of one of his striking poems, entitled the "Heart's Home," is subjoined: —

> Where is thy home? Thus to my heart appealing
> I spake. Say thou, who hast had part
> In all my inmost being's deepest feeling,
> Where is thy proper home? Tell me, my heart!
> Is it where peaceful groves invite to leisure,
> And silvery brooklets lapse in easy measure?
>   No, no, my heart responded, No!
> . . . . . .
>
> Where is thy home? Perchance, where tropic splendor,
> In golden luxury of light, calls forth
> The purple grape; perchance, 'midst roses tender,
> Thou revellest in the beauty of the South.
> Is that thy home, beneath the palm-tree shadows?
> And ever-verdant summer's flowery meadows,
>   Still, still my heart made answer, No!
>
> Where is thy home? Is it 'mid icebergs hoary,
> The crags and snow-fields of the Arctic strand,
> Where the midsummer's midnight sees the glory
> Of sunset and of sunrise, hand in hand.
> Where 'twixt the pine-trees gleams the snow-drift's whiteness,
> And starry night flames with auroral brightness?
>   But still my whispering heart said, No!
> . . . . . .
>
> Where is thy home? Say, if perchance it lieth
> In that prefigured land of love and light,
> Whither, they say, the soul enfranchised flieth,
> When earthly bonds no longer check her flight?

>     Is there thy home, — those unknown realms elysian,
>     Which shine beyond the stars, a heavenly vision?
>         Then first my heart made answer, Yes!
>     There is my home, it said, with quick emotion;
>     My primal home, to which I am akin.
>     Though earthly fires may call forth my devotion,
>     Yet I forget not Heaven's pure flame within.
>     Amidst the ashes still a spark surviveth
>     Which ever yearneth heavenward, ever striveth
>         To be with God, who is my home!

In attempting to gather up the sounds of the never-ceasing chorus, we shall perceive a common creed, pervading most of the songs, — heart-echoes are they from one age and nation to another. Tracing to their common source these lyric-bursts of Christian heroes and saints of the long-forgotten past, we thus come into sympathy with the music of their souls, and may even offer our worship in their very words. Some morbid, ascetic Christians there are, who seem to be the living representatives of cloister, cowl, and convent; they prefer to remain voiceless, while they dissipate their days, which should be dedicated to thanksgiving and charity, in gloom and sadness. But Christianity is the patron of all that is cheerful and hope-inspiring, while its native language is that of psalm and song. If "light is sown for the righteous, and gladness for the upright in heart," surely the Christian should gather the golden harvest. We have already referred to the fact that Niebuhr's great mind solaced itself, amidst its intense labors and researches, by murmuring a hymn of thanksgiving, or some such plaintive appeal as the following : —

>     So give us peace: peace in the church and school,
>     Peace to the powers who o'er our country rule,
>     Peace to the conscience, peace within the heart,
>         Do Thou impart.

What a lesson has Luther left us, of bravery and cheerful trust, and love of song! Holland — whose claim to the invention of printing has been established, which is the home of classics, painters, men of science, — such names as Erasmus, Grotius, Lipsius, and Boerhaave — has also had her sons of song. Here is a neat little homily in verse, translated from the Dutch of L. van Welthem: —

> Know that holiness keeps her throne
> Not in cloisters or temples alone;
> The temple where she loves to dwell
> Is a pure spirit's sacred cell.

Another and more noted poet of the Netherlands was Dirk Rafael Kamphuyzen, who was born in 1586, and died 1626. While at the University of Leyden, he received instruction from the renowned Arminius, whose doctrines he embraced. He wrote a "Paraphrase of the Psalms," and a collection of poems. His religious poetry is superior to any which preceded it: there is in it a pure and earnest feeling throughout, an intense conviction of truth. His "May-Morning" is one of the most popular productions of the Dutch poets. Here are two or three of its fifteen stanzas (Sir John Bowring's translation): —

'Tis May! whose fragrant breath and dyes so far o'er earth are
    gone,
That memory all her charms supplies, ere she herself comes on.
'Tis May! the loveliest of the year, who with fresh beauty glows;
The air is sweet, the sunbeams clear, the wished-for zephyr blows.
The earth with varied flowers is dight, the bees with honey pass,
The larks chirp gaily, and alight upon the new-born grass.

Joost van den Vondel (born 1587, died 1679), as a poet, has never been rivalled in Holland. His tragedies, thirty-two in number, are perhaps the grandest in Dutch literature. His "Lucifer" has been often compared to Milton's "Paradise Lost;" and some have supposed it might have suggested the latter. Vondel's character was deeply imbued with religious enthusiasm. From the Bible he took almost all the subjects of his tragedies. He was, at first, eagerly in favor of Arminianism, and afterwards embraced Catholicism. Here is an extract from his "Lucifer:" —

> Who sits above heaven's heights sublime,
>   Yet fills the grave's profoundest place,
> Beyond eternity, or time,
>   Or the vast round of viewless space?
> Who on Himself alone depends,
>   Immortal, glorious, but unseen,
> And in His mighty Being blends
>   What rolls around or flows within?
>     .    .    .    .    .
> The tongue Thy peerless name hath spoken,
>   No space can hold that awful name;
> The aspiring spirit's wing is broken:
>   Thou wilt be, wert, and art the same!
> Language is dumb; imagination,
>   Knowledge, and science helpless fall;
> They are irreverent profanation,
>   And Thou, O God! art all in all.

It was on a Palm Sunday, about seven hundred and fifty years after the midnight song of Paul and Silas, at Philippi, that the Emperor Louis, "the *debonnaire*," and his court, were on their way to the cathedral at Mentz, in full procession, when, passing a dungeon, there issued from the prison-bars a hymn, which, in our vernacular, began: —

Glory and honor and praise to Thee, our Redeemer and King!
To whom little children sang lays, to whom our hosannas we bring.

. . . . . . .

Fragrant to Thee was their praise: oh, smile on the offering we bring!
Thy joy is in all pleasant lays, Thou blessed and all-gracious King:

This was the prison-song of Theodulph of Orleans, afterwards canonized as a saint. His hymn touched the heart of Charlemagne's imperial son, and the persecuted bishop found the joy of deliverance coming after his song. The "beloved disciple," in his sea-girt prison of Patmos, had his soul refreshed with the ecstatic songs of the Celestial City; and his inspired record of the vision is itself the grandest of all hymns. There was a Belgian poet, who died in the year of grace 1300, so prolific in his gifts, that he made a poetical translation of the Bible, from the Latin of Comestor, into the Dutch language. The poet's name is Jacob van Maerlant, and he entitled his performance "Rymbybel." A copy of this Rhyme-Bible is in the Astor Library.

After the great ecclesiastical Reformation had burst the iron barriers of Romish superstition, the grand chorus of sacred song resounded from many other lands beside Germany and Sweden: Italy, France, and Spain soon took up the burden of the refrain. Madame Guyon sang some of her sweetest devotional lyrics, even in the Bastille; and Geneva was a citadel of strength for the friends of religious liberty and truth. Geneva — the beautiful city of the Swiss lake, once covered with the dense darkness of the papacy, and anon the "beacon of the Church, and a bulwark of Christianity"— is replete with storied and traditional interest. Once it was the asylum for refugees of religious persecution, the "school of the prophets," and the headquarters for the printing and disseminating of the proscribed Bible; and, ere long, we find it again under eclipse, its glory departed, and actually arraying itself in antagonism with the very truth of which it was lately the defence and depository for the world. Yes: with its proud, ancestral faith, its creeds and symbols inscribed by the hand of Calvin himself, Geneva had, indeed, "lost all the Reformation had conferred upon it, and only retained the boast of its historic name in a lifeless and insolent Rationalism." For apostolic, vital Christianity, it had substituted the subtle poison of the modern infidelity of Voltaire, Gibbon, and Rousseau; and the inevitable result was spiritual desolation and death. It was, however, at this juncture, in 1816, at the close of the protracted wars which had so distracted and devastated the continent of Europe, that Mr. Robert Haldane, of Scotland, moved with a zeal for the mitigation of this spiritual destitution, reached Geneva. "At the period of Mr. Haldane's visit, both clergy and professors ridiculed the idea of the divinity of Jesus of Nazareth; and countenanced, by their lives, the gayety and frivolity by which people in general sought to drown all thoughts of eternity. Here and there a feeble voice was heard, bearing witness to the ancient faith; but it was soon stifled. A meeting of infidel students, presided over by M. Merle D'Aubigné, protested against "the odious aggression," as they styled a very moderate assertion of the cardinal doctrines of Christianity. In the face of such determined opposition, Haldane was in despair, and abandoned his project; but, having halted at Berne, he was persuaded to return and renew the effort. A second time he was on the eve of abandoning it, when, providentially, he was led into conversation with a student of the theological seminary, on the subject of religion. This young man, Mr. James, afterwards pastor at Brede, was profoundly ignorant of the gospel, but displayed a deep interest in Mr. Haldane's conversation. On the morrow he returned, bringing with him another student, Mr. C. Rieu. Both of them became evidently awakened, and Haldane made arrangements at once to prolong his stay. The sequel may best be related in his own words: " The two students with whom I first conversed brought six others, in the same state of mind with themselves, with whom I had many and long conversations. Their visits became so frequent, and at such different hours, that I proposed they should come together; and it was arranged that they should do so three times a week, from six to eight o'clock in the evening. This gave me time to converse with others, who, from the report of the students, began to visit me. After having proceeded in this manner about a fortnight, with these eight students, I was earnestly solicited, in the name of the other students, to begin anew. I complied with the request; and during the whole of the winter, and until the termination of their studies in the following summer, almost all the students of theology regularly attended, and God was graciously pleased to accompany his Word with power." It seems the constituted "faculty" stirred up an opposition to this movement on the part of Mr. Haldane, and they attempted to instigate the government to banish him from the canton; and, this failing, they sought to have him impeached, but popular sentiment overruled this also. The first-fruits of this awakening was Cæsar Malan, one of the pastors of the city, who had been first quickened by a conversation with Dr. Mason, of New York, who passed through Geneva on his travels at this time; "but Mr. Haldane was honored to lead him as an awakened sinner to a knowledge of the Saviour. Once himself enlightened, "his eloquent words dropped on the leaden slumbers of his audience like bolts of fire: pastors, professors, syndics, and private citizens were cut to the heart, and almost gnashed on him with their teeth, as Dr. Malan descended from the pulpit, and passed through their own ranks, unrecognized, an avoided and rejected man!"\* Dejected and overwhelmed, the preacher hastened homeward, and at his own door was met by Mr. Haldane, who, greeting him with a cordial grasp of the hand, said, "Thank God, the gospel has been once more preached in Geneva." M. Gaussen also (a neighboring pastor) boldly preached the truth. The heresy of Geneva was now fairly unveiled, and the persecuted young students at once became earnest and successful preachers of the Word of Life. A new church organization was soon effected by the aid of Mr. Henry Drummond, a young English gentleman of fortune, "whose heart the Lord had touched," and who arrived at Geneva just as Mr. Haldane was leaving. It is, of course, impossible to estimate the amount of good which has resulted from the missionary emprise of Mr. Haldane. It was the initial step in a work which has spread over Europe, and which has even reached to this continent, in the Swiss mis-

\* Waymarks in the Wilderness.

sions to the Lower Canadians. The mere enumeration of their names, long since endeared to us for their "works' sake," would evince something of the greatness of this missionary work. Among a much longer list, were Merle d'Aubigné. F. Monod, C. Rieu, Cæsar Malan, Gouthier, Mejanel, Felix Neff, and M. Olivier.

Our discursive pen has, almost unconsciously, lingered about this interesting "Home of Calvin" so long, that we are fain to ask forgiveness for the digression, albeit its collateral interest may well atone for the detention. Now let us return to the singers. And, first, let us listen to some of the prison-songs of the saintly Madame Guyon, whose melodies, despite their mysticism, are very charming ; for example : —

> Thy love, O God ! restores me,
>   From sighs and tears, to praise ;
> And deep my soul adores Thee,
>   Nor thinks of time or place.
> I ask no more, in good or ill,
> But union with Thy holy will.
> 'Tis that which makes my treasure,
>   'Tis that which brings my gain ;
> Converting woe to pleasure,
>   And reaping joy from pain.
> Oh ! 'tis enough, whate'er befall,
> To know that God is all in all.

> .     .

> 'Tis Love unites what sin divides ;
> The centre where all bliss resides ;
> To which the soul once brought,
> Reclining on the First Great Cause,
> From His abounding sweetness draws
> Peace passing human thought.
> Sorrow foregoes its nature there,
> And life assumes a tranquil air,

> Divested of its woes.
> There sovereign goodness soothes the breast,
> Till then incapable of rest,
> In sacred, sure repose.

She seldom refers to the outward events of her life in her hymns. The following stanzas are, we believe, the only exception; and these exhibit an unreserved acquiescence and resignation of spirit that is truly exemplary.

> Nor exile I, nor prison, fear; love makes my courage great;
> I find a Saviour everywhere, His grace in every state.
> Nor castle-walls, nor dungeons deep, exclude His quickening beams;
> There I can sit, and sing, and weep, and dwell on heavenly themes!

Her first imprisonment by the Romanists, on account of her proclivity to Protestantism, was in 1688, in a convent. Some seven years afterwards she was again imprisoned, it was in the Castle of Vincennes; and, in 1698, she was taken to the Bastille, where she was confined four years, and then banished to Blois. Bossuet was especially opposed to her doctrine, seeing in it only a revival of the Gnostic heresy. Fénelon, on the contrary, became a convert to it, and spoke and wrote in defence of it, and of his new friend; and thus brought upon himself banishment, and upon his book papal censure. To Cowper, who found some resemblance between the tried life of Madame Guyon and his own, we are indebted for admirable translations of some of the best of her religious poems. One of her prose works, "A Short and Easy Method of Prayer," contains her account of the "Prayer of Silence," in which not only is there no utterance by the voice, but even the mind concentrates its whole energies in one desire, "Thy will be done." This work was feared by the Romanists, who collected it by hundreds, and burned it.

From the French of C. Malan, we have these beautiful lines: —

> No, no, it is not dying, to go unto our God;
>     The glowing earth forsaking,
> Our journey homeward taking along the starry road.
> No, no, it is not dying, heaven's citizen to be;
>     The crown eternal wearing,
> And rest unbroken sharing, from care and conflict free.
> No, no, it is not dying, to hear the precious Word,
>     " Receive the Father's blessing,
> For evermore possessing the favor of the Lord."

The following plaintive lines, translated from the French, were found amongst the private papers of the Queen of Scots, when her cabinet was plundered at Chartley, shortly before her death.

> Alas, what am I? what my life become?
> A corpse existing when the pulse hath fled!
> An empty shadow, mark for conflicts dread,
> Whose only hope of refuge is the tomb.
> Cease to pursue, O foes! with envious hate;
> My share of this world's glories hath been brief;
> Soon will your ire on me be satiate,
> For I consume and die of mortal grief.
> And ye, my faithful friends, who hold me dear,
> In dire adversity, and bonds, and woe,
> I lack the power to guerdon love sincere;
> Wish, then, the close of all my ills below,
> That, purified on earth, with sins forgiven,
> My ransomed soul may share the joys of heaven.*

The name of the hapless queen reminds us of her last pathetic hymn or prayer: —

* Savile's Lyra Sacra.

"O Domine Deus! Speravi in Te!
O care mi Jesu! nunc libera me," etc.

---

O Lord God! I've trusted in Thee!
O Jesus beloved! now liberate me;
In fetters so galling, in tortures appalling, I long after Thee!
In moaning, in groaning, on bent knee atoning,
I adore Thee! I implore Thee to liberate me.

In the sixteenth century there was no evangelist, among women at least, more active in the cause of pure Christianity, than was the Queen of Navarre. "The goodness of her heart, the purity of her life, and the abundance of her works, spoke eloquently to those about her of the beauty of the gospel."[*] She wrote some religious verses and ballads, to which many of the nobility of France owed their first religious impressions. The following is a translation of one of her pieces: —

Who would be a Christian true, must his Lord's example follow;
Every worldly good resign, and earthly glory count but hollow:
    Honor, wealth, and friends so sweet,
    He must trample under feet;
    But, alas! to few 'tis given
    Thus to tread the path to heaven!

With a willing, joyful heart, his goods among the poor divide;
Others' trespasses forgive; revenge and anger lay aside:
    Be good to those who work you ill;
    If any hate you, love them still;
    But, alas! to few 'tis given
    Thus to tread the path to heaven!

He must hold death beautiful, and over it in triumph sing;
Love it with a warmer heart than he loveth mortal thing;
    But, alas! to few 'tis given
    Thus to tread the path to heaven!

[*] D'Aubigné's Reformation.

Clement Marot, who was the friend of Calvin, and attached to the court of Francis I., made a French version of fifty of David's Psalms, and also wrote much religious poetry, which long continued to be popular in Paris and Geneva, among the Protestant churches. His sacred lyrics were sung alike by prince and peasant, and even children chanted them in the streets of Paris, and elsewhere. Clement Marot's metrical version of the Psalms was sung by the persecuted Huguenots and Protestants of Holland, as they gathered in multitudes under the shelter of the woods. They became, indeed, battle-songs, like those of ancient Israel by the Red Sea; or the army of Jehoshaphat, before which the enemy fled as from a charge. Bayle ranks Marot among the best of the French poets. It is very remarkable that his poetry should have been so completely ignored, while the hymns of Germany have been so frequently translated. We offer a literal prose rendering of two of his minor pieces, as specimens: —

### A PRAYER AFTER MEALS.

Eternal Father, who commandest us not to be anxious for the morrow! we give Thee thanks for the good things which Thou givest us for this day. As Thou hast now been pleased to open Thy hand, and given to our bodies food and drink, be pleased also to nourish our souls with the bread of heaven for the glory of Thy name.

### LITTLE CHRISTIAN DEVICES.

Is Christ dead? Yes, certainly! What caused His death? Perfect charity. What was the occasion? Ardent love! For whom? For us, sinners, who have offended Him! For what purpose? To merit for us His Paradise, which, without Him, we could not have acquired by austerity, fasting, watching, shame, suffering, and torments. He saved poor Adam, most justly condemned, with his posterity, procuring for him the high heaven, of which, by his sin, he was disinherited; and he who will believe this truth, which is beyond the sense and the understanding, — loving, with a heart full of purity, — will, with great clearness, vitally know that by God alone he has his unmerited salvation.

Fénelon (1651-1715) preached his first sermon at the early age of fifteen, before a select assembly convened at Paris, whither he had been called by his uncle, the marquis. He afterwards formed an acquaintance with the celebrated quietist, Madame Guyon, who was, at first, in high favor at the court of Louis XIV. But this did not last long: Bossuet instigated a series of persecutions against her, which resulted in her long imprisonment. Fénelon, however, befriended and defended her, as already stated; for which good service he was placed under ban, and denounced as a heretic. This is one of his hymns: —

> Living or dying, Lord, I would be Thine!
> Oh, what is life?
> A toil, a strife,
> Were it not lighted by Thy love divine.
> I ask not wealth,
> I crave not health:
> Living or dying, Lord, I would be Thine!
>
> Oh, what is death,
> When the poor breath
> In parting can the soul to Thee resign!
> While patient love
> Her trust doth prove,
> Living or dying, Lord, I would be Thine!
>
> Throughout my days,
> Be constant praise
> Uplift to Thee from out this heart of mine;
> So shall I be
> Brought nearer Thee:
> Living or dying, Lord, I would be Thine!

It is a singular and noteworthy fact, that neither France, Switzerland, nor Scotland, possesses, like Germany, any hymn-literature, born of the Reformed Church, either Lutheran or Calvinistic. The Church at Geneva used David's Psalter, and so did Scotland; and so the Scottish Church still cherishes her rugged Scotch version of them, "with all the sacred associations which two centuries of such a church history as that of Scotland has gathered round the song of to-day, mingling it with echoes from mountain gatherings, and martyrs' prisons, and scaffolds, and joyful death-beds: probably no hymn-book could be ever one-half so musical or poetical to Scottish ears and hearts, as those strange, rough verses."\*

We pass the other great poets of mediæval Italy, Tasso, and his successors, because they cannot be properly classed among sacred lyric poets. Petrarch did not write much that may be so characterized. We find but one or two of his sonnets of this class.

Petrarch, in his later days, lived in peace and retirement at Milan: it was in a sequestered quarter, near the Church of St. Ambrose. "My life," he says, in a letter to a friend, "has been uniform ever since age tamed the fervor of youth, and extinguished that fatal passion which so long tormented me. Like a weary traveller, I quicken my steps as I proceed. I read and write, day and night, one occupation relieving another: this is all my amusement and employment. My eyes are worn out with reading, my fingers weary with holding the pen. One thing only is a source of disquietude: I am esteemed more than I deserve, so that a vast concourse of people

\* Mrs. Charles.

come to see me." Yes: he was honored by all men, and courted by monarchs. He died in 1374, seated in his library, his head resting on a book.

This sublime vision of Future Blessedness is from the Italian of Petrarch:—

> The time will come when every change shall cease,
> This quick revolving wheel shall rest in peace;
> No summer then shall glow, nor winter freeze;
> Nothing shall be to come, and nothing past,
> But an eternal now shall ever last!
> Though Time shall be no more, yet space shall give
> A nobler theatre to love and live.
> Then, all the lying vanities of life, —
> The sordid source of envy, hate, and strife, —
> Ignoble as they are, shall then appear
> Beneath the searching beam of Truth severe.
> Then souls, from sense refined, shall see the fraud
> That led them from the living way of God.
> Blest is the pile that marks the hallowed dust,
> There, at the resurrection of the just,
> When the last trumpet, with earth-shaking sound,
> Shall wake her sleepers from their couch profound;
> How will the beatific sight display
> All heavenly beauty in these climes of day!

The following sonnet is from the same source:—

> I live lamenting my departed years,
>   Spent in the vain love of an earthly thing;
>   No flight essaying, though my soaring wing
> Hath borne me on, perchance, to lofty spheres.
> O Thou, who seest my misery and tears,
>   Invisible, eternal, heavenly King!
>   Help for this soul, feeble and wandering,
> Support her weakness and allay her fears.
> So that, if I have lived in storm and strife,
>   Sheltered in peaceful haven I may rest;
> And my last hour, oh, be Thou near to aid!
> On Thee, thou knowest, my only hope is staid.

The following is from the Italian of Dante, whose glowing and gloomy pen seemed to linger so spellbound over the terrors of the lost. His great poems are a reflex of the purgatorial creed of the Middle Ages.

> The King of kings, whose goodness knows no bounds,
> In recompensing ills His servants bear,
> Makes me discard all anger, care, and grief,
> And to the court of heaven direct mine eyes;
> And while I muse upon the glorious choir
> Of citizens, who dwell where all is pure,
> In praising my Creator, I, His creature,
> Am more inflamed with love, the more I praise;
> For if I contemplate the promised bliss
> To which my God invites the Christian race,
> For me there seems nought else to be desired.
> But, friend beloved, for thee I truly grieve,
> Who disregard'st the life and world to come,
> And losest, for a shadow, bliss secure!

We present part of one of the hymns of Savonarola, the Romish reformer and martyr of Italy, thus anglicized by Mrs. H. Beecher Stowe: —

> Alas, how oft this sordid heart hath wounded Thy pure eye!
> Yet for this heart, upon the cross, Thou gav'st Thyself to die.
> . . . . . . . .
> Burn in my heart, celestial flame, with memories of Him,
> Till, from earth's dross refined, I rise to join the seraphim.
> Ah, vanish each unworthy trace of earthly care or pride,
> Leave only graven on my heart the Cross, the Crucified!

Ariosto discovers so much devotional feeling in the following sonnet, that we cannot refrain from quoting it: —

> How shall my cold and lifeless prayer ascend,
> Father of Mercies! to Thy seat on high,
> If, while my lips for Thy deliverance call,
> My heart against that liberty contend?

Do Thou, who knowest all, Thy rescue send,
Though every power of mine the help deny.
Eternal God! oh, pardon that I went
Erring so long! whence have mine eyes been smit
With darkness, nor the good from evil known.
To spare offenders, being penitent,
Is even ours ; to drag them from the pit,
Themselves resisting, — Lord, is Thine alone!

Michel Angelo, in one of his letters to his friend and biographer, Vasari, wrote the following sonnet, introducing it with these words : " I know you will tell me that, being old, I am unwise to attempt the making of sonnets; but since they say I am in my dotage, I do but perform my proper office."

Now in frail bark, and on the storm-tossed wave,
Doth this, my life, approach the common port,
Whither all haste to render up account
Of every act, — the erring and the just.
Wherefore I now do see, that by the love
Which rendered Art mine idol and my Lord,
I did much err. Vain are the loves of man,
And error lurks within his every thought.
Light hours of this my life, where are ye now,
When towards a twofold death my foot draws near?
The one well-known, the other threatening loud.
Not the erst worshipped-art, can now give peace
To him whose soul turns to that love divine
Whose arms shall lift him from the Cross to Heaven.

Another of his fine sonnets we subjoin, translated by Wordsworth : —

The prayers I make will then be sweet indeed,
 If Thou the spirit give by which I pray ;
 My unassisted heart is barren clay,
That of its native self can nothing feed.
Of good and pious works Thou art the seed
 That quickens only where Thou say'st it may.
 Unless Thou show to us Thine own true way,

No man can find it : Father, Thou must lead.
Do Thou, then, breathe those thoughts into my mind
  By which such virtue may in me be bred,
  That in Thy holy footsteps I may tread ;
The fetters of my tongue do Thou unbind,
  That I may have the power to sing of Thee,
  And sound Thy praises everlastingly!

Michel Angelo, one of the most extraordinary men of Italy, was born in 1474. He was painter, sculptor, architect, and poet, and in each department of science alike illustrious and unsurpassed. The building of St. Peter's, at Rome, which he directed many years, and the marvellous painting of the Sistine Chapel, are works, either of which is enough for immortality. He died at Rome, 1564. His sonnets were the amusement of his leisure hours, and an elegant pastime they were.

Like the sonnets of Michel Angelo, those of Vittoria Colonna derive a singular interest from that spirit of devotion which breathes through the religious section of them. Scripturally simple and ascetically austere, they are so truly Protestant as to have earned for her the reputation of ranking as a disciple of the Reformation.

Vittoria Colonna, of the sixteenth century, was the most distinguished poetess of Italy. She was possessed of great beauty, both of person and character. Of noble lineage and endowed with great wealth, this " most brilliant woman of Italy " passed a life of singular tranquillity, amid scenes of great political tumult. Like Petrarch's, her numerous sonnets breathe an undying affection, and are the eloquent story of her great sorrow, for she became a widow at the early age of thirty-six years. Although she remained in the communion of the Romish Church, her later poems afford unequivocal evidence of her possession of a pure Protestant faith. The following sonnets are a sufficient proof of this: —

    Deaf would I be to earthly sounds, to greet
        With thought intent, and fixed on things above,
    The high angelic strains, the accent sweet,
        In which true peace accords with perfect love;
    Each living instrument, the breath that plays
    Upon its strings, from chord to chord conveys,
        And to one end so perfectly they move,
    That nothing jars the eternal harmony;
    Love melts each voice, love lifts its accents high,
        Love beats the time, presides o'er every string.
    The angelic orchestra one signal sways;
    The sound becomes more sweet, the more it strays
    Through varying changes, in harmonious maze;
        He who the song inspired, prompts all who sing!

---

    Father of Heaven! if by Thy mercy's grace
    A living branch I am of that True Vine
    Which spreads o'er all, — and would we did resign
    Ourselves entire by faith to its embrace! —
    In me much drooping, Lord, Thine eye will trace,
    Caused by the shade of these rank leaves of mine,
    Unless in season due Thou dost refine
    The humor gross, and quicken its dull pace.
    So cleanse me, that, abiding e'er with Thee,
    I feed me hourly with the heavenly dew,
    And with my falling tears refresh the root.
    Thou saidst, and Thou art truth, Thou'dst with me be:
    Then willing come, that I may bear much fruit,
    And worthy of the stock on which it grew.

---

    Would that mine ears were deaf to earthly sound,
        That every thought might more intently dwell
        On the sweet tones and notes angelical
    Which love and peace upraise the world around:

Nature is all attuned, and still is found
  To breathe o'er every chord a living spell,
  So that, concerted, all together swell,
  And pure ethereal harmonies rebound.
But love attunes each voice : love rules the choir,
  Beats time, and gives the burden all must bear :
  'Tis love leads nature's choir, nor leads it wrong.
Sweet and more sweet the grateful notes aspire :
  All nature joins in one harmonious song,
  And tells of love; for God has given the air.

From Bowring's Batavian poetry, we select the following stanzas, translated from Kamphuyzen, of the seventeenth century : —

  If there be one whose thoughts delight to wander
  In pleasure's fields, where love's bright streams meander,
    If there be one who longs to find,
    Where all the purer blisses are enshrined,
  A happy resting-place of virtuous worth,
  A blessed paradise on earth, —

  Let him survey the joy-conferring union
  Of brothers who are bound in fond communion,
    And not by force of blood alone,
    But by their mutual sympathies are known ;
  And every heart and every mind relies
  Upon fraternal, kindred ties.

  Oh, blessed abode, where love is ever vernal,
  Where tranquil peace and concord are eternal,
    Where none usurp the highest claim,
    But each with pride asserts the other's fame, —
  Oh! what are all earth's joys compared to thee,
  Fraternal unanimity!

  .   .   .   .   .   .

  God, in his boundless mercy, joys to meet it ;
  His promises of future blessings greet it,
    And fixed prosperity, which brings
    Long life, and ease, beneath its shadowing wings,
  And joy and fortune that remain sublime
  Beyond all distance, change, and time.

The following sonnet is a translation from the Spanish of Lope de Vega, by Longfellow:—

> Lord, what am I, that, with unceasing care,
> Thou didst seek after me? that Thou didst wait,
> Wet with unhealthy dews, before my gate,
> And pass the gloomy nights of winter there?
> Oh, strange delusion, that I did not greet
> Thy blessed approach! and oh, to heaven how lost,
> In my ingratitude's unkindly frost,
> Has chilled the bleeding wounds upon Thy feet!
> How oft my guardian angel gently cried,
> " Soul, from thy casement look, and thou shalt see
> How He persists to knock and wait for thee ! "
> And, oh! how often to that voice of sorrow,
> " To-morrow we will open," I replied;
> And when to-morrow came, I answered still, " To-morrow."

Lope de Vega was born at Madrid, in 1562 : he was a prodigy of wit in his early days; and he kept up his reputation as a man of many words, till the end of his days. It is said that he read Latin at five years old; and such was his passion for verses, that, before he could use a pen, he bribed his elder schoolmates, with a portion of his breakfast, to write to his dictation, and then exchanged his effusions with others, for prints and hymns. Thus truly he lisped in numbers; and, as he was the most prolific and voluminous of poets, he kept himself diligently exercised in that line, to the end of his life.

Don Jorge Manrique, of Spain, flourished in the latter half of the fifteenth century. He followed the profession of arms, and died on the field of battle, in the year 1479. His grand funeral hymn, or ode, was written in memory of his father's death. The translation is by Professor Longfellow. The ode extends to eighty-four stanzas; we present eight of them : —

Oh, let the soul her slumbers break;
Let thought be quickened, and awake, —
Awake to see
How soon this life is past and gone,
And death comes softly stealing on,
How silently!

. . . . .

Let no one fondly dream again,
That Hope, and all her shadowy train,
Will not decay:
Fleeting as were the dreams of old,
Remembered like a tale that's told,
They pass away.

Our lives are rivers, gliding free
To that unfathomed, boundless sea,
The silent grave!
Thither all earthly pomp and boast
Roll, to be swallowed up and lost
In one dark wave.

Thither the mighty torrents stray,
Thither the brook pursues its way,
And tinkling rill.
They all are equal: side by side
The poor man and the son of pride
Lie calm and still.

I will not here invoke the throng
Of orators and sons of song,
The deathless few;
Fiction entices, and deceives,
And, sprinkled o'er her fragrant leaves,
Lies poisonous dew.

To One alone my thoughts arise,
The Eternal Truth, the Good and Wise:
To Him I cry,
Who shared on earth our common lot,
But the world comprehended not
His Deity!

> Yes: the glad Messenger of love,
> To guide us to our home above,
> The Saviour came.
> Born amid mortal cares and fears,
> He suffered, in this vale of tears,
> A death of shame.
>
> Did we but use it as we ought,
> This world would school each wandering thought
> To its high state!
> Faith wings the soul beyond the sky,
> Up to that better world on high,
> For which we wait!

This sonnet, anglicized by the same elegant pen, is from the Spanish of Francisco de Aldana: —

> Clear fount of light! my native land on high,
> Bright with a glory that shall never fade!
> Mansion of Truth! without a vale or shade;
> Thy holy quiet meets the spirit's eye.
> There dwells the soul in its ethereal essence,
> Gasping no longer for life's feeble breath;
> But, sentinelled in heaven, its glorious presence
> With pitying eye beholds, yet fears not, death.
> Beloved country! banished from thy shore,
> A stranger in this prison-house of clay,
> The exiled spirit weeps and sighs for thee!

The remarkable ode to the Divine Being, by Derzhavin, who has been styled the Russian Pindar, is luxuriant with ornament and imaginative power. This poem has been translated into several European languages, and also into the Chinese and Japanese. It is stated that a copy of it, printed in gold letters, on white satin, is hung up in the palace of the Emperor of China, and another in the Temple of Jeddo.* Here follows a portion of the stanzas: —

* Golownin's Japan.

O Thou Eternal One! whose presence bright
    All space doth occupy, all motion guide ;
Unchanged through Time's all-devastating flight,
    Thou only God! there is no God beside.
Being above all beings, Mighty One,
    Whom none can comprehend, and none explore ;
Who fill'st existence with Thyself alone ;
    Embracing all ; supporting, ruling o'er ;
    Being whom we call God, — and know no more!
In its sublime research, philosophy
    May measure out the ocean deep, may count
The sands, or the sun's rays ; but, God! for Thee
    There is no weight nor measure : none can mount
Up to Thy mysteries : reason's brightest spark,
    Though kindled by Thy light, in vain would try
To trace Thy counsels, infinite and dark ;
    And thought is lost ere thought can soar so high,
    Even like past moments in eternity.
Thou from primeval nothingness didst call
    First chaos, then existence ; Lord, on Thee
Eternity had its foundation : all
    Sprung forth from Thee, of light, joy, harmony,
Sole origin : all life, all beauty, Thine.
    Thy word created all, and doth create ;
Thy splendor fills all space with rays divine !
    Thou art, and wert, and shalt be, glorious, great,
    Life-giving, life-sustaining Potentate !
Thy chains the unmeasured universe surround,
    Upheld by Thee, by Thee inspired with breath,
Thou the beginning with the end hast bound,
    And beautifully mingled life and death !
As sparks mount upward from the fiery blaze,
    So suns are born, so worlds sprung forth from Thee !
And as the spangles in the sunny rays
    Shine round the silver snow, the pageantry
Of heaven's bright army glitters in Thy praise.
A million torches lighted by Thy hand
    Wander unwearied through the blue abyss ;
They own Thy power, accomplish Thy command,
    All gay with life, all eloquent with bliss.

What shall we call them ?   Piles of crystal light,
  A glorious company of golden streams,
Lamps of celestial ether, burning bright,
  Suns lighting systems with their joyous beams ?
But Thou to these art as the noon to night.
Yes : as a drop of water in the sea,
  All this magnificence in Thee is lost :
What are ten thousand worlds compared to Thee ?
  And what am *I* then ?   Heaven's unnumbered host,
Though multiplied by myriads, and arrayed
  In all the glory of sublimest thought,
Is but an atom in the balance ; weighed
  Against Thy greatness, is a cipher brought
  Against infinity !   O, what am I then ?   Nought !
Nought ! yet the effluence of Thy light divine,
  Pervading worlds, hath reached my bosom too ;
Yes ! in my spirit doth thy Spirit shine,
  As shines the sunbeam in a drop of dew.
Nought ! yet I live, and on hope's pinions fly
  Eager towards Thy presence ; for in Thee
I live, and breathe, and dwell ; aspiring high,
  Even to the throne of Thy Divinity.
  I am, O God, and surely Thou must be !
Thou art ! — directing, guiding all, — Thou art !
  Direct my understanding then to Thee,
Control my spirit, guide my wandering heart ;
  Though but an atom 'midst immensity,
Still I am something fashioned by Thy hand :
  I hold a middle rank 'twixt heaven and earth ;
On the last verge of mortal being stand,
  Close to the realms where angels have their birth,
Just on the boundaries of the spirit-land !

 . . . . . .

Creator, — yes !   Thy wisdom and Thy word
  Created *me.*   Thou source of life and good,
Thou Spirit of my spirit, and my Lord !
  Thy light, Thy love, in their bright plenitude,
Filled me with an immortal soul, to spring
  O'er the abyss of death, and bade it wear
The garments of eternal day, and wing

Its heavenly flight beyond this little sphere,
Even to its source, — to Thee, its Author there.

Gabriel Romanovitch Derzhavin, the most distinguished lyric poet of Russia, was born in 1743, and died in 1816. In 1791, Catherine bestowed on him the office of Secretary of State. Two years later, he was elected to the Senate: various other appointments he successively occupied; after holding which some time, he retired on full pension. His far-famed "Address to the Deity," for wealth of imagery, grandeur, and sublimity, is said to be unsurpassed by any known ode. Its mastery of language, and splendor of conception, are its distinguishing characteristics.

The well-known lines on the "Celestial Sabbath," translated by Bowring from the Russian, are sung at midnight, in the Greek churches, the week before Easter: —

> The golden palace of my God,
>   Towering above the clouds, I see;
> Beyond, the cherubs' bright abode,
>   Higher than angels' thoughts can be:
> How can I in those courts appear,
>   Without a wedding-garment on?
> Conduct me, Thou Life-Giver, there, —
>   Conduct me to Thy glorious throne!
> And clothe me with Thy robes of light,
> And lead me through sin's darksome night,
>   My Saviour and my God!

From the same source, we derive the following extract: —

> The hollowest vessels sound the loudest,
>   The richest treasures deepest lie;
> Yet piled up wealth. and rank the proudest,
>   Are but tumultuous vanity.

I am a prince, with princely spirit,
  A ruler, if I rule my heart;
  A titled heir, if I inherit
    Of virtue, wisdom, truth, a part.

The following is Bowring's translation of a "Song of the Cherubim," from the Russian of Khernvimij, which is chanted in the Greek churches during the procession of the Cup: —

  See the glorious cherubim
    Thronging round the Eternal's throne;
  Hark! they sing their holy hymn,
  To the unknown Three in One, — All-supporting Deity!
    Living Spirit, praise to Thee!

  Rest, ye worldly tumults, rest;
    Here let all be peace and joy;
  Grief no more shall rend the breast,
    Tears no more bedew the eye.

  Heaven-directed spirits, rise
    To the temple of the skies!
  Join the ranks of angels bright,
    Near the Eternal's dazzling light.

The following ode, or paraphrase, of a passage from the book of Job, is quoted from Bowring's translation from the Russian of Lomonossov: —

  O Man! whose weakness dares rebel
    Against the Almighty's strength, draw nigh
  And listen, for my tongue shall tell
    His message from the unclouded sky!
  'Midst rain and storm and hail He spoke,
  Around the piercing thunder broke;
  At His proud word the clouds disperse,
  And thus He shakes the universe!
  "Come forth, then, in thy pride and power, —
    Come answer me, thou son of earth:
  Where wert thou in that distant hour
    When first I gave creation birth?

When all the mountains' heights were reared,
When all the heavenly hosts appeared, —
My wisdom and my strength's display?
Man! let thy towering wisdom say:
" Where wert thou when the stars, new born,
　Sprung into light at my command,
And filled the bounds of eve and morn,
　And sung the Intelligence that planned
Their course sublime? When first the sun
On wings of glory had begun
His race, and oceans of pure light
Wafted mild Luna through the night?
" Who bid the ascending mountains rise?
Who fixed the boundary of the sea?
Who, when the waves attacked the skies,
　Confined their fluvious revelry?

　　.　　.　　.　　.　　.

" Say, hast thou scaled the mountains' height,
Or sounded ocean's vast abyss, —
Or measured all that infinite
　Immensity that o'er thee is?"

The memory of the amiable but hapless Princess Elizabeth, daughter of James I., who became Queen of Bohemia, is associated, as a hymnist, with the names of the celebrated Dr. Donne, George Wither, and others. Her history is a sad and eventful one. "She went a happy bride to her husband's hereditary palace at Heidelberg, became a happy mother at eighteen, saw her husband placed on the throne of Bohemia, and realized the dream of her youthful ambition, — a crown. But scarcely had she shown her queenly presence in Bohemia, before her husband was driven from his royalty. She fled for her life, and entered on the dark succession of misfortunes which crowded on her the rest of her days. Widowed at last, beggared, tortured by her father's crooked policy; living to hear of her brother Charles's death on the scaffold; parting with her children, for lack of means to support them; treated with cold neglect by the only son who could help her; having her sound Protestant heart smitten at the perversion of others of her children to Romanism, — yet her hopeful, buoyant heart kept up until, after forty sorrowful years of exile, and thirty years of desolate widowhood, she returned, at the age of sixty-five, to finish her checkered career in the land of her infancy." She died in Leicester House, London; leaving the relics of her royal furniture to be preserved in that same Combe Abbey, which had witnessed the pleasures of her youth, and that piety which had solaced her to the end.

> This is joy, this is true pleasure,
> If we best things make our treasure,
> And enjoy them at full leisure,
> Evermore in richest measure.
> God is only excellent;
> Let up to Him our love be sent;
> Whose desires are set or bent
> On aught else, shall much repent.
>
> . . . . .
>
> God most holy, high, and great,
> Our delight doth make complete,
> When in us He takes His seat;
> Only then are we replete.
>
> Why should vain joys us transport?
> Earthly pleasures are but short,
> And are mingled in such sort,
> Griefs are greater than the sport.
>
> . . . . .
>
> When thy heart is fullest fraught
> With heaven's love, it shall be caught
> To the place it loved and sought,
> Which Christ's precious blood hath bought.

These lines are from a hymn of thirty-three stanzas, written while under her sore tribulation.

Petöfi, the "Burns of Hungary," was born on the first dawn of the year 1823. In the spring of 1844, he reached Pesth, where he introduced himself to Vörösmarty, the then most renowned of the Magyar poets. He was at first coldly received, and deemed rude and intrusive; but, after hearing him read some of his verses, his host exclaimed, "Hungary never had such lyrics: you must be cared for." From that moment his literary fame and fortune were established, his merits recognized. The popular voice also awarded him renown; for, says a contemporary, "he never went to bed at night, or arose in the morning, without hearing his songs from the multitudinous passengers in the streets." In the beginning of the year 1849, he joined Bem, whose adjutant he became, in the patriot army. He was present at the fearful slaughter in Segesvár; and, in the memorable retreat of the Magyar army, he was killed.

We select three little pearls from Sir J. Bowring's translation of his poems:—

> Round the dark green circle of the woods I wander,
> Looking on the flowers the high oaks blooming under;
> Birds among the branches, bees among the flowers,
> Music all around us bursting from the bowers;
> Flowers and trees are still, yet seem alive and wary,
> Listening to the hymns of nature's sanctuary.
> Is all sleeping here,—the forest, flowers, and furrows?
> Let me stand and muse, forgetful of my sorrows.

---

> Why should Death an image bring, mouldering and perishing?
>     Death, which is the charioteer,
> Our freed spirits to convey, over an ascending way,
>     To the heavens all bright and clear.

When I look upon the sky, in its blue immensity,
    Fancy fashions out a road,
Fading in the distance far, where, from smiling star to star,
    We are welcomed up to God.

---

And what is sorrow? 'tis a boundless sea.
    And what is joy!
A little pearl in that deep ocean's bed:
I sought it, found it, held it o'er my head,
    And, to my soul's annoy,
It fell into the ocean's depth again;
And now I long and look for it in vain.

Queen Maria of Hungary's "Song of the Cross" was probably composed in 1526, when she was compelled to flee from Buda, on account of her adherence to the Reformed doctrine, after the battle of Mohacz, in which her husband and the flower of the Hungarian nobility fell, in defending their country against the Turks.

Can I my fate no more withstand, nor 'scape the hand
That for my faith would grieve me?
This is my strength, that well I know,
    In weal or woe,
God's love the world must leave me.
God is not far, though hidden now:
He soon shall rise, and make them bow,
    Who of His Word bereave me.

Judge as ye will my cause this hour, yours is the power:
God bids me strive no longer;
I know what mightiest seems to-day
    Shall pass away;
Time than your rule is stronger.
The Eternal Good I rather choose,
And, fearless, all for this I lose;
    God help me thus to conquer!

We conclude our desultory ramble over these far-apart countries in quest of sacred song, by citing part of a poetic waif, — rather a splendid poem, culled from, — where think you, gentle reader? — the Sandwich Islands! It is from the "Honolulu Friend," April, 1868, and is entitled "The Soul's Dreamings."

Wings of beauty! wings immortal! hovering o'er me in death's night,
Ye will bear me onward ever, through the bowers of pure delight!
I shall pass the sable portal, only changed to form of light,
Leaving earth, to soar a spirit, boundless in its trackless flight.
Clay may feel a pang at parting, as the spirit brighter glows,
As the phœnix mounts in rapture from the ashes of its woes;
Then, away, a pure thought fleeting where vast worlds their lore disclose,
Where love's vestal lights flame brightly, hopes with folded wings repose.
Through vast space, on freedom's pinions, seeking knowledge evermore;
Its wide home, the blue empyrean, the eternal spirit shore;
There the twinkling stars are pages, gemmed with wisdom's boundless store,
Where the records of the ages yield in light their spirit lore.
. . . . . . . .
Kindred spirits there are meeting, will-winged thoughts that God-like move,
In their radiant robes electric, through the starry isles they rove.
Wings of beauty! wings immortal! hovering o'er me in death's night,
Ye will bear me onward ever, through the bowers of pure delight!
I shall pass the sable portal, only changed to form of light,
To dust returning what is mortal, seeking God in boundless flight!

# SIXTH EVENING.

## EARLY ENGLISH.

# SIXTH EVENING.

## EARLY ENGLISH.

WE have hitherto been listening to the sweet stream of sacred music, as it welled up from the Reformed churches of Germany, and other States of Continental Europe. It now remains for us to trace the meanderings of that same stream, in its fertilizing course along the shores of the island-homes of Great Britain.

The earliest utterances of Christian bards in England were the rugged Saxons; then came the Normans, and with them the "Miracle Plays," and other poems of the fourteenth century. Afterwards, the minstrel-monk, Chaucer, strung his lute to the high themes of Holy Writ; then followed the "divine Spenser," whose florid allegories, like a series of richly emblazoned frescoes, have not yet ceased to enchant us by their exuberant imagery and surpassing beauty. As one might infer from his "Faerie Queene," Spenser was a pure and noble-minded Christian gentleman, whose intellectual vigor and spiritual culture were much in advance of his age. His rare sonnets on the Seasons are unique cabinet pictures, and are among the most melodious in the language. Milton was an especial admirer of his "Hymn of Heavenly Love," which, like most of his poetry, has a peaceful rhythmical flow, like the ripple of a rivulet. But we are anticipating: let us then return to Chaucer. He lived from A.D. 1328 till 1400, was the prototype of Milton, and presents to us many fine examples of sacred poetry, including the lamentation of Mary Magdalene, lines on the Soul, and the beautiful story of the Christian Martyr, in the "Canterbury Tales."

Chaucer is the earliest of the Anglican bards who have sung to us in intelligible English. Of him the courtly Sidney said, he marvelled that " he should have seen so distinctly in that gray and misty morning of literature." As an artist, he has portrayed to us the thoughts, habits, and people of his time; and his sweet pastoral sketches are fragrant with the dews and freshness of spring. Chaucer inclined to Protestantism and to Wickliffe's Bible, which is much in his favor: he was a Christian monk, and a genius. We shall only recite his stanzas, believed to have been written on his death-bed: —

> Fly from the crowd, and be to virtue true,
>   Content with what thou hast, though it be small:
> To hoard brings hate ; nor lofty thoughts pursue ;
>   He who climbs high, endangers many a fall.
>     .    .    .    .    .    .    .
> Be thou serene, nor at thy lot repine :
>   He 'scapes all ill whose bosom is resigned ;
> Nor way, nor weather, will be always fine ;
>   Beside, thy home's not here, a journey this ;
> A pilgrim thou, then hie thee on thy way ;
>   Look up to God, intent on heavenly bliss,
> Take what the road affords, and praises pay.
>   Shun brutal lusts, and seek thy soul's high sphere.
> So truth shall shield thee or from hurt or fear.

Edmund Spenser (1553–1598), towards the close of his life, wrote four beautiful hymns besides his celebrated "Faerie Queene." From one of these hymns we extract the following, modernized: —

> Love! lift me up upon thy golden wings,
>     From this base world unto thy heaven's height,
> Where I may see those admirable things
>     Which there Thou workest by Thy sovereign might;
> Far above feeble reach of earthly sight,
>     That I thereof an heavenly hymn may sing,
> Unto the God of Love, high heaven's King!
>
> .    .    .    .    .    .    .
>
> Learn Him to love, that lovèd thee so dear,
> And in thy breast His blessèd image bear;
> With all thy heart, with all thy soul and mind,
>     Thou must Him love, and His behests embrace;
> All other loves with which the world doth blind
>     Weak fancies, and stir up affections base,
> Thou must renounce and utterly displace,
> And give thyself unto Him full and free,
> That full and freely gave Himself to thee.
> Then thou shalt feel thy spirit so possessed,
>     And ravished with devouring great desire
> Of His dear self, that shall thy feeble breast
>     Inflame with love, and set thee all on fire
> With burning zeal through every part entire,
> That in no earthly thing thou shalt delight
> But in His sweet and amiable sight.

The claim of Spenser to be regarded as a sacred poet does not rest upon his hymns alone, although these would be enough to embalm and consecrate the volume that contains them. Spenser may be styled the representative of one class of our sacred poetry, while Milton is that of the other. The former, indeed, should be read, as Warton loved to read him, —

> "At the root of mossy trunk reclined."

"The lineaments of his Christian character will not be darkened," writes Willmott, "to any thoughtful eye, by those 'allegorical devices' in which the poet loved cloudily to enwrap them. His pictures glow with a southern sunshine; but their richest colors are frequently employed to heighten and embellish virtue, and his most gorgeous descriptions often point their moral to the heart."

We select two more beautiful passages: they are from that rich storehouse of poetic fancy, his "Faerie Queene," in the original orthography: —

### ON THE MINISTRY OF ANGELS.

And is there care in heaven? And is there love
In heavenly spirits to these creatures bace,
That may compassion of their evils move?
There is: else much more wretched were the cace
Of men then beasts: but O the exceeding grace
Of Highest God! that loves His creatures so,
And all His workes with mercy doth embrace,
That blessed angels he sends to and fro,
To serve to wicked man, to serve His wicked foe!

How oft do they their silver bowers leave
To come to succour us that succour want!
How oft do they with golden pineons cleave
The flitting skyes, like flying pursuivant,
Against fowle feendes to ayd us militant!
They for us fight, they watch, and dewly ward,
And their bright squadrons round about us plant;
And all for love, and nothing for reward;
O why should hevenly God to men have such regard!

### IMPERSONATION OF FAITH.

She was arrayèd all in lily white,
In her right hand she bore a cup of gold,
With wine and water filled up to the height;

> In which a serpent did himself unfold,
> That horror made to all that did behold;
> But she no whit did change her constant mood:
> And in her other hand she did fast hold
> A book that was both signed and sealed with blood,
> Wherein dark things were writ, hard to be understood.

The gallant but hapless Sir Walter Raleigh, who was born in 1552, during his long imprisonment composed some of his terse and trenchant hymns: here is a specimen:—

> Rise, O my soul! with thy desires to heaven,
> And, with divinest contemplation, use
> Thy time, where time's eternity is given,
> And let vain thoughts no more thy thoughts abuse,
> But down in midnight darkness let them lie;
> So live thy better, let thy worst thoughts die.
> And thou, my soul, inspired with holy flame,
> View, and review, with most regardful eye,
> That holy cross whence thy salvation came,
> On which thy Saviour, and thy sin did die;
> For in that sacred object is much pleasure,
> And in that Saviour is thy life, thy treasure.
> To Thee, O Jesu! I direct mine eyes.
> To Thee, my hands, to Thee, my humble knees,
> To Thee, my heart shall offer sacrifice:
> To Thee, my thoughts. who my thoughts only sees,
> To Thee, myself, myself and all, I give;
> To Thee I die, to Thee I only live!

The following lines were written in 1603, just after his condemnation. They form only the commencement of a much longer medley, entitled "The Pilgrimage."

> Give me my scallop-shell of quiet,
>   My staffe of faith to walk upon,
> My scrip of joye (immortal diet!)
>   My bottle of salvation,
> My gown of glory, hope's true gage;
> And thus I take my pilgrimage.

Some of the tender and earnest numbers of Southwell, the martyr-monk, now are before us. The prevailing tone of his poetry is somewhat a reflex of his life, which, though short, was full of sorrow and suffering. Like many other noble works of which the world is justly proud, most of Southwell's productions were written in prison.

In one of his letters to a friend, he thus wrote from his cell: "We have sung the canticles of the Lord in a strange land, and in this desert we have sucked honey from the rock, and oil from the hard stone; but we now sow the seed with tears, that others may hereafter with joy carry in the sheaves to the heavenly granaries." His expressive lines, entitled "Preparative to Prayer," are a homily to all thoughtful minds: —

> When thou dost talk with God, — by prayer, I mean, —
>   Lift up pure hands, lay down all lust's desires;
> Fix thoughts on heaven, present a conscience clean;
>   Since holy blame to mercy's throne aspires,
> Confess faults' guilt, crave pardon for thy sin,
> Tread holy paths, call grace to guide therein.
> It is the spirit with reverence must obey
>   Our Maker's will, to practise what He taught:
> Make not the flesh thy counsel when thou pray,
>   'Tis enemy to every virtuous thought:
> It is the foe we daily feed and clothe,
> It is the prison that the soul doth loathe.

Wonderfully vigorous and terse are the following selections: —

> Not always fall of leaf, nor even spring,
> Not endless night, nor yet eternal day;
> The saddest birds a season find to sing,
> The roughest storm a calm may soon allay;
> Thus, with succeeding turns, God tempereth all,
> That man may hope to rise, yet fear to fall.

My conscience is my crown, contented thoughts my rest,
My heart is happy in itself, my bliss is in my breast.
Enough, I reckon wealth; a mean, the surest lot,
That lies too high for base contempt, too low for envy's shot.
My wishes are but few, all easy to fulfil,
I make the limits of my power the bounds unto my will.
I have no hopes but one, which is of heavenly reign;
Effects attained, or not desired, all lower hopes refrain.
I feel no care of coin, well-doing is my wealth,
My mind to me an empire is, while grace affordeth health.

. . . . . . . .

Spare diet is my fare, my clothes more fit than fine;
I know I feed and clothe a foe, that, pampered, would repine.

Here is another beautiful passage of his: —

> When words are weak, and foes encountering strong,
> Where mightier do assault than do defend,
> The feebler part puts up enforcèd wrong,
> And silent sees that speech could not amend.
> Yet higher powers must think, though they repine;
> When sun is set, the little stars will shine.

Sir Philip Sidney, in company with his sister, the Countess of Pembroke, made a metrical version of the Psalms of David, portions of which comprise some fine passages. Here is an example: —

O Lord! in me there lieth naught but to Thy search revealed lies;
For when I sit, Thou markest it. no less Thou notest when I rise:
Yea, closest closet of my thought hath opened windows to thine eyes.

> Thou walkest with me when I walk;
> When to my bed for rest I go,
> I find Thee there, and everywhere!

A decade of years, and we find another group of illustrious names, — Lord Bacon and his contemporaries. The prose of the "father of modern inductive philosophy" is replete with poetic beauties; but he wrote, towards the close of life, a paraphrastic version of seven of the Psalms of David, which contains some remarkable lines. Here are passages from his Psalm civ. : —

>  Father and King of powers both high and low,
>  Whose sounding fame all creatures serve to blow;
>  My soul shall with the rest strike up Thy praise,
>  And carol of Thy works and wondrous ways.
>
>  . . . . . . .
>
>  I know that He my words will not despise;
>  Thanksgiving is to Him a sacrifice!

Giles Fletcher (1584–1650) has said much and well, in a single stanza, upon a theme of surpassing interest: —

>  Sweet Eden was the arbor of delight,
>    Yet in its honey flowers our poison blew:
>  Sad Gethsemane, the bower of baleful night,
>    Where Christ a health of poison for us drew,
>    Yet all our honey in that poison grew;
>  So we, from sweetest flower, could suck our bane,
>  And Christ, from bitter venom, could again
>  Extract life out of death, and pleasure out of pain!

His terse lines on "The Excellency of Christ" are a characteristic specimen of the antithetical style of his day: —

>  He is a path, if any be misled;
>  He is a robe, if any naked be;
>  If any chance to hunger, He is bread;
>  If any be a bondman, He is free;
>  If any be but weak, how strong is He!
>  To dead men, life He is; to sick men, health;
>  To blind men, sight; and, to the needy, wealth;
>  A pleasure without loss, a treasure without stealth.

There is a calm the poor in spirit know,
That softens sorrow and that sweetens woe;
There is a peace that dwells within the breast,
When all without is stormy and distrest;
There is a light that gilds the darkest hour,
When dangers thicken, and when tempests lower:
That calm to faith and hope and love is given,
That light shines down to man direct from heaven.

Towards the latter part of his life, he was rector of Alderton, Suffolk, where, according to quaint old Fuller, "his clownish and low-parted parishioners (having nothing but their shoes high about them) valued not their pastor according to his worth, which disposed him to melancholy, and hastened his dissolution." He died about the year 1623.

These quaint and honest lines on Self-control are by Phineas Fletcher:—

Ah, silly man, who dream'st thy honor stands
In ruling others, not thyself! Thy slaves
Serve thee, and thou thy slaves; in iron bands
Thy servile spirit, pressed with wild passions, raves.
Wouldst thou live honored?—clip ambition's wing;
To reason's yoke thy furious passions bring:
Thrice noble is the man who of himself is king!

Giles Fletcher — who, with his brother Phineas, were the two most gifted followers of Spenser — wrote some of the finest religious poems of the Elizabethan age. We present this brief extract from "The Purple Island," by the latter:—

The cheerful lark, mounting from early bed,
  With sweet salutes awakes the drowsy night;
The earth she left, and up to heaven is fled,—
  There chants her Maker's praises out of sight.

While at Trinity College, Cambridge, Giles composed his principal poem, "Christ's Victorie," from which we select the following: —

> As when the cheerful sun, enlamping wide,
>   Glads all the world with his uprising ray,
> And wooes the widowed earth afresh to pride,
>   And paints her bosom with the flowery May,
>   Her silent sister steals him quite away;
> Wrapped in a sable cloud from mortal eyes,
> The hasty stars at noon begin to rise;
> And headlong to his early roost the sparrow flies.
>
> But soon as he again disshadowed is,
>   Restoring the blind world his blemished sight,
> As though another day were newly his,
>   The cozened birds busily take their flight,
>   And wonder at the shortness of the night:
> So Mercy once again herself displays
> Out from her sister's cloud, and open lays
> Those sunshine looks whose beams would dim a thousand days.

Among the multitudinous gems that sparkle over the great dramas of Shakspeare, we have but space for a few. Here they are: —

> Look, how the floor of heaven
> Is thick inlaid with patines of bright gold;
> There's not the smallest orb, which thou behold'st,
> But in his motion like an angel sings,
> Still quiring to the young-eyed cherubins:
> Such harmony is in immortal souls;
> But, whilst this muddy vesture of decay
> Doth grossly close it in, we cannot hear it.

---

> The cloud-capt towers, the gorgeous palaces,
> The solemn temples, the great globe itself,
> Yea, all which it inherit, shall dissolve;
> And, like this insubstantial pageant faded,
> Leave not a rack behind!

Sweet are the uses of adversity;
Which, like the toad, ugly and venomous,
Wears yet a precious jewel in his head.

---

'Tis the mind that makes the body rich;
And as the sun breaks through the darkest clouds,
So honor peereth in the meanest habit.
What, is the jay more precious than the lark,
Because his feathers are more beautiful?
Or is the adder better than the eel,
Because his painted skin contents the eye?
Oh, no, good Kate! neither art thou the worse
For this poor furniture, and mean array.

---

To-morrow, and to-morrow, and to-morrow,
Creeps in this petty pace from day to day,
To the last syllable of recorded time;
And all our yesterdays have lighted fools
The way to dusty death. Out, out, brief candle!
Life's but a walking shadow; a poor player,
That struts and frets his hour upon the stage,
And then is heard no more: it is a tale
Told by an idiot, full of sound and fury,
Signifying nothing.

---

Poor soul, the centre of my sinful earth,
    Fooled by those rebel powers that thee array,
Why dost thou pine within, and suffer dearth,
    Painting thy outward walls so costly gay?
Why so large cost, having so short a lease,
    Dost thou upon thy fading mansion spend?
Shall worms, inheritors of this excess,
    Eat up thy charge? Is this thy Body's end?
Then, Soul, live thou upon thy servant's loss,
    And let that pine, to aggravate thy store;
Buy terms Divine in selling hours of dross;
    Within be fed, without be rich no more:
So shalt thou feed on Death, that feeds on men;
And, Death once dead, there's no more dying then!

Those who are familiar with Izaak Walton's charming biography of Dr. Donne, will remember, that, after his troublous, busy life, he solaced his declining age "by many divine sonnets, and other high, holy, and harmonious composures." Among them, this "heavenly hymn, written on his sick-bed:" —

> Wilt Thou forgive that sin where I begun,
>   Which was my sin, though it were done before?
> Wilt Thou forgive that sin through which I run,
>   And do run still, though still I do deplore?
> When Thou hast done, Thou hast not done, for I have more.
>
> Wilt Thou forgive that sin, which I have won
>   Others to sin, and made my sin their door?
> Wilt Thou forgive that sin which I did shun
>   A year or two, but wallowed in a score?
> When Thou hast done, Thou hast not done, for I have more.
>
> I have a sin of fear, that, when I've spun
>   My last thread, I shall perish on the shore:
> But swear by Thyself, that, at my death, Thy Son
>   Shall shine as He shines now, and heretofore;
> And having done that, Thou hast done: I fear no more!

The worthy doctor caused this hymn to be set to solemn music, and to be frequently sung by the choristers of St. Paul's, at the evening service.

John Donne was born in London, in 1573. He deserves to be noted as a worthy divine, having been Dean of St. Paul's, a learned man, and the leader of the so-called metaphysical poets of England. His life was one of vicissitude and trial. It seems that he was endowed with a small salary and a large family, the inconvenience of which was not relieved by his imprisonment. Writing to his spouse, he once signed himself, "John Donne, undone." He left this world of trial, for one of rest, in 1631, when his mortal remains were buried in Westminster Abbey.

It is of Dr. Donne that Sir Henry Wotton quaintly said, "That body, which was once a temple of the Holy Ghost, and is now become a small quantity of Christian dust, I shall see reanimated."

The principal poem of Sir John Davis (1570–1626) is that on the "Immortality of the Soul," which Willmott designates "our first and noblest didactic poem." It is a series of philosophical arguments, solid in thought and unanswerable in reasoning, to establish the great and consoling truth of man's immortality. We extract these lines: —

> O ignorant, poor man! what dost thou bear
>    Locked up within the casket of thy breast?
> What jewels and what riches hast thou there?
>    What heavenly treasure in so weak a chest?
>
> . . . . . .
>
> Think of her worth, and think that God did mean
>    This worthy mind should worthy things embrace;
> Blot not her beauties with thy thoughts unclean,
>    Nor her dishonor with thy passion base.
>
> Kill not her quickening power with surfeitings;
>    Mar not her sense with sensuality;
> Cast not her serious wit on idle things;
>    Make not her free-will slave to vanity.

Very good counsel, in a compact form, is given us in these stanzas by Thomas Randolph, of this epoch:

> First worship God: he that forgets to pray,
> Bids not himself good morrow nor good day;
> Let thy first labor be to purge thy sin,
> And serve Him first, whence all things did begin.
>
> . . . . . . .

So live with men, as if God's curious eye
Did everywhere into thine actions spy;
Strive to live well; tread in the upright ways,
And rather count thy actions than thy days.

Another fragment comes to us from one Peter Heylyn, on the Sacred Oracles: —

If thou art merry, here are airs;
If melancholy, here are prayers;
If studious, here are those things writ
Which may deserve thy ablest wit;
If hungry, here is food divine;
If thirsty, nectar, heavenly wine.

Read, then; but, first, thyself prepare
To read with zeal and mark with care;
And when thou read'st what here is writ,
Let thy best practice second it:
So twice each precept read shall be, —
First, in the book, and, next, in thee.

In strong, terse, and quaint measure, George Sandys, born 1577, chants his appeal to the Saviour, written at the Holy Sepulchre at Jerusalem: —

Saviour of mankind, Man-Immanuel!
Who, sinless, died for sin; who vanquished hell;
The first-fruits of the grave; whose life did give
Light to our darkness; in whose death we live, —
Oh, strengthen Thou my faith, convert my will,
That mine may Thine obey! protect me still,
So that the latter death may not devour
My soul, sealed with Thy seal; so, in the hour
When Thou, whose body sanctified the tomb,
Unjustly judged, a glorious Judge shall come,
To judge the world with justice: by that sign
I may be known, and entertained for Thine.

When on his sick-bed, Sir Henry Wotton wrote some remarkable lines, in which he uses the beautiful metaphor of Christ's blood being the bath of sin: —

O Thou great Power! in whom I move,
    For whom I live, to whom I die,
Behold me through Thy beams of love,
    Whilst on this couch of tears I lie;
And cleanse my sordid soul within
By Thy Christ's blood, the Bath of Sin!

No hallowed oils, no grains, I need;
    No rags of saints, no purging fire:
One rosie drop from David's seed
    Was worlds of seas to quench Thine ire.
Oh, precious ransom, which, once paid,
That *consummatum est* was said!

And said by Him, that said no more,
    But sealed it with His sacred breath:
Thou, then, that hast discharged my score,
    And, dying, wast the death of Death,
Be to me now — on Thee I call —
My life, my strength, my joy, my all.

Sir Henry Wotton, born in 1588, is recorded as one of England's poets. He was ambassador at Venice, and afterwards Provost of Eton; the friend of Izaak Walton, and an early discoverer of Milton's transcendent merit.

Here are two of the exquisite sonnets of Drummond, of Hawthornden (1585–1649), so much admired by Milton: —

Look how the flower, which lingeringly doth fade,
The morning's darling late, the summer's queen,
Spoiled of that juice which kept it fresh and green,
As high as it did raise, bows low the head;
Right so my life (contentments being dead,
Or in their contraries but only seen),
With swifter speed declines, than erst it spread,
And (blasted) scarce now shows what it hath been.
As doth the pilgrim, therefore, whom the night
By darkness would imprison on his way,

Think on thy home, my soul, and think aright
Of what yet rests thee of life's wasting day:
Thy sun posts westward, passèd is thy morn,
And twice it is not given thee to be born.

---

Sweet bird, that sing'st away the early hours,
Of winters past or coming, void of care;
Well pleased with delights which present are, —
   Fair seasons, budding sprays, sweet-smelling flowers, —
   To rocks, to springs, to rills, from leafy bowers,
Thou thy Creator's goodness dost declare,
And what dear gifts on thee He did not spare,
   A stain to human sense in sin that lowers.
What soul can be so sick, which, by thy songs
   (Attired in sweetness) sweetly is not driven
Quite to forget earth's turmoils, spites, and wrongs,
   And lift a reverent eye and thought to heaven?
Sweet artless songster, thou my mind dost raise
To airs of spheres, — yes, and to angels' lays.

In the year 1588 was born the Puritan poet George Wither, who wrote numerous hymns and poems, notable for their quiet simplicity, rather than for impressiveness and force. These hymns, over three hundred in number, are designed for an incredible variety of subjects, — every season of nature and of the Church, and for all imaginable accidents of life. The titles of some, indeed, border on the ludicrous: "For a Widower or Widow delivered from a Troublesome Yokefellow," "For a Cripple," "For a Sailor," "For a Poet," "For one whose Beauty is much praised," "For one upbraided with Deformity," &c.

Wither's poem for "Anniversary Marriage-Days" was, doubtless, suggested by his sentiments of devoted attachment to his wife: —

Lord, living here are we, as fast united yet,
As when our hands and hearts by Thee together first were knit;
And in a thankful song now sing we will Thy praise,
For that Thou dost as well prolong our loving, as our days.

Wither's "Rocking Hymn" has outlived its author, as well as the storms that beset his latter days. But, turning from the lullaby to its writer, we notice that his portrait has come down to us, surrounded by the quaint motto, "I grow and wither, both together." His career was eventful and changeful, for he lived in troublous times, — more storm-cloud than sunshine seemed to have been his earthly portion; but, amidst his sorrows and sufferings, his Muse oft beguiled and solaced his sorely tried spirit. His best pieces were penned in prison. One more extract from this source must suffice: —

### THE MARIGOLD.

When with a serious musing I behold
The graceful and obsequious Marigold, —
How duly, every morning, she displays
Her open breast when Phœbus spreads his rays;
How she observes him in his daily walk,
Still bending towards him her small slender stalk;
How, when he down declines, she droops and mourns,
Bedewed, as 'twere, with tears, till he returns;
And how she veils her flowers when he is gone,
As if she scornèd to be looked upon
By an inferior eye, or did contemn
To wait upon a meaner light than him:
When this I meditate, methinks the flowers
Have spirits far more generous than ours,
And give us fair examples, to despise
The servile fawnings and idolatries,
Wherewith we court these earthly things below,
Which merit not the service we bestow.

Robert Herrick, whose anacreonic poems have given him fame with the world at large, deserves, also, to be placed in the category of religious poets, for his later contributions to our Christian anthology, which deserve the title originally given to them, — "Noble Numbers." In the year 1648, when he was fifty-seven years of age, he was ejected from his living on account of his adhesion to the Royalist cause. "In a good many of his poems, he touches the heart of truth; in others, even those of epigrammatic form, he must be allowed to fail in point as well as in meaning. But his verses are brightened by a certain almost childishly quaint and innocent humor."[*] His exquisite Litany to the Holy Spirit commences, —

> In the hour of my distress,
> When temptations me oppress,
> And when I my sins confess,
>     Sweet Spirit, comfort me.
>
> When I lie within my bed,
> Sick at heart and sick in head,
> And with thoughts discomforted,
>     Sweet Spirit, comfort me.
>
> When the house doth sigh and weep,
> And the world is drowned in sleep,
> Yet mine eyes the watch do keep,
>     Sweet Spirit, comfort me.
>
> When the tapers now burn blue,
> And the comforters are few,
> And that number more than true,
>     Sweet Spirit, comfort me.
>
> When the priest his last hath prayed,
> And I nod to what is said,
> Because my speech is now decayed,
>     Sweet Spirit, comfort me.

[*] England's Antiphon.

Herrick's lyrics to Primroses and Daffodils are known to all lovers of true poetry, as, indeed, are his chastely beautiful lines to Blossoms: —

Fair pledges of a fruitful tree, why do ye fall so fast?
    Your date is not so past
But you may stay yet here awhile to blush and gently smile,
    And go at last.
What, were ye born to be an hour or half's delight,
    And so to bid good-night?
'Tis pity nature brought ye forth, merely to show your worth,
    And lose you quite.
But you are lovely leaves, where we may read how soon things have
    Their end, though ne'er so brave;
And, after they have shown their pride, like you, awhile, they glide
    Into the grave.

We subjoin a few of his striking epigrams, — gems without the setting: —

    God's rod doth watch while men do sleep; and then
    The rod doth sleep while vigilant are men.

---

    A man's transgression God does then remit,
    When man He makes a penitent for it.

---

    Humble we must be, if to heaven we go:
    High is the roof there, but the gate is low.

---

    Heaven is not given for our good works here;
    Yet it is given to the laborer.

Henry King, who was Bishop of Rochester in the reign of Charles II., wrote a remarkable poem on the death of his wife, which has often been quoted as a most finished specimen of elegiac poetry: —

> Accept, thou shrine of my dead saint,
> Instead of dirges, this complaint;
> And for sweet flowers to crown thy hearse,
> Receive a strew of weeping verse,
> From thy grieved friend, whom thou might'st see
> Quite melted into tears for thee!

Quaint old Quarles, who lived A.D. 1592–1644, is known to students by his "Emblems," and his "Enchiridion," as well as his religious verse, which, to our modern ear, sounds somewhat inharmonious. It is, however, forceful and significant. He was a devout and worthy man; and, in his closing hours, delivered some excellent counsel to his friends, wishing them "to have a care of the expense of their time, and every day to call themselves to an account." He expressed great sorrow for his sins; and, when it was told him that he did himself much harm thereby, he replied, "They be not my friends who deny me leave to be penitent." His penitence, he well knew, was the best preparative for a peaceful and happy death; and such was his. His brief but well-spent life is fruitful of instruction. Such was the charm of his conversation, that it was said to "distil pleasure, knowledge, and virtue on all who shared his friendship." Despite his occasional obscurity, and the ruggedness of his measures, his poetry abounds with noble thoughts. We cull a few extracts: —

> Farewell, ye gilded follies, pleasing troubles;
> Farewell, ye honored rags, ye glorious bubbles!
> Fame's but a hollow echo; gold, pure clay;
> Honor, the darling but of one short day;
> Beauty, the eye's idol, but a damasked skin;
> State, but a golden prison to live in,
> And torture free-born minds; embroidered trains,
> Merely but pageants for proud-swelling veins;

And blood allied to greatness, is alone
Inherited, not purchased, nor our own:
Fame, honor, beauty, state, train, blood, and birth
Are but the fading blossoms of the earth.
Welcome, pure thoughts; welcome, ye silent groves;
These guests, these courts, my soul most dearly loves:
Now the winged people of the sky shall sing
My cheerful anthems to the gladsome spring:
A prayer-book now shall be my looking-glass,
In which I will adore sweet virtue's face.

---

I love (and have some cause to love) the earth;
She is my Maker's creature, therefore good;
She is my mother, for she gave me birth;
She is my tender nurse, she gave me food;
   But what's a creature, Lord, compared with Thee?

I love the air; her dainty sweets refresh
My drooping soul, and to new sweets invite me;
Her shrill-mouthed choir sustain me with their flesh,
And with their polyphonian notes delight me;
   But what's the air or all the sweets that she
   Can bless my soul withal, compared to Thee?
. . . . . . .
To heaven's high city I direct my journey,
Whose spangled suburbs entertain mine eye:
Mine eye, by contemplation's great attorney,
Transcends the crystal pavement of the sky;
   But what is heaven, great God, compared to Thee?
   Without Thy presence heaven's no heaven to me.

---

And what's a life? A weary pilgrimage,
Whose glory in one day doth fill the stage
With childhood, manhood, and decrepid age.
And what's a life? The flourishing array
Of the proud summer meadow, which to-day
Wears her green flush, and is, to-morrow, hay.

Enter, right welcome and thrice-honored George Herbert, rector of Bemerton, and minstrel of the

Church Catholic! Thou dost, indeed, nobly sustain the illustrious line of succession of England's church worthies. George Herbert, who was not only a favorite with his contemporaries, — Bishop Andrews, Dr. Donne, and Lord Bacon, — but also of his affectionate biographer, "honest Izaak Walton," and a host of others in succession, was born in 1593, and died of consumption in 1632, in the meridian of his days. He took orders, was married, and, after a few years, was presented with the living of Bemerton, near Salisbury, into which he was inducted in 1630, — too short an interval, yet how well improved, albeit his work but half done. This pious parish priest was a spare, gaunt personage, his face long and sharp-featured, and yet his aspect cheerful and "his speech and motion did both declare him a gentleman; for they were all so meek and obliging, that they purchased love and respect from all that knew him. Of a stature inclining towards tallness, his body was very straight, and, so far from being cumbered with too much flesh, he was lean to an extremity." Referring to his priestly office, he quaintly remarks: "I am so proud of His service, that I will always observe and obey and do His will, and always call Him 'Jesus, my Master;' and I will always contemn my birth, or any title or dignity that can be conferred upon me, when I shall compare them with my title of being a priest, and serving at the altar of Jesus, my Master." "And that he did so," continues Walton, "may appear in many parts of his book of Sacred Poems; especially in that which he calls 'The Odour,' in which he seems to rejoice in the thought of that word Jesus, and to say, that the adding these words, 'my Master,' to it, and the often repetition of them, seemed to perfume his mind, and leave an oriental fragrance in his very breath."

This godly man was so passionately fond of music, that he was accustomed, twice a week, to walk to Salisbury Cathedral, to attend divine service; and, on his return, would say "that his time spent in prayer, and cathedral-music, elevated his soul, and was his heaven upon earth." He would often also say, "Religion does not banish mirth, but only moderates and sets rules to it." His death was as beautiful, peaceful, and, may we not add, picturesque, as his brief life had been. The Sunday preceding his decease, he rose suddenly from his couch, called for one of his instruments, and, having tuned it, played and sung one of his own stanzas : —

> The Sundays of man's life,
> Threaded together on Time's string,
>   Make bracelets to adorn the wife
> Of the eternal glorious King;
>   On Sundays, heaven's door stands ope;
> Blessings are plentiful and rife;
>   More plentiful than hope.

"Thus," adds his biographer, "he sang on earth such hymns and anthems as the angels and he and Mr. Ferrar now sing in heaven!"

> "All must to their cold graves;
> But the religious actions of the just
> Smell sweet in death, and blossom in the dust."

Walton relates an anecdote of one of his walks to Salisbury. When Herbert was some way on his journey, he overtook a poor man, standing by a "poorer horse," that had fallen down beneath too heavy a burden; and, seeing the distress of the one, and the suffering of the other, he put off his canonical dress, and helped the man to unload, and, afterwards, to reload the horse. Then giving him money to refresh himself and the animal, he departed, at the same time telling him, that, if he loved himself, he should be merciful to his beast. This incident afforded a subject to the Royal Academician, Cooper, for an interesting picture.

The history of his poems is most touching and beautiful. In his last sickness, he presented them to a friend, in these words: "Sir, I pray deliver this little book to my dear brother Ferrar, and tell him he shall find in it a picture of the many spiritual conflicts that have passsed betwixt God and my soul, before I could subject mine to the will of Jesus my Master; in whose service I have now found perfect freedom. Desire him to read it; and then, if he can think it may turn to the advantage of any poor, dejected soul, let it be made public; if not, let him burn it, for I, and it, are less than the least of God's mercies."

Baxter's opinion of Herbert's poems was a high one. "I confess," he says, "that next to the Scripture poems, there are none so savory to me as Mr. George Herbert's, because he speaks to God, like a man that really believeth in God, and whose business in the world is most with God; heart-work and heaven-work make up his books."

Willmott, with a loving spirit, adds also a like tribute to his consecrated Muse; summing up in the words of Walton's quaint eulogy, the reading of which will "still keep those sacred fires burning upon the altar of so pure a heart as shall free it from the anxieties of this world, and keep it fixed upon things that are above."

His sacred melodies are ever instinct with spiritual life and power to the Christian; while their homely quaintness, strange conceits, and rich arabesque effect no less endear them to the lover of lyrical art. It has been justly remarked that "the divine mind of Herbert was ever tending to seek God everywhere and in every thing; no writer before him has shown such a love to God, — such a childlike confidence in Him." When recovering from sickness, he sings, —

>And now in age I bud again;
>After so many deaths, I live and write;
>I once more smell the dew and rain,
>And relish versing. Oh, my only Light!
>It cannot be, that I am he
>On whom Thy tempests fell all night!

One of his characteristic pieces is entitled "Man's Medley:" —

>In soul, he mounts and flies; in flesh, he dies!
>He wears a stuff, whose thread is coarse and round,
>But trimmed with curious lace,
>And should take place
>After the trimming, not the stuff and ground:
>Not that he may not here
>Taste of the cheer;
>But as buds drink, and straight lift up their head,
>So must he sip, and think of better drink
>He may attain to after he is dead.

He taught the noble truth that a man is what he is in himself, not what the world may consider him from the accident of birth or circumstances. Hear him again: —

Teach me, my Lord and King! in all things Thee to see;
And what I do in any thing, to do it as for Thee.
All may of Thee partake, nothing can be so mean,
But for this tincture (for Thy sake) will not grow bright and clean.
This is the famous stone, that turneth all to gold;
For that which God doth touch and own, cannot for less be told.

---

    O day most calm, most bright!
  The fruit of this, the next world's bud;
    The endorsement of supreme delight,
  Writ by a Friend, and with His blood!
    The couch of Time, care's balm and bay!
  The week were dark, but for Thy light:
    Thy torch doth show the way.

. . . . .

  Sundays the pillars are,
On which heaven's palace archèd lies;
  The other days fill up the spare
And hollow room with vanities.
  They are the fruitful beds and borders
Of God's rich garden: that is bare
  Which parts their ranks and orders.

  Thou art a day of mirth;
And where the week-days trail on ground,
  Thy flight is higher, as thy birth.
Oh, let me take thee at the bound,
  Leaping with thee from seven to seven,
Till that we both, being tossed from earth,
  Fly hand in hand to heaven!

---

In time of service seal up both thine eyes,
  And send them to thy heart; that, spying sin,
They may weep out the stains by them did rise;
  Those doors being shut, all by the ear comes in.
Who marks in church-time others' symmetry,
Makes all their beauty his deformity.

Sweet Peace, where dost thou dwell? I humbly crave
    Let me once know.
I sought thee in a secret cave,
    And asked if peace were there,
A hollow wind did seem to answer, "No!
    Go seek elsewhere."

I did; and, going, did a rainbow note:
    Surely, thought I,
This is the lace of Peace's coat:
    I will search out the matter.
But while I looked, the clouds immediately
    Did break and scatter.

Then I went to a garden, and did spy
    A gallant flower,
The crown imperial. "Sure," said I,
    "Peace at the root must dwell."
But when I digged, I saw a worm devour
    What showed so well.

At length I met a reverent good old man;
    Whom when for peace
I did demand, he thus began:
    "There was a prince of old
At Salem dwelt, who lived with good increase
    Of flock and fold."

---

Lord, with what care hast Thou begirt us round!
    Parents first season us; then schoolmasters
Deliver us to laws; they send us bound
    To rules of reason, holy messengers,

Pulpits and Sundays, sorrow dogging sin,
    Afflictions sorted, anguish of all sizes,
Fine nets and stratagems to catch us in,
    Bibles laid open, millions of surprises,

Blessings beforehand, ties of gratefulness,
    The sound of glory ringing in our ears;
Without, our shame; within, our consciences;
    Angels and grace, eternal hopes and fears:

Yet all these fences, and their whole array,
One cunning bosom-sin blows quite away.

---

Sweet day! so cool, so calm, so bright,
    The bridal of the earth and sky;
The dews shall weep thy fall to-night;
    For thou must die.

Sweet rose! whose hue, angry and brave,
    Bids the rash gazer wipe his eye;
Thy root is ever in its grave;
    And thou must die.

Sweet spring! full of sweet days and roses;
    A box where sweets compacted lie;
Thy music shows ye have your closes;
    And all must die.

Only a sweet and virtuous soul,
    Like seasoned timber, never gives;
But, though the whole world turn to coal,
    Then chiefly lives.

---

O day! with holy duties thickly blossomed,
    And every blossom dropping precious balm;
    Sermon and prayer, and sweetly-chanted psalm,
And privy thoughts, to God alone unbosomed, —
    I would have stayed thee with a fond constraining,
    Fain such an antepast of Heaven to eke,
    And stretch its sweetness through the weary week,
Six days of dearth — to one of bread! — remaining;
    But could not clip one pinion of thy flight
That borrowed, from thy bliss, an unwont fleetness:
    So while thy beauty fadeth from my sight,
I must content to win a sacred meetness,
From thy divinest influence, for all
The week's sharp toils and cares, that to my hap may fall!

---

By all means, use sometimes to be alone;
    Salute thyself; see what thy soul doth wear;
Dare to look in thy chest, for 'tis thine own;
    And tumble up and down what thou find'st there.

"A man must be a giant, like Shakspeare or Milton, to cast off his age's faults. Indeed, no man has more of the 'quips and cranks and wanton wiles' of the poetic spirit of his time than George Herbert, but with this difference from the rest of Dr. Donne's school, that such is the indwelling potency, that it causes even these to shine with a radiance such that we wish them still to burn and not be consumed. We could not bear to part with his most fantastic oddities: they are so interpenetrated with his genius as well as his art." \*

We confess we linger with a loving reverence about this saintly singer; and, in imagination, would seek out and fondly gaze upon the little church that has become hallowed to us by the sweet memories of Herbert and Norris. The name of Norris is now seldom heard, even in the retirement of the scholar; but Willmott has not ignored him: on the contrary, has devoted a delightful chapter to his memory. Norris was born in 1657, and, in 1691, obtained the living of Bemerton, which he held for twenty years, and died in 1711, in the fifty-fourth year of his age, having exhausted his strength by intense application and long habits of severe reasoning. On the south side of Bemerton Church, a marble tablet commemorates his piety and his genius. The words of the epitaph are melancholy, yet appropriate: *Bene latuit.* "Here he lay, concealed from the pomp and vanity of life; here he sent up daily, to the gate of heaven, the music of a gentle and contented heart! The old and tranquil parsonage was, to him, a happy hiding-place." We present one stanza of his poem,

\* England's Antiphon.

entitled "The Parting," which is remarkably beautiful: —

> How fading are the joys we dote upon,
> Like apparitions seen and gone;
>   But those who soonest take their flight,
> Are the most exquisite and strong.
>   Like angels' visits short and bright;
> Mortality's too weak to bear them long.

"The exquisite comparison of human joys to the visits of angels, after having been engrafted into 'The Grave,' of Blair, was transferred by Campbell to the 'Pleasures of Hope,' and has now passed into a poetical proverb; but the beauty of the image belongs to Norris."

Edmund Waller, whose mother was the sister of John Hampden and cousin to Oliver Cromwell. Although a member of the Parliament, he was a royalist at heart; for, being implicated in a plot on behalf of the king, he was exiled ten years, and fined ten thousand pounds. These beautiful lines were, it is believed, the last he ever penned: —

> The seas are quiet when the winds are o'er,
> So calm are we when passions are no more!
> For then we know how vain it is to boast
> Of fleeting things, so certain to be lost.
>
> Clouds of affection from our younger eyes
> Conceal that emptiness which age descries:
> The soul's dark cottage, battered and decayed,
> Lets in new light through chinks that time has made.
>
> Stronger by weakness, wiser men become
> As they draw near to their eternal home;
> Leaving the old, both worlds at once they view,
> That stand upon the threshold of the new.

Izaak Walton, who wielded pen and fishing-rod with equal love and skill, was born at Stafford, in 1593. His "Angler" is redolent of sweet country air and wild flowers: it is a prose poem, and, like "The Pilgrim's Progress," must ever live. He died at the ripe age of ninety, in 1683. We owe a large debt of gratitude to Izaak Walton for the portraitures of Donne, Herbert, Hooker, and others, he has sketched so minutely. If we think of him more often by his "Angler," it is because that is the book that comes home to the hearts and bosoms, not of all anglers merely, but of all thinkers. It is a pleasant pastoral, babbling, like the sequestered streams it tells about, very musically, and very ramblingly.

We cite a prose passage, at random, from his "Angler," which is as good as many a poetical one that passes current, if not much better: —

"Well, scholar, having now taught you to paint your rod, and we having still a mile to Tottenham High-Cross, I will, as we walk towards it, in the cool shade of this sweet honeysuckle hedge, mention to you some of the thoughts and joys that have possessed my soul since we two met together. That you may also join with me, in thankfulness to the Giver of every good and perfect gift, for our happiness. . . . Every misery that I miss is a new mercy, and therefore let us be thankful. There have been, since we met, others that have met disasters of broken limbs, and many other miseries that threaten human nature; let us, therefore, rejoice and be thankful. We are free from the unsupportable burden of an accusing conscience, — a misery that none can bear; therefore, let us praise Him for His preventing grace. . . . Let me tell you, scholar, I have a rich neighbor that is always so busy, that he has no leisure to laugh; the whole business of his life is to get money, more money! Yet it was wisely said by one of great observation: 'That there be as many miseries beyond riches, as on this side of them.' Let us not repine, or so much as think the gifts of God unequally dealt, if we see another abound with riches: we see but the outside of the rich man's happiness; but let us be thankful for health and a competence, and, above all, for a quiet conscience."

Take another little homily of his: —

"Affliction is a divine diet, which, though it be not pleasing to mankind, yet Almighty God hath often, very often, imposed it as good though bitter physic to those children whose souls are dearest unto Him."

Crashaw, who wrote "Steps to the Temple"— a series of sacred poems — "for Happy Souls to climb Heaven by," wrote also some fine lines on a Prayer-book, which Coleridge thought were among the finest in the realm of sacred song. We annex an extract from the poem, although, fully to appreciate its spiritual beauty, it should be read entire.

> It is, in one choice handful, heaven, and all
> Heaven's royal hosts encamped thus small;
> To prove that true, schools used to tell,
> A thousand angels in one point can dwell.
> It is love's great artillery,
> Which here contracts itself, and comes to lie,
> Close couched in your white bosom, and from thence,
> As from a snowy fortress of defence,
> Against your ghostly foe to take your part,
> And fortify the hold of your chaste heart.
>
> It is an armory of light;
> Let constant use but keep it bright,
>   You'll find it yields,
> To holy hands and humble hearts,
>   More swords and shields
> Than sin hath snares, or hell hath darts.
>   Only be sure
>   The hands be pure
> That hold these weapons, and the eyes
>   Those of turtles, chaste and true,
> Wakeful and wise.
>     .    .    .    .    .    .

> Dear soul, be strong:
> Mercy will come ere long,
> And bring her bosom full of blessings, —
> Flowers of never-fading graces;
> To make immortal dressings
> For worthy souls, whose wise embraces
> Store up themselves for Him who is alone
> The Spouse of virgins, and the Virgin's Son!

Here is a beautiful stanza from his "Hymn to the Nativity:" —

> Welcome to our wandering sight!
> Eternity shut in a span!
> Summer in winter, day in night!
> Heaven in earth, and God in man!
> Great Little One, whose glorious birth
> Lifts earth to heaven, stoops heaven to earth.

Crashaw, who was born, it is believed, in the year of Shakspeare's death, has been compared with Shelley and Keats for the music and delicacy of his verse. It has been, indeed, objected to his poetry, that it is too redolent of imagery, and too "fantastically beautiful." We present one of his "Divine Epigrams," which is excellent: —

> Two went to pray? Oh, rather say,
> One went to brag, the other to pray:
> One stands up close, and treads on high,
> Where the other dares not lend his eye:
> One nearer to God's altar trod,
> The other to the altar's God.

Jeremy Taylor, who has been styled our "Shakspeare in Theology," was born in the year 1613. Although his prose is more poetic than his verse, he yet wrote some short lyrics and hymns. Here is his melody for Christmas: —

Awake, my soul, and come away:
  Put on thy best array,
  Lest, if thou longer stay,
Thou lose some minutes of so blest a day.

. . . . . .

He that begirt each zone,
To whom both poles are one,
Who grasped the zodiac in His hand,
And made it move or stand,
Is now, by nature, Man!
By stature but a span;
Eternity is now grown short;
A King is born without a court;
The water thirsts, the fountain's dry;
And life, being born, made apt to die!

He shared the tribulations of his time: fine and imprisonment fell heavily upon him at various times during the ascendency of the Puritans, against whom he spoke and wrote very strongly. He died 1667.

"It is good," are the words of Bishop Taylor, "that we transplant the instruments of fancy into religion; and, for this reason, music was brought into churches, and comely garments and solemnities, that the wandering eye and heart may be bribed, and may so be disposed to cherish a more spiritual affection."

Love, on the Saviour's dying head,
  Her spikenard drops, unblamed, may pour;
  May mount His cross, and wrap Him dead
    In spices from the golden shore;
  Risen, may embalm His sacred name
With all a painter's art, and all a minstrel's flame!\*

He wrote the following nervous lines, entitled "The Offering:" —

\* Christian Year.

> They gave to Thee
>   Myrrh, frankincense, and gold ;
> But, Lord, with what shall we
> Present ourselves before Thy majesty,
>   Whom Thou redeemedst when we were sold ?
> We've nothing but ourselves, and scarce that neither, —
>   Vile dirt and clay ;
> Yet it is soft, and may impression take.
> Accept it, Lord, and say, this Thou hadst rather ;
>   Stamp it, and on this sordid metal make
> Thy holy image, and it shall outshine
> The beauty of the golden mine.  Amen.

How grandly Habington's lines on the Firmament commence ! listen : —

> When I survey the bright celestial sphere
>   So rich with jewels hung, that night
> Doth like an Ethiop bride appear,
> My soul her wings doth spread, and heavenward flies,
>   The Almighty's mysteries to read
>   In the large volume of the skies !
> For the bright firmament shoots forth no flame
>   So silent, but is eloquent
>   In speaking the Creator's name.
> No unregarded star contracts its light
>   Into so small a character,
>   Removed far from our human sight,
> But, if we steadfast look, we shall discern
>   In it, as in some holy book,
> How man may heavenly knowledge learn.

Shirley, the latest of the Elizabethan dramatists, is the author of this grand dirge : —

> The glories of our birth and state
>   Are shadows, not substantial things ;
> There is no armor against fate :
>   Death lays his icy hand on kings !

>     Sceptre and crown
>     Must tumble down,
>     And in the dust be equal made
>     With the poor crooked scythe and spade.
>
>     .   .   .   .   .
>
>     The garlands wither on your brow,
>       Then boast no more your mighty deeds;
>     Upon death's purple altar, now,
>       See where the victor-victim bleeds.
>         All heads must come
>         To the cold tomb:
>     Only the actions of the just
>     Smell sweet, and blossom in the dust!

The mind that dictated the above incomparable lines could scarcely be insensible to moral excellence and religious feeling. The same may be predicated of the subjoined, also from his pen: —

>     Hark! how chimes the passing bell!
>     There's no music to a knell:
>     All the other sounds we hear
>     Flatter, and but cheat the ear.
>     This doth put us still in mind
>     That our flesh must be resigned;
>     And, a general silence made,
>     The world be muffled in a shade.
>     Orpheus' lute, as poets tell,
>     Was but a moral of this bell.

We now hail that chief of the tuneful throng, the great and good Milton, whom a brother bard beautifully apostrophizes as one —

>     That rode sublime
>     Upon the seraph-wings of Ecstasy,
>     The secret of the abyss to spy;
>     Who passed the flaming bounds of place and time;
>     The living Throne, the sapphire blaze,
>     Where angels tremble, while they gaze,
>     He saw; but, blasted with excess of light,
>     Closed his eyes in endless night!

Yes: the first thought that is suggested to us by the magic name of Milton is his wondrous spiritual vision, coupled with his bodily blindness. Yet the Christian philosophy with which he endured the privation of sight, and the dignified strain in which he repelled the foul charge of his assailants, that it was a judgment from heaven for his republican opinions, are beyond all praise. What nobility of mind, and what splendor of diction, he discovers in the following eloquent passage: "It is not so wretched to be blind," he says, "as it is not to be capable of enduring blindness. Let me be the most feeble creature alive, as long as that feebleness serves to invigorate the energies of my rational and immortal spirit; as long as, in that obscurity in which I am enveloped, the light of the Divine Presence more clearly shines; and, indeed, in my blindness I enjoy, in no inconsiderable degree, the favor of the Deity, who regards me with more tenderness and compassion in proportion as I am able to behold nothing but *Himself*. For the Divine Law not only shields me from injury, but almost renders me too sacred to attack, as from the overshadowing of those heavenly wings which seem to have occasioned this obscurity." Milton's greatness is seen in the fact that he forgot self: his master-mind sought to look outward and upward. "He is ever soaring towards the region beyond perturbation, — the true condition of soul; that is, wherein a man shall see things even as God would have him see them. He has no time to droop his pinions, and sit moody, even on the highest pine: the sun is above him; he must fly upwards." *

* England's Antiphon.

At the age of forty-five, he thus writes concerning his blindness, one of his noblest sonnets: —

>When I consider how my light is spent
>>Ere half my days, in this dark world and wide,
>>And that one talent, which is death to hide,
>Lodged with me useless, though my soul more bent
>To serve therewith my Maker, and present
>>My true account, lest He, returning, chide:
>>"Doth God exact day-labor, light denied?"
>I fondly ask. But Patience, to prevent
>That murmur, soon replies: "God doth not need
>>Either man's work, or His own gifts; who best
>>Bear His mild yoke, they serve Him best; His state
>Is kingly; thousands at His bidding speed,
>>And post o'er land and ocean without rest;
>>They also serve who only stand and wait."

Among Milton's fine lyrics, the following is, perhaps, less familiar to the reader than the preceding extract: —

>Fly, envious Time, till thou run out thy race;
>Call on the lazy, leaden-stepping hours,
>Whose speed is but the heavy plummet's pace,
>And glut thyself with what thy womb devours, —
>Which is no more than what is false and vain,
>And merely mortal dross;
>So little is our loss!
>So little is thy gain!
>For when as each thing bad thou hast entombed,
>And, last of all, thy greedy self consumed,
>Then long eternity shall greet our bliss
>With an individual kiss,
>And joy shall overtake us as a flood:
>When every thing that is sincerely good,
>And perfectly divine,
>With truth and peace and love, shall ever shine
>About the supreme throne
>Of Him to whose happy-making sight alone

> When once our heavenly guided soul shall climb, —
> Then, all this earthly grossness quit,
> Attired with stars, we shall for ever sit
> Triumphing over Death, and Chance, and thee, O Time!

Milton's passionate love of music inspired some of his grandest outbursts of song. Glimpses of the great poet's life may be seen in the opening passages of certain books of his epic; the most pathetic of these is the sad but beautifully patient lament on the blindness of his old age. This, and the sonnets on his blindness, and on the Waldenses, if less grand, are among the most beautiful and touching of his writings. Milton was engaged upon the great epic seven years (1658–1665). The first rough sketches of the poem took the shape of a tragedy, or "mystery," on the "Fall of Man," the manuscripts of which are still extant in the Library of Cambridge University, where also is still to be seen the mulberry-tree planted by the poet when he was a student. He was no less illustrious as a man than as a poet: his character stands out from the men of his age, and indeed of any age, in moral sublimity. The world's liberty owes as much to his mighty pen as to Cromwell's weighty sword. Milton's personal habits were simple and pure, yet majestic and Christian. We can form some idea of the noble man by the following sketch: "He was found in a small chamber, hung with rusty green, sitting in an elbow-chair, and dressed neatly in black : pale, but not cadaverous; his hands and feet gouty. In his latter years, he retired every night at nine o'clock, and lay till four in summer, till five in winter; and, if not disposed then to rise, he had some one to sit at his bedside, and read to him. When he rose, he had a chapter of the Hebrew Bible read to him; and, with the intervention of breakfast, he studied till twelve. He then dined, took some exercise for an hour, — generally in a chair, in which he used to swing himself, — and afterwards played on the organ, or the bass-viol, and either sang himself, or made his wife sing, who, as he said, had a good voice, but no ear. He then resumed his studies till six, from which hour, till eight, he conversed with those who came to visit him. He finally took a light supper, smoked a pipe of tobacco, and drank a glass of water, after which he retired to rest." * So calmly passed the days of the blind old poet, until, before the completion of his sixty-sixth year, he passed away from earth with scarcely a pang. It was on Sunday, Nov. 8, 1674. His ashes repose in the Church of St. Giles, Cripplegate.

It seems supererogatory, if not absurd, to attempt any tribute to his genius, at this late day, when Macaulay has expressed such a beautiful one among his noble historic sketches, where he says: "A mightier poet, tried at once by pain, danger, poverty, obloquy, and blindness, meditated, undisturbed by the obscene tumult which raged all around him, a song so sublime and so lofty, that it would not have misbecome the lips of those ethereal Virtues whom he saw, with that inner eye, which no calamity could darken, flinging down on the jasper pavement their crowns of amaranth and gold."

Milton's splendid Hymn to the Nativity, written at the early age of twenty-one years, remains unrivalled for its sublimity and classic elegance. Listen to a stanza or two: —

* Collier's Eng. Lit.

No war, or battle's sound,
Was heard the world around;
The idle spear and shield were high uphung;
The hookèd chariot stood
Unstained with hostile blood;
The trumpet spake not to the armèd throng;
And kings sat still with awful eye
As if they surely knew their sovereign Lord was by!

. . . . . .

The oracles are dumb,
No voice or hideous hum
Runs through the archèd roof in words deceiving;
Apollo from his shrine
Can no more divine,
With hollow shriek the steep of Delphos leaving;
No nightly trance, or breathèd spell,
Inspires the pale-eyed priest from the prophetic cell.

The chief of sacred singers, it is known, held the post of Latin Secretary under Cromwell; at the Restoration, he was, of course, dismissed. He was now poor and blind; and, in addition to these trials, Charles II. fined him, and doomed his writings, on Liberty, to be publicly burned. Undaunted, however, by these accumulated afflictions, the great poet produced "Paradise Lost." After enduring the ills of poverty several years, the king invited him to resume his former post, with all its honors, emoluments, and court favors; but Milton, well knowing that this honor must involve silence on the question of human liberty, did not hesitate, but, with noble magnanimity, refused the tempting bribe. He preferred the principle of right, although it entailed poverty, to a mean ambition, with the splendors of court patronage. How grandly the heroism of the man with the genius of the poet unite in the "Poet of Paradise"!

One of the best, if not the best, of Milton's famous sonnets, is that "On the late Massacre in Piemont:"—

> Avenge, O Lord, Thy slaughtered saints, whose bones
>   Lie scattered on the Alpine mountains cold!
>   Even them who kept Thy truth so pure of old,
> When all our fathers worshipped stocks and stones,
> Forget not! in Thy book record their groans,
>   Who were Thy sheep, and in their ancient fold
>   Slain by the bloody Piemontese, that rolled
> Mother with infant down the rocks.  Their moans
>   The vales redoubled to the hills, and they
> To heaven.  Their martyred blood and ashes sow
>   O'er all the Italian fields, where still doth sway
> The triple tyrant; that from these may grow
>   A hundred-fold, who, having learned Thy way,
> Early may fly the Babylonian woe.

In his eloquent defence of sacred poetry, Milton declares the proper office of the poet to be "to celebrate, in glorious and lofty hymns, the throne and equipage of God's almightiness; and what He works and what He suffers to be wrought with high providence in His Church; to sing victorious agonies of saints and martyrs, the deeds and triumphs of just and pious nations doing valiantly, through faith, against Christ's enemies; to deplore the general relapses of kingdoms and states from justice and God's true worship." Here are his exquisite lines on church music:—

> But let my due feet never fail
> To walk the studious cloisters pale,
> And love the high embowèd roof,
> With antique pillars massy proof,
> And storied windows richly dight,
> Casting a dim religious light;
> There let the pealing organ blow
> To the full-voiced choir below,

In service high, and anthems clear,
As may with sweetness, through mine ear,
Dissolve me into ecstasies,
And bring all heaven before mine eyes.

We have only space for a few passages from his great epic: the "Hymn to the Creator," like a true picture, loses none of its freshness and richness by reperusal.

These are Thy glorious works, Parent of good,
Almighty! Thine this universal frame,
Thus wondrous fair; Thyself how wondrous then!
Unspeakable, who sitt'st above these heavens
To us invisible, or dimly seen
In these Thy lowest works; yet these declare
Thy goodness beyond thought, and power divine.

Speak, ye who best can tell, ye sons of light,
Angels; for ye behold Him, and with songs
And choral symphonies, day without night,
Circle His throne rejoicing; ye in heaven:
On earth join, all ye creatures, to extol
Him first, Him last, Him midst, and without end.
Fairest of stars, last in the train of night,
If better thou belong not to the dawn,
Sure pledge of day, that crown'st the smiling morn
With thy bright circlet, praise Him in thy sphere,
While day arises, that sweet hour of prime.
Thou sun, of this great world both eye and soul,
Acknowledge Him thy greater; sound His praise
In thy eternal course, both when thou climb'st,
And when high noon hast gained, and when thou fall'st.
. . . . . .
Ye mists and exhalations, that now rise
From hill or steaming lake, dusky or gray,
Till the sun paint your fleecy skirts with gold,
In honor to the world's Great Author rise;
Whether to deck with clouds the uncolored sky,
Or wet the thirsty earth with falling showers,
Rising or falling still advance his praise.
. . . . . .

> His praise, ye winds that from four quarters blow,
> Breathe soft or loud; and wave your tops, ye pines,
> With every plant, in sign of worship wave.
> Fountains, and ye that warble, as ye flow,
> Melodious murmurs, warbling tune his praise.

Now for his majestic chant for "Evening in Paradise:"—

> Now came still evening on, and twilight gray
> Had in her sober livery all things clad:
> Silence accompanied; for beast and bird,
> They to their grassy couch, these to their nests,
> Were slunk; all but the wakeful nightingale;
> She all night long her amorous descant sung;
> Silence was pleased: now glowed the firmament
> With living sapphires; Hesperus, that led
> The starry host, rode brightest, till the moon,
> Rising in clouded majesty, at length,
> Apparent queen, unveiled her peerless light,
> And o'er the dark her silver mantle threw!

---

> Nor think, though men were none,
> That heaven would want spectators, God want praise.
> Millions of spiritual creatures walk the earth
> Unseen, both when we wake and when we sleep.
> All these with ceaseless praise His works behold,
> Both day and night. How often from the steep
> Of echoing hill or thickets have we heard
> Celestial voices to the midnight air,
> Sole, or responsive to each other's note,
> Singing their great Creator! Oft in bands,
> While they keep watch, or nightly rounding walk,
> With heavenly touch of instrumental sounds
> In full harmonic numbers joined, their songs
> Divide the night, and lift our thoughts to Heaven.

Much curious speculation has been entertained concerning the origin of Milton's "Paradise Lost." Some have supposed that it was suggested by the "Divine Weekes" of De Bartas; others, with no more plausibility, think to trace it to an earlier source,—that of Avitus, one of the Fathers of the Church, who was consecrated, in the year 490, Archbishop of Vienna, in Dauphiny; and who is said to have converted Clovis, king of France, and Sigismund, of Burgundy, to Christianity. He wrote five sacred poems on "The Creation," "The Fall," "The Deluge," &c., and died in A.D. 525. Milton is supposed to have been acquainted with these Latin poems, and possibly derived the idea of his epic therefrom.

There is still another conjecture,—that of the renowned Dutch poet, Vondel, an Anabaptist, who was lowly born and without education, but whose genius was most remarkable. His "Lucifer" may be considered the precursor of "Paradise Lost," which it anticipated fourteen years. There is no evidence to show, however, that the incomparable Milton kindled his flame at that of his illustrious contemporary.

We scarcely need refer to his "Sonnet to Cromwell," or to his "Il Penseroso," "Comus," "L' Allegro," or to his fine sonnets on "May Morning," to "The Nightingale," &c.: they are too well known.

A clergyman at Hull was stepping into a boat with a young couple, whom he was going to marry. The event took place early in the seventeenth century. The weather was calm, and there was the promise of a bright voyage; but a mysterious premonition of coming danger oppressed the good parson's heart, and, throwing his cane on shore as the boat went off, he cried, "Ho, for heaven!" The shout was prophetic: neither himself, bridegroom, nor bride ever returned. The son of that prophetic pastor lived to give us one of the best boat-songs that ever floated with the sailor over the waters, or charmed the dwellers on the land. This son was Andrew Marvell, the friend of Milton. His deep sympathy with the suffering and persecuted for conscience' sake may be seen in his beautiful poem: —

> Where the remote Bermudas ride,
> In th' ocean's bosom unespied,
> From a small boat that rowed along,
> The listening winds received this song.
>
> . . . . . .
>
> What should we do, but sing His praise,
> That led us through the watery maze,
> Unto an isle so long unknown,
> And yet far kinder than our own?

Sir Thomas Browne, contemporary with Waller, has given us a fine hymn in his "Religio Medici:" it occurs in the midst of prose, as the prayer every night before he yields to the "death of sleep." Sleep is "so like death," he says, "that I dare not trust it without my prayers, and an half-adieu unto the world, and take my farewell in a colloquy with God."

> The night is come: like to the day,
> Depart not Thou, great God, away.
> Let not my sin, black as the night,
> Eclipse the lustre of Thy light.
> Keep still in my horizon: to me
> The sun makes not the day, but Thee.
> Thou, whose nature cannot sleep,
> On my temples sentry keep;
> Guard me 'gainst those watchful foes
> Whose eyes are open while mine close:
> Let no dreams my head infest,
> But such as Jacob's temples blest.
> While I do rest, my soul advance;
> Make my sleep a holy trance,

> That I may, my rest being wrought,
> Awake unto some holy thought,
> And with as active vigor run
> My course, as doth the nimble sun.
> Sleep is a death: oh, make me try,
> By sleeping, what it is to die!
> And as gently lay mine head
> On my grave, as now my bed.
> Howe'er I rest, great God, let me
> Awake again, at last with Thee;
> And, thus assured, behold, I lie
> Securely, or to wake or die.

"This is the dormitive," he continues, "I take to bedward: I need no other *laudanum* than this to make me sleep; after which I close mine eyes in security, content to take my leave of the sun, and sleep unto the resurrection." These lines present a remarkable analogy to the celebrated Evening Hymn of Bishop Ken.

The most sublime and splendid passage from the pen of Dryden, according to Warton, is this:—

> So when of old the Almighty Father sate,
> In council, to redeem our ruined state,
> Millions of millions, at a distance round,
> Silent the sacred consistory crowned,
> To hear what Mercy, mixed with Justice, could propound:
> All prompt, with eager pity, to fulfil
> The full extent of their Creator's will!
> But when the stern conditions were declared,
> A mournful whisper through the hosts was heard;
> And the whole Hierarchy, with heads hung down,
> Submissively declined the ponderous proffered crown.
> Then, not till then, the Eternal Son from high,
> Rose in the strength of all the Deity,—
> Stood forth to accept the terms, and underwent
> A weight which all the frame of Heaven had bent,
> Nor He himself could bear, but as Omnipotent!

Dryden's exquisite translation of "Veni, Creator Spiritus" is one of the finest compositions in the language: —

> Creator Spirit, by whose aid
> The world's foundations first were laid,
> Come visit every pious mind;
> Come pour thy joys on human kind;
> From sin and sorrow set us free,
> And make Thy temples worthy Thee.
> . . . . . .
> Plenteous of grace, descend from high,
> Rich in thy sevenfold energy!
> Thou strength of His almighty hand,
> Whose power does heaven and earth command!
> . . . . . .
> Refine and purge our earthly parts;
> But, oh, inflame and fire our hearts!
> Our frailties help, our vice control,
> Submit the senses to the soul;
> And when rebellious they are grown,
> Then lay Thy hand, and hold them down.
>
> Chase from our minds the infernal foe,
> And peace, the fruit of love, bestow;
> And, lest our feet should step astray,
> Protect and guide us in the way.
>
> Make us eternal truths receive,
> And practise all that we believe:
> Give us Thyself, that we may see
> The Father, and the Son, by Thee.

The opening of his poem, "Religio Laici," written to defend episcopacy against dissent, is solemn and majestic in its flow: —

> Dim as the borrowed beams of moon and stars
> To lonely, weary, wandering travellers,
> Is Reason to the Soul: and, as on high
> Those rolling fires discover but the sky,

> Not light us here; so Reason's glimmering ray
> Was lent, not to assure our doubtful way,
> But guide us upward to a better day.
> And as those nightly tapers disappear,
> When day's bright lord ascends our hemisphere;
> So pale grows Reason at Religion's sight:
> So dies, and so dissolves, in supernatural light!

Here we close our Evening with the Elizabethan poets, those magnates of the British Muse; and, as we recede from the Augustan Age of England's poetic glory, let us, with a gentle and loving reverence, thank them in our hearts, for the refined pleasure and exaltation of feeling which their noble numbers have inspired in us. In conning over their glowing and pictorial melodies, we seem to be admitted to the presence-chamber of the mighty spirit host, — those "God-anointed kings of thought," convened from that great age and clime; and, as we cannot better express our sense of obligation, let us cherish and conserve, with miser care, the good things they have bequeathed to us.

# SEVENTH EVENING.

## LATER ENGLISH.

# SEVENTH EVENING.

## LATER ENGLISH.

"BLESS the Lord, O my soul! and all that is within me bless His holy name!" Thus sang the Psalmist. Thus should we sing too. "We should, with him, issue this, one of the grandest invocations that can be uttered, addressed to one of the noblest audiences that can be convoked. The Psalmist peals a summons through all the chambers of his being, and calls forth every capacity of his nature, that, one and all, they might join in a vast chorus, of which the name of God should be the theme, and the glory of God the end. It seems as though he gathered into some one vast inner chamber his powers of thought and memory and hope and fear and love, and that he gave charge to his soul to be the leader of this choir, yea, to be the very soul to it, breathing life and sense into its melody, to give the key-note to its chants and to rule its song. Yes: as David did, so let us do also. Each man has within his own bosom the materials for a choir, as tuneful as any which ever stood in surpliced array beneath the cathedral's fretted roof; a choir with full, deep, rich voices, whose anthems can swell, whose choruses can peal, upward, upward, upward, far above the din and turmoil of the earth, until they float into the presence of God Himself, and mingle, it may be, with the myriad voices of those whose praises are ever heard around the throne." *

As introductory to our talk about English hymn-writers and their hymns, it may not be inappropriate to premise a few words as to what properly constitutes a hymn. In most of our church collections may be found many sacred poems, many admonitory rhymes or poetical homilies, intermingled with what are really true hymns of praise and adoration. A true hymn is either prayer or praise, — a heart-utterance of praise to the Divine Being, — and not a response from the pew to the pulpit. "Hymns are not meant to be theological statements," remarks a recent English hymnist, "expositions of doctrine, or enunciations of precepts: they are utterances of the soul in its manifold moods of hope and fear, joy and sorrow, love, wonder, and aspiration. A hymn should not consist of comments on a text, or of remarks on an experience; but of a central and creative thought, shaping for itself melodious utterance, and with every detail subordinated to its clear and harmonious presentation. Herein a true hymn takes rank as a poem. Hymns are utterances of the religious affections, not theological statements or doctrinal expositions. All true hymns have grown out of a deep and true theology."† The "Te Deum" was praised by Luther as a good symbol, not less than as a perfect hymn. While, therefore, hortatory hymns are usually unsuitable for congregational singing, others, again, are equally unadapted for the use of a mixed audience, because of the use of too great famili-

---

\* Power on the Psalms.      † Gill's Golden Chain of Praise.

arity of expression as applied to our Lord; instances of which are noticeable in some of Watts's pieces in his "Horæ Lyricæ," and in some of the Moravian hymns. All such addresses should be expressions of "humble love joined with holy fear."

"Hymns are the exponents of the inmost piety of the Church," observes a glowing and forcible writer; * "they are the crystalline tears, or blossoms of joy, or holy prayers, or incarnated raptures. They are jewels, which the Church has worn, — the pearls, the diamonds, and precious stones, formed into amulets, more potent against sorrow and sadness than the most famous charms of wizard or magician. Angels sat at the grave's mouth; and so hymns are the angels that rise up out of our griefs and darkness and dismay." Yes: very many of our most cherished hymns are those which, expressive of the heart-struggles and aspirations of Christian life, as well as those of joy and sorrow, hope or fear, have, for the most part, had their birth amid the shadows of the chamber of sorrow. These soul-utterances in song have usually emanated from those who have been taught "the divine art of carrying sorrow and trouble as wonderful food, as an invisible garment that clothed them with strength, as a mysterious joy; so that they suffered gladly, so that they might see nobler realities than sight could reach." So prolific have been our English hymnists, during the seventeenth and eighteenth centuries, that, according to a recent authority,† no less than seven hundred names in this department of English poetry have been enumerated. We can, of course, refer only to the most renowned.

* H. W. Beecher. † Sedgwick.

When the Reformation dawned on England, the common people did not require much persuasion to induce them to sing hymns in the mother tongue. Congregational singing soon found its way into parish churches and chapels; for Geneva had set the fashion, where "all the congregation — men, women, and boys — sing together," and the "sweet infection" soon spread over seas. It is remarkable that the Baptists, after the Reformation, were very generally opposed to singing in their congregations: it was not until a score of years or more after, that the practice obtained with them. The Baptist communion was much divided on this question of singing; to such a degree, indeed, as to put both parties out of tune.

When the Pilgrim Fathers reached the long-wished-for Western world, who would not like to have listened to that united, hearty hymn of thanksgiving, that would put to shame much of our modern psalm-singing, in which the ear, rather than the heart, seems to be most concerned? During the great revival which took place under Edwards, Whitefield, and others, singing formed a prominent and a most influential part in divine worship; as it also did in the spiritual crusade of the Wesleys, Doddridge, and others, in England.

In making our selections, the difficulty that confronts us at the outset is, what to indicate, and what to omit, the claimants being so numerous; and yet the precise information that we seek is by no means of ready access.

Not seldom do we dare perils and dangers, make long pilgrimages over land and ocean, to gaze upon some sainted shrine, or linger in the precincts of some spot hallowed to us by genius. A kindred interest is awakened by the recital of whatever is associated with those productions of the pen that have won for themselves our admiration and esteem. This is especially true with respect to our poets and hymn-writers. Who does not feel a deeper interest in perusing those touching stanzas, "God moves in a mysterious way," when he recalls the occasion which produced them,—the dark clouds that overshadowed the gentle spirit of the Christian bard, when those plaintive strains first welled up from his tempest-tossed heart?

In presenting the results of our researches pertaining to the hymn-writers and their hymns, we would premise that the incidents we shall adduce will, of necessity, be very brief and select. First, then, in the order of time, we meet with the well-known names of Sternhold and Hopkins. The first-named was an officer in the Court of Henry VIII., and Hopkins was a clergyman in Suffolk. Jointly, they were the authors of the first psalter attached to the Book of Common Prayer, which appeared in 1562. This version of the Psalms was, in 1696, superseded by that of Brady and Tate.

The fine old hymn, "All people that on earth do dwell," which has been often ascribed to Hopkins, is now believed to have been composed by one Kethe, who was an exile with Knox, at Geneva, in 1555.

Richard Baxter, who was born A.D. 1615, is well known as the author of "The Saint's Everlasting Rest." He wrote poetry, as well as solemn prose, to beguile, doubtless, his sad and solitary hours, which were not few. He was often harassed by threats and fines and imprisonment; and at length, after a trial before the notorious Jeffries, was condemned, for his "Paraphrase on the New Testament," to pay a fine of five hundred marks. Being unable to pay the amount, he was committed to prison. He bore his tribulations with wonderful patience; and when, during his last sickness, he was asked by a friend how he did, he replied, "Almost well." His end was as peaceful as his earthly life had been troublous. His most popular hymn reads, —

> Lord, it belongs not to my care, whether I die or live.

It is part of a sacred lyric, commencing, —

> My whole though broken heart, O Lord! from henceforth shall be Thine.

A contemporary of the forenamed was Mason, the author of the well-known "Treatise on Self-Knowledge," who wrote some hymns, like Quarles' and Herbert's for quaintness, but "luminous with imagery." Take a specimen stanza, from his "Evening Song of Praise:" —

> Man's life's a book of history,
> The leaves thereof are days,
> The letters, mercies closely joined,
> The title is Thy praise.

John Mason was one of the earlier hymn-writers to whom Dr. Watts was indebted. The lines,

> What shall I render to my God,
> For all his gifts to me?

are to be found identical in both collections.

Mason, whom Baxter styled "the glory of the Church of England," became, in 1674, rector of Water-Stratford, Bucks, where he spent his devoted and useful life; he "finished his course with joy," in 1694. Of his sacred songs, Montgomery says, "The style is a middle tint between the raw coloring of Quarles and the daylight clearness of Watts and the Wesleys."

Honest John Bunyan's name ought to be mentioned here; for, although a writer of very poor verse, in his prose he was essentially a poet, as his immortal allegory attests. He was born twenty years after Milton; yet, although two men could scarcely be more dissimilar as to the outward accidents of life, — the one a profound scholar, the other an uneducated tinker, — yet each has enriched our English literature far beyond the average of writers.

It is remarkable that John Bunyan, who had to endure twelve long years' imprisonment in Bedford jail for preaching the gospel, was the first of the nonconformists to receive a license so to do from the British government. It was dated the 9th of May, 1672. Would you not have liked to have seen and heard him, in his rude pulpit, after his release from captivity?

> "When such a man, familiar with the skies,
> Has filled his urn where the pure waters rise,
> And once more mingles with us, meaner things,
> 'Tis e'en as if an angel shook his wings."

Bunyan was eminently a Bible-man, — "the man of one book," and that one the "Book of books," —

> "A book wherein his Saviour's Testament,
> Written with golden letters, rich and brave, —
> A work of wondrous grace, and able souls to save."

Henry Vaughan's sacred verse, although, like Herbert's, disfigured with the conceits of his time, is yet eminently spiritual, and replete with rare beauty, both of thought and expression. We subjoin a few extracts from his finest poems: —

I saw Eternity the other night,
Like a great ring of pure and endless light,
All calm as it was bright;
And round beneath it, Time in hours, days, years,
Driven by the spheres,
Like a vast shadow moved, in which the world
And all her train were hurled.

### THE SECOND ADVENT.

Ah! what time wilt thou come? when shall that crie,
The Bridegroome's Comming! fill the sky?
Shall it in the Evening run
When our words and works are done?
Or will thy all-surprizing light
Break at midnight,
When either sleep, or some dark pleasure
Possesseth mad man without measure?
Or shall these early, fragrant hours
Unlock thy bowres?
And with their blush of light descry
Thy locks crowned with eternitie?

Professor Longfellow says, "It was in an hour of blessed communion with the souls of the departed that the sweet poet wrote those few lines which have made death lovely. He spoke well who said 'that graves are the footsteps of angels.'" Listen to these fine stanzas: —

I see them walking in an air of glory,
Whose light doth trample on my days, —
My days, which are at best but dull and hoary,
Mere glimmerings and decays.
O holy hope, and high humility,
High as the heavens above!
These are your walks, and you have showed them me,
To kindle my cold love.
Dear, beauteous Death! the jewel of the just!
Shining nowhere but in the dark!
What mysteries do lie beyond thy dust,
Could man outlook that mark!

Vaughan's "Hymn to the Rainbow" is only surpassed by that of Campbell, who plagiarized from his predecessor: —

> Still young and fine! but what is still in view
> We slight as old and soiled, though fresh and new.
> How bright wert thou, when Shem's admiring eye
> Thy burnished, flaming arch did first descry!
> When Terah, Nahor, Haran, Abram, Lot, —
> The youthful world's gray fathers in one knot, —
> Did, with intentive looks, watch every hour
> For thy new light, and trembled at each shower!
> When thou dost shine, darkness looks white and fair,
> Forms turn to music, clouds to smiles and air;
> . . . . . . .
> Bright pledge of peace and sunshine! the sure tie
> Of thy Lord's hand, the object of His eye!
> When I behold thee, though my light be dim,
> Distant, and low, I can in thine see Him
> Who looks upon thee from His glorious throne,
> And minds the covenant 'twixt all and One.

His poem, "The Retreat," bears great analogy, in its mystic philosophy, to Wordsworth's ode on "Immortality." Both these poets seem to think that this is not our first stage of existence, — that we are haunted by dim memories of a former state. He enjoyed a tranquil, happy life (1621–1695) at Newton, Wales. Listen to his ghostly counsel: —

> When first thy eyes unvail, give thy soul leave
>   To do the like; our bodies but forerun
> The spirit's duty; true hearts spread and heave
>   Unto their God, as flowers do to the sun:
> Give Him thy first thoughts then; so shalt thou keep
> Him company all day, and in Him sleep.
>
> Yet never sleep the sun up; prayer should
>   Dawn with the day; there are set, awful hours
> 'Twixt heaven and us: the manna was not good

After sun-rising, for day sullies flowers;
Rise to prevent the sun; sleep doth sins glut,
And heaven's gate opens when the world's is shut.

. . . . . . . .

Mornings are mysteries; the first world's youth,
Man's resurrection, and the future's bud,
Shroud in their births; the crown of life, light, truth,
Is styled their star; the stone and hidden food;
These blessings wait upon them, one of which
Should move: they make us holy, happy, rich.

Good Bishop Ken (1637–1711), whose name suggests the "Morning and Evening Hymns" and the "Doxology," endured many trials and afflictions "for conscience' sake." After his death and burial, it is recorded that his sorrowing attendants saluted the opening day with the strains of his own Morning Hymn. The doxology, "Praise God, from whom all blessings flow," "is a masterpiece of compression and amplification," says Montgomery: there is, probably, no other stanza in existence that has been so often, and is still, sung by all denominations of Christians. We subjoin his paraphrase on "Charity:"—

Blest Charity! the grace long-suffering, kind,
Which envies not, has no self-vaunting mind,
Is not puffed up, makes no unseemly show,
Seeks not her own, to provocation slow,
No evil thinks, in no unrighteous choice
Takes pleasure, doth in truth rejoice,
Hides all things, still believes, and hopes the best,
All things endures, averse to all contest.
Tongues, knowledge, prophecy, shall sink away
At the first glance of beatific ray,—
Then charity its element shall gain,
And with the God of love eternal reign.

"In him," it has been beautifully said, "doctrine and life melted harmoniously into each other. Poetry, with him, was only a recreation from graver pursuits; but he has bequeathed to us a Morning and Evening Hymn, which will only perish with the religion that inspired them."* An eloquent writer † thus refers to the character of this eminent divine: "We shall hardly find in all ecclesiastical history a greener spot than the later years of this courageous and affectionate pastor; persecuted alternately by both parties, and driven from his station in his declining age; yet singing on, with unabated cheerfulness, to the last."

Among the hymns of Addison that have become classic is this: —

When all Thy mercies, O my God! my rising soul surveys,
Transported with the view, I'm lost in wonder, love, and praise!
Oh, how shall words, with equal warmth, the gratitude declare,
That glows within my ravished breast? But Thou canst read it there.
Through every period of my life, Thy goodness I'll pursue;
And, after death, in distant worlds, the glorious theme renew.

Our literature owes much to Addison, for he refined, polished, and purified it more than any writer of his own or perhaps any former age; even Pope, who was his rival and satirist, admits that "no whiter page than Addison's remains."

What a noble passage is his "Cato's Soliloquy on the Immortality of the Soul"! —

It must be so, — Plato, thou reason'st well, —
Else whence this pleasing hope, this fond desire,
This longing after immortality?
Or whence this secret dread and inward horror
Of falling into nought? Why shrinks the soul
Back on herself, and startles at destruction?
'Tis the Divinity that stirs within us;

* Willmott.  † Quarterly Review.

'Tis Heaven itself that points out an hereafter,
And intimates eternity to man.
Eternity! thou pleasing, dreadful thought!
Through what variety of untried being,
Through what new scenes and changes must we pass!
. . . . . . . .
The soul, secured in her existence, smiles
At the drawn dagger, and defies its point.
The stars shall fade away, the sun himself
Grow dim with age, and nature sink in years;
But thou shalt flourish in immortal youth,
Unhurt amidst the war of elements,
The wreck of matter, and the crush of worlds.

Addison's famous lyric, "The spacious firmament on high," first appeared in the "Spectator" in 1712, at the close of an article by him, on "The Right Means to strengthen Faith."* His paraphrase on the twenty-third psalm accompanied an essay on "Trust in God," about the same time, when his powers had reached their highest cultivation and development. About this time, also, he wrote his "Traveller's Hymn," consisting of ten stanzas,—of which this is one,—of great beauty:—

>    Thy mercy sweetened every soil,
>      Made every region please,—
>    The hoary Alpine hills it warmed,
>      And smoothed the Tyrrhene seas.

To praise or criticise Addison would be alike immodest and superfluous. Tickell's elegy may best speak his tribute:—

>    If, pensive, to the rural shades I rove,
>    His form o'ertakes me in the vernal grove;
>    'Twas there of just and good he reasoned strong,
>    Cleared some great truth, or raised some serious song;

---

* It has been doubted, by some critics, whether Andrew Marvell did not write it.

> There, patient, showed us the wise course to steer,
> A candid censor, and a friend sincere;
> There taught us how to live, and — oh, too high
> The price of knowledge! — taught us how to die.

Some two centuries ago, there was, in the town of Southampton, the son of a deacon of an Independent Church, whose ear for melody suffered something like what a person of sensitive nerve feels at the sound of a file sharpening a saw; and he complained that the hymnists of his day were sadly out of taste. "Give us something better, young man," was the reply. The young man did it; and the Church was invited to close its evening service with a new hymn, which commenced, —

> Behold the glories of the Lamb, amidst His Father's throne;
> Prepare new honors for His name, and songs before unknown.

This was Isaac Watts's first hymn. To him is the credit due of creating a people's hymnal; for he taught them to sing, and supplied them with sacred songs. It is true the Wesleys share largely the honor of contributing to our hymnology; and they, in common with Watts, have unquestionably done more to embalm in the hearts and memories of Christians the great scriptural truths of our faith, than any that had preceded them. Their testimony is an imperishable one, like the truth they lived and sang.

"He was," says Montgomery, "almost the inventor of hymns in our language, so greatly did he improve upon his few almost forgotten predecessors in the composition of sacred song." The weakness and suffering of his later years afforded him protracted seasons of retirement, and these he made prolific of profit to the

Christian world in the rich contributions thus conferred. As he approached his closing hours, he expressed himself as "waiting God's leave to die," and thus he entered into his rest, Nov. 25, 1748. There is a tradition touching the hymn which begins, "There is a land of pure delight," which connects it with Southampton, and says that it was while "looking out upon the beautiful scenery of the harbor and river, and the green glades of the New Forest on its farther bank, that the idea suggested itself to Dr. Watts, of 'a land of pure delight,' and of 'sweet fields beyond the swelling flood, dressed in living green,' as an image of the heavenly Canaan."

Watts's famous work was his "Logic," prepared primarily for the use of his pupil, the son of Sir John Hartopp, at Stoke Newington. When he attained his twenty-fourth year, he preached his first sermon at the Independent "Meeting-house," in Mark Lane, London; but his frequent attacks of indisposition caused him, after some dozen years, to relinquish the position. Sir Thomas Abney invited him on a visit to his house, at Theobalds; whither he went to spend a week, and remained for six-and-thirty years, until his death.

In spite of his acknowledged artistic defects, Watts's hymns are among the very best extant; and they will continue to form the vehicles of utterance for assembled worshippers as well as for Christian retirement. By their quickening and inspiring influence, Congregationalism in England and America was rescued, to a great extent, from the formalism that prevailed during the eighteenth century. Watts's hymns have found their way into the Episcopal, and all other orthodox communions. How many of his expressive stanzas recur to us, often involuntarily, with a sanative and soothing power! such as these: —

> Be earth, with all her scenes, withdrawn,
> Let noise and vanity be gone:
> In secret silence of the mind
> My heaven, and there my God, I find.

---

> When I survey the wondrous cross
> On which the Prince of Glory died!*

---

> Death, like a narrow sea, divides
> This heavenly land from ours.

We learn, from a recent authority,† that the well-known hymn, —

> Before Jehovah's awful throne,
> Ye nations, bow with sacred joy, —

was written by John Wesley, although it is usually credited to Watts; his hymn reads, —

> Nations, attend before His throne,
> With solemn fear and sacred joy.

The note-book of a London-City missionary contains the narrative of a Jewess, who, seeing part of the hymn, beginning, "Not all the blood of beasts," read it, and became so deeply impressed by its teaching, that she was induced to consult diligently her Bible, and soon she discovered in the despised Nazarene, the true Messiah. In consequence of this, her husband repudiated her, obtained a divorce; went to India, and married again, and then — died. She suffered privation, patiently and cheerfully, like those faithful few at Jerusalem of old.

---

\* A writer of one of the "Oxford Essays" fixes on this as Watts's finest hymn.
† Miller.

The hymn commencing, "My God, the spring of all my joys," has been pronounced, by critics, one of the very best of its author's numerous Christian lyrics. Another very striking and impressive one is "Absent from flesh! oh, blissful thought!" Watts's lines, —

> When I can read my title clear
> To mansions in the skies, —

Cowper seems to have adopted, in his poem on "Truth," in the comparison of the condition of the wealthy, sceptical Voltaire, with that of the poor, believing cottager: —

> Just knows, and knows no more, her Bible true, —
> A truth the brilliant Frenchman never knew;
> And in that charter reads, with sparkling eyes,
> Her title to a treasure in the skies.

Doddridge mentions the powerful effect of singing the hymn of Watts, "Give me the wings of faith to rise," after the sermon he had preached, on Hebrews vi. 12. The hymn gave such emphasis to the sermon, that many were too much moved to continue singing it, while most sang it with tears.

Dr. Watts's version of Psalm cxlvi., "I'll praise my Maker with my breath," has a special interest as being uttered, when very near his end, by John Wesley. From among many who have expressed their sense of indebtedness to the worthy doctor, we may mention the name of the celebrated Colonel Gardiner, whose testimony is strong and decided. In a letter to Dr. Doddridge, he expresses his fear lest the poet should die before he had an opportunity of thanking him; a fear, however, not realized. This "Poet of the

Sanctuary," as we have said, wrote many if not most of his inspiring hymns in the chamber of sickness. Although he never married, yet he loved children, and is their friend to this day by his " Divine Songs." The writer has lingered reverently over his tomb, — not far from that of John Bunyan, in the burial-ground of Bunhill Fields, London, — the *Campo Santo* of Dissenters.

Next in the procession of the sacred poets comes the author of "Night Thoughts,"— Young, who, from his austere gravity, it is difficult to believe ever was *young*. His flowers are sometimes intermingled with weeds, — with the golden grain we find oft-times the gaudy and noxious poppy, the hemlock with the vine : all is displayed with a boundless and indiscriminate prodigality. But let us turn to his picture-pages, albeit they have less of bright lights than of shadows. Our first extract is, however, a splendid one : —

> A Deity believed, is joy begun ;
> A Deity adored, is joy advanced ;
> A Deity beloved, is joy matured.
> Each branch of piety delight inspires.
> Faith builds a bridge from this world to the next
> O'er death's dark gulf, and all its horrors hides.
> Praise, the sweet exhalation of our joy,
> That joy exalts, and makes it sweeter still ;
> Prayer ardent opens heaven, lets down a stream
> Of glory on the consecrated hour
> Of man in audience with the Deity !

---

> At thirty, man suspects himself a fool ;
> Knows it at forty, and reforms his plan ;
> At fifty, chides his infamous delay,
> Pushes his prudent purpose to resolve ;
> In all the magnanimity of thought

Resolves, and re-resolves ; then dies the same !
And why ? because he thinks himself immortal.
All men think all men mortal but themselves :
Themselves, when some alarming shock of fate
Strikes through their wounded hearts the sudden dread ;
But their hearts wounded, like the wounded air,
Soon close ; where passed the shaft, no trace is found,
As from the wing no scar the sky retains,
The parted wave no furrow from the keel :
So dies in human hearts the thought of death !
E'en with the tender tear, which nature sheds
O'er those we love, we drop it in their grave !

This fine triplet has often been admired : —

Talk they of morals ? O Thou bleeding Love !
Thou maker of new morals to mankind !
The grand morality is love of Thee !

There are some splendid thoughts in this passage : —

The chamber where the good man meets his fate,
Is privileged beyond the common walk
Of virtuous life, quite on the verge of heaven.
. . . . . .
Here tired dissimulation drops her mask,
Here real and apparent are the same.
You see the man ; you see his hold on heaven ;
Heaven waits not the last moment, owns its friends
On this side death, and points them out to men ;
To vice, confusion ; and, to virtue, peace !
Whatever farce the boastful hero plays,
Virtue alone has majesty in death.

By a sort of concatenation, we turn from the author of "Night Thoughts" to that of "The Grave." Both are poets of a sombre hue, and yet, as quaint old Fuller used to say, "to smell to a turf of fresh earth is wholesome for the body; no less are thoughts of mortality cordial to the soul. Earth thou art, and unto earth shalt thou return." Robert Blair, and his contemporary Young, although in their poetry melancholic, and shrouded with the shadows of death, were yet, in their private life, of cheerful and happy mood enough. Campbell remarks, "Blair may be a homely and even gloomy poet in the eye of fastidious criticism; but there is a masculine and pronounced character, even in his gloom and homeliness, that keeps it most distinctly apart from either dulness, or even vulgarity. His style pleases us, like the powerful expression of a countenance without regular beauty." Here is a specimen passage of his Muse: —

> How shocking must thy summons be, O Death!
> To him that is at ease in his possession;
> Who, counting on long years of pleasure here,
> Is quite unfurnished for that world to come!
> In that dread moment, how the frantic soul
> Raves round the walls of her clay tenement,
> Runs to each avenue, and shrieks for help,
> But shrieks in vain! How wishfully she looks
> On all she's leaving, now no longer hers!
> A little longer, yet a little longer,
> Oh, might she stay, to wash away her stains,
> And fit her for her passage! Mournful sight!
> Her very eyes weep blood; and every groan
> She heaves is big with horror: but the foe,
> Like a stanch murd'rer, steady to his purpose,
> Pursues her close through every lane of life,
> Nor misses once the track, but presses on;
> Till, forced at last to the tremendous verge,
> At once she sinks to everlasting ruin.

Pope's celebrated lyric, "Vital spark of heavenly flame," like some other productions of his pen, is an imitation. "The original source of this hymn is supposed to be a poem composed by the Emperor Adrian, who, dying A.D. 138, thus gave expression to his mingled doubts and fears. His poem begins thus:—

> Animula vagula blandula,
> Hospes comesque corporis.

("Sweet spirit, ready to depart, guest and companion of the body.")

It is afterwards found freely rendered in a piece by a poet of some note in his own day,— Thomas Flatman, of London,— a barrister, poet, and painter. Flatman's poem is called "A Thought of Death;" and, as he died in the year Pope was born, 1688, and the poems are very similar, there can be little doubt that Pope has imitated his predecessor. From Pope's correspondence, we learn that on Nov. 7, 1712, he sent a letter to Mr. Steele, for insertion in the "Spectator," on the subject of Adrian's last words; to which Steele responded by asking him to make of them an ode, in two or three stanzas, for music. He replied immediately, saying that he had done as required, and sent the piece."*

To show how close is the parallel between the poets, we put a stanza of each side by side:—

| | |
|---|---|
| Full of sorrow, full of anguish, | Vital spark of heavenly flame! |
| Fainting, gasping, trembling, crying, | Quit, oh, quit this mortal frame! |
| Panting, groaning, shrinking, dying,— | Trembling, hoping, ling'ring, flying, |
| Methinks I hear some gentle spirit say, | Oh, the pain, the bliss of dying! |
| "Be not fearful, come away!" | Cease, fond Nature, cease thy strife, |
| | And let me languish into life! |

It has been urged by critics, that it is inconsistent and inconceivable that a dying man should hold such a soliloquy with his soul,— it is altogether too studied

* Miller's Our Hymns.

and rhetorical, too artificial. Although undoubtedly a grand poem, yet it cannot be regarded strictly as a hymn, any more than Toplady's famous production, "Deathless principle! arise," judged by the rule of St. Augustine, who tells us "a hymn must be *praise*, — the praise of God, and this in the form of song." Pope's "Universal Prayer" has been considered justly amenable to criticism for its defective theology; and yet, it cannot be denied, it is to be preferred to the artificial, flamboyant style of his sacred eclogue, "The Messiah." A few short extracts we subjoin : —

> Thou great First Cause, least understood ! who all my sense confined
> To know but this, that Thou art good, and that myself am blind :
> Yet give me in this dark estate, to see the good from ill ;
> And binding nature fast in fate, let free the human will.
> What conscience dictates to be done, or warns me not to do,
> This, teach me more than hell to shun, that, more than heaven pursue.
>    .    .    .    .    .    .    .
> Save me alike from foolish pride, or impious discontent,
> At aught Thy wisdom has denied, or aught Thy goodness lent.
> Teach me to feel another's woe, to hide the faults I see ;
> That mercy I to others show, that mercy show to me.
>    .    .    .    .    .    .    .
> To Thee, whose temple is all space, whose altar, earth, sea, skies !
> One chorus let all beings raise ! all nature's incense rise !

Warburton informs us that Pope wrote his "Universal Prayer" to silence the cavils which his "Essay on Man" had elicited; not thinking, probably, that the "Prayer" itself would subject him to animadversions scarcely less formidable. The incongruous and irreverent mingling of the name of a pagan god with that of the Divine Being, in the last line of the first stanza; the uncouth combination of fate and free-will in the second and third verses, expressed, too, in bad grammar; and the hyperbole bordering on profanity in the fourth stanza, — are grave defects in a poem otherwise worthy of great critical praise.

Pope's "Essay on Man" was Bolingbroke in verse, for the mind of the former dwelt under the shadow of the latter. This explains the infidel tendencies of much of his seductive verse. What but the deistical fallacy of the sufficiency of natural religion, as it is called, and the equally sophistical sentiment of a spurious liberality, is in these lines? —

> Slave to no sect, who takes no private road,
> But looks through nature, up to nature's God!

Or, again, how unsound are those lines so often quoted with unthinking approval! —

> For forms of government let fools contest;
> Whate'er is best administered is best.
> For modes of faith, let senseless zealots fight;
> He can't be wrong, whose life is in the right.

As if the administration of a government did not greatly depend upon its form; as if the rectitude of life did not depend upon its faith.

Recalling the pure and almost inspired Muse of Milton, we can scarcely read the seductive lines of the great satirist, with unalloyed pleasure or profit. It has been said that "when Milton lost his eyes, Poetry lost hers."

Having taken our exceptions to his erratic theology, we gladly accord to him all praise for the masterly passages which follow: —

> O blindness to the future! kindly given,
> That each may fill the circle marked by heaven.
> .    .    .    .    .    .    .

> Hope humbly, then, with trembling pinions soar,
> Wait the great teacher, Death; and God adore.
> What future bliss, He gives not thee to know,
> But gives that hope to be thy blessing now.
> Hope springs eternal in the human breast;
> Man never *is*, but always *to be* blest:
> The soul, uneasy and confined from home,
> Rests and expatiates in a life to come.

> What nothing earthly gives, or can destroy,
> The soul's calm sunshine and the heart-felt joy,
> Is Virtue's prize.

Although Pope's style was didactic, — he having left untouched the two higher orders of poetry, the epic and dramatic, — yet in this department he was the master unsurpassed. No other poet, not even Cowper, has combined such powers of reasoning with such splendid decorations of fancy. His works have been more frequently edited than those of any other British poet, except Shakspeare. He does not seem to have been a very lovable character, however, as his caustic satires would lead us to suspect. His person was small and deformed; and his temper of mind often, also, crooked. His friend, Bishop Atterbury, once referring to his irascibility, described him as "mens curva in corpore curvo." In justice to the poet, however, we ought to cite his noble couplet on his friend:

> How pleasing Atterbury's softer hour!
> How shined his soul unconquered in the Tower!

There is a familiar hymn, beginning, —

> Rise, my soul, and stretch thy wings,
> Thy better portion trace,

which is often erroneously ascribed to Malan: it is by Robert Seagrave, who deserves honorable mention among hymnists.

One Byrom, born in 1691, has left several hymns, which are more remarkable for their metaphysics than their melody. We present two of his epigrams:—

> Think, and be careful what thou art within;
> For there is sin in the desire of sin:
> Think, and be thankful, in a different case;
> For there is grace in the desire of grace.

---

> Faith, Hope, and Love were questioned what they thought
> Of future Glory, which religion taught:
> Now Faith believed it firmly to be true,
> And Hope expected so to find it too;
> Love answered, smiling with a conscious glow,
> "'Believe?' 'Expect?' I know it to be so!"

One of Thomson's finest bursts of poetic inspiration is his "Hymn of the Seasons:" how sublimely it opens!—

> These, as they change, Almighty Father, these
> Are but the varied God. The rolling year
> Is full of Thee. Forth in the pleasing spring
> Thy beauty walks, Thy tenderness and love.
> Wide flush the fields; the softening air is balm;
> Echo the mountains round; the forest smiles;
> And every sense and every heart is joy.
> Then comes Thy glory in the summer months,
> With light and heat refulgent. Then Thy sun
> Shoots full perfection through the swelling year;
> And oft Thy voice in dreadful thunder speaks;
> And oft at dawn, deep noon, or falling eve,
> By brooks and groves, in hollow-whispering gales.
> Thy bounty shines in autumn unconfined,
> And spreads a common feast for all that lives.
> In winter awful Thou! with clouds and storms
> Around Thee thrown, tempest o'er tempest rolled,
> Majestic darkness! on the whirlwind's wing
> Riding sublime, Thou bidst the world adore,
> And humblest nature with Thy northern blast!

That exquisite poem on Winter, by Thomson, abounds in fine passages: here is one, which is inscribed on his tomb: —

> Father of light and life, Thou God supreme!
> Oh, teach me what is good, — teach me Thyself!
> Save me from folly, vanity, and vice,
> From every low pursuit; and feed my soul
> With knowledge, conscious peace, and virtue pure,
> Sacred, substantial, never-fading bliss!

Thomson's sublime hymn, with which his "Seasons" closes, has been said to concentrate the essential beauty of his epic, as if in "a cloud of fragrance, and by the breath of devotion, it directed it up to heaven." The poet was born, A.D. 1700, at Ednam, in Roxburghshire; and in that land of picturesque beauty and wild romance he gave the first promise of poetic wealth. He is described as a "fine, fat fellow, not without his errors; but a loving brother, a fast friend, a sharp and accurate observer of men and things, and gave hope, in his last hours, that he died in the faith."

A large, sorrow-stricken crowd was gathered around an open grave in the well-known Bunhill-Fields burying-ground, London, in the spring of 1768. The funeral address and prayer being ended, the multitude lifted up their voices and sang, —

> Sons of God by blest adoption, view the dead with steady eyes;
> What is sown thus in corruption shall in incorruption rise;
> What is sown in death's dishonor shall revive to glory's light;
> What is sown in this weak manner shall be raised in matchless
>   might.
> Earthly cavern, to thy keeping we commit our brother's dust:
> Keep it safely, softly sleeping, till our Lord demand thy trust.
> Sweetly sleep, dear saint, in Jesus; thou with us shalt wake from
>   death;
> Hold he cannot, though he seize us: we his power defy by faith!

"The funeral-hymn had been written by the one whose dust was now covered. The grave was closed, and the stone which was laid upon it is still there; and those who visit the spot should linger awhile, and think of the youthful errors and sins, the dark conflicts, the bitter tears, the spiritual struggles, the sound conversion, the consecrated talents, the faithful ministry, and the fresh and fruitful hymns of Joseph Hart. And when they have caught the fragrance of his memory, and hear the songs of those who still thank God for his ministry in the old 'meeting-house' of Jewin Street, they may be ready to chant the soothing and assuring hymn, which arose, in some solemn moments, nearly fifty years ago, from the heart of Milman." *

> Brother, thou art gone before us, and thy saintly soul is flown
> Where tears are wiped from every eye, and sorrow is unknown:
> From the burden of the flesh, and from care and fear released,
> Where the wicked cease from troubling, and the weary are at rest.

Another worthy gentleman, one of Lady Huntington's select friends, was Philip Doddridge, whose winning address and gentleness of spirit caused him to be so tenderly beloved by Dr. Watts. He lived for his humble parish of Kebworth, in Northampton, and seems to have been very happy in his seclusion from the din and stir of city life. "I live like a tortoise," he writes, "shut up in its shell, almost always in the same town, the same house, and the same chamber: yet I live like a prince, not indeed in the pomp of greatness, but the pride of liberty,—master of my books, master of my time, and, I hope I may add, master of myself." He wrote, at the suggestion of Dr. Watts, "The Rise and Progress of Religion in

* Christophers' Hymn-writers.

the Soul," which was published in 1745; a book that still continues to win trophies to the gospel, not merely among the Wilberforces of our day, but also among the multitudes unknown to earthly fame. In the autumn of 1751, Doddridge, at the age of fifty, ceased from his "labors of love," at Lisbon, and his ashes rest in the English burying-ground there. Doddridge deserves our tribute, also, as "the sweet lyrist of God's people." Has he not given voice to the most cherished emotions of the soul? Has he not been with us on our covenant days, and, with exquisite pathos, bid

> The glowing heart rejoice,
> And tell its raptures all abroad?

Should the reader be sceptical as to the controlling influence of a mother's training, his faith might be quickened were he to read the noble testimony of Augustine to his sainted mother, Monica; or the records of the heroic mother of Cromwell; the mother of our own Washington; or of her who taught her son theology by the rude pictorial process of Dutch tiles. Who can justly estimate the value of maternal counsel and instruction in the instance of the embryo author of the "Rise and Progress of Religion in the Soul," the "Family Expositor," and the imperishable hymns bequeathed to us by Philip Doddridge? We have, doubtless, thousands of true and exemplary mothers who are equal to their responsibilities; but who does not see that our modern habits of thought are adverse to their growth and increase? Folly and fashion seem well-nigh to have superseded the reign of the gentler graces and virtues of true womanhood; leaving us, instead, — as illustrative of this age of progress, — a splendid exterior, but no inner life.

"The North British Review" pronounces Doddridge's "Rise and Progress of Religion" the best book of the eighteenth century; very high praise, when so many great pens were enriching our literature. It has been rendered into the leading languages of Europe. Who can tell how many have ascribed their conversion to its perusal?

The life-record of Doddridge is a beautiful and instructive study. His private deportment, as well as his public ministrations, alike evinced the amiability and spiritual culture of this estimable servant of God. With what wonderful devotion to the good of others did he fill up the brief days of his earthly career! how pure and exalted his aims! No wonder that the great Robert Hall should declare him to be his prime favorite among divines; or that his name is to the Church at large as a household word.

The contributions of Doddridge to our hymnology are numerous, and include many familiar devotional lyrics. Critically judged, they are, for the most part, not distinguished for literary skill, or generally quite equal to the compositions of Dr. Watts, his contemporary. Doddridge's name will always be honored in connection with the history of the founding of Dissenting Colleges. His overtasked and useful life was terminated all too soon for the interests of the good work to which he devoted himself.

Doddridge's most esteemed hymns include those commencing, "Awake, my soul, stretch every nerve!" "Ye golden lamps of heaven, farewell," "Grace, 'tis a charming sound," "Hark! the glad sound, the Saviour comes!" "Thine earthly Sabbaths, Lord, we love." Doddridge's hymns were often supplementary epitomizings of his sermons. After he had completed the study of some biblical topic for the pulpit, he would throw the leading thoughts into a few stanzas; the hymn commencing, "Jesus, I love Thy charming name," was the condensation of his sermon on 1 Pet. ii. 7. Thus, while most of the sermons to which they pertained have disappeared for ever, "these sacred streams, at once beautiful and buoyant, are destined to carry the devout emotions of Doddridge to every shore where His Maker is loved, and where his mother tongue is spoken. If amber is the germ of fossil-trees, fetched up and floated off by the ocean, hymns like these are a spiritual amber." *

Doddridge's epigram on his family motto, "Dum vivimus vivamus," so highly eulogized by Johnson, is familiar to most readers : —

"Live while you live," the epicure would say,
"And seize the pleasures of the present day."
"Live while you live," the sacred preacher cries,
"And give to God each moment as it flies."
Lord, in my life let both united be :
I live in pleasure while I live to Thee!

As a Christian lyrist, Doddridge deserves our grateful regard. One of the best of his hymns, as we have intimated, commences, —

Ye golden lamps of heaven, farewell, with all your feeble light;
Farewell, thou ever-changing moon, pale empress of the night!
And thou, refulgent orb of day, in brighter flames arrayed,
My soul, that springs beyond thy sphere, no more demands thy aid.
Ye stars are but the shining dust of my divine abode, —
The pavement of those heavenly courts, where I shall reign with
    God!

Doddridge seems to have *enjoyed* his religion, — to have made the most of it : his letters to his wife reveal

* Dr. J. Hamilton.

this. His faith was, it seems, equivalent to a realization. He has preserved to us this impressive record (Sept. 13, 1747): "I must record this day as one of the most blessed of my life. God was pleased to meet me in my secret retirement in the morning, and poured into my soul such a flood of consolation in the exercise of faith and love, as I was hardly able to contain. It would have been a relief to me to have been able even to have uttered strong cries of joy."

Nor is this an isolated instance. He seems to have enjoyed, in an eminent degree, that "peace of God which passeth all understanding." His waking hours were so frequently employed on devotional themes, that they were sometimes interwoven with the still hours of repose, and mingled with his dreams. His recent biographer * gives an illustration of this, as showing under what impressions he conposed a fine hymn, — following a remarkable dream which he had, after a conversation with the Rev. Dr. Clarke, on the state of the soul after death.

"He dreamed that he was dead, and that his spirit soared away into those deep regions of the infinite, which oftentimes awaken our trembling curiosity. He felt, as he lost sight of this noisy, busy world, how vain and empty are the objects which excite its inhabitants so much; and, while musing on the theme, and committing himself to the care of the Divine Pilot, as he embarked on the ocean of immensity, and sailed amidst islands of stars, he fancied he was met on the shores of heaven by an angel-guide, who conducted him to a palace which had been assigned for his abode. The dreamer wondered at the place, for it

* Harsha.

made him think that heaven was not so unlike earth as the teachings of Scripture had led him to expect; but he was told that there he was to be gradually prepared for unknown glories afterwards to be revealed. In the inner apartment of the palace stood a golden cup, with a grape-vine embossed on it, which he learned was meant to signify the living union of Christ and His people. But as he and his guide were talking, a gentle knock at the door, before him, announced the approach of some one, when, the portals unfolding, revealed the majestic presence of the Redeemer of the Church. The now glorified disciple immediately fell at the feet of his gracious Lord, but was raised with assurances of favor, and of the kind acceptance which had been vouchsafed to all his loving services. Then taking up the cup, and drinking out of it, the Saviour put it in His servant's hands, inviting him to drink, who shrunk from the amazing honor; but was told, 'If thou drink it not, thou hast no part with me.' He was ready to sink under the transport of gratitude and joy which was thus produced, when that condescending One, in consideration of his weakness, left him for a while, with the assurance that He would soon return; directing him, in the mean time, to look and meditate upon the objects that were around; and lo! there were pictures hung all about, illustrative of his own pilgrim-life; scene after scene of trial and deliverance, of conflict and victory, meeting his eyes, and filling his heart with love and wonder. And, as he gazed on them, he thought,—what we often fancy will be the saint's first thought in heaven,—how all the perils of his former life were now for ever over. Exulting in his new-found safety, a burst of joy broke the enchantment of his celestial dream; and he awoke again, amidst a flood of tears, to the consciousness that he was in the body still."

It was under the inspiration of this dream, that he wrote that beautiful hymn : —

> While on the verge of life I stand,
> And view the scene on either hand,
> My spirit struggles with its clay,
> And longs to wing its flight away.
>
> . . . . .
>
> Come, ye angelic convoys, come, —
> And lead the willing pilgrim home ;
> Ye know the way to that bright throne,
> Source of my joys, and of your own.
>
> . . . . .
>
> Oh, for a seraph's voice to sing!
> To fly, as on a cherub's wing!
> Performing, with unwearied hands,
> A present Saviour's high commands.
> Yet, with these prospects full in sight,
> I'll wait Thy signal for my flight:
> And in Thy service here below,
> Confess that heavenly joys may grow.

Nor had he to wait long for the full fruition of his desire.

Doddridge's prose is, we think, even better than his verse. Listen to his good counsel : "Let it be our great care to give up ourselves to the Redeemer, in the bonds of an everlasting covenant. While we are in this world, let it be our growing concern, by the assistance of His grace, to be more and more transformed into His image, and to subserve the purposes of His glory. Let us pass the days of our pilgrimage here, in frequent converse with Him, in continual devotedness to Him, and in the longing expectation of that happy hour, which will dismiss us from the labors and sorrows of this mortal state, and raise us to the fullest and brightest visions of that glory, which, even in this distant and imperfect prospect, is sufficient to eclipse all the splendors of life, and to disarm all the terrors of death!"

It is often said that genius is allied to madness, and we have something like a verification of the case in the two following instances. The first extract is said to have been composed by a person partially insane, at Cirencester, in 1779: —

> Could we with ink the ocean fill,
> Were the whole earth of parchment made,
> Were every single stick a quill,
> Were every man a scribe by trade;
> To write the love of God alone,
> Would drain the ocean dry;
> Nor would the scroll contain the whole,
> Though stretched from sky to sky.

The other example is that of Christopher Smart, who lived about the same time (1722-1771), and was constitutionally predisposed to the same malady. On one occasion, when confined in an insane asylum, during a lucid interval, he composed the following remarkable poem on David, consisting of nearly one hundred stanzas. Being deprived of pen and ink, it is said, he was obliged to indent his lines with a key upon the wainscot of his room.

> Sublime invention, ever young,
> Of vast conception, towering tongue,
> To God, the eternal theme;

Notes from your exaltation caught,
Unrivalled royalty of thought,
  O'er meaner thoughts supreme.

He sang of God, the mighty source
Of all things; that stupendous force
  On which all strength depends;
From whose right arm, beneath whose eyes,
All period, power, and enterprise
  Commences, reigns, and ends.

. . . .

The world, the clustering spheres, He made,
The glorious light, the soothing shade,
  Dale, champaign, grove, and hill;
The multitudinous abyss,
Where secrecy remains in bliss,
  And wisdom hides her skill.

"Tell them I AM," Jehovah said
To Moses; while earth heard in dread;
  And, smitten to the heart,
At once above, beneath, around,
All Nature, without voice or sound,
  Replied, "O Lord, Thou art!"

We meet, in our poetic rambles, with these sublime lines, addressed to the Deity, written by Boyse, who lived in the early part of the eighteenth century: —

Exalted Power, invisible, supreme!
Thou sovereign, sole, unutterable name!
As round Thy throne Thy flaming seraphs stand,
And touch the golden lyre with trembling hand;
Too weak Thy pure effulgence to behold, —
With their rich plumes their dazzled eyes infold;
Transported with the ardors of Thy praise,
The "Holy, holy, holy!" anthem raise.
To them responsive, let creation sing
Thee, — indivisible, eternal King!

Two of our most popular hymns, commencing "Sweet the moments, rich in blessing," and "Lord, dismiss us with thy blessing," were written by the Rev. Walter Shirley, of Galway, Ireland. The following is the only hymn known to have been written by Hervey, author of "Meditations among the Tombs:"—

> Since all the downward tracts of time
>   God's watchful eye surveys,
> Oh, who so wise to choose our lot
>   And regulate our ways?
>
> Since none can doubt His equal love,
>   Unmeasurably kind,
> To His unerring, gracious will
>   Be every wish resigned.
>
> Good when he gives, supremely good;
>   Nor less, when he denies;
> Even crosses, from His sovereign hand,
>   Are blessings in disguise.

Byron considered Gray's "Elegy" the corner-stone of his glory, and he is not alone in the estimate of this masterpiece of song. Let us rehearse some of the majestic stanzas:—

> Beneath those rugged elms, that yew-tree's shade,
>   Where heaves the turf in many a mouldering heap,
> Each in his narrow cell for ever laid,
>   The rude forefathers of the hamlet sleep.
>
> The breezy call of incense-breathing Morn,
>   The swallow twittering from the straw-built shed,
> The cock's shrill clarion, or the echoing horn,
>   No more shall rouse them from their lowly bed.
>
>     .    .    .    .    .    .
>
> The boast of Heraldry, the pomp of Power,
>   And all that Beauty, all that Wealth e'er gave,
> Await alike the inevitable hour:
>   The paths of glory lead but to the grave.

Nor you, ye proud, impute to these the fault,
  If Memory o'er their tomb no trophies raise,
Where, through the long-drawn aisle and fretted vault,
  The pealing anthem swells the note of praise.

Can storied urn, or animated bust,
  Back to its mansion call the fleeting breath?
Can Honor's voice provoke the silent dust,
  Or Flattery soothe the dull, cold ear of Death?

Perhaps in this neglected spot is laid
  Some heart once pregnant with celestial fire,—
Hands that the rod of empire might have swayed,
  Or waked to ecstasy the living lyre.

   .   .   .   .   .   .

Full many a gem of purest ray serene
  The dark, unfathomed caves of ocean bear:
Full many a flower is born to blush unseen,
  And waste its sweetness on the desert air.

What must the excellence of the finished poem be, from which the author deliberately rejected two such stanzas as these, after they had been once inserted!—

  Hark, how the sacred calm that breathes around,
    Bids every fierce, tumultuous passion cease,—
  In still, small accents breathing from the ground
    A grateful earnest of eternal peace.

And this, descriptive of the rustic tomb of the village scholar:—

  There scattered oft, the earliest of the year,
    By hands unseen, are showers of violets found:
  The red-breast loves to build and warble there,
    And little footsteps lightly print the ground.

Hazlitt considered the "Elegy" "one of the most classical productions ever penned by a refined and thoughtful mind, moralizing on human life." There are two manuscripts of it in existence : in 1854, they were sold at auction, — one, for one hundred pounds ; and the other, which contained five additional stanzas, never printed in the published editions, for one hundred and thirty pounds. The old tower of Upton Church (Gray's "ivy-mantled tower") is still a most picturesque object, although fast falling into decay. The memory of the bard is, however, even more closely associated with another locality, that of Stoke Pogis. It was here he wrote, wandered, and died; and here, too, all that was mortal of him sleeps, under "the yew-tree's shade." After recovering from the dazzling fascination of these beautiful stanzas, and on returning to the "Elegy," deliberately to scan its words, we find no intimations of a "life beyond life." This omission and defect, in one of the grandest odes of our English anthology, has tempted an American pen, with much success, to supply, —

> Though they, each tome of human lore unknown,
> The brilliant path of science never trod,
> The sacred volume claimed their hearts alone,
> Which taught the way to glory and to God.
>
> Here they from Truth's eternal fountain drew
> The pure and gladdening waters, day by day;
> Learnt. since our days were evil, fleet, and few,
> To walk in wisdom's bright and peaceful way.
>
> .     .     .     .     .     .
>
> When life flowed by, and, like an angel, Death
> Came to release them to the world on high,
> Praise trembled still on each expiring breath,
> And holy triumph beamed from every eye.
>
> Then gentle hands their "dust to dust" consign,
> With quiet tears the simple rites are said, —
> And here they sleep, till, at the trump divine,
> The earth and ocean render up their dead.

In good old times, when hymn-books were scarce, it was the custom in many of the dissenting churches for the clerk to read out a line or couplet of a hymn, so that those who were without books might unite in the singing. There is a story told of an officiating minister of a Methodist chapel in Georgia, years ago, who, having left his spectacles at home on one occasion, intended to announce to the congregation that the singing would be dispensed with: he arose, and said, —

> My eyes are dim, I cannot see;

and immediately the chorister commenced singing the words to the tune of "Old Hundred." Surprise and mortification made the clergyman almost speechless; but he made an effort to stammer out, —

> I meant but an apology.

This line was taken up by the congregation in the same manner; when the dominie, becoming much excited, exclaimed, —

> Forbear, I pray: my sight is dim.

But all remonstrance seemed to be vain: the singing went on; while, in accents of despair, he again cried out, —

> I do not mean to read a hymn;

a declaration so palpable, that at length it had the effect of restraining the ardor, and silencing the vociferous singers.

We Americans ought to be a musical, psalm-singing people; for the first press "put up" in Cambridge, in 1639, by Stephen Day, was devoted to the printing "The Psalms in Metre: faithfully translated for the use, edification, and comfort of the saints, in public and private, especially in New England." And a worthy act it was, on the part of the Pilgrim Fathers, that they accorded to that same Stephen Day the grant of "three hundred acres of land, where it may be convenient without prejudice to any town," as an acknowledgment of his good services in the department of psalmody.

Instances are upon record of discord having occurred between the pulpit and the choir; but perhaps the least said on this subject, the better. We might mention the case, however, of a strange clergyman, who had been invited to officiate in a New-England church, in the absence of the pastor. Not being familiar with some of the rules of the choir, he caused them so much offence, that they would not sing. After several efforts, the preacher determined not to be discomfited, and read the verse, —

"Let those refuse to sing who never knew our God;
But children of the heavenly King may speak their joys abroad."

This roused the entire congregation, who waited not for the choir to lead them.

Among our English hymnists, the Wesleys — Charles and John — shine as twin stars, and stars also of the first magnitude. John was educated at Oxford; and subsequently, impelled by missionary zeal, he went, in company with his brother Charles, in 1735, on a mission to Georgia, to preach to the settlers and Indians. But, though unsuccessful, this mission to America was attended with most important results to the Wesleys, through the spiritual benefits they derived from the Moravian Christians, who sailed with them in the same ship. On his return to England, in 1738, John Wesley formed, in conjunction with Whitefield and others, the first Methodist society, at the Moravian chapel, in Fetter Lane, London. From that period to the end of his long and laborious life, he was constantly engaged in going from place to place to preach the gospel. He met with much opposition, and sometimes personal violence; but this did not deter him from prosecuting his great work. John translated several hymns from the German; but his brother Charles composed the multitude\* of beautiful hymns that bear the name of Wesley. He at least equalled Watts, in the average excellence of his hymns: in these respects, he stands foremost among the priesthood of Christian minstrelsy.

Though the eighteenth century was rife with sceptics and doubters, it had also valiant defenders of Christianity. It had "its hearts of faith and tongues of fire." The age of Rousseau and Voltaire was also the age of Whitefield and Wesley,— two names not to be ignored; men who, although they have passed away, yet live in the loving memories of thousands, nay, hundreds of thousands, of persons. With the advent of Methodism came a new and deeper outburst of sacred song in the Church; and with it a pentecostal baptism of both its clerical and lay members. Most of the numerous hymns of the Wesleys are eminently lyrical; some, however, are fine poems.

To attempt an enumeration of their finest lyrical productions would be no easy task, where there are so many of varied excellence. The following are beyond

---

\* Charles Wesley published 4,100 hymns, and left upwards of 2,000 others in manuscript.

the pale of criticism, and need only time to render them classic: it will suffice to mention the first lines of some of the best.

> O Love Divine, how sweet Thou art!
>
> Jesus, Lover of my soul!
>
> The heavens declare Thy glory, Lord.
>
> Hark! the herald angels sing,
> Glory to the new-born King!

or, rather, as the author originally wrote it, —

> Hark! how all the welkin rings, —
> Glory to the King of kings!

All must feel the force and poetry of such lines as these: —

> On faith's strong eagle-pinions rise,
> And force your passage to the skies,
> And scale the mount of God.

---

I want a principle within of jealous, godly fear,
A sensibility of sin, a pain to feel it near;
I want the first approach to feel of pride or fond desire,
To catch the wandering of my will, and quench the kindling fire.
From Thee that I no more may part, no more Thy goodness grieve,
The filial awe, the fleshly heart, the tender conscience give.

The spot where Charles Wesley composed that fine hymn,

> Lo! on a narrow neck of land,
> 'Twixt two unbounded seas I stand

(so eminently suggestive of the grand thought), was the last projecting point of rock at Land's-End, Cornwall, stretching out between the Bristol and English Channel. It is really "a narrow neck of land," jutting out into the Atlantic. With scarcely a foot-room beneath you, you have on either side a precipice, with the sea raging and roaring at its base; and, whether you turn to the right hand or the left, your eye meets a vast expanse of ocean. Montgomery says of this hymn: "It is a sublime contemplation, — solemn, collected, unimpassioned thought, — but thought occupied with that which is of everlasting import to a dying man standing on the lapse of a moment between two eternities."

Southey thought Charles Wesley's hymn, "Stand the omnipotent decree," the finest lyric in the English language.

Were we to indicate two or three others of his most successful hymns, they would include the following: "Light of life, seraphic fire," "Shrinking from the cold hand of Death," and "Love Divine, all loves excelling."

When Wesley was preaching, on one occasion, in Kelso churchyard, Walter Scott was arrested by his appeals: he lingered and listened, and returned home to ponder the great subject of personal religion.

About twenty years ago, on a winter's night, a heavy gale set in upon the precipitous, rock-bound coast near the Bristol Channel. A little coasting vessel struggled bravely, but in vain, with the tempest. One dark, fearful headland could not be weathered, — the bark must go ashore. Then came the last desperate effort of the captain and his ship's crew. Their toiling at the oars was soon over, — their boat was swamped. They were supposed to have all sunk together: for, in the morning, they were found lying side by side upon a reedy rock. On visiting the wreck, and going below to the cabin, there was found lying on the table the captain's hymn-book, opened at the page containing that delightful hymn, —

> Jesus, Lover of my soul!
> Let me to Thy bosom fly, —
> While the nearer waters roll,
> While the tempest still is high.

It is stated that the great British statesman, Cobden, left the world with the lines of one of John Wesley's hymns upon his lip. It is one of his translations from the German, and reads thus: —

> Thee will I love, my Joy, my Crown!
> Thee will I love, my Lord, my God!
> Thee will I love, beneath Thy frown
> Or smile, Thy sceptre or Thy rod :
> What though my flesh and heart decay,
> Thee shall I love in endless day.

John Wesley wrote one hymn which is supposed to mark some phases of his personal experience. It commences, —

> How happy is the pilgrim's lot!
> How free from every anxious thought!
> From worldly hope and fear.

Referring to this hymn, Mr. Christophers relates a remarkable instance of the conversion of a singular character, who lived in the West of England, and to whom the words might fitly be applied. It seemed as if the hymn were made expressly for him, since there was scarcely a day, through his somewhat lengthened life, in which some stanza of it was not on his lips. "Foolish Dick" people called him; for in early life he was quite unequal to any kind of labor requiring mental exercise. But he proved to be susceptible of religious impressions, notwithstanding his seeming idiocy. Dick was one morning on his way to the well for water, when an aged Christian, who was leaning over the garden-gate, said, "So you are going to the well for water, Dick."—"Yes, sir."—"Well, Dick, the woman of Samaria found Jesus Christ at the well."—"Did she, sir?" That was enough: a quickening thought had struck into his half-awakened mind; and when he came to the well, he said to himself, yet loud enough to be heard by his Saviour, "Why should not I find Jesus Christ at the well? Oh that I could find Him! Will He come to me?" His prayer was heard; and Dick returned, not only bearing his full pitcher, but also that "well of water springing up into everlasting life."

John Wesley, the theologian, every year travelled many thousand miles; and even on horseback he was at his book, and at the stopping-places was ready with pen and voice. He wrote upon a great variety of subjects, but religion was indeed the predominating one. He was the father of the system of cheap books for the people. From the sale of his publications, he derived the chief means of his great charities. To his honor be it recorded, the amount ascertained to have been given away by him exceeded a hundred thousand dollars. Consistently enough might he preach that close and judicious sermon "Money," under the three heads: "gain all you can, save all you can, and give all you can." It is less difficult with many to adopt the first two heads, than the last. At the age of seventy even, he preached in the open air, to thirty thousand persons, so clear and strong was his voice. He must have been a picturesque old man, from the descriptions given of his *personnel*,— with his clear forehead, white hair, and piercing eye; even his dress was characteristic, — the perfection of neatness and simplicity. He is said to have been the originator of the phrase, "cleanliness is next to godliness." One book he always carried with him in his journeys, besides the Bible: it was his "Diary."

Would we learn what view of life this worthy minister of the gospel took? He tells us on his eighty-sixth birthday : "This day, I enter on my eighty-sixth year; and what cause have I to praise God, as for a thousand spiritual blessings, so for bodily blessings also. How little have I suffered yet by the rush of numerous years. . . . I am not conscious of any decay in writing sermons, which I do as readily, and, I believe, as correctly as ever. To what cause can I impute this, that I am as I am? First, doubtless, to the power of God, fitting me for the work to which I am called, as long as He pleases to continue me therein; and next, subordinately to this, the prayers of His children. May we not impute it as inferior means: first, to my constant exercise and change of air; second, to my never having lost a night's sleep, sick or well, at land or at sea, since I was born; third, to my having sleep at command, so that whenever I feel myself almost worn out, I call it, and it comes day or night; fourth, to my having constantly, for about sixty years, risen at four in the morning; fifth, to my constant preaching at five in the morning for above fifty years; sixth, to my having had so little pain in my life, and so little sorrow, or anxious care? Even now, though I find pain daily in my eye, or temple, or arm, yet it is never violent, and seldom lasts many minutes at a time. Whether or not this is sent to give me warning that I am shortly to quit this tabernacle, I do not know; but be it one way, or the other, I have only to say, —

> My remnant of days I spend to His praise,
> Who died the whole world to redeem;
> Be they many or few, my days are His due,
> And they all are devoted to Him!"

So it proved, three years afterwards: in 1791, at the age of eighty-eight, he breathed his last, with a hymn of praise on his lips. With the little strength remaining, he cried out to his friends watching his departure, "The best of all is, God is with us;" and could only whisper the first two words of a favorite psalm, "I'll praise, I'll praise," and Wesley's kindly voice was to be heard no more. At the time of his death, more than one hundred thousand persons looked to him as their guide to heaven; since then, that number has become a million.

Said Southey, half a century ago. "There may come a time when the name of Wesley will be more generally known, and in remoter regions of the globe, than that of Frederick, or of Catharine. For the works of such men survive them, and continue to operate, when nothing remains of worldly ambition but the memory of its vanity and its guilt." That prophecy has already been accomplished; and "the fragrance of that name grows richer with the lapse of time." Even the minor events and incidents of such a life as that of the greatest evangelist of modern times are replete with interest to us; and, as these have been garnered up by a loving pen,[*] we cull a few for our entertainment.

[*] Wakeley's Wesley.

Many of the clerical celebrities of the past age have furnished no little amusement by their eccentricities: but here is an instance of the comic, concerning a clerk of the Rev. Samuel Wesley, father of his more renowned sons. This clerk was susceptible of a weak point,—vanity: he believed his rector was the greatest man in the parish, if not in the country, and that he himself stood next to him in importance. He took a fancy of wearing Mr. Wesley's cast-off clothes and wigs; for the latter of which his head was far too small, and the figure he cut in it was ludicrously grotesque. One morning, before church-time, Mr. Wesley said, "John, I shall preach on a particular subject to-day, and shall choose my own psalm, of which I shall give out the first line, and you shall proceed as usual. John was pleased; and the service went forward, as usual, till they came to the singing, when Mr. W. gave out the following line:—

"Like to an owl in ivy bush,"—

This was sung, and the following line. John, peering out of the huge canonical wig in which his head was half lost, gave out, with an audible voice, and an appropriate connecting twang,—

"That rueful thing am I!"

The whole congregation saw and felt the force of the similitude, and their gravity was turned into irresistible laughter. This same Samuel Wesley is portrayed by his biographers as a most exemplary and noble Christian minister, and one of the most affectionate fathers that ever lived. He was a persevering man also; struggling with poverty, and bending under the weight of seventy years, he was endeavoring to bring out his elaborate work, written in Latin, on the book of Job, — a work which occupied his studious hours for a quarter of a century, — when his right hand was stricken with paralysis, and he could no longer hold a pen. In this emergency, his faith and courage did not desert him: he calmly says, "I have already lost one hand in the service, yet, I thank God, *non deficit altera;* * and I begin to put the other hand to school this day, to learn to write, in order to help its lame brother."

Not the father of the Wesleys only was noble, but the mother was no less excellent. She was, indeed, justly called "the Mother of Methodism;" for, during her husband's absence in London, attending convention, Mrs. Wesley held meetings in the parsonage, at which the family and servants attended; and daily the numbers increased, till the rooms were crowded to excess. These meetings were held, "because she thought the end of the institution of the Sabbath was not fully answered by attending church, unless the intermediate spaces of time were filled up by acts of devotion." Who can tell the influence those meetings of their mother in the parsonage had upon John and Charles in future years? This excellent woman, writing to her son John, says, "Would you judge of the lawfulness or unlawfulness of pleasure, of the innocence or malignity of actions? Take this rule: Whatever weakens your reason, impairs the tenderness of your conscience, obscures your sense of God, or takes off the relish of spiritual things; in short, whatever increases the strength and authority of your body over

* The other does not fail me.

your mind, that thing is sin to you, however innocent it may be in itself." Good counsel this for the present day.

John Wesley's life-story seems to have illustrated the beautiful lines of "Festus" Bailey : —

> "He most lives,
> Who thinks most, feels the noblest, acts the best;"

for assuredly few human lives were so richly endowed, and so prolific of good to others, as his. His aims and ideas were all on a grand scale; the world at large was his parish, as he himself once said; and his audiences were tenfold the extent of most other ministers of the Cross. As to his bodily presence, he was small; yet, as to his mental and spiritual power, he was gigantic. The words of a friend, "The Bible knows nothing of a solitary religion : you must find some companions, or make them," seemed to have had a controlling influence upon Wesley's whole after life; and thence upon the destiny of, maybe, millions of souls.

Mr. Wesley was, at first, a reader of sermons, and thought he could preach in no other way; but, fortunately for his great success, he was compelled by an accident to preach on one occasion extempore. "It is fifty years since I first preached in this church" (All-hallows Church, London), said Mr. W. : "I remember it, from a peculiar circumstance that occurred at that time. I came without a sermon; and, going up into the pulpit-stairs, I hesitated, and returned into the vestry, under much mental confusion and agitation. A woman that was there, noticing this, said, 'Pray, sir, what is the matter with you?' I replied, 'I have not brought a sermon with me.' Putting her hand upon my shoulder, she said, 'Is that all? Cannot you trust God for a sermon?' That question had such an effect upon me, that I ascended the pulpit and preached extempore, with great freedom to myself, and acceptance to the people; and I have never since taken a written sermon into the pulpit."

Wesley was earnestly opposed to "screaming" in the pulpit. "Speak with all your heart," he says in his letter to one of his associates, "but with a moderate voice. It was said of our Lord, 'He shall not cry,'— the word means *scream*. Herein be a follower of me, as I am of Christ." One secret of Mr. Wesley's wonderful power in preaching consisted in its adaptation, directness, simplicity, and earnestness; characteristics which also distinguish our modern Wesley,—Spurgeon. No wonder Mr. Wesley had fruit from the first sermon he preached on his father's tombstone. One of his hearers, on that occasion, was a gentleman who boasted that he had not been to church in thirty years. The churchyard scene—a man preaching in the midst of graves, and over the dust of his father —led him to attend and hear Mr. Wesley. When the sermon was ended, the gentleman stood as if he was transfixed, looking up to heaven. Mr. Wesley inquired of him, "Are you a sinner?" With a tearful eye, quivering lip, and faltering voice, he answered, "Sinner enough!" and he remained looking up till his friends thrust him into his carriage, and hurried him home. Ten years after, Mr. Wesley saw him, and was agreeably surprised to find him "strong in faith, though feeble in body, and giving glory to God." His first sermon, in the open fields, was preached at Kingswood, and from this singularly apposite text, — the rain descending in torrents, as he stood under a sycamore-tree, — "As the rain cometh down and the snow from heaven, and returneth not thither, but watereth the earth, and maketh it to bring forth and bud, that it may give seed to the sower and bread to the eater," &c.

Wesley was methodical, and therefore he accomplished more than most other men, opportunities being equal. His maxim was, "Always in haste, but never in a hurry." He said, "Leisure and I have taken leave of each other." "Make the most of a short life," was another of his wise saws. Wesley was a great lover of nature: he could find

> "Books in the running brooks,
> Sermons in stones, and good in every thing."

On one occasion, he, with some friends, was admiring the fine scenery near Chatham, when he exclaimed, "Why should we give the landscape all the praise, and the Author none?" and he sang, and the rest joined in singing, Watts's beautiful hymn, —

> Praise ye the Lord: 'tis good to raise
> Your hearts and voices in His praise:
> His nature and His works invite
> To make this duty our delight.

John Wesley considered that hymn of his brother, "Come, let us join our friends above," the sweetest he ever wrote. As the shadows of evening were gathering around him, he, on one occasion, ascended the pulpit at City-road Chapel, London, and, for some moments looking up to heaven, as if communing with the mighty dead, broke the solemn stillness by giving out the words of this same hymn. There was another great favorite with him, written also by his brother Charles, called "Wrestling Jacob:" "Come, O Thou Traveller unknown!"

Mr. Wesley was on a visiting tour, and, before preaching at a certain missionary station, he gave out the words, and as he proceeded his speech began to falter, and tears flowed down his cheeks: the entire audience was deeply affected, sorrowing most of all because they were persuaded that they should see his face no more. That hymn it was, which Watts, with great nobility of spirit, said was worth all the verses which he had ever written. What a fine couplet is this, also from his pen! —

> The cross, on which He bows His head,
> Shall lift us to the skies.

The distinguished Moravian, Peter Boehler, during his visit to England, was not only useful to John Wesley, but also to his brother Charles. When he was sick, in London, in 1737, he sent for his friend, who promptly obeyed the summons. On Wesley's recovery, and conversion to the doctrines of faith, his German friend rebuked his disinclination publicly to confess it, by saying, "If you had a thousand tongues, you should publish it with them all." It is said that the composition of his well-known hymn,

> Oh for a thousand tongues, to sing
> My great Redeemer's praise!

was written in commemoration of the anniversary of his spiritual birth.

Handel composed tunes expressly for several of Charles Wesley's hymns: for instance, he set to music those beginning, "Sinners, obey the gospel word,"

"O Love Divine, how sweet thou art!" and "Rejoice, the Lord is King."

The musical manuscripts, in Handel's own handwriting, are preserved in the Library of Cambridge University. Wesley thus refers to the great composer of "The Messiah," in his fine elegy on the death of Dr. Boyce, — as striking his golden harp with angels and archangels before the throne of God : —

> The generous, good, and upright heart,
>   That sighed for a celestial lyre,
> Was tuned on earth, to bear a part
>   Symphonious with that warbling choir
> Where Handel strikes the golden strings,
> And plaintive angels strike their wings.

Charles Wesley's last hymn was written the day that he lay silent for some time, "in age and extreme feebleness:" he called his wife, and requested her to write the following lines, as he dictated them : —

> In age and feebleness extreme,
> Who shall a helpless worm redeem?
> Jesus, my only hope Thou art,
> Strength of my failing flesh and heart:
> Oh, could I catch a smile from Thee,
> And drop into eternity!

Was there ever a better dying song?

Wilberforce may be classed among the friends of Wesley. They met for the first time at Hannah More's house, Clifton, near Bristol. "I went in 1786 to see Hannah More," says Wilberforce; "and, when I came into the room, Charles Wesley arose from the table, around which a numerous party sat at tea, and, coming forward, he gave me his solemn blessing. I was scarcely ever more affected. Such was the effect of his manner and appearance, that it altogether overset me; and I burst into tears, unable to restrain myself." *

One of the most interesting incidents illustrating the power of a hymn, that we have met with, is the following. The only daughter of an English nobleman, some years ago, although brought up in the lap of luxury and worldly splendor, was led by a series of circumstances to visit a Methodist Church in London, and shortly afterwards became a devoted Christian. She was the idol of her father; and it was with deep regret that he noticed the change that had taken place in her views and conduct. He placed at her disposal large sums of money, hoping to induce her to return to the gay life of dissipation and pleasure that her former associates indulged. After failing in all his projects to win her back to worldly vanities, he determined to introduce her into company, under circumstances that would compel her to join in the amusements of the party, or give high offence. It was arranged that, on a festive occasion, several young ladies should each accompany a performance on the piano-forte with a song. The hour arrived, the party assembled, several had performed their pieces; and all were waiting with eager expectation for our heroine. With wonderful serenity she took her seat at the instrument, ran her fingers over its keys, and commenced playing, singing, in a sweet air, the words of Charles Wesley,—

> No room for mirth or trifling here,
> For worldly hope, or worldly fear,
>  If life so soon is gone;

\* Life of Wilberforce.

> If now the Judge is at the door,
> And all mankind must stand before
>   The inexorable Throne.
>
> No matter which my thoughts employ,
> A moment's misery or joy:
>   But, oh, when both shall end,
> Where shall I find my destined place?
> Shall I my everlasting days
>   With fiends or angels spend?

She rose from her seat: the whole party were subdued; not a word was spoken. Her father wept aloud. One by one the visitors left the house. Soon afterwards, both father and daughter rejoiced together with a new joy. During his union with the Church, he is said to have contributed to benevolent enterprises a sum equal to over half a million of dollars.

More than half a century ago, when itinerant Methodist ministers fared roughly, there occurred in Louisiana a little incident worth noting, to show the good effect a hymn may sometimes produce. A travelling minister was one evening reduced to the very verge of starvation; he had spent the preceding night in a swamp, and had taken no food for thirty-six hours, when he reached a plantation. He entered the house, and asked for food and lodging. The mistress of the house, a widow, with several daughters and negroes, refused him. He stood warming himself by the fire a few minutes, and began singing a hymn, commencing, —

> Peace, my soul, thou needst not fear:
> The great Provider still is near.

He sang the whole hymn; and, when he looked round, they were all in tears. He was forthwith invited to stay a week with them.

William Williams (1717-1791), at the age of twenty-three, was ordained deacon, and began his ministry at Llanwrtyd, and afterward he became an itinerant Methodist minister, in which capacity he labored for half a century. For the variety and uniform excellence of his hymns, he has been styled the "Watts" of Wales. These are his: —

> O'er the gloomy hills of darkness
> Guide me, O Thou great Jehovah!

The former is especially interesting, as being a noble missionary hymn, composed before the founding of the modern missionary societies.

John Cennick, whose life has been briefly sketched by Matthew Wilks, was connected with the Moravians, in London; and he twice visited their community in Germany. To Cennick we are indebted for two of the finest hymns ever written, — "Rise, my soul, and stretch thy wings," and "Lo! He comes, with clouds descending." The last-named first appeared in a "Collection of Sacred Hymns," 1752. This hymn is undoubtedly suggested by the "Dies Iræ." In some church collections, this hymn is attributed to Thomas Olivers.

Beddome's Collection of Hymns — originally written for the use of the Baptist Church at Bourton, in Gloucestershire — comprises some which have become universal favorites. Among the number might be instanced the following: "Did Christ o'er sinners weep?" "Faith, 'tis a precious grace," "Let party names no more," and "Witness, ye men and angels now."

Robert Hall says, in his "Introduction" to these

Hymns, "The man of taste will be gratified with the beautiful and original thoughts which many of them exhibit; while the experimental Christian will often perceive the most sweet movements of his soul strikingly delineated, and sentiments portrayed which will find their echo in every heart." The esteemed author devoted the whole of his useful life to the church at Bourton, — a pastoral service of more than half a century. He was born in 1717, and died 1795.

Samuel Davies, who lived from 1724 until 1761, was an American by birth. He was licensed to preach, in 1745, by the Presbytery of Newcastle, Del. Afterwards, he was appointed by the trustees of the College of New Jersey to visit England; subsequently, he succeeded Jonathan Edwards as president of Princeton College. He wrote a hymn, admirable for its simplicity, force, and comprehensiveness, — "Great God of wonders! all Thy ways."

Thomas Haweis, chaplain to the Countess of Huntingdon (1734–1820), was one of the founders of the London Missionary Society, and author of several important theological works : he wrote also some favorite hymns, as "O Thou from whom all goodness flows," "Enthroned on high, Almighty Lord."

Haweis wrote above two hundred and fifty hymns; and in his preface to the collection he complains that, in his day, "the voice of joy and gladness is too commonly silent, unless in that shameful mode of psalmody, now almost confined to the wretched solo of a parish clerk, or to a few persons huddled together in one corner of the church, who sing to the praise and glory of themselves, for the entertainment, or oftener for the weariness, of the rest of the congregation, — an absurdity too glaring to be overlooked, and too shocking to be ridiculous."

Thomas Olivers (1725-1799) was of humble origin, but ultimately became known and honored as "a sweet singer in Israel." He was deprived of both his parents when he was but four years old, and was placed under the protection of a distant relative. At eighteen, he was apprenticed to a shoemaker; but, owing to his bad conduct, he was compelled to leave the neighborhood. At Bristol, where he had gone to carry on his trade, he heard Whitefield preach, and became a Christian. Subsequently, he met with Mr. Wesley, and joined the corps of itinerant Methodist preachers in Cornwall. In his various journeys on horseback, during twenty-five years, he travelled about one hundred thousand miles; often meeting with opposition and violence in his good work.

"During a conference, in Wesley's time, Thomas Olivers, one of the preachers, came down to him, and, unfolding a manuscript, said, 'Look at this: I have rendered it from the Hebrew, giving it, as far as I could, a Christian character; and I have called on Leoni, the Jew, who has given me a synagogue melody to suit it. Here is the tune, and it is to be called "Leoni." I read the composition, and it was that well-known, grand imitation of ancient Israel's hymns:—

> 'The God of Abraham praise,
>   Who reigns enthroned above;
>   Ancient of everlasting days,
>   And God of love.'"

The entire hymn consists of twelve stanzas; and Montgomery says of it, "There is not in our language a lyric of more majestic style, more elevated thought, or more glorious imagery: its structure, indeed, is unattractive; but, like a stately pile of architecture, severe and simple in design, it strikes less on the first view than after deliberate examination, when its proportions become more graceful, its dimensions expand, and the mind itself grows greater in contemplating it." This fine hymn is said to have had great influence upon the mind of Henry Martyn, when contemplating his important missionary career. Olivers lived to a good old age: in his earlier years, he preached, but his latter were devoted to authorship. It is remarkable, that, although Olivers and his associate, Wesley, were in sweetest harmony with their contemporary, Toplady, in their hymnic utterances, yet in their theology they were bitter opponents. Their poetry, who would let die; their polemics, who would care to retain? It is pleasant, however, to add that they were personal friends.

# EIGHTH EVENING.

## LATER ENGLISH.

(*Continued.*)

# EIGHTH EVENING.

## LATER ENGLISH.

*(Continued.)*

IN the storied and picturesque city of Oxford, might have been seen, about a century and a half since, a young man paying his way, as servitor, at Pembroke College. He shunned his classmates, because they were inclined to "riotous living." He had heard of the young men there, "who lived by rule and method," called Methodists; and, for more than a year, he yearned to be acquainted with them; but a sense of his inferior condition kept him back. At length the great object of his desires was effected. A pauper had attempted suicide; and a person was sent to inform Charles Wesley, that he might visit him, and administer spiritual medicine. The messenger was charged not to say who sent her: but, contrary to these orders, she told his name; and Charles Wesley, who had seen him frequently walking by himself, and heard something of his character, invited him to breakfast the next morning. An introduction to this little fellowship soon followed; and he also, like them, "began to live by rule, and pick up the very fragments of his time, that not a moment of it might be lost."

This young man was George Whitefield; and thus has the graphic pen of Wesley's biographer described his first introduction to that little society, whose members afterwards stamped their influence so broadly on that and subsequent times.

After leaving Oxford, and taking deacon's orders, he began to preach at Bristol, and to exhibit "that impassioned eloquence which moved and melted both the Old World and the New." Above the average in stature, of a graceful deportment, a musical voice, to these natural endowments he added the conviction of the grandeur of his solemn vocation as a messenger of God to men. His maxim was to preach, as Apelles painted, for eternity! Whitefield differed from his associate Wesley, as to some minor doctrinal points; but they loved each other with true brotherly affection, for their souls glowed with the warm charities of the gospel. After he returned from his third visit to America, he was, in 1749, appointed chaplain to Lady Huntingdon, whose mansion in Park Street, London, was opened for Whitefield's ministry. Lords Chesterfield, Bolingbroke, the Marquis of Lothian, and others of the nobility, attended his preaching,—some to profit, and some to reject and scorn.

The spiritual crusade of Whitefield, Wesley, Watts, Doddridge, and others associated with the Countess of Huntington, formed an important era in the history of Christianity in Great Britain. The earnest preaching, the electric appeals, of these Home-missionaries of the Cross, kindled anew the dying faith of the churches, and made converts of multitudes who had been hitherto either indifferent or hostile to its claims. Lady Huntingdon's wealth and position naturally gave to her a controlling influence; for her fortune of one hundred thousand pounds was, like her life-service, devoted to the good cause. Among her ladyship's intimate friends was a personage small of stature, modest in bearing, but fluent in thought and speech: he was troubled with a feeble body, and was a great lover of solitude, — to such an extent, indeed, that he never married. He has taught us all to sing, from the nursery ditties of our infant days, to the aspirations of Christian manhood, and to the full maturity of age. Need we introduce this remarkable personage by name? Is it not the venerable pastor of the church at Stoke Newington, — Dr. Watts? He was born in the stormiest days of nonconformity; and we find him nursed in the arms of his sorrowing mother, on a stone by the prison-walls which confine his father, a "godly man and a deacon," suffering persecution for conscience' sake.

But we have already held with him our quiet colloquy. Closely associated with the names of Wesley and Whitefield is that of Lady Huntingdon, at whose house the first Methodist Conference was held, in June, 1744. The celebrated Romaine, when expelled from St. George's, Hanover Square, was invited by the countess to preach at her house. On the death of the earl, in 1746, she had the entire command of her fortune, which she devoted very liberally to religious purposes. She died at her house in Moorfields, adjoining the chapel, in 1791, at the ripe age of eighty-four years. At the time of her death, there were more than sixty chapels in her "connection." We possess several fine hymns from her pen, including the following: "Oh, when my righteous Judge shall come!" "We soon shall hear the midnight cry," "Come, Thou Fount of every blessing."

A quaint mixture of wit, sense, and bluntness, with real piety, was John Berridge, whose life, although a bachelor, it were a misnomer to call lonely; "for it was as stirring as a hundred miles' riding, with ten or twelve sermons a week, could make it, and that for a period of nearly five-and-twenty years. At home, his table was ever ready for his hearers, many of whom came from a distance; his stables open to their horses; while houses and barns, in every direction, were rented and taken care of for the lay-preachers employed at his expense. The richness and originality of his mind made him an especial favorite; while his sturdy sticking to his own notions of duty never gave offence to those who understood the depth and singleness of his piety."*

As a specimen of his earnest style, read the following extract from his letter of condolence to Lady Huntingdon, on the death of her daughter: —

> She has gone to pay a most blessed visit, and you will see her again, never to part more. Had she crossed the sea, you could have borne it; but now she has gone to heaven, it is almost intolerable. Wonderful, strange love is this! . . . I cannot soothe you, and I must not flatter you. I am glad the dear creature has gone to heaven before you. Lament, if you please; but glory, glory, glory be to God, says
> 
>                                         JOHN BERRIDGE.

Daniel Turner (1710-1798), a Baptist minister at Abington, England, wrote some notable hymns; among them, that sometimes attributed to Grigg, "Beyond the glittering starry skies." As we have already intimated, Watts and Doddridge often used

* Knight's Huntingdon, &c.

to write hymns as a sequel to their sermons. This curious custom has long since ceased, however. Other clerical eccentricities lingered later, with Swift, Sydney Smith, and Roland Hill; but these are now becoming forgotten.

There is a story told of a certain eccentric clergyman of Cambridge, England, years ago, who, when challenged to preach against intemperance, is said to have improvised the following short sermon, under a wayside tree, on the word "Malt." He commenced by stating that he had chosen a short text, which could not be divided into sentences, there being none; nor into words, there being but one. He therefore divided it into letters; thus, M is moral, A is allegorical, L is literal, and T is theological. His exposition ran as follows: the moral is to teach you good manners; therefore, M, my masters, A, all of you, L, leave off, T, tippling. The allegorical is when one thing is spoken of, and another meant. The thing spoken of is malt, which you make. M, your meat, A, your apparel, L, your liberty, and T, your Trust. The literal is, according to the letters, M, much, A, ale, L, little, T, trust. The theological is, according to the effects it works in some, M, murder; in others, A, adultery; in all, L, looseness of life; and, in many, T, treachery. Rather a roundabout way of proving that "gin is a snare," as well as all spirituous drinks. But temperance is one of the Christian virtues. It is a remarkable fact that the burden of Biblical instruction is against the use of stimulating drinks. Although St. Paul's advice to take a little wine medicinally is often urged, few are aware how many instances are on record in which wine and all strong drinks are prohibited in the Bible.

When the Children of Israel were travel-worn and thirsty, Moses smote the rock Horeb; and water, not wine, rolled in living streams at their feet. When the drunken king spread rich viands and wine before Daniel, he refused to drink any thing save water. When Hagar and her child were perishing with thirst, an angel directed them to a well of water in the wilderness. When the Gideonites were chosen to go out and meet the hosts of Midian, three hundred cold-water drinkers were the men picked for that special service. Samson, a man of great physical strength, and John the Baptist, the mightiest born of woman, were each commanded to drink neither wine nor strong drink. Now turn we from libations to long sermons.

Dr. Isaac Barrow once preached so long, that all his congregation dropped off, leaving the sexton and himself alone. The sexton, finding the doctor apparently no nearer a conclusion, is reported to have said to him: "Sir, here are the keys; please to lock up the church, when you get through your discourse!" Long sermons are the bane of the pulpit's power; but then, sometimes, under short sermons, some people will become drowsy.

Even Whitefield found it sometimes necessary to rouse nodding heads and half-shut eyes with the cry of "Fire, fire!" and when his alarmed people cried out, "Where, sir? where?" he would earnestly and solemnly reply: "In hell, for those who sleep under the preaching of the Word." Swift, taking the misfortune of Eutychus for his argument, began a sermon with: "I have chosen these words with design, if possible, to disturb some part in this audience of half an hour's sleep, for the convenience and exercise thereof, this place at this season of the day is very much celebrated." Then he goes on, in allusion to Eutychus sleeping in the window: "The preachers now in the world, however they may exceed St. Paul in the art of setting men to sleep, do extremely fall short of him in the power of working miracles; therefore, hearers are become more cautious, so as to choose more safe and convenient stations and postures for their repose, without hazard of their persons, and upon the whole matter choose rather to trust their destruction to a miracle than their safety."

The Rev. James Bonnar, of Auchtermuchty, of the Relief Kirk, hit upon a very pleasant means of rousing a drowsy congregation. "It was a very warm day, the church closely packed; the occasion, the Monday following communion. He observed, with some annoyance, many of the congregation nodding and sleeping in their pews whilst he was preaching. He took his measures accordingly, and introduced the word 'hyperbolical' into his sermon; but he paused, and said: 'Now, my friends, some of you may not understand this word "hyperbolical:" I'll explain it. Suppose that I were to say that this congregation were *all* asleep in this church at the present time, I would be speaking hyperbolically; because' (looking round) 'I don't believe much more than one-half of you are sleeping.' The effect was instantaneous; and those who were nodding recovered themselves, and nudged their sleeping neighbors, and the preacher went on as if nothing had happened."

In Crabbe's time, it seems people sometimes slept in church; for he describes the effects of the vehemence of a certain preacher thus: —

> He such sad coil with words of vengeance kept,
> That our best sleepers startled as they slept;

Doubtless, the reader has noticed the name of Steele in our hymnology: we have a few things to mention respecting it. Anne Steele was the daughter of a Baptist minister, who, in 1757, had the pastoral charge of a congregation, meeting in the village of Broughton, in Hampshire, on the spot where their fathers had worshipped from the time of the Commonwealth.* The good pastor writes in his diary: "1757, Nov. 29. This day, Nanny sent a part of her composition to London, to be printed. I entreat a gracious God, who enabled and stirred her up to such a work, to direct in it, and bless it for the good and comfort of many. . . . I pray God to make it useful, and keep her humble." A quaint and beautiful expression of a Christian parent's grateful solicitude and joy. The benediction invoked upon the collection of her spiritual songs seems to have been bountifully bestowed. Who can doubt this, on reading that noble hymn? —

> Jesus, my Lord, in Thy dear name unite
>   All things my heart calls great or good or sweet;
>   Divinest springs of wonder and delight,
> In Thee, Thou fairest of ten thousand, meet.

Here is another of her sweet hymns: —

> Father, whate'er of earthly bliss Thy sovereign will denies,
> Accepted at Thy throne of grace, let this petition rise:
> Give me a calm, a thankful heart, from every murmur free;
> The blessings of Thy grace impart, and make me live to Thee;
> Let the sweet hope that I am Thine, my life and death attend;
> Thy presence through my journey shine, and crown my journey's end.

---

* There is an incident on record, relating to the predecessor of Mr. Steele, his uncle, who was so popular a preacher, that the parson of the parish reported, at the episcopal visitation, that his parochial province was sadly invaded by the dissenter. "How can I best oppose him?" was his query to Bishop Burnett. "Go home," said the wise diocesan, "and preach better than Henry Steele, and the people will return."

These are the soft, plaintive utterances of one sorely tried in this earthly life; whose songs, from out the "furnace of affliction,"

> "Rose like an exhalation, with the sound
> Of dulcet symphonies and voices sweet."

More than a century ago, a young man was impressed into the British navy. His mind had already been poisoned by sceptical reading; and the influences which met him on board a man-o'-war were not adapted to counteract those false views. After a series of sins and sufferings, we find him on the coast of Africa, in the employment of a slave-dealer, reduced to wants which made him a literal representative of the prodigal son. He was a very outcast, ready to perish. Unexpectedly rescued from this degradation, it was only to encounter the imminent danger of shipwreck. During the terrors of the storm, he had nearly gone overboard, when a friendly hand rescued him; and shortly afterwards finding, in the ship's cabin, a copy of "Thomas à Kempis," his conscience became awakened, and, like the prodigal, "he arose and came to his Father." This was John Newton. The name of John Newton, as associated with that of Cowper, the poet, suggests to us their joint production, entitled "Olney Hymns." Cowper's portion consisted of sixty-two, and Newton's two hundred and eighty-six hymns. The "Olney Collection" was published in 1779, before Cowper was known as a poet. Living at Mrs. Unwin's house, which was close to the vicarage, Cowper exchanged visits almost daily with Newton; and it was during this time, 1767–1779, that the Olney hymns were prepared. It was not long, however, after Cowper had commenced his labors, before he was visited with a second attack of insanity, which compelled him to desist from his work. His translations from the mystic poems of Madame Guyon were done at the request of his friend, Rev. Mr. Bull, who succeeded Mr. Newton on his departure for London, his native place. This eminent servant of God (to quote from the epitaph he wrote for himself) was "once an infidel and libertine, a servant of slaves in Africa." He was an only child, and had the misfortune to lose his mother in his seventh year; a circumstance that at once became a bond of sympathy between these remarkable men. Newton's mother trained up her son carefully, "having it in her heart" that he would be one day engaged in the Christian ministry, — a work to which she had devoted him. Young Newton's father and stepmother did not carry on this good work, but he was "much left to himself, to mingle with idle and wicked boys, and soon learned their ways."

After some years of seafaring life, and many rough adventures, he was shipwrecked in a terrible storm, as already intimated. "The ship outrode the storm, and the awakened sinner was saved to serve God in the world." In the year 1764, when in his thirty-ninth year, he entered upon a regular ministry, having been, by the Earl of Dartmouth, presented to the vicarage of Olney. His prose writings are much esteemed for their experimental and evangelical piety; and his "Narrative" is especially interesting, as a minute "record of a series of most remarkable special providences by which his life was spared, just when it seemed about to be taken, and by which his course was diverted into the path of safety, just when its persistency in the downward way seemed inevitable. At the venerable age of eighty-two, Newton "laid down his life and labor together, and fell asleep in Jesus." It is scarcely requisite to indicate even the best of his numerous lyrics. The most popular of his hymns include the following: "How sweet the name of Jesus sounds," "Day of judgment, day of wonders."

One of the most admirable of Newton's hymns is that on the name of Jesus: some of its stanzas, especially the fifth, possess the terseness and vigor of the old Latin hymns.

> Jesus! my Shepherd, Husband, Friend,
>   My Prophet, Priest, and King,
> My Lord, my Life, my Way, my End,
>   Accept the praise I bring.
>
> Weak is the effort of my heart,
>   And cold my warmest thought;
> But when I see Thee as Thou art,
>   I'll praise Thee as I ought.
>
> Till then I would Thy love proclaim
>   With every fleeting breath;
> And may the music of Thy name
>   Refresh my soul in death.

There was a stricken deer, who had long been panting for the water-brooks, but he had yet found no comfort; till one day, listlessly taking up the New Testament, he opened it at the words, "Whom God hath set forth to be a propitiation, through faith in His blood," &c.; and peace flowed into his soul like a river. That "stricken deer," need we add, was William Cowper.

Undoubtedly, the most beautiful of Cowper's minor poems is that on his Mother's Picture. It was Cowper's misfortune to lose his mother before he was six years of age. A picture of her was sent to him when he was nearly sixty. At the sight of it, there started up images and recollections and feelings, which had slept for more than half a century. Time and forgetfulness were baffled by a sister-art; and the work was completed by Poetry, in as touching lines as ever recorded the movements of a poet's memory into the shadowy regions of childhood.

> Oh, that those lips had language! Life has passed
> With me but roughly since I heard thee last.
> Those lips are thine: thy own sweet smile I see, —
> The same that oft in childhood solaced me.

Cowper's deep affection for his mother lasted with him through life. On receipt of her likeness, he wrote to Lady Hesketh, "I had rather possess my mother's picture than the richest jewel in the British crown; for I loved her with an affection that her death, fifty years since, has not in the least abated."

Poor, melancholy Cowper was not of choice a bachelor: his projected union with his cousin was interdicted by the father of his choice, Theodora Jane, second daughter of Ashley Cowper. As the attachment was mutual, they each suffered deeply this disappointment of their wishes. It is supposed to have aggravated his disease.

Well has it been said, that, "when bodily darkness fell on the footsteps of Milton, he imagined it the overshadowing of heavenly wings; and we might ascribe to a like cause the spiritual darkness of poor Cowper's days." The gloomy thought that had taken possession of him was never relinquished; but often it seemed to fade away into the unreal wretchedness of a distressing dream. There is great interest, too, in tracing how his imagination extracted melody from his madness, — the evil spirit that troubled him charmed to rest by the harpings of his Muse. It did not please Heaven to unweave the tangled meshes of poor Cowper's brain. The dark delusion of despair hung over his mind to the very verge of his long life of just threescore years and ten."* His last original piece, "The Castaway," is, indeed, under all the circumstances, one of the most affecting ever composed. He had been reading, in "Anson's Voyages," an account of a man lost overboard in a gale. That appalling casualty, which often consigns the sailor to a helpless fate, is told in vivid stanzas, closing with the saddest possible moralizing: —

> No poet wept him; but the page of narrative sincere,
> That tells his name, his worth, his age, is wet with Anson's tear;
>     And tears, by bards or heroes shed,
>     Alike immortalize the dead.
> I therefore purpose not, or dream descanting on his fate,
> To give the melancholy theme a more enduring date;
>     But misery still delights to trace
>     Its semblance in another's case.
> No voice Divine the storm allayed, no light propitious shone,
> When, snatched from all effectual aid, we perished each alone;
>     But I beneath a rougher sea,
>     And whelmed in deeper gulfs than he!

Very many of Cowper's hymns, like passages in his longer poems, have become "household words." Some of his most remarkable hymns have a history. For example: Cowper "thought it was the Divine will" that he should go to a particular part of the river Ouse, and drown himself; but the driver of the vehicle, missing his way, diverted him from his

---

* Henry Reed.

purpose; and thereupon were composed those memorable lines, "God moves in a mysterious way,"—composed, as Montgomery remarks, "under circumstances of awful interest,—in the twilight of departing reason." It was the last hymn he compiled for the "Olney Collection." Among the hymns that will ever live are those pathetic utterances of his so expressive of the conflicts of Christian life; as, "Oh for a closer walk with God!" and "O Lord, my best desires fulfil!" The much-admired hymn, "To Jesus, the crown of my hope," was, it is believed, the last hymn Cowper wrote.

It adds no little to the interest with which we recite some of Cowper's plaintive melodies, when we remember the circumstances that gave them birth. One of his thanksgiving hymns—"How blest Thy creature is, O God!"—was written, we are informed by his biographer, immediately upon his recovery from his second attack of mental derangement; and the second strain, in which he poured forth the grateful feelings of his heart, was that beginning, "Far from the world, O Lord! I flee."

Cowper—the great Christian poet of England, and, as Willmott justly remarks, pre-eminently the poet of the affections, above any writer in our language—has enriched sacred literature by so many exquisite bursts of poetic inspiration, that it is no easy task to determine which are the best. We must be allowed simply to follow our vagrant fancy in the selection, hoping it will please:—

>    The path of sorrow, and that path alone,
>    Leads to the land where sorrow is unknown!
>    No traveller e'er reached that blest abode,
>    Who found not thorns and briers in his road.

Worldlings may dance along the flowery plain,
Cheered, as they go, by many a sprightly strain;
Where nature has her mossy velvet spread,
With unshod feet, they yet securely tread;
Admonished, scorn the caution and the friend,
Bent on all pleasure, heedless of its end.
But He, who knew what human hearts would prove,
How slow to learn the dictates of His love,
That, hard by nature, and of stubborn will,
A life of ease would make them harder still,
In pity to the souls His grace designed
To rescue from the ruins of mankind,
Called for a cloud to darken all their years,
And said, "Go spend them in the vale of tears."

---

The Soul, reposing on assured belief,
Feels herself happy amidst all her grief;
Forgets her labors, as she toils along,
Weeps tears of joys, and bursts into a song.

Beattie (1735–1803), although of humble origin, yet, by his industry and the sterling Christian elements of his character, attained to the professorship of moral philosophy in Marischal College, Aberdeen, when only in his twenty-sixth year. He is best known by his "Minstrel," a poem of great gracefulness of imagery and beauty of diction. After a life of Christian usefulness, the poet and philosopher died, it is said, broken-hearted, under the severe pressure of domestic afflictions. Here are three fine stanzas from his "Hermit." Alluding to the return of spring after the desolations of winter, the poet thus points us to the light of Immortality:—

'Tis night, and the landscape is lovely no more;
I mourn, but, ye woodlands, I mourn not for you;
For morn is approaching, your charms to restore,
Perfumed with fresh fragrance and glittering with dew.

Nor yet for the ravage of winter I mourn;
Kind nature the embryo blossom will save,
But when shall spring visit the mouldering urn!
Oh, when shall it dawn on the night of the grave!

'Twas thus, by the glare of false science betrayed, —
That leads, to bewilder; and dazzles, to blind, —
My thoughts wont to roam, from shade onward to shade,
Destruction before me, and sorrow behind.
"Oh, pity, great Father of Light!" then I cried,
"Thy creature, who fain would not wander from Thee;
Lo, humbled in dust, I relinquish my pride:
From doubt and from darkness Thou only canst free."

And darkness and doubt are now flying away,
No longer I roam in conjecture forlorn,
So breaks on the traveller, faint, and astray,
The bright and the balmy effulgence of morn.
See Truth, Love, and Mercy in triumph descending,
And nature all glowing in Eden's first bloom!
On the cold cheek of Death smiles and roses are blending,
And beauty immortal awakes from the tomb.

Here is one fine descriptive stanza from his "Minstrel:" —

But who the melodies of morn can tell?
The wild brook babbling down the mountain-side;
The lowing herd; the sheepfold's simple bell;
The pipe of early shepherd dim descried
In the lone valley; echoing far and wide
The clamorous horn along the cliffs above;
The hollow murmur of the ocean-tide;
The hum of bees; the linnet's lay of love;
And the full choir that wakes the universal grove.

His description of a morning landscape is much admired; especially this famous stanza, which was Dr. Chalmers's great favorite:—

Oh, how canst thou renounce the boundless store
    Of charms, which Nature to her votary yields!
The warbling woodland, the resounding shore,
    The pomp of groves, the garniture of fields;

> All that the genial ray of morning gilds,
> And all that echoes to the song of even, —
>   All that the mountain's sheltering bosom shields,
> And all the dread magnificence of heaven, —
> Oh, how canst thou renounce, and hope to be forgiven?

That soul-stirring lyric, by Robinson, of Cambridge, England, —

> Come, Thou Fount of every blessing,
> Tune my heart to sing Thy grace, —

has a sad history. Its author — of whom Robert Hall remarked, that he "could say *what* he pleased, *when* he pleased, and *how* he pleased" — was possessed of versatile and popular talents; but he became the victim of a love of change and eccentricity. By turns, he was Calvinistic, Methodist, Independent, Baptist, and Socinian.

In our church-books may be found some hymns by Blacklock, a minister of the Church of Scotland, who lived during the latter part of the eighteenth century. He lost his sight in early life; but such was his facility in composition, that he is said to have dictated his sermons and hymns as fast as they could be written. One of his hymns commences, "Come, O my soul! in sacred lays." The familiar hymn beginning, "O Thou, my soul! forget no more," acquires especial interest from the fact that it is a translation of the Christian hymn written by a Hindoo, — Khrishna Pal, at Serampore.

Thomas Green, of Ware, one of our hymn-writers, composed, in 1774, when only ten years of age, the hymn commencing, "Jesus, and can it ever be?" As a marvel of precocious talent, it takes its place along with Milton's psalm ("Let us with a gladsome mind," &c.) written at the age of fifteen.

Amid the rich slopes and hills of Devonshire, in a sequestered hamlet, stands the quiet parish-church of Broad Hembury; within whose walls, on the Sabbath-days of a century ago, might have been seen the vicar officiating at the altar of worship, — fervently leading his rustic audience in the service of homily, praise, and prayer. The preacher was Augustus Toplady, who is described as having an "ethereal countenance, and light, immortal form. His voice was music. His vivacity would have caught the listener's eye; and his soul-filled looks and movements would have interpreted his language, had there not been such commanding solemnity in his tones as made apathy impossible, and such simplicity in his words that to hear was to understand. From easy explanations, he advanced to rapid and conclusive arguments, and warmed into importunate exhortations, till conscience began to burn, and feelings to take fire from his own kindled spirit; and himself and his hearers were together drowned in sympathetic tears." He entered upon his pastoral duties in 1768, and it was in the rural retreat of Broad Hembury that most of his soul-stirring hymns were composed.

Toplady, when a lad of sixteen, and on a visit to Ireland, had strolled into a barn, where an illiterate layman was preaching, — but preaching reconciliation to God through the death of His Son. The homely sermon took effect; and, from that hour, the gospel wielded all the powers of his brilliant and active mind. Toplady became very learned; and at the early age of thirty-eight years he died, — more widely read in Fathers and Reformers than most academic dignitaries can boast when their heads are hoary. His splendid and expressive hymns, a rich embodiment of religious experience, are his imperishable memorial. During his last illness, he seemed to be in the very vestibule of glory. To a friend's inquiry, he replied, with sparkling eye. "I cannot tell the comforts I feel in my soul: they are past expression. The consolations of God are so abundant, that he leaves me nothing to pray for: my prayers are all converted into praise. I enjoy a heaven already in my soul."

This eminent Christian poet and minister has left us, not only many sweet songs of Zion, but a beautiful moral lesson by his example, — both in his life and his death. When near his departure from earthly scenes, on being told that his pulse was becoming weaker and weaker, he replied: "Why, that is a good sign that my death is fast approaching; and, blessed be God, I can add, that my heart beats, every day, stronger and stronger for glory." And, after many other beautiful Christian words, when close to his end, bursting into tears of joy, as he said, "It will not be long before God takes me; for no mortal man can live after the glories which God has manifested to my soul." Thus he died, in the thirty-eighth year of his age. How short a life, and yet how richly freighted with blessing to the world!

"Toplady," remarks Montgomery, "evidently kindled his poetic torch at that of his contemporary, Charles Wesley. Like Bruce, Kirke White, and McCheyne, Toplady was early called to join the heavenly choirs; but he has left us the inheritance of his Muse, in some imperishable sacred lyrics." We scarcely need indicate them: they are familiar as the name of their author, — nay, more so; for example, those almost peerless hymns beginning, "Deathless principle, arise," "Rock of Ages, cleft for me," who will forget?

This last-named hymn, so justly prized by the Christian Church, was written in 1776, entitled "A Living and Dying Prayer for the holiest Believer in the world." These expressive stanzas gave consolation to the late lamented Prince Consort, in his dying hour; and in how many unrecorded instances they have ministered to the spiritual comfort of others, living and dying, is known only to the Omniscient. "Dr. Pomeroy relates that a few years ago, when in an Arminian Church, at Constantinople, the people were singing, the language of their hymn was foreign; but it was evident that the singers were in earnest, and that there was deep feeling in the words of their song. The music was a simple melody: all sang with closed eyes; but, as the strain continued, tears were starting and trickling down many, many a cheek. Dr. Pomeroy would fain have joined in the plaintive, tender, yet glowing hymn."* What were they singing? An Arabic version of "Rock of Ages, cleft for me!"

This hymn is supposed to have been the offspring of one of those seasons of depression, which seem, from the revelations of his diary, to have marked the character of his religious life.

Mr. Gladstone has made a Latin translation of this great hymn; it may be found in Schaff's "Christ in Song." — a rich collection of our best sacred poetry. All critics regard Toplady's grand lyric poem, "Death-

* Christophers.

less principle, arise!" as worthy of the high praise Lady Huntingdon bestowed upon it, when it was first sent to her by the author,

Mrs. Barbauld, who lived from 1743 till 1825, issued her first lyrics during her residence with her father, Dr. Aiken, in a Dissenting Academy, at Warrington. She subsequently became the wife of the Rev. Mr. Barbauld, a French Protestant minister; when she wrote "Early Lessons for Children," "Hymns in Prose," and other pieces.

Mrs. Barbauld's poetry included among its admirers Charles James Fox; though not of the highest order, her versification is graceful, musical, and infused with religious fervor. Her "Address to the Deity" is one of her fine poems; here are the opening lines: —

> I read God's awful name emblazoned high,
> With golden letters on the illumined sky;
> Nor less the mystic characters I see,
> Wrought in each flower, inscribed on every tree;
> In every leaf that trembles to the breeze
> I hear the voice of God among the trees.

The closing lines have the solemn cadence of the tolling bell: —

> And when the last, the closing hour draws nigh,
> And earth recedes before my swimming eye, —
> When trembling on the doubtful verge of fate
> I stand, and stretch my view to either state, —
> Teach me to quit this transitory scene,
> With resignation and a look serene;
> Teach me to fix my ardent hopes on high,
> And having lived to Thee, in Thee to die!

What heart does not respond to this beautiful prayer?—

If friendless, in a vale of tears I stray,
Where briers wound, and thorns perplex my way,
Still let my steady soul Thy goodness see,
And, with strong confidence, lay hold on Thee:
With equal eye, my various lot receive,
Resigned to die, or resolute to live;
Prepared to kiss the sceptre, or the rod,
While God is seen in all, and all in God.

Her beautiful lines on the death of the virtuous were singularly applicable to her own tranquil death: —

Sweet is the scene when Christians die,
  When holy souls retire to rest;
How mildly beams the closing eye!
  How gently heaves the expiring breast!

So fades a summer cloud away;
  So sinks the gale when storms are o'er;
So gently shuts the eye of day;
  So dies a wave along the shore.

Triumphant smiles the victor's brow,
  Fanned by some guardian angel's wing;
O Grave! where is thy victory now?
  And where, insidious Death, thy sting?

Both Wordsworth and Rogers much admired this stanza in her poem on Life: —

Life! we've been long together,
Through pleasant, and through cloudy weather;
'Tis hard to part when friends are dear, —
Perhaps 'twill cost a sigh, a tear:
  Then steal away, give little warning,
Choose thine own time,
Say not "Good-night," but in some brighter clime
  Bid me "Good-morning."

The excellent Hannah More, so well known by her multifarious writings, — educational, moral, and religious, — left at her death ten thousand pounds in legacies to charitable and religious institutions, not to mention her long continued benefactions while living. Although she was never married, she has left some admirable counsel for those who are; and to all such the lines especially are commended.

> The angry word suppressed, the taunting thought;
> Subduing and subdued, the petty strife
> Which clouds the color of domestic life;
> The sober comfort, all the peace which springs
> From the large aggregate of little things, —
> On these small cares of daughter, wife or friend,
> The almost sacred joys of home depend.

Here are two more extracts from her pen: —

> *Here*, bliss is short, imperfect, insecure;
> But total, absolute, and perfect *there*.
> *Here*, time's a moment, short our happiest state;
> *There*, infinite duration is our date.
> *Here*, Satan tempts, and troubles e'en the best;
> *There*, Satan's power extends not to the blest.
> In a weak simple body, *here* I dwell;
> But *there* I drop this frail and sickly shell.
> *Here*, my best thoughts are stained with guilt and fear;
> But love and pardon shall be perfect *there*.
> *Here*, my best duties are defiled with sin;
> *There*, all is ease without and peace within.
> *Here*, feeble faith supplies my only light;
> *There*, faith and hope are swallowed up in sight.
> *Here*, love of self my fairest works destroys;
> *There*, love of God shall perfect all my joys.
> *Here*, things, as in a glass, are darkly shown;
> *There*, I shall know as clearly as I'm known.
> Frail are the fairest flowers which bloom below;
> *There*, freshest palms on roots immortal grow.
> *Here*, wants and cares perplex my anxious mind;
> But spirits *there* a calm fruition find.

The soul on earth is an immortal guest,
Condemned to starve at an unreal feast:
A spark, which upwards tends by Nature's force;
A stream, diverted from its parent source;
A drop, dissevered from the boundless sea;
A moment, parted from eternity;
A pilgrim, panting for the rest to come;
An exile, anxious for his native home.

Among the more distinguished names of the Baptist denomination, that of Dr. Ryland holds an honored place. He was associated with Carey, Fuller, Sutcliffe, and others, in organizing the Baptist Missionary Society, at Kettering, in 1792. Two years afterwards, he was appointed to the presidency of the Baptist College, Bristol, and the pastorate at Broadmead Chapel; which duties he continued to discharge until his death, in 1825. The event was signalized by the high eulogium passed upon his character by the two most celebrated men in the Baptist communion of their time, — John Foster and Robert Hall. Ryland's hymns are not, as a rule, remarkable for poetic fire or finish; the best known, and perhaps deservedly so, is, " Sovereign Ruler of the skies," which consists of nine stanzas; and also " O Lord! I would delight in Thee!" of which he says, " I recollect deeper feelings of mind in composing this hymn, than perhaps I ever felt in making any other."

The celebrated Dr. Dwight, of Yale College, came of a noble stock, his excellent mother having been a daughter of Jonathan Edwards. In 1771, he entered upon his duties as tutor in Yale College; six years later he married, and, in 1783, he became the pastor of the church at Greenfield, Conn., and also conducted an academy with great success. Besides many works in prose, Dr. Dwight wrote some hymns for the Presbyterian hymn-book; among them the well-known lines, "I love Thy kingdom, Lord."

Sometimes, a verse of a hymn possesses a talismanic charm, and acts as a spell to recall the past. An affecting illustration of this is on record, of an incident which occurred during the war in Canada, more than a century ago. The Indians, then allies with the French, made frequent hostile incursions; and, on one occasion, they made a descent upon the town of Carlisle, Penn., where a poor German family lived. Here the savages instantly killed the father and son. The mother was fortunately absent at the time; but they took two little girls into cruel captivity. After many years, one of these, surviving the hardships of her fate, together with about four hundred other poor captives, was released, at the instance of the English officer, Bouquet, who had achieved a victory over the savages. These poor creatures were placed in a line, and the mothers and friends of the town and its suburbs were invited to the inspection, in order that the liberated captives might be identified and taken home. Among the visitors was the mother of the two little captive girls; but bitter was her disappointment when she failed to discover her lost children. On the colonel's inquiring whether she could not remember something by which they might recognize her, she replied, that she used to sing to them a hymn beginning, —

>    Alone, yet not alone am I,
>       Though in this solitude so drear;
>    I feel my Saviour always nigh,
>       He comes the weary hours to cheer.
>    I am with Him, and He with me;
>    Even here, alone I cannot be.

She began to sing the hymn; but scarcely had she sung the first two lines, when her lost one came rushing from the crowd to her arms, and joined in singing the charmed syllables that so happily restored the loved and lost to each other.

The following sweet lines are by Crabbe, the "poet of the poor," whose pictures of humble life have charmed so many sympathetic hearts: —

Pilgrim, burdened with thy sin, come the way to Zion's gate;
There, till Mercy speaks within, knock and weep and watch and
    wait:
Knock, He knows the sinner's cry; weep, He loves the mourner's
    tears;
Watch, for saving grace is nigh; wait till heavenly grace appears.
Hark! it is the Saviour's voice, "Welcome, pilgrim, to thy rest."
Now within the gate rejoice, safe and owned and bought and blest:
Safe, from all the lures of vice; owned, by joys the contrite know;
Bought, by Love, and life the price; blest, the mighty debt to owe.
Holy pilgrim, what for thee in this world can now remain?
Seek that world from which shall flee sorrow, shame, and tears and
    pain:
Sorrow shall for ever fly, shame from glory's view retire,
Tears be wiped from every eye, pain in endless bliss expire.

Blake, the painter and poet, has been considered partially insane, from his strange and wild caprice, alike with his pen, as his pencil. Some of his "Songs of Innocence," published in the year 1789, were engraved, accompanied with his illustrations on copper, by the author. One of these lyrics, on Sympathy, is charming for its touching simplicity; here are three of the stanzas: —

> Can I see another's woe,
> And not be in sorrow too?
> Can I see another's grief,
> And not seek for kind relief?
>   .    .    .    .

And can He, who smiles on all,
Hear the wren, with sorrows small,
Hear the small bird's grief and care,
Hear the woes that infants bear,
And not sit beside the nest,
Pouring pity in their breast?
And not sit the cradle near,
Weeping tear on infant's tear?

. . . . .

Think not thou canst sigh a sigh,
And thy Maker is not by;
Think not thou canst weep a tear,
And thy Maker is not near.

Very beautiful it seems, at this distance of time and space, to recall the peaceful, almost patriarchal, scenes of old Scottish homes; especially on the Sabbath. With what reverence, loyalty, and love was its due observance regarded! Scotia's bards have portrayed the beautiful picture, — Burns in his "Cotter's Saturday Night," and Graham in his charming poem on the Sabbath. With the dawn of the holy day, went up the glad orisons of thanksgiving; and when soft twilight lingered on the hill-side, or threw its shadows on the peaceful moor, and motley groups might be seen wending their way homeward from the house of their solemnities, pæans of praise burst upon the Sabbath stillness, ever and anon, as the shadows increased. Such sweet Sabbath scenes have passed away, and with them the charm they diffused over the way-worn spirit, which was soothing and refreshing as the fragrant breath of flowers.

Speaking of the "Cotter's Saturday Night," touching and picturesque as is that beautiful domestic poem, it has been doubted whether it ever taught any person to pray. The sentiment of piety, and piety itself, are very distinct things. Sir Walter Scott would sometimes take his visitors to an arbor on his lawn, at a certain hour in the evening, to listen to the music of a Covenanter's melody, the cadences of which fell with a strange fascination upon the ear of the great minstrel himself; but it only touched his ear. He and his visitors went back to the saloons of Abbotsford, not to raise, with their better skill, the evening hymn of thanksgiving; but regarded it merely through the medium of a romantic imagination, and it was doubtless soon forgotten amid the mazes of the dance and the music and merriment of fashion's throng.

Poor Burns, erratic as he was, had some knowledge of, and reverence for, a nobler life, as some of his poems indicate. But the poet had many melancholy hours, as a foil to his gay and giddy ones. "There was a certain part of my life," he says, " that my spirit was broke by repeated losses and disasters, which threatened, and indeed effected, the ruin of my fortune. My body, too, was attacked by that most dreadful distemper, a hypochondria, or confirmed melancholy. In this wretched state, the recollection of which makes me shudder, I hung my harp upon the willow-trees, except in some lucid intervals, in one of which I composed the following:"—

> O Thou Great Being! what Thou art, surpasses me to know;
> Yet sure I am that known to Thee are all Thy works below.
> Thy creature here before Thee stands, all wretched and distrest;
> Yet sure those ills that wring his soul, obey Thy high behest.
>
> . . . . . . . . .
>
> But if I must afflicted be, to suit some wise design,
> Then man my soul with firm resolves to bear, and not repine.

It is pleasant indeed to think, with Professor Wilson, who, speaking of the closing days of Burns, says that "he died under the ægis of the Christian faith, and that he had his Bible with him in his lodgings, and he read it almost continually; often, when seated on a bank, from which he had difficulty in rising without assistance, for his weakness was extreme, and in his emaciation he was like a ghost. To the last, he loved the sunshine, the grass, and the flowers; to the last, he had a kind look and word for the passers-by, who all knew it was Burns. His sceptical doubts no longer troubled him, — they had never been more than shadows; and he had at last the faith of a confiding Christian."

Burns's prayer, in the prospect of death, is full of touching pathos: —

O Thou unknown, almighty Cause of all my hope and fear!
In whose dread presence, ere an hour, perhaps I must appear;
If I have wandered in those paths of life I ought to shun, —
As something loudly in my breast remonstrates I have done, —
. . . . . . . . .
Where human weakness has come short, or frailty stept aside,
Do Thou, All Good! — for such Thou art! — in shades of darkness hide.
Where with intention I have erred, no other plea I have,
But Thou art good, and Goodness still delighteth to forgive.

Hear his judgment of charity, —

Who made the heart, 'tis He alone decidedly can try us;
He knows each chord, its various tone; each spring, its various bias;
Then at the balance let's be mute, we never can adjust it;
What's *done* we partly may compute, but know not what's resisted.

Graham, the author of the beautiful poem of "The Sabbath," is said to have written that work, and got it published, without his wife knowing any thing about it; and one evening he brought home a copy to her, requesting her to read it. As his name did not appear on its titlepage, she did not dream that he had any thing to do with its authorship: accordingly, she read on with evident interest, while the sensitive author paced up and down the room. At length, she broke out in praise of the poem, and, turning to him, said, "Ah, James, if you could but produce a poem like this!" The disclosure of his secret, it is said, overwhelmed her with surprise and pleasure.

> The setting orb of night her level ray
> Shed o'er the land, and on the dewy sward
> The lengthened shadows of the triple cross
> Were laid far stretched,— when in the east arose,
> Last of the stars, day's harbinger: no sound
> Was heard, save of the watching soldier's foot:
> Within the rock-barred sepulchre, the gloom
> Of deepest midnight brooded o'er the dead,
> The Holy One: but, lo! a radiance faint
> Began to dawn around His sacred brow:
> The linen vesture seemed a snowy wreath,
> Drifted by storms into a mountain cave:
> Bright and more bright the circling halo beamed
> Upon that face, clothed in a smile benign,
> Though yet exanimate. Nor long the reign
> Of death; the eyes that wept for human griefs
> Unclose, and look around with conscious joy.
> Yes; with returning life, the first emotion
> That glowed in Jesus' breast of love, was joy
> At man's redemption, now complete; at death
> Disarmed; the grave transformed into the couch
> Of faith; the resurrection and the life.
> Majestical He rose: trembled the earth;
> The ponderous gate of stone was rolled away;
> The keepers fell; the angel, awe-struck, sunk
> Into invisibility, while forth

> The Saviour of the world walked, and stood
> Before the sepulchre, and viewed the clouds
> Empurpled glorious by the rising sun.

Campbell relates a little incident touching Graham's love of singing: he says, "We had agreed to sit up all night, and go together to Arthur's Seat to see the sun rise. We sat, accordingly, all night in his delightful parlor, the seat of so many happy remembrances. We then went and saw a beautiful sunrise. I returned home with him, for I was living in his house at the time. He was unreserved in all his devoutest feelings before me; and, from the beauty of the morning scenery, and the recent death of his sister, our conversation took a serious turn, — on the proofs of infinite benevolence in the creation, and the goodness of God. As I retired to my own bed, I overheard his devotions, — not his prayer, but a hymn which he sang, and with a power and inspiration beyond himself and beyond any thing else."

It is remarked by an eminent divine, Robertson, that "the mysticism, the obscurity of thought and expression, which belong to Browning, Tennyson, and Wordsworth, is but a protest and witness for the infinite in the soul of man." Let us listen to the Muse of the last named.

It seems almost like profanation to mutilate his magnificent "Ode on the Intimations of Immortality," but we have only space for a few lines of it: —

> Our birth is but a sleep and a forgetting:
> The soul that rises with us, our life's star,
> Hath had elsewhere its setting,
> And cometh from afar.
> Not in entire forgetfulness,
> And not in utter nakedness,

But trailing clouds of glory do we come,
    From God who is our home.
Heaven lies about us in our infancy!
Shades of the prison-house begin to close
    Upon the growing boy;
But he beholds the light, and whence it flows,
    He sees it in his joy.
The youth, who daily farther from the east
    Must travel, still is Nature's priest,
    And by the vision splendid
    Is on his way attended;
At length the man perceives it die away,
And fade into the light of common day.

 . . . . . .

O joy! that in our embers
Is something that doth live,
That Nature yet remembers
What was so fugitive.
The thought of our past years in me doth breed
Perpetual benediction; not indeed
For that which is most worthy to be blest;
Delight and liberty, the simple creed
Of childhood, whether busy or at rest,
With new-fledged hope still fluttering in his breast:
    Not for these I raise
    The song of thanks and praise;
But for those obstinate questionings
Of sense and outward things,
Fallings from us, vanishings;
Blank misgivings of a creature
Moving about in worlds not realized;
High instincts, before which our mortal nature
Did tremble like a guilty thing surprised;
But for those first affections,
Those shadowy recollections,
    Which, be they what they may,
Are yet the fountain-light of all our day,
Are yet a master-light of all our seeing;
    Uphold us, cherish, and have power to make
Our noisy years seem moments in the being
    Of the eternal silence; truths that wake,

To perish never;
Which neither listlessness nor mad endeavor,
Nor man, nor boy,
Nor all that is at enmity with joy,
Can utterly abolish or destroy!

His "Ode to Duty" is a fine piece of poetry; here are two of the stanzas: —

Stern daughter of the Voice of God,
O Duty, if that name thou love,
Who art a light to guide, a rod
To check the erring, and reprove;
Thou who art victory and law
When empty terrors overawe,
From vain temptations dost set free,
And calm'st the weary strife of frail humanity.

. . . . . . .

Serene will be our days, and bright,
And happy will our nature be,
When love is an unerring light,
And joy its own security.
And they a blissful course may hold
Even now, who, not unwisely bold,
Live in the spirit of this creed,
Yet seek thy firm support, according to their need.

Here is one of his fine hymns: —

Not seldom, clad in radiant vest,
Deceitfully goes forth the morn;
Not seldom evening in the west
Sinks smilingly forsworn.

The smoothest seas will sometimes prove,
To the confiding bark, untrue;
And if she trust the stars above,
They can be treacherous too.

The umbrageous oak, in pomp outspread,
Full oft, when storms the welkin rend,
Draws lightnings down upon the head
It promised to defend.

But Thou art true, incarnate Lord!
  Who didst vouchsafe for man to die;
  Thy smile is sure, Thy plighted word
  No change can falsify.

I bent before Thy gracious throne,
  And asked for peace with suppliant knee;
  And peace was given, — nor peace alone,
  But faith and hope and ecstasy!

Wordsworth's life was eminently beautiful and poetic. It was in strict accordance with his own idea of what a poet's life should be: it was lived in the very presence of Nature, — Nature in all her glory; and "a holy calm rests over it, like sunshine upon a Sabbath day." We feel that it was true and great, the reflex of a true and great man. It was a life in which the spiritual rather than the material and the practical obtain the ascendency. His quiet, contemplative days glided on like the peaceful lake or river, making its own gentle music as it wends its modest way. Wordsworth, Southey, and Coleridge, — the poetic triad, — from their locality, on the lakes of Cumberland, have been styled the "Lake-poets." Wordsworth's "Ode to Immortality" is the most admired of his pieces. He says, "Having to wield some of its elements, when I was impelled to write this poem on the 'Immortality of the Soul,' I took hold of the notion of pre-existence, as having sufficient foundation in humanity for authorizing me to make for my purpose the best use of it I could as a poet."

This note and the poem itself reveal the character of Wordsworth's philosophy, and the secret of his habit of thought. The mystic spiritualism which imbues his poetry is that which distinguishes him from merely descriptive and didactic poets. "Were this element wanting in him," writes one of his biographers, "we should have a fine reporter of Nature's doings, a fine painter of objective effects, but no creator, no idealist; and therefore, properly speaking, no poet, in the high signification of the term." He, however, was eminently possessed of the spiritual faculty: all nature to him was symbolical.

Wordsworth seems to have been a very amiable and excellent man. The quiet of his Grasmere life was relieved by frequent excursions in the neighborhood and elsewhere. In 1802, after his visit to France, he was married to Mary Hutchinson, of Penrith, — not a beauty, but one of the most lovable of women. Every one knows the beautiful lines he addressed to her, beginning, —

> She was a phantom of delight,
> When first she gleamed upon my sight;

and it is pleasant to add that the illusive charm of his first love never died out of his heart. Our philosophic poet was a great lover of locomotion; and, as he studied and composed in the open air, he made good use of his legs, which, however, we are informed, were not so ornamental as useful. De Quincey informs us he had read that Milton's surviving daughter, when she saw the crayon drawing representing the likeness of her father, in Richardson the painter's octavo volume of Milton, burst out in a rapture of passionate admiration, exclaiming, "This is my father! this is my dear father!" And when De Quincey had procured this book, he saw in this likeness of Milton a perfect portrait of Wordsworth. The poet's domestic life was a very felicitous one.  In his home there were no jars or discords; but it seems to have been a temple of the graces and the virtues.  Some of his sweetest lyrics date their origin to incidents connected with his home-life.  He closed his earthly life on the twenty-third of April, 1850, the birthday and deathday of Shakspeare.

He has undoubtedly written much poetry that may be thought very prosaic; yet some of his productions — his "Ode to Immortality," some of his sonnets, and a few of his minor pieces — are unsurpassed, and likely to remain so.  As Byron and Moore recede, Milton and Wordsworth will advance in popular renown; and a good sign it is, for it indicates that the moral is asserting its just authority over the sensuous.

It was Wordsworth's custom to compose in the open air.  His servant once said to a visitor: "This, sir, is my master's library: his study is out of doors."  He had a great dislike to writing; and his sister, or some other member of his family, was always at hand to perform for him the office of amanuensis.

We must take our leave of Nature's great bard, rehearsing his fine admonitory sonnet: —

> The world is too much with us; late and soon,
> Getting and spending, we lay waste our powers.
> Little we see in Nature that is ours:
> We have given our hearts away, — a sordid boon!
> This sea that bares her bosom to the moon;
> The winds that will be howling at all hours,
> And are up-gathered now, like sleeping flowers, —
> For this, for every thing, we're out of tune;
> It moves us not.  Great God! I'd rather be
> A Pagan, suckled in a creed outworn,

So might I, standing on this pleasant lee,
Have glimpses that would make me less forlorn;
Have sight of Proteus coming from the sea,
Or hear old Triton blow his wreathèd horn.

Montgomery, who was born at Irvine, in Ayrshire, 1771, is, from his long residence in Sheffield, often supposed to have been an Englishman. His father was a Moravian missionary, who died at the island of Tobago. Montgomery's first volume of poems was called "The Wanderer of Switzerland, and other Poems;" but his later productions, including his "Songs of Zion," which have cheered many a Christian heart, are his most characteristic and popular works.

The beautiful sacred lyrics of Montgomery live not only in our church-books of psalmody, but some are also embalmed in the common heart of Christendom. Who does not remember his fine poem, "Oh, where shall rest be found?" And where shall we find a nobler burst of elevated sentiment in song than is to be found in his Advent hymn, "Angels, from the realms of glory"? Others might be referred to in which are passages of a high order of poetry; as in his noble missionary hymn, commencing, "O Spirit of the living God," and especially the Miltonic stanza: —

>    O Spirit of the Lord, prepare
>    All the round earth her God to meet;
>    Breathe Thou abroad, like morning air,
>    Till hearts of stone begin to beat.

His deep interest in the missionary emprise may be seen in his noble pæan, "Hark! the song of Jubilee!"

His popular poem, "The Common Lot," consisting of ten stanzas, was written during a country walk in the snow, on his thirty-fourth birthday anniversary. Montgomery's earlier days were troublous and disturbed, — little suited to the contemplative habits of a poet. But he was, indeed, more than a poet, he was a philanthropist; and, because of his conscientious opposition to slavery, and other then existing abuses, he became the victim of political persecution. In 1797, a volume of his minor poems was published, under the significant title of "Prison Amusements." Religious and benevolent objects found in him an earnest and zealous advocate; and even his secular poems possessed a religious tendency and aim. If the reader is acquainted with the published memoirs of the poet, he will recall the touching incident of his friend, Dr. Holland, reciting his hymns to him, when advanced in years, and seriously ill. "Read on," he said, "I am glad to hear you : the words recall the feelings which first suggested them ; and it is good for me to feel affected and humbled by the terms in which I have endeavored to provide for the expression of similar religious experience in others. As all my hymns embody some portions of the history of the joys or sorrows, the hopes and the fears of this poor heart, so I cannot doubt but that they will be found an acceptable vehicle of expression of the experience of many of my fellow-creatures who may be similarly exercised during the pilgrimage of their Christian life." That beautiful description of Prayer — which, by some strange fatuity, is placed in our Collections among hymns of prayer or praise — is really only a descriptive poem. We refer to the well-known lines, commencing, "Prayer is the soul's sincere desire."

His Muse, like Cowper's, has contributed numerous sacred lyrics; free from dogmas, and being inspired by the religion of love, they are eminently designed to diffuse the love of religion.

A love of poetry was kindled in Montgomery by hearing Blair's "Grave" read to him in his school-days. From his early school-days, therefore, he may be said to have wooed the Muse. It has been well said that "his history affords a fine example of virtuous and successful perseverance, and of genius devoted to pure and noble ends, — not a feverish, tumultuous, and splendid career, like that of some greater poetical heirs of immortality, but a course ever brightening as it proceeded, — calm, useful, and happy."

Montgomery's "Stranger and his Friend" has been esteemed one of the most beautiful of his sacred poems : —

> A poor wayfaring Man of grief
> Hath often crossed me on my way,
> Who sued so humbly for relief,
> That I could never answer, " Nay : "
> I had not power to ask his name,
> Whither he went, or whence he came ;
> Yet there was something in his eye
> That won my love, I knew not why.
>
> Once, when my scanty meal was spread,
> He entered, — not a word he spake, —
> Just perishing for want of bread ;
> I gave him all : he blessed it, brake,
> And ate, — but gave me part again.
> Mine was an angel's portion then ;
> For, while I fed with eager haste,
> That crust was manna to my taste.

I spied him where a fountain burst
Clear from the rock: his strength was gone;
The heedless water mocked his thirst,
He heard it, saw it hurrying on:
I ran to raise the sufferer up;
Thrice from the stream he drained my cup,
Dipt, and returned it running o'er;
I drank, and never thirsted more.

'Twas night,— the floods were out,— it blew
A winter hurricane aloof;
I heard his voice abroad, and flew
To bid him welcome to my roof:
I warmed, I clothed, I cheered my guest,
Laid him on my own couch to rest;
Then made the hearth my bed, and seemed
In Eden's garden while I dreamed.

Stript, wounded, beaten, nigh to death,
I found him by the highway-side;
I roused his pulse, brought back his breath,
Revived his spirit, and supplied
Wine, oil, refreshment; he was healed;
I had myself a wound concealed;
But from that hour forgot the smart,
And Peace bound up my broken heart.

There are two more exquisite stanzas which close the poem.

Montgomery's "Death of Adam" has been considered one of his finest poems, alike for its conception, imagery, and language; but his most popular pieces are those already cited, and his lines "Via Crucis, via Lucis," "Oh, where shall rest be found?" and the beautiful hymn, —

What are these in bright array,
This innumerable throng,
Round the altar night and day,
Hymning one triumphant song, —

"Worthy is the Lamb once slain,
  Blessing, honor, glory, power,
Wisdom, riches, to obtain
  New dominion every hour"?
These through fiery trials trod;
  These from great affliction came;
Now before the throne of God,
  Sealed with His almighty name;
Clad in raiment pure and white,
  Victor-palms in every hand,
Through their dear Redeemer's might,
  More than conquerors they stand.

His hymn commencing, "Spirit, leave thy house of clay," was composed during his political persecution in York Castle; and was occasioned by the death of one of his fellow-prisoners, who, with seven others, had suffered the loss of all worldly goods for conscience' sake. The following simple, touching lines, may not be familiar to the reader, not being included in his collected works: —

  "Father, thy will, not mine, be done," —
So prayed on earth Thy suffering Son:
    So, in His name, I pray;
  The spirit fails, the flesh is weak,
  Thy help in agony I seek;
    Oh, take this cup away!

  If such be not Thy sovereign will,
  Thy better purpose then fulfil,
    My wishes I resign;
  Into thy hands my soul commend,
  On Thee for life or death depend;
    Thy will be done, not mine!

Our familiarity with his lines on Night does not lessen their impressive beauty: listen to one or two of the stanzas, — what a hushed feeling of sadness they seem to convey! —

Night is the time for rest: how sweet, when labors close,
To gather round an aching breast the curtain of repose,
   Stretch the tired limbs, and lay the head
   Upon our own delightful bed!

   .    .    .    .    .

Night is the time to muse : then from the eye the soul
Takes flight, and, with expanding views, beyond the starry pole
   Descries, athwart the abyss of night,
   The dawn of uncreated light!

Night is the time to pray: our Saviour oft withdrew
To desert mountains far away ; so will His followers do, —
   Steal from the throng to haunts untrod,
   And hold communion there with God.

His impressive lines on the Grave, so familiar, are yet ever fresh with the inspiration of the theme : —

   There is a calm for those who weep,
   A rest for weary pilgrims found ;
   And while the mouldering ashes sleep
      Low in the ground, —

   .    .    .    .    .

   The soul, of origin divine, —
   God's glorious image freed from clay, —
   In heaven's eternal sphere shall shine,
      A star of day!

   The sun is but a spark of fire,
   A transient meteor in the sky ;
   The soul, immortal as its Sire,
      Shall never die!

Replete with tender pathos are his lines on the " Death of a Friend : " —

Friend after friend departs ! who hath not lost a friend ?
There is no union here of hearts, that finds not here an end:
   Were this frail world our final rest,
   Living or dying, none were blest.

Beyond the flight of Time, beyond the reign of Death,
There surely is some blessed clime, where Life is not a breath!
    Nor life's affections, transient fire,
    Whose sparks fly upward and expire.

There is a world above, where parting is unknown!
A long eternity of love, formed for the good alone:
    And faith beholds the dying here
    Translated to that glorious sphere!

Our last selection shall be his Funeral chant: —

    Servant of God, well done! Rest from thy loved employ;
    The battle o'er, the victory won, — enter thy Master's joy!
    The cry at midnight came, he started up to hear;
    A mortal arrow pierced his frame: he fell, but felt no fear.
    His spirit with a bound left its encumbering clay;
    His tent, at sunrise, on the ground a darkened ruin lay.

The above suggests the beautiful tribute to the departed, by Lord Lyttleton: —

    Forgive, blest shade, the tributary tear
      That mourns thy exit from a world like this;
    Forgive the wish that would have kept thee here,
      And stayed thy progress to the seats of bliss.
    No more confined by grovelling scenes of night,
      No more a tenant pent in mortal clay;
    Now should we rather hail thy glorious flight,
      And trace thy journey to the realms of day!

That beautiful lyric prayer, "Guide me, O Thou great Jehovah," was composed in his native tongue, by William Williams, a Welsh Methodist minister, who, for half a century, travelled, and preached the gospel in the Principality. He was born in 1717, and died in 1791. "O'er those gloomy hills of darkness" is another of his hymns.

Coleridge considered the sonnet on "Night and Death," by the Rev. J. Blanco White, — a proselyte from Romanism, — the finest and most grandly conceived in the language: —

>  Mysterious Night! When our first parent knew
>     Thee from report Divine, and heard thy name,
>     Did he not tremble for this lovely frame,
>  This glorious canopy of light and blue?
>  Yet 'neath a curtain of translucent dew,
>     Bathed in the rays of the great setting flame,
>     Hesperus, with the host of heaven, came,
>  And lo! Creation widened in man's view.
>  Who could have thought such darkness lay concealed
>     Within thy beams, O Sun! or who could find,
>     Whilst fly and leaf and insect stood revealed,
>  That to such countless orbs thou mad'st us blind?
>  Why do we, then, shun death with anxious strife?
>  If light can thus deceive, wherefore not life?

Coleridge (1772–1834), one of the finest minds England has produced, has been compared to an unfinished cathedral, — grand in its proportions, but defective, because incomplete. And yet no man of letters since Johnson has perhaps been more admired by his countrymen. His scholarship, like his conversation, was great. But for his sad proclivity to the baneful drug that had well-nigh been his ruin, he would have been one of the greatest of England's scholars. True poet as he is, yet most of his subjects do not come within the range of our selections. Here is a striking passage from his poems: —

>     In some hour of solemn jubilee
>     The massy gates of paradise are thrown
>     Wide open, and forth come, in fragments wild,
>     Sweet echoes of unearthly melodies,
>     And odors snatched from beds of amaranth,
>     And they that from the crystal river of life

> Sprung up on freshenèd wing, ambrosial gales!
> The favored good man in his lonely walk
> Perceives them, and his silent spirit drinks
> Strange bliss, which he shall recognize in heaven.

His "Hymn on Chamouni" has been called the grandest burst of poetic praise in the language. Listen to the closing lines, thus apostrophizing Mont Blanc:

> Rise, oh, ever rise!
> Rise, like a cloud of incense, from the earth,
> Thou kingly spirit throned among the hills,
> Thou dread ambassador from earth to heaven!
> Great hierarch! tell thou the silent sky,
> And tell the stars, and tell yon rising sun,
> Earth, with her thousand voices, praises God.

His "Youth and Age," like his "Ancient Mariner" and "Genevieve," it is presumed, we all know.

Hartley Coleridge, the gifted son of a gifted father, was born in 1796, and died in 1849. The following sweetly worded sonnet is his:—

### SHE LOVED MUCH.

> She sat and wept beside His feet. The weight
> Of sin opprest her heart; for all the blame,
> And the poor malice of the worldly shame,
> To her was past, extinct, and out of date;
> Only the sin remained,—the leprous state.
> She would be melted by the heat of love,
> By fires far fiercer than are blown to prove
> And purge the silver ore adulterate.
> She sat and wept, and with her untressed hair
> Still wiped the feet she was so blest to touch;
> And He wiped off the soiling of despair
> From her sweet soul, because she loved so much!
> I am a sinner, full of doubts and fears;
> Make me a humble thing of love and tears!

The following is also his:—

If I have sinned in act, I may repent:
If I have erred in thought, I may disclaim
My silent error, and yet feel no shame;
But if my soul, big with an ill intent,
Guilty in will, by fate be innocent,
Or, being bad, yet murmurs at the curse
And incapacity of being worse,
That makes my hungry passion still keep Lent
In keen experience of a carnival:
Where, in all worlds, that round the sun revolve
And shed their influence on this passive ball,
Abides a power that can my soul absolve?
Could any sin survive, and be forgiven,
One sinful wish would make a hell of heaven.

Southey wrote these admirable counsels to the afflicted:—

The wounded heart is prone to entertain
Presumptuous thoughts, and feelings which arraign
The appointed course of things; but what are we,
Short-sighted creatures of an hour,
That we should judge? In part alone we see,
And this but dimly. He who ordereth all,
Beholdeth all, at once, and to the end:
Upon His wisdom and His power,
His mercy and His boundless love, we rest;
And, resting thus in humble faith, we know,
Whether the present be for weal or woe,
For us whatever is must needs be best.

---

Methinks, if ye would know
How visitations of calamity
Affect the pious soul, 'tis shown you here:
Look yonder at the cloud, which, through the sky
Sailing along, doth cross in her career
The rolling moon: I watched it as it came,
And deemed the deep opaque would blot her beams,

But, melting like a wreath of snow, it hangs
In folds of wavy silver round, and clothes
The orb with richer beauties than her own ;
Then, passing, leaves her in her light serene.

What an impressive prayer is this ! —

Lord ! who art merciful as well as just,
Incline Thine ear to me, a child of dust.
Not what I would, O Lord ! I offer Thee,
    Alas ! but what I can.
Father Almighty ! who hast made me man,
And bade me look to heaven, for Thou art there, —
Accept my sacrifice and humble prayer.
Four things, which are not in Thy treasury,
I lay before Thee, Lord, with this petition :
    My nothingness, my wants,
    My sins, and my contrition.

Mrs. Southey's touching stanzas on the "Pauper's Death-bed" are very impressive. Here is an extract : —

Tread softly, — bow the head, in reverent silence bow, —
No passing bell doth toll, yet an immortal soul
    Is passing now.
Stranger, however great, with lowly reverence bow ;
There's one in that poor shed, one by that paltry bed,
    Greater than thou.

. . . . . . . .

O change, O wondrous change ! burst are the prison-bars,
This moment, there so low, so agonized, and now
    Beyond the stars.
O change, stupendous change ! there lies the soulless clod :
The sun eternal breaks, the new immortal wakes, —
    Wakes with his God !

· These lines are also from her pen : —

I weep, but not rebellious tears; I mourn, but not in hopeless woe;
I droop, but not with doubtful fears; for whom I've trusted, Him I know.
 Lord, I believe,—assuage my grief,
 And help, oh, help, mine unbelief!
My days of youth and health are o'er, my early friends are dead and gone;
And there are times it tries me sore to think I'm left on earth alone;
 But then Faith whispers, "'Tis not so:
 He will not leave, nor let thee go."

Campbell's polished and elaborate poems are among the best lyrics in the language; we refer especially to his "Last Man," "What's Hallowed Ground," "The Rainbow," &c. We have only space to admit portions of his "Last Man":—

 All worldly shapes shall melt in gloom,
  The sun himself must die,
 Before this mortal shall assume
  Its immortality.
 I saw a vision in my sleep,
 That gave my spirit strength to sweep
  Adown the gulf of Time:
 I saw the last of human mould,
 That shall creation's death behold,
  As Adam saw her prime.
 The sun's eye had a sickly glare,
  The earth with age was wan,
 The skeletons of nations were
  Around that lonely man.
 Some had expired in fight, the brands
 Still resting in their bony hands;
  In plague and famine, some:
 Earth's cities had no sound nor tread,
 And ships were drifting with the dead
  To shores where all was dumb.
 Yet, prophet-like, that lone one stood,
  With dauntless words and high,
 That shook the sere leaves from the wood,
  As if a storm passed by,—

Saying, "We are twins in death, proud Sun,
Thy face is cold, thy race is run,
  'Tis Mercy bids thee go.
For thou, ten thousand thousand years,
Hast seen the tide of human tears,
  That shall no longer flow.

. . . .

E'en I am weary in yon skies
  To watch thy fading fire;
Test of all sumless agonies,
  Behold not me expire.
My lips shall speak thy dirge of death;
Their rounded gasp and gurgling breath
  To see thou shalt not boast.
The eclipse of nature spreads my pall,
The majesty of darkness shall
  Receive my parting ghost.
This spirit shall return to Him
  Who gave its heavenly spark;
Yet think not, Sun, it shall be dim
  When thou thyself art dark:
No: it shall live again, and shine
In bliss unknown to beams of thine,
  By Him recalled to breath,
Who captive led Captivity,
Who robbed the grave of victory,
  And took the sting from death.
Go, Sun, while Mercy holds me up,
  On nature's awful waste,
To drink this last and bitter cup
  Of grief that man shall taste,—
Go, tell the night that hides thy face,
Thou saw'st the last of Adam's race,
  On earth's sepulchral clod,
The darkening universe defy
To quench his immortality,
  Or shake his trust in God."

Campbell's estimate of posthumous fame is strikingly impressive: he said, "When I think of the existence which shall commence when the stone is laid over my head, how can literary fame appear to me, to any one, but as nothing? I believe, when I am gone, justice will be done to me in this way, — that I was a pure writer. It is an inexpressible comfort, at my time of life, to be able to look back, and feel that I have not written one line against religion or virtue."

There is an impressive sonnet on "Immortality," by our American artist-poet, Washington Allston: —

> To think for aye! to breathe immortal breath,
> And know nor hope, nor fear, of ending death;
> To see the myriad worlds that round us roll
> Wax old and perish, while the steadfast soul
> Stands fresh and moveless in her sphere of thought;
> O God omnipotent! who in me wrought
> This conscious world, whose ever-growing orb,
> When the dead Past shall all in time absorb,
> Will be but as begun, — oh, of Thine own
> Give of the holy light that veils Thy throne,
> That darkness be not mine, to take my place
> Beyond the reach of light, a blot in space!
> So may this wondrous life, from sin made free,
> Reflect Thy love for aye, and to Thy glory be!

Some of the sacred lyrics of Moore are exquisite. Here are two or three: —

> As down in the sunless retreats of the ocean,
>   Sweet flowers are springing no mortal can see,
> So, deep in my soul, the still prayer of devotion,
>   Unheard by the world, rises silent to Thee,
>     My God! silent to Thee!
>     Pure, warm, silent to Thee.
>
> As still to the star of its worship, though clouded,
>   The needle points faithfully o'er the dim sea,
> So, dark as I roam, in this wintry world shrouded,
>   The hope of my spirit turns trembling to Thee,
>     My God! trembling to Thee!
>     True, fond, trembling to Thee.

Oh Thou who dry'st the mourner's tear,
    How dark this world would be,
If, when deceived and wounded here,
    We could not fly to Thee!
The friends who in our sunshine live,
    When winter comes, are flown;
And he who has but tears to give,
    Must weep those tears alone;
But Thou wilt heal that broken heart,
    Which, like the plants that throw
Their fragrance from the wounded part,
    Breathes sweetness out of woe.
When joy no longer soothes or cheers,
    And even the hope that threw
A moment's sparkle o'er our tears,
    Is dimmed and vanished too.
Oh, who would bear life's stormy doom,
    Did not Thy wing of love
Come brightly wafting through the gloom
    One Peace-branch from above!
Then sorrow, touched by Thee, grows bright,
    With more than rapture's ray,
As darkness shows us worlds of light
    We never saw by day.

---

This world is all a fleeting show,
    For man's illusion given:
The smiles of joy, the tears of woe,
Deceitful shine, deceitful flow:
    There's nothing true but heaven!

And false the light on glory's plume,
    As fading hues of even —
And love and hope and beauty's bloom
Are blossoms gathered for the tomb:
    There's nothing bright but heaven!

Poor wanderers of a stormy day,
    From wave to wave we're driven;
And fancy's flash, and reason's ray,
Serve but to light the troubled way:
    There's nothing calm but heaven!

One of the best of Moore's sacred lyrics is the following: —

The bird let loose in Eastern skies, when hastening fondly home,
Ne'er stoops to earth her wing, nor flies where idle warblers roam.
But high she shoots through air and light, above all low delay,
Where nothing earthly bounds her flight, nor shadow dims her way.
So grant me, God, from every care and stain of passion free,
Aloft through virtue's purer air to hold my course to Thee !
No sin to cloud, no lure to stay my soul, as home she springs ;
Thy sunshine on her joyful way, Thy freedom in her wings !

---

Angel of charity, who, from above,
  Comest to dwell a pilgrim here,
Thy voice is music, thy smile is love,
  And Pity's soul is in thy tear.
When on the shrine of God were laid
  First-fruits of all most good and fair
That ever bloomed in Eden's shade,
  Thine was the holiest offering there.
Hope, and her sister, Faith, were given
  But as our guides to yonder sky ;
Soon as they reach the verge of Heaven,
  There, lost in perfect bliss, they die.
But long as Love, almighty Love,
  Shall on His throne of thrones abide,
Thou, Charity, shalt dwell above,
  Smiling for ever by His side.

---

Come, ye disconsolate, where'er you languish,
  Come, at God's altar fervently kneel ;
Here bring your wounded hearts, here tell your anguish, —
  Earth has no sorrow that Heaven cannot heal.
Joy of the desolate, Light of the straying,
  Hope, when all others die, fadeless and pure,
Here speaks the Comforter, in God's name saying,
  Earth has no sorrow that Heaven cannot cure.

The Muse of Moore, like that of Byron, seems too often to have revelled and luxuriated amidst the seductive scenes of vice; yet when religion does inspire her song, her strains are so sweet that we cannot but regret that her flights had not been more often heavenward. Another of his most admired sacred pieces is "Miriam's Song:"—

> Sound the loud timbrel o'er Egypt's dark sea!
> Jehovah has triumphed, His people are free!
> Sing, for the pride of the tyrant is broken;
>   His chariots, his horsemen, all splendid and brave, —
> How vain was their boast! for the Lord hath but spoken,
>   And chariots and horsemen are sunk in the wave.
> Sound the loud timbrel o'er Egypt's dark sea!
> Jehovah has triumphed, His people are free!
> Praise to the Conqueror, praise to the Lord!
> His Word was our arrow, His breath was our sword!
> Who shall return to tell Egypt the story
>   Of those she sent forth in the hour of her pride?
> For the Lord hath looked out from His pillar of glory,
>   And all her brave thousands are dashed in the tide.
> Sound the loud timbrel o'er Egypt's dark sea!
> Jehovah has triumphed, His people are free!

Scarcely less beautiful is the following, from the same source:—

> Is it not sweet to think, hereafter,
>   When the spirit leaves this sphere,
> Love, with deathless wing, shall waft her
>   To those she long hath mourned for here?
>
> Hearts, from which 'twas death to sever;
>   Eyes, this world can ne'er restore, —
> There, as warm, as bright as ever,
>   Shall meet us, and be lost no more.
>        .     .     .     .     .
> Hope still lifts her radiant finger,
>   Pointing to the eternal home;
> Upon whose portal yet they linger,
>   Looking back for us to come.

Horace Smith's "Hymn to the Flowers" is replete with delicate and impressive imagery: let us con over some of the stanzas:—

> Day-stars! that ope your frownless eyes, to twinkle
>   From rainbow-galaxies of earth's creation,
> And dew-drops on her lonely altars sprinkle,
>   As a libation!
>
> Ye matin worshippers! who, bending lowly
>   Before the uprisen sun — God's lidless eye —
> Throw from your chalices a sweet and holy
>   Incense on high.
>
> Ye bright mosaics! that with storied beauty
>   The floor of Nature's temple tessellate,
> What numerous emblems of instructive duty
>   Your forms create!
>
> . . . . . . . .
>
> Your voiceless lips, O flowers! are living preachers:
>   Each cup a pulpit, and each leaf a book,
> Supplying to my fancy numerous teachers
>   From loneliest nook.
>
> . . . . . . . .
>
> Ephemeral sages! what instructors hoary
>   For such a world of thought could furnish scope?
> Each fading calyx a *memento mori*,
>   Yet fount of Hope!
>
> . . . . . . . .
>
> Were I in churchless solitudes remaining,
>   Far from all voice of teachers or divines,
> My soul would find in flowers of God's ordaining
>   Priests, sermons, shrines.

Dear to every section of the Christian Church are the sweet measures of the poet-bishop, Heber, who lived 1783–1826. Some of them are odes, but all are infused with the poetic element to the highest degree. "From Greenland's icy mountains" is an instance in point; and so is his beautiful "Epiphany Hymn;" it is really an apostrophe to a star, rather than a hymn,— "Brightest and best of the sons of the morning." The former was written at Hodnet, Shropshire, in 1820, and was sung by his congregation after a sermon appealing to them on behalf of missions. This remarkable hymn explains Heber's devoted course in India, since he could not

>     to men benighted
> The lamp of life deny.

When sailing to Madras, with a detachment of invalid troops on board, Bishop Heber acted as their pastor. "I have too little in my situation," said he, "of those pastoral duties, which are as useful to the minister as to his people; and I am delighted at the opportunity thus unexpectedly afforded me." And so, with his Prayer-book in his hand, he went below, from time to time, to minister to the sufferers.

His exquisite stanzas at a funeral present a remarkable instance of poetic compression, the closing stanza especially:—

> Thou art gone to the grave! but 'twere vain to deplore thee,
> When God was thy ransom, thy guardian, thy guide;
> He gave thee, He took thee, and He will restore thee,
> And death hath no sting since the Saviour hath died.

We are all familiar with Byron's brilliant apostrophe to the genius of Henry Kirke White; yet it will bear repeating, for its intrinsic beauty, and it will best introduce a name that claims our admiration and our pity.

> Unhappy White! when life was in its spring,
> And thy young Muse just waved her joyous wing,
> The spoiler swept that soaring lyre away,
> Which else had sounded an immortal lay.

Oh, what a noble heart was here undone,
When Science' self destroyed her favorite son!
. . . . . .
'Twas thine own genius gave the final blow,
And helped to plant the wound that laid thee low!
So the struck eagle, stretched upon the plain,
No more through rolling clouds to soar again,
Viewed his own feather on the fatal dart,
And winged the shaft that quivered to his heart.

His excessive studies, pursued too often by the light of the midnight lamp, gave to him high rank in the halls of learning; although the achievement was purchased by the sacrifice of his life, at the early age of twenty-three years.

His splendid poem, the "Star of Bethlehem," is destined to live in the memories and hearts of all lovers of sacred song: —

When marshalled on the nightly plain
  The glittering host bestud the sky,
One star alone of all the train
  Can fix the sinner's wandering eye:
Hark, hark! to God the chorus breaks,
  From every host, from every gem,
But one alone the Saviour speaks, —
  It is the Star of Bethlehem!

Once on the raging seas I rode;
  The storm was loud, the night was dark;
The ocean yawned, and rudely blowed
  The wind that tossed my foundering bark:
Deep horror then my vitals froze,
  Death-struck, I ceased the tide to stem;
When suddenly a star arose, —
  It was the Star of Bethlehem!

It was my guide, my light, my all,
  It bade my dark forebodings cease;
And, through the storm and danger's thrall,
  It led me to the port of peace.

> Now, safely moored, my perils o'er,
>   I'll sing, first in night's diadem,
> For ever and for evermore,
>   The Star, the Star of Bethlehem!

There is a hymn, written by Dr. Andrew Reed, commencing, "There is an hour when I must part." This hymn was recited to Dr. Reed, at his own request, when he was approaching his end: after listening to it, he said, "That hymn I wrote at Geneva: it has brought comfort to many, and now it brings comfort to me."

Andrew Reed is a name deservedly honored in the churches; alike for his eminent services as a philanthropist, an author, and a successful minister of the gospel. Few men have accomplished so much for the poor and the distressed as he, in the establishment of no less than five great national benevolent institutions in England; and who shall compute the amount of spiritual benefaction his protracted ministry has conferred? He was born in London, 1787, and died in 1862. He visited this country, in company with Dr. Matheson, as a deputation from the Congregational Union of England to the Churches in America, in 1834; and during his stay he received the diploma of D.D. from Yale College. He published several theological works, also the narrative of his official "Visit to the American Churches," and his popular work, "No Fiction."

Frederika Bremer, the Swedish authoress, is the writer of these vigorous lines: the translation is by Mary Howitt.

> Cheek grow pale, but heart be vigorous;
>   Body fall, but soul have peace;
> Welcome, pain, thou searcher rigorous!
>   Slay me, but my faith increase.

Sin, o'er sense so softly stealing;
　Doubt, that would my strength impair,—
Hence at once from life and feeling!
　Now my cross I gladly bear.

Up, my soul! with clear sedateness
　Read Heaven's law, writ bright and broad;
Up! a sacrifice to greatness,
　Truth, and goodness,—up to God!

Up to labor! from thee shaking
　Off the bonds of sloth, be brave!
Give thyself to prayer and waking;
　Toil some fainting soul to save.

Sir R. Grant, who was British Governor of Bombay, died in 1834. He wrote some impressive and stirring Christian lyrics; amongst them, his "Litany," "Saviour! when in dust to Thee, low we bend the adoring knee," "When gathering clouds around I view," and "O Saviour! whose mercy, severe in its kindness," are great favorites.

One of the most beautiful of his poems is "The Brooklet:"—

Sweet brooklet, ever gliding,
Now high the mountain riding,
The lone vale now dividing,
　　Whither away?
"With pilgrim course I flow,
Or in summer's scorching glow,
Or o'er moonless wastes of snow:
　　Nor stop nor stay;
For, oh, by high behest, to a bright abode of rest,
In my parent Ocean's breast,
　　I hasten away!"

Many a dark morass,
Many a craggy mass,
Thy feeble force must pass;
　　Yet, yet delay!

"Though the marsh be dire and deep,
Though the crag be stern and steep,
On, on my course must sweep:
    I may not stay;
For, oh, be it east or west,
To a home of glorious rest,
In the bright sea's boundless breast,
    I hasten away!"

The warbling bowers beside thee,
The laughing flowers that hide thee,
With soft accord they chide thee, —
    Sweet brooklet, stay!
"I taste of the fragrant flowers,
I respond to the warbling bowers,
And sweetly they charm the hours
    Of my winding way;
But ceaseless still in quest
Of that everlasting rest,
In my parent's boundless breast,
    I hasten away!"

Knowest thou that dread abyss?
Is it a scene of bliss?
Oh, rather cling to this, —
    Sweet brooklet, stay!
"Oh, who shall fitly tell
What wonders there may dwell?
That world of mystery well
    Might strike dismay;
But I know 'tis my parent's breast;
There held I must needs be blest;
And with joy to that promised rest,
    I hasten away!"

That was a strange crisis in the life-story of the American missionary to Burmah. Two unbelieving friends pursue their travels hither and thither, and, seemingly by the merest accident, cross each other's path, or rather meet, but meet unconsciously, and, unknown to each other, occupying adjoining chambers, — the one to die, the other to be awakened, by that death, out of his unbelieving reverie, and to seek a better preparation for both living and dying than a sceptical philosophy could give him. This survivor was Judson, whose earnest piety is sufficiently attested by the devotion of six-and-thirty years of unwearied toil to the salvation of idolatrous Burmah.

Dr. Judson, the pioneer missionary to the East, was, in company with his first wife and others, sent forth to India by the American Congregationalist Board of Commissioners. On their way, they became Baptists; and, after meeting with much opposition from the East India Company, they at length, to avoid reshipment to England, sailed from Madras, in a vessel bound to Rangoon. Thus they reached Burmah, where it was found that Providence had a great work for them to do. Their mission was commenced about the year 1815; and Judson labored, in connection with the American Baptists, until the breaking out of the Burmese war with the British, in 1824; when Dr. Judson was seized with violence by the natives, cruelly bound, and cast into prison; and it was not until April, 1826, that he was liberated. During his painful incarceration, like Paul and Silas, he solaced his prison hours with Christian songs. It was during this period that he composed the paraphrase, "Our Father, God, who art in heaven," which is said to be comprised in fewer words even than the original Greek. He was a scholar and linguist, having translated the Bible into Burmese, and constructed a Burmese and English Dictionary. He died in peace, at sea, on the 19th of April, 1850, aged sixty-two years; his remains being committed to the deep.

# NINTH EVENING.

## MODERN ENGLISH AND AMERICAN.

# NINTH EVENING.

## MODERN ENGLISH AND AMERICAN.

BYRON, next in the order of time, blazed, comet-like, on the literary hemisphere; and for his poetic productions received from his publisher not less than fifteen thousand pounds sterling, and a revenue of popular applause. But he was a misanthropic man, — at issue with himself, with his home, and the world at large. As England looked to him, so he looked to her, as his last, sad verses, written at Missolonghi, testify : —

> My days are in the yellow leaf;
> The flowers and fruits of love are gone;
> The worm, the canker, and the grief
>     Are mine alone!
> The fire that on my bosom preys
> Is lone, as some volcanic isle.

Referring to Byron's writings, Professor H. Reed remarks: "Never had our poetry been so profaned. There had been one phase of infidelity with Bolingbroke and his disciples, and another with Paine and his crew; but the most insidious was that which came from the bright, dark fancy of Byron!"

Three things, at least, are chargeable against the seductive verse of Byron, — its direct atheistical tendency, its moral depreciation of women, and its glorifying vice with the attributes of virtue. And yet passages of the highest poetry can be found throughout his writings; but they have been justly compared to the crown of a volcano, "glistening with brilliant sunshine amid yawning rents of inconceivable darkness."

Byron found a faithful friend in Scott, who, on one occasion, had the moral courage to admonish him against his erratic course. "Would you have me turn Methodist?" said Byron. "No," was the reply: "I cannot conceive of your being a Methodist; but you might be a catholic Christian." Byron seems to have entertained the sincerest respect for his friend, if not for his counsel. How little Byron knew, when he shrank from what he thought to be Scott's recommendation of Methodism, that a Methodist preacher would be honored as more than his equal in true "Hebrew Melodies." And how little Scott thought, when he found himself arrested by Wesley's preaching in Kelso churchyard, that the name of one of Wesley's itinerant companions would stand in the lists of immortality above his own, on the line of Israelitish hymnists.

An incident in the life of Lord Byron, which occurred at Falmouth in the year 1809, brought the poet and a Methodist minister, Mr. Shepherd, unexpectedly together; who were until then unknown to each other. Upon the poet inquiring if he could be accommodated with some novel, the minister replied, "I have a book here that might interest you, and one that I am sure will not only refine your taste, but do your heart good: it is the Bible." The poet started in astonishment; and soon his gayety of manner was changed into an expression of thoughtful gravity, while his companion gave him some lessons on the Bible, and from the Bible. "I have not the pleasure of knowing your name, sir," said the host, as his visitor rose to depart; "but I pray God to bless you." "Thank you," was his parting reply: "my name is George Lord Byron; good-by." It was the future poet on his way to Lisbon; and who knows how far the quiet Methodist's lesson "on the Bible and from the Bible" influenced his after thought and feeling, as the author of "Hebrew Melodies"? Was it the echo of that worthy man's touching appeal that sometimes in after days, and in other climes, made him "silent and solemn"? — as when he said, in the presence of his friend Shelley: "Here is a little book which somebody has sent me about Christianity, that has made me very uncomfortable: the reasoning seems to me very strong, the proofs are very staggering. I don't think you can answer it, Shelley: at least, I am sure I can't; and, what is more, I don't wish it."* Alas, that he did not make a better use of his convictions! But let us turn from the regretful memory of the poet's personal errors to some of his beautiful pictorial utterances. These include "The Destruction of Sennacherib," "Hebrew Melodies," "Vision of Belshazzar," in which he has so admirably caught the spirit of the original.

Byron's "Vision of Belshazzar" is wonderfully pictorial and brilliant. We need scarcely repeat it, however; for who has not read it?

> The king was on his throne, the satraps thronged the hall:
> A thousand bright lamps shone o'er that high festival.
> A thousand cups of gold, in Judah deemed divine;
> Jehovah's vessels hold the godless heathen's wine!

* Christophers' Hymns.

In that same hour and hall, the fingers of a hand
Came forth against the wall, and wrote as if on sand;
The fingers of a man, a solitary hand
Along the letters ran, and traced them like a wand.
The monarch saw and shook, and bade no more rejoice;
All bloodless waxed his look, and tremulous his voice:—
"Let the men of lore appear, the wisest of the earth,
And expound the words of fear which mar our royal mirth."

What a grand passage is the following!—

> Between two worlds life hovers like a star,
> 'Twixt night and morn, upon the horizon's verge:
> How little do we know that which we are!
> How less what we may be! The eternal surge
> Of time and tide rolls on, and bears afar
> Our bubbles: as the old burst, new emerge,
> Lashed from the foam of ages; while the graves
> Of empires heave but like some passing waves.

Another of his fine poems is "The Destruction of Sennacherib's Army:"—

> The Assyrian came down like a wolf on the fold,
> And his cohorts were gleaming in purple and gold;
> And the sheen of their spears was like stars on the sea,
> When the blue wave rolls nightly on deep Galilee.
>
> Like the leaves of the forest when summer is green,
> That host with their banners at sunset were seen;
> Like the leaves of the forest when autumn hath blown,
> That host on the morrow lay withered and strown.
> . . . . . . .
> And there lay the rider distorted and pale,
> With the dew on his brow, and the rust on his mail;
> And the tents were all silent, the banners alone,
> The lances uplifted, the trumpets unblown.
>
> And the widows of Ashur are loud in their wail,
> And the idols are broke in the temple of Baal;
> And the might of the Gentile, unsmote by the sword,
> Hath melted like snow in the glance of the Lord!

How sublime is his apostrophe to the Ocean! —

> Roll on, thou deep and dark blue ocean, roll!
> Ten thousand fleets sweep over thee in vain;
> Man marks the earth with ruin; his control
> Stops with the shore; upon the watery plain
> The wrecks are all thy deed, nor doth remain
> A shadow of man's ravage, save his own,
> When, for a moment, like a drop of rain,
> He sinks into thy depths with bubbling groan,
> Without a grave, unknelled, uncoffined, and unknown.
>
> . . . . . . .
>
> Thou glorious mirror, where the Almighty's form
> Glasses itself in tempests; in all time,
> Calm or convulsed, in breeze or gale or storm,
> Icing the pole, or in the torrid clime
> Dark-heaving; boundless, endless, and sublime,
> The image of eternity, the throne
> Of the Invisible; even from out thy slime
> The monsters of the deep are made: each zone
> Obeys thee; thou goest forth, dread, fathomless, alone.

Keble, the popular author of the "Christian Year," has enriched our sacred literature by his Muse. Although expressly written for the service of the Episcopal Church, these sacred lyrics have found many admirers among other communions. We cull a few brilliants from his collection: they need no setting.

### RELIGION OF DAILY LIFE.

> There are in this loud, stunning tide
>   Of human care and crime,
> With whom the melodies abide
>   Of the everlasting chime,
> Who carry music in their heart
> Through dusky lane and wrangling mart;
> Plying their daily task with busier feet,
> Because their secret souls a holy strain repeat.

### FLOWERS.

Sweet nurslings of the vernal skies,
  Bathed in soft airs, and fed with dew,
What more than magic in you lies
  To fill the heart's fond view?
In childhood's sports companions gay,
In sorrow, on life's downward way,
How soothing! in our last decay,
  Memorials prompt and true.

Relics ye are of Eden's bowers,
  As pure, as fragrant, and as fair,
As when ye crowned the sunshine hours
  Of happy wanderers there.

His voice is hushed, but his rare and beautiful melodies will perpetuate his memory as long as the "service of song" shall minister solace to the sons and daughters of sorrow. It was but recently that he left the ranks of the Church Militant to join the hymnists of the "upper sanctuary;" and well has it been remarked, that those who kept him company little thought that he would so soon realize the consoling prophecy of his own verse.

Then, fainting soul, arise and sing;
Mount, but be sober on the wing:
Mount up, for Heaven is won by prayer;
Be sober, for thou art not there.
Till death the weary spirit free,
Thy God hath said 'tis good for thee
To walk by faith, and not by sight:
  Take it on trust a little while;
Soon shalt thou read the mystery right,
  In the full sunshine of His smile!

Dean Milman was born in 1791, was educated at Eton and Oxford, in 1821 was appointed to the professorship of poetry in the University of Oxford, and in 1849 became Dean of St. Paul's. His "Fall of Jerusalem" is one of his noted poems. We subjoin two extracts: —

> When God came down from Heaven, the Living God ¡
> What signs and wonders marked His stately way?
> Brake out the winds in music where He trod?
>   Shone o'er the heavens a brighter, softer day?
> The dumb began to speak, the blind to see,
>   And the lame leaped, and pain and paleness fled;
> The mourner's sunken eye grew bright with glee,
>   And from the tomb awoke the wondering dead!
> When God went back to Heaven, the Living God!
>   Rode He the heavens upon a fiery car?
> Waved seraph wings along His glorious road?
>   Stood still to wonder each bright wandering star?
> Upon the cross He hung, and bowed His head,
>   And prayed for them that smote, and them that curst;
> And drop by drop His slow life-blood was shed,
>   And His last hour of suffering was His worst!

---

>     What means yon blaze on high?
>     The empyrean sky,
> Like the rich veil of some proud fane, is rending;
>     I see the star-paved land
>     Where all the angels stand,
> Even to the highest height in burning rows ascending;
>     Some with their wings dispread,
>     And bowed the stately head,
> As on some mission of God's love departing,
> Like flames from midnight conflagration starting;
> Behold! the appointed messengers are they,
> And nearest earth they wait to waft our souls away.

Hood, although generally known by his sparkling wit and humorous poems, has yet given us some of the most deeply pathetic and impassioned stanzas in the language. He was born in 1798, and died in

1845. His variously gifted pen touched alike the springs of laughter and of tears.

### RUTH.

She stood breast-high amid the corn,
Clasped by the golden light of morn,
Like the sweetheart of the sun,
Who many a glowing kiss had won.

On her cheek an autumn flush
Deeply ripened; such a blush
In the midst of brown was born, —
Like red poppies grown with corn.

Round her eyes her tresses fell,
Which were blackest none could tell;
But long lashes veiled a light
That had else been all too bright;

And her hat with shady brim,
Made her tressy forehead dim:
Thus she stood amid the stooks,
Praising God with sweetest looks.

Sure, I said, Heaven did not mean
Where I reap thou should'st but glean;
Lay thy sheaf adown, and come,
Share my harvest and my home.

Here is another exquisite little poem of his: —

We watched her breathing through the night, her breathing soft and low,
As in her breast the wave of life kept heaving to and fro.
So silently we seemed to speak, so slowly moved about,
As we had lent her half our powers to eke her living out.
Our very hopes belied our fears, our fears our hopes belied;
We thought her dying when she slept, and sleeping when she died.
For when the morn came, dim and sad, and chill with early showers,
Her quiet eyelids closed, — she had another morn than ours!

Moir (better known as the "Delta" of "Blackwood") was born 1798, and died in 1851. This busy surgeon of Musselburgh found time to cultivate a poetic genius of the first order. He wrote among other poems one remarkable for its touching pathos and exquisite feeling, entitled "Casa Wappy" (the self-conferred pet-name of an infant son of the poet, snatched away after a brief illness). Here are a few of the stanzas: —

> And hast thou sought thy heavenly home, our fond, dear boy, —
> The realms where sorrow dare not come, where life is joy?
>     Pure at thy death, as at thy birth,
>     Thy spirit caught no taint from earth:
>     Even by its bliss we mete our dearth, Casa Wappy!
>
> Despair was in our last farewell, as closed thine eye;
> Tears of our anguish may not tell when thou didst die;
>     Words may not paint our grief for thee,
>     Sighs are but bubbles on the sea
>     Of our unfathomed agony, Casa Wappy!
>
> Thou wert a vision of delight to bless us given;
> Beauty embodied to our sight, a type of heaven;
>     So dear to us thou wert, thou art
>     Even less thine own self than a part
>     Of mine and of thy mother's heart, Casa Wappy!
>
> Thy bright, brief day knew no decline, 'twas cloudless joy;
> Sunrise and night alone were thine, beloved boy!
>     This moon beheld thee blithe and gay,
>     That found thee prostrate in decay,
>     And ere a third shone, clay was clay, Casa Wappy!
>
> Gem of our hearth, our household pride, earth's undefiled!
> Could love have saved, thou hadst not died, our dear, sweet child!
>     Humbly we bow to Fate's decree;
>     Yet had we hoped that time should see
>     Thee mourn for us, not us for thee, Casa Wappy!
>
>     . . . . . . .
>
> The nursery shows thy pictured wall, thy bat, thy bow,
> Thy cloak and bonnet, club and ball; but where art thou?

A corner holds thine empty chair;
Thy playthings idly scattered there,
But speak to us of our despair, Casa Wappy!

. . . . . .

Snows muffled earth when thou didst go, in life's spring bloom,
Down to the appointed house below,—the silent tomb!
But now the green leaves of the tree,
The cuckoo and the "busy bee,"
Return, but with them bring not thee, Casa Wappy!

'Tis so: but can it be (while flowers revive again)
Man's doom, in death that we and ours for aye remain?
Oh! can it be, that o'er the grave
The grass renewed should yearly wave,
Yet God forget our child to save,—Casa Wappy?

It cannot be: for were it so thus man could die,
Life were a mockery, Thought were woe, and Truth a lie;
Heaven were a coinage of the brain,
Religion frenzy, Virtue vain,
And all our hopes to meet again Casa Wappy!

The late Lord Jeffrey, in writing to Moir, said of his domestic verses: "I cannot resist the impulse of thanking you with all my heart for the deep gratification you have afforded me, and the soothing, and I hope bettering, emotions which you have excited. I am sure that what you have written is more genuine pathos than any thing almost I have ever read in verse, and is so tender and true, so sweet and natural, as to make all lower recommendations indifferent."

Knox, a Scottish poet, who lived from 1789 to 1825, wrote some splendid lyrics,—"verses alive with sacred fire, and breathing of scriptural simplicity and tenderness." The feelings of the young poet's heart, at a particular crisis of his family history, are seen in these lines:—

Harp of Zion, pure and holy, pride of Judah's eastern land!
May a child of guilt and folly strike thee with a feeble hand?
May I to my bosom take thee, — trembling from the prophet's touch, —
And, with throbbing heart, awake thee to the strains I love so much?
I have loved thy thrilling numbers since the dawn of childhood's day;
Since a mother soothed my slumbers with the cadence of thy lay;
Since a little blooming sister clung with transport round my knee,
And my glowing spirit blessed her, with a blessing caught from thee!
Mother, sister, both are sleeping where no heaving hearts respire,
Whilst the eve of age is creeping round the widowed spouse and sire.
He and his, amid their sorrow, find enjoyment in thy strain;
Harp of Zion, let me borrow comfort from thy chords again!

This same Knox was the author of that exquisite poem on "Mortality," which the late President Lincoln so much admired. It begins, —

>   Oh, why should the spirit of mortal be proud?
>   Like a fast-flitting meteor, a fast-flying cloud,
>   A flash of the lightning, a break of the wave, —
>   He passes from life to his rest in the grave!
>
>   .   .   .   .   .   .   .
>
>   The hand of the king who the sceptre hath borne,
>   The brow of the priest who the mitre hath worn,
>   The eye of the sage, and the heart of the brave,
>   Are hidden and lost in the depths of the grave!
>
>   .   .   .   .   .   .   .
>
>   The saint who enjoyed the communion of heaven,
>   The sinner who dared to remain unforgiven,
>   The wise and the foolish, the guilty and just,
>   Have quietly mingled their bones in the dust!
>
>   .   .   .   .   .   .   .
>
>   And the smile and the tear, and the song and the dirge,
>   Still follow each other, like surge upon surge:
>   From the gilded saloon, to the bier and the shroud, —
>   Oh, why should the spirit of mortal be proud?

David Gray, a self-taught Scottish peasant, wrote this fine sonnet: —

> Why are all fair things at their death the fairest?
> Beauty the beautifullest in decay?
> Why doth rich sunset clothe each closing day
> With ever-new apparelling the rarest?
> Why are the sweetest melodies all born
> Of pain and sorrow? Mourneth not the dove,
> In the green forest gloom, an absent love?
> Leaning her breast against the cruel thorn,
> Doth not the nightingale, poor bird, complain,
> And integrate her uncontrollable woe
> To such perfection, that to hear is pain?
> Thus Sorrow and Death — alone realities —
> Sweeten their ministration, and bestow
> On troublous life a relish for the skies!

Listen to Allan Cunningham's beautiful lyric tribute to the Sabbath : —

Dear is the hallowed morn to me, when village bells awake the day,
And, by their sacred minstrelsy, call me from earthly cares away.
And dear to me the wingèd hour, spent in thy hallowed courts, O Lord!
To feel devotion's soothing power, and catch the manna of Thy word.

. . . . . . . .

Oft when the world, with iron bands, has bound me in its six days' chain,
This bursts them, like the strong man's hands, and lets my spirit loose again.

. . . . . . . .

Go, man of pleasure, strike the lyre, of Sabbaths broken sing the charms ;
Ours are the prophet's car of fire, which bears us to a Father's arms !

The Scottish poet, Pollok, has something of Miltonic grandeur in much of his verse. Here is his delineation of what all would possess, but only few secure, — true happiness : —

True Happiness had no localities,
No tones provincial, no peculiar garb.
Where Duty went, she went, with Justice went,
And went with Meekness, Charity, and Love.
Where'er a tear was dried, a wounded heart
Bound up, a bruised spirit with the dew
Of sympathy anointed, or a pang
Of honest suffering soothed, or injury
Repeated oft, as oft by love forgiven;
Where'er an evil passion was subdued,
Or Virtue's feeble embers fanned; where'er
A sin was heartily abjured and left;
Where'er a pious act was done, or breathed
A pious prayer, or wished a pious wish,—
There was a high and holy place, a spot
Of sacred light, a most religious fane,
Where Happiness, descending, sat and smiled.

Here is a very touching and beautiful description of a dying Christian:—

The dying eye,—that eye alone was bright,
And brighter grew, as nearer death approached;
. . . . . . .
She made a sign
To bring her babe; 'twas brought, and by her placed.
She looked upon its face, that neither smiled,
Nor wept, nor knew who gazed upon 't, and laid
Her hand upon its little breast, and sought
For it, with look that seemed to penetrate
The heavens, unutterable blessings,— such
As God to dying parents only granted,
For infants left behind them in the world.
"God keep my child," we heard her say, and heard
No more: the Angel of the Covenant
Was come, and, faithful to His promise, stood
Prepared to walk with her through death's dark vale.
And now her eyes grew bright and brighter still,—
Too bright for ours to look upon, suffused
With many tears,— and closed without a cloud!
They set,—as sets the morning star, which goes

Not down behind the darkened west, nor hides
Obscured among the tempests of the sky,
But melts away into the light of heaven!

Pollok, who is known to us by his "Course of Time," was born in 1799, and died in 1827, at the early age of twenty-seven years. His too ardent devotion to study superinduced consumption, which soon laid him low. He had only just completed his great poem and commenced his public ministry, when he was removed to the south of England, for the benefit of his health, where, alas! he died. In a letter to his brother about this time (1826), he says, "It is with much pleasure that I am now able to tell you that I have finished my poem. Since I wrote to you last, I have written about three thousand five hundred verses; which is considerably more than a hundred every successive day. This, you will see, was extraordinary expedition to be continued so long; and I neither can nor wish to ascribe it to any thing but an extraordinary manifestation of Divine goodness. Although some nights I was on the border of fever, I rose every morning equally fresh, without one twitch of headache; and, with all the impatience of a lover, hasted to my study. Towards the end of the tenth book, — for the whole consists of ten books, — where the subject was overwhelmingly great, and where I. indeed, seemed to write from immediate inspiration, I felt the body beginning to give way. . . . I am convinced that summer is the best season for great mental exertion; because the heat promotes the circulation of the blood, the stagnation of which is the great cause of misery to cogitative men. The serenity of mind which I have possessed is astonishing. Exalted on my native mountains, and writing often on the top of the very highest of them, I proceeded, from day to day, as if I had been in a world in which there was neither sin nor sickness nor poverty."

Pollok, like Kirke White, adds one more to the list of great minds too early quenched by the excessive ardor of their intellectual pursuits. He has been described as tall, well-proportioned, of a dark complexion, " sicklied o'er with the pale cast of thought," with deep-set eyes, heavy eyebrows, and black, bushy hair. "A smothered light burned in his dark orbs, which flashed with a meteor brilliancy, whenever he spoke with enthusiasm and energy."

Motherwell, the "melancholy" Scottish bard, who died in 1835, at the early age of thirty-eight, has written a sweet poem, "The water, the water!" from which we give an extract: —

> The water, the water! the dear and blessed thing,
> That all day fed the little flowers, on its banks blossoming:
> The water, the water! that murmured in my ear
> Hymns of a saint-like purity, that angels well might hear;
>     And whispered in the gates of heaven,
>     How meek a pilgrim had been shriven.
>
> The water, the water! the mournful, pensive tone
> That whispered to my heart, how soon this weary life was done.
> The water, the water! that rolled so bright and free,
> And bade me mark how beautiful was its soul's purity;
>     And how it glanced to heaven its wave,
>     As, wandering on, it sought its grave!

We cull the following poetic flowers from the pen of the late Bishop Doane, of New Jersey: —

### EVENING.

> Softly now the light of day
> Fades upon my sight away;
> Free from care, from labor free,
> Lord! I would commune with thee.

Thou, whose all-pervading eye
  Naught escapes, without, within,
Pardon each infirmity,
  Open fault and secret sin.

. . . . .

Thou who, sinless, yet hast known
  All of man's infirmity;
Then, from Thy eternal throne,
  Jesus, look with pitying eye!

### THE CHRISTIAN'S DEATH.

Lift not thou the wailing voice,
  Weep not, 'tis a Christian dieth, —
Up, where blessed saints rejoice,
  Ransomed now, the spirit flieth;
High, in heaven's own light, she dwelleth,
Full the song of triumph swelleth;
Freed from earth, and earthly failing,
Lift for her no voice of wailing.

### THE BANNER OF THE CROSS.

Fling out the Banner! let it float skyward and seaward, high and wide;
The sun, that lights its shining folds, the cross on which the Saviour died.
Fling out the Banner! angels bend, in anxious silence, o'er the sign,
And vainly seek to comprehend the wonder of the Love divine!
Fling out the Banner! heathen lands shall see, from far, the glorious sight,
And nations, crowding to be born, baptize their spirits in its light.

What a beautiful spirit of Christian resignation breathes throughout the last lines composed by Mrs. Hemans! — the "Sabbath Sonnet," written a few days prior to her decease: —

How many blessed groups this hour are bending
Through England's primrose meadow-paths their way,
Towards spire and tower, midst shadowing elms ascending,
Whence the sweet chimes proclaim the hallowed day.

> The halls from old heroic ages gray
> Pour their fair children forth; and hamlets low,
> With whose thick orchard-blooms the soft winds play,
> Send out their inmates in a happy flow,
> Like a freed vernal stream. I may not tread
> With them those pathways, — to the feverish bed
> Of sickness bound; yet, O my God! I bless
> Thy mercy, that with Sabbath peace hath filled
> My chastened heart, and all its throbbings stilled
> To one deep calm of lowliest thankfulness!

In less than one month after giving utterance to the above "soul-sonnet," Felicia Hemans passed away; and her memorial, in St. Ann's Church, Dublin, has inscribed over her mortal remains these fitting stanzas, from her own pen: —

> Calm on the bosom of thy God,
>   Fair spirit, rest thee now.
> Even while with us thy footsteps trod,
>   His seal was on thy brow.
> Dust to its narrow house beneath,
>   Soul to its home on high!
> They that have seen thy look in death,
>   No more may fear to die.

This gifted writer excelled as much in her linguistic skill as in her poetical productions; having rendered into English verse many pieces from eminent Continental writers. Her life, overcharged with cares and privations, and neglected by her natural protector, succumbed, in the unequal strife, in 1835.

The Rev. W. Crosswell, of Boston, wrote several beautiful sacred lyrics, which, like those of Bishop Coxe, of New York, are exquisitely musical, brilliant, and stirring. Here are some extracts: —

> I saw them in their synagogue, as in their ancient day,
> And never from my memory the scene shall fade away;
> For dazzling on my vision still the latticed galleries shine
> With Israel's loveliest daughters, in their beauty half divine.

It is the holy Sabbath eve: the solitary light
Sheds, mingled with the hues of day, a lustre nothing bright;
On swarthy brow and piercing glance it falls with saddening tinge,
And dimly gilds the Pharisee's phylacteries and fringe.
The two-leaved doors slide slow apart before the Eastern screen,
As rise the Hebrew harmonies, with chanted prayers between;
And 'mid the tissued veils disclosed, of many a gorgeous dye,
Enveloped in their jewelled scarfs the sacred records lie.
Robed in his sacerdotal vest, a silvery-headed man,
With voice of solemn cadence, o'er the backward letters ran;
And often yet, methinks, I see the glow and power that sate
Upon his face, as forth he spread the roll immaculate.
And fervently, that hour, I prayed that from the mighty scroll
Its light, in burning characters, might break on every soul;
That on their hardened hearts the veil might be no longer dark,
But be for ever rent in twain, like that before the ark;
For yet the tenfold film shall fall, O Judah! from thy sight,
And every eye be purged to read thy testimonies right,—
When thou, with all Messiah's signs in Christ distinctly seen,
Shalt, by Jehovah's nameless name, invoke the Nazarene!

Rev. Dr. Crosswell's death was remarkable: while engaged in the public Sabbath afternoon service, at the conclusion of the last collect, instead of rising from his knees, he sank upon the floor, and shortly afterwards expired.

Among our American poets, we think the late George W. Bethune well deserves a place of honor. What glad sunshine gleams through the following musical stanzas:—

I love to sing when I am glad,—song is the echo of my gladness:
I love to sing when I am sad, till song makes sweet my very sadness:
'Tis pleasant time when voices chime to some sweet rhyme in concert only;
And song to me is company, good company, when I am lonely.
Whene'er I greet the morning light, my song goes forth in thankful numbers;
And 'mid the shadows of the night I sing to me my welcome slumbers:

My heart is stirred by each glad bird whose notes are heard in summer bowers;
And song gives birth to friendly mirth around the hearth in wintry hours.
Man first learned song in Paradise, from the bright angels o'er him singing;
And in our home above the skies glad anthems are for ever ringing.
God lends His ear, well pleased to hear the songs that cheer his children's sorrow;
Till day shall break, and we shall wake where love will make unfading morrow.

. . . . . . . .

Then let me sing, while yet I may, like him God loved, — the sweet-toned Psalmist,
Who found in harp and holy lay the charm that keeps the spirit calmest;
For sadly here I need the cheer, while sinful fear with promise blendeth:
Oh, how I long to join the throng who sing the song that never endeth!

On one occasion, when in his pulpit awaiting the arrival of his congregation, he pencilled off on a scrap of paper the lines commencing, "Oh for the happy hour!" On the day preceding his death, which took place at Florence, Italy, in 1862, he wrote some affecting lines, of which the following are the commencement: —

> When time seems short, and death is near,
> And I am pressed by doubt and fear,
> And sins, an overflowing tide,
> Assail my peace on every side, —
> This thought my refuge still shall be,
> I know the Saviour died for me!

The beauty of the following poem, by Bethune, will be recognized by all who read it: —

I am alone ; and yet in the still solitude there is a rush
Around me, as were met a crowd of viewless wings : I hear a gush
    Of uttered harmonies, — heaven meeting earth,
    Making it to rejoice with holy mirth.
Ye winged mysteries, sleeping before my spirit's conscious eye,
Beckoning me to arise, and go forth from my very self, and fly
With you far in the unknown, unseen immense
Of worlds beyond our sphere, — what are ye ? whence ?
Ye eloquent voices, now soft as breathings of a distant flute,
Now strong as when rejoices the trumpet in the victory and pursuit :
Strange are ye, yet familiar, as ye call
My soul to wake from earth's sense and its thrall.
I know you now : I see, with more than natural light, ye are the good,
The wise departed ; ye are come from heaven to claim your brotherhood
With mortal brother, struggling in the strife
And chains which once were yours in this sad life.

Mrs. Barrett Browning's religious poetry abounds with splendid metaphors and high aspirations, expressed with masterly power : in some instances, the language may seem somewhat turgid and obscure, but the soul of true poetry is infused through all. Here are two fine passages : —

    What are we set on earth for ? Say to toil !
    Nor seek to leave thy tending of the vines
    For all the heat o' the sun, till it declines,
    And death's mild curfew shall from work assoil.
    God did anoint thee with His odorous oil
    To wrestle, not to reign ; and He assigns
    All thy tears, ever like pure crystallines,
    Unto thy fellows, working the same soil,
    To wear for amulets. So others shall
    Take patience, labor, to their heart and hand,
    From thy hand and thy heart and thy brave cheer,
    And God's grace fructify through thee to all !
    The least flower with a brimming cup may stand
    And share its dew-drop with another near.

### COMFORT.

Speak low to me, my Saviour, low and sweet,
From out the hallelujahs, sweet and low,
Lest I should fear and fall, and miss thee so,
Who art not missed, by any that entreat.
Speak to me as to Mary at Thy feet;
And if no precious gums my hands bestow,
Let my tears drop, like amber, while I go
In search of Thy divinest voice, complete
In humanest affection; thus, in sooth,
To lose the sense of losing! As a child,
Whose song-bird seeks the wood for evermore,
Is sung to, in its stead, by mother's mouth;
Till sinking on her breast, love reconciled,
He sleeps the faster that he wept before.

From a couch of sickness went forth those earnest, scholarly, and artistic poems of Mrs. Barrett Browning, which have won for her such pre-eminent fame. This gifted daughter of genius left our world, after enriching it with many an imperishable tribute of her Muse, in the midsummer of 1861; and her "sacred dust" sleeps under the blue sky of that land —

"Where the poet's lip and the painter's hand
　Are most divine."

Whoever of us may hereafter chance to visit Florence will not be likely to forget that poet-shrine in the English burying-ground there; associating it with her own plaintive and prophetic words, so familiar to us all, —

And friends, dear friends, when it shall be
That this low breath is gone from me,
And round my bier ye come to weep, —
Let one, most loving of you all,
Say, "Not a tear must o'er her fall, —
'He giveth His beloved sleep.'"

We have, however, begun her beautiful poem with the last stanza : let us recite one or two of those preceding : —

> Of all the thoughts of God, that are
> Borne inward unto souls afar,
> Along the Psalmist's music deep,
> Now tell me if there any is,
> For gift or grace, surpassing this, —
> "He giveth His beloved sleep."
>
> What would we give to our beloved?
> The hero's heart to be unmoved,
> The poet's star-tuned heart to sweep,
> The Senate's shouts to patriot's vows,
> The monarch's crown to light the brows, —
> "He giveth His beloved sleep."

How affectingly beautiful are her lines on Cowper's Grave! — too long, however, for insertion here, and too excellent to be marred by abridgment.

Proctor (known by the pseudonym of Barry Cornwall) was born in 1790. He has published "Dramatic Sketches," and various other volumes of lyrics; some of which exhibit a happy combination of religious feeling with poetic skill. For example, the following : —

> We are born; we laugh; we weep;
> We love; we droop; we die;
> Ah! wherefore do we laugh or weep?
> Why do we live or die?
> Who knows that secret deep?
> Alas! not I.
>
> Why doth the violet spring
> Unseen by human eye?
> Why do the radiant seasons bring
> Sweet thoughts that quickly fly?
> Why do our fond hearts cling
> To things that die?

> We toil, through pain and wrong;
>   We fight — and fly;
> We love; we lose; and then, ere long,
>   Stone-dead we lie.
> O life! is *all* thy song
> "Endure and die"?

---

> There is a land immortal, the beautiful of lands;
> Beside the ancient portal a sentry grimly stands.
> He only can undo it, and open wide the door,
> And mortals who pass through it are mortals never more.
>
> . . . . . . . .
>
> Their sighs are lost in singing, they're blessed in their tears,
> Their journey homeward winging, they leave to earth their fears.
> Death like an angel seemeth, — "We welcome thee," they cry;
> Their face with glory beameth, 'tis life with them to die!*

Here is a little lyric gem, from the facile and picturesque pen of Charles Kingsley: —

> My fairest child, I have no song to give you;
> No lark could pipe to skies so dull and gray;
> Yet, ere we part, one lesson I can leave you,
>   For every day:
> Be good, sweet maid, and let who will be clever;
> Do noble things, not dream them, all day long;
> And so make life, death, and that vast forever
>   One grand, sweet song!

Harriet Winslow List is the author of these beautiful lines: —

> Why thus longing, thus for ever sighing,
>   For the far-off, unattained, and dim,
> While the beautiful, all round thee lying,
>   Offers up its low, perpetual hymn?
>
> Wouldst thou listen to its gentle teaching,
>   All thy restless yearnings it would still;
> Leaf and flower and laden bee are preaching,
>   Thine own sphere, though humble, first to fill.
>
> . . . . . . . .

---

* Flavel beautifully said, "Heaven is epitomized in holiness, and it is the true badge and livery of the heaven-born."

Not by deeds that win the crowd's applauses,
    Not by works that give thee world-renown,
Not by martyrdom or vaunted crosses,
    Canst thou win and wear the immortal crown.

Daily struggling, though unloved and lonely,
    Every day a rich reward will give;
Thou wilt find, by hearty striving only,
    And truly loving, thou canst truly live.

The late Adelaide H. Proctor, daughter of the well-known poet of that name, has left us some rare Christian lyrics: we quote a few lines from her hymn on Thankfulness:—

My God, I thank Thee who hast made the earth so bright;
So full of splendor and of joy, beauty and light;
So many glorious things are here, noble and right.
I thank Thee, too, that Thou hast made joy to abound;
So many gentle thoughts and deeds circling us round;
That in the darkest spot of earth some love is found.
I thank Thee more that all our joy is touched with pain;
That shadows fall on brightest hours; that thorns remain;
So that earth's bliss may be our guide, and not our chain.
For Thou, who knowest, Lord, how soon our weak heart clings,
Hast given us joys, tender and true, yet all with wings;
So that we see, gleaming on high, diviner things.

Here is a little admonitory gem of hers:—

One by one the sands are flowing, one by one the moments fall;
Some are coming, some are going; do not strive to grasp them all.
One by one thy duties wait thee,—let thy whole strength go to each:
Let no future dreams elate thee; learn thou first what these can teach.

. . . . . . . . . .

Every hour that flits so slowly has its task to do or bear;
Luminous the crown, and holy, if thou set each gem with care.
Hours are golden links, God's token, reaching heaven; but one by one
Take them, lest the chain be broken ere thy pilgrimage be done.

R. M. Milnes (Lord Houghton) has published several fine pieces; among them, some lines on "The Worth of Hours," — which end as follows: —

> So should we live that every hour
> May die, as dies the natural flower, —
> A self-reviving thing of power;
>
> That every thought and every deed
> May hold within itself the seed
> Of future good and future meed;
>
> Esteeming sorrow, whose employ
> Is to develop, not destroy,
> Far better than a barren joy.

In the olden time, the hum of Babel did not reach to the scholar's hermitage. "When all is still and quiet in a man, then will God speak to him, in the cool of the day," is the beautiful remark of Norris, of Bemerton; "and, in that calm and silence of the passions, the Divine voice will be heard." It would be well for us, of these days of tumult and strange excitement, could we steal away awhile from the thronged thoroughfares of life, at quiet eventide, and muse over the suggestive lives and instructive pages of the worthies who have bequeathed to us the wealth of their experience in their Christian melodies. Ben Jonson, inspired by the genius of his age, remarked, "Good men are the stars of the world." One of these stars, Owen Feltham, justly observes, "The acts of our famous predecessors are beacons set upon hills to summon us to the defence of virtue." He says elsewhere, — in one of his letters, late in life, — "I have lived in such a course, as my books have ever been my delight and recreation; and that which some men call idleness, I will call the sweetest part of my life, — and that is my thinking." The movements of the age are somewhat swifter now than then; yet that is no reason why we should deny ourselves all repose and reflection.

Fittingly does the laurel-crown adorn the brow of Alfred Tennyson, — a minstrel worthy to be successor to William Wordsworth. Our poet's early days were passed amid the fens of Lincolnshire and Cambridge; and there, in his earlier poems, he pictured his landscapes; but the productions of his maturer years have taken tone and color from the richer scenery around Alum Bay, Carisbrook, and his beautiful home adjacent, — Farringford, in the Isle of Wight. Within this quiet, rural retreat by the sea, Tennyson lives among his children and his books; extracting, ever and anon, from his wayside rambles, many an illuminated and beautiful thought, for the delectation of his readers. His ideal and elegiac poems are well known; indeed, so are his "Locksley Hall," "Idyls of the King," &c. We might easily increase the store, had we space to spare; but here are a few brilliants from the pictorial pages of Tennyson: —

> More things are wrought by prayer
> Than this world dreams of. Wherefore let thy voice
> Rise like a fountain for me night and day.
> For what are men better than sheep or goats,
> That nourish a blind life within the brain,
> If, knowing God, they lift not hands of prayer,
> Both for themselves and those who call them friend?
> For so the whole round earth is every way
> Bound by gold chains about the feet of God.

### VICTORIOUS FAITH.

> I cannot hide that some have striven,
> Achieving calm, to whom was given
> The joy that mixes man with heaven;

Who, rowing hard against the stream,
Saw distant gates of Eden gleam,
And did not dream it was a dream;
But heard, by secret transports led,
Even in the charnels of the dead,
The murmur of the fountain-head:
Which did accomplish their desire,
Bore and forbore, and did not tire,
Like Stephen, an unquenched fire.
He heeded not reviling tones,
Nor sold his heart to idle moans,
Though cursed and scorned, and hissed, with stones:
But looking upward, full of grace,
He prayed, and from a happy place
God's glory smote him on the face.

Who that has ever lingered by some rippling brook, in a shady retreat, and listened to its sweet music, does not recall Tennyson's expressive lyric, as liquid in its ripple as the stream it describes? —

I come from haunts of coot and hern, I make a sudden sally,
And sparkle out among the fern, to bicker down a valley,
I chatter over stony ways, in little sharps and trebles,
I bubble into eddying bays, I babble on the pebbles.
With many a curve my banks I fret, by many a field and fallow,
And many a fairy foreland set with willow-weed and mallow.
. . . . . . . . .
I chatter, chatter, as I flow to join the brimming river,
For men may come and men may go, but I go on for ever.
I wind about, and in and out, with here a blossom sailing,
And here and there a lusty trout, and here and there a grayling,
And here and there a foamy flake upon me, as I travel,
With many a silvery waterbreak above the golden gravel,
And draw them all along, and flow to join the brimming river,
For men may come and men may go, but I go on for ever.

Bernard Barton, the Quaker poet (1784–1849), deserves a place among the Christian minstrels, for his many refined and musical lyrics. Some specimen lines follow, from his poem on Human Life: —

I walked the fields at morning's prime, the grass was ripe for mow-
    ing;
The skylark sang his matin chime, and all was brightly glowing.
"And thus," I cried, "the ardent boy, his pulse with rapture beat-
    ing,
Deems life's inheritance a joy, the future proudly greeting."
I wandered forth at noon: alas! on earth's maternal bosom
The scythe had left the withering grass, and stretched the fading
    blossom.
And thus, I thought, with many a sigh, the hopes we fondly cher-
    ish,
Like flowers, which blossom but to die, seem only born to perish.
. . . . . . . .
Once more at eve abroad I strayed, through lonely hay-fields
    musing,
While every breeze that round me played, rich fragrance was dif-
    fusing.

His vigorous lines on "The Sabbath" remind us of George Herbert: —

>Types of eternal rest, fair buds of bliss,
>    In heavenly flowers unfolding week by week;
>The next world's goodness imaged forth in this;
>    Days of whose worth the Christian's heart can speak!
>. . . . . . .
>Days fixed by God for intercourse with dust,
>    To raise our thoughts and purify our powers;
>Periods appointed to renew our trust;
>    A gleam of glory after six days' showers!
>. . . . . . .
>Foretastes of heaven on earth, pledges of joy
>    Surpassing fancy's flights and fiction's story;
>The preludes of a feast that cannot cloy,
>    And the bright out-courts of immortal glory!

One of the most industrious and skilful of literary benefactors to our sacred anthology is Sir John Bowring. In the department of Letters he has been a laborious worker. Besides various translations from the

Russian, Hungarian, Bohemian, and other national poets, he has published " Matins and Vespers," "Hymns," and other works in prose. He was appointed British Governor at Hong Kong, and subsequently to a special mission to Siam; and in 1859 retired from public service, with distinguished honor and a pension.

His hymns are much admired; for example, these: "In the cross of Christ I glory," "Watchman, tell us of the night."

Bowring's lyrics are charming. Here is one of the choicest: —

Sweet are the joys of home, and pure as sweet; for they,
Like dews of morn and evening, come to wake and close the day.
The world hath its delights, and its delusions too;
But home to calmer bliss invites, more tranquil and more true.

. . . . . . .

Life's charities, like light, spread smilingly afar;
But stars approached become more bright, and home is life's own star.
The pilgrim's step in vain seeks Eden's sacred ground;
But in home's holy joys again an Eden may be found.
A glance of heaven to see, to none on earth is given;
And yet a happy family is but an earlier heaven!

His song on the beauties of creation ends with this choice stanza: —

> And if thy glories here be found
> Streaming with radiance all around,
>   What must the FOUNT OF GLORY be?
> In Thee we'll hope; in Thee confide;
> Thou mercy's never-ebbing tide!
> Thou Love's unfathomable sea!

Mrs. Craik (better known as Miss Muloch), author of "John Halifax," and numerous other popular works, has contributed some exquisite little lyrics to our sacred poetry. We have annexed two examples; the first is founded upon a Russian proverb, and is entitled " Labor and Rest : " —

Two hands across the breast, and work is done;
Two pale feet crossed in rest, the race is run!
Two eyes with coin-weights shut, and all tears cease;
Two lips where grief is mute, and wrath at peace:
So pray we oftentimes mourning our lot;
God in His kindness answering not!

Two hands to work addressed, aye for His praise;
Two feet that never rest, walking His ways;
Two eyes that look above, still through all tears;
Two lips that speak but love, never more fears:
So cry we afterwards, low at our knees, —
Pardon those erring prayers! Father, hear these!

### MORTALITY.

Ye dainty mosses, lichens gray,
  Pressed each to each in tender fold,
And peacefully thus day by day
  Returning to their mould:
Brown leaves, that with aërial grace
  Slip from your branch like birds a-wing,
Each having in the appointed place
  Its bud of future spring:
If we, God's conscious creatures, knew
  But half your faith in our decay,
We should not tremble as we do
  When summoned clay to clay.
But with an equal patience sweet,
  We should put off this mortal gear;
In whatsoe'er new form is meet,
  Content to reappear.
Knowing each germ of life He gives
  Must have in Him its source and rise;
Being that of His being lives
  May change, but never dies.

Ye dead leaves, dropping soft and slow,
Ye mosses green and lichens fair,
Go to your graves, as I will go,
For God is also there.

Mrs. Charles, whose accomplished and versatile pen has enriched our sacred literature with so many productions in prose and verse, is the author of these musical and instructive lines: —

Is thy cruse of comfort failing? rise and share it with another,
And through all the years of famine it shall serve thee and thy brother.
Love Divine will fill thy storehouse, or thy handful still renew;
Scanty fare for one will often make a royal feast for two.
For the heart grows rich in giving; all its wealth is living grain;
Seeds, which mildew in the garner, scattered, fill with gold the plain.
Is thy burden hard and heavy? do thy steps drag wearily?
Help to bear thy brother's burden; God will bear both it and thee.
Numb and weary on the mountains, wouldst thou sleep amidst the snow?
Chafe that frozen form beside thee, and together both shall glow.
Art thou stricken in life's battle? many wounded round thee moan;
Lavish on their wounds thy balsams, and that balm shall heal thine own.
Is the heart a well left empty? None but God its void can fill;
Nothing but a ceaseless Fountain can its ceaseless longings still.
Is the heart a living power? Self-entwined, its strength sinks low;
It can only live in loving, and by serving love will grow.

Archbishop Trench, whose beautiful translations of mediæval hymns and other cognate works are so highly esteemed, is the author of the following sonnets: —

CARPE DIEM!

We live not in our moments or our years;
  The present we fling from us like the rind
  Of some sweet future, which we after find
Bitter to taste, or bind *that* in with fears,

And water it beforehand with our tears, —
    Vain tears for that which never may arrive;
    Meanwhile the joy whereby we ought to live,
Neglected, or unheeded, disappears.
    Wiser it were to welcome and make ours
Whate'er of good, though small, the present brings,—
    Kind greetings, sunshine, songs of birds, sweet flowers,
With a child's pure delight in little things;
    And of the griefs unborn to rest secure,
    Knowing that mercy ever will endure.

---

Lord, what a change within us one short hour
    Spent in Thy presence will avail to make!
    What heavy burdens from our bosoms take;
What parchèd grounds refresh, as with a shower!
We kneel, and all around us seems to lower;
    We rise, and all the distant and the near
    Stands forth in sunny outline, brave and clear!
We kneel, how weak! we rise, how full of power!
Why, therefore, should we do ourselves this wrong,
Or others, that we are not always strong;
That we are ever overborne with care;
    That we should ever weak or heartless be,
Anxious or troubled, when with us is prayer,
    And joy and strength and courage are with *Thee?*

Dr. Bonar is a prominent clergyman of the Free Church of Scotland, and author of many beautiful sacred lyrics. His "Hymns of Faith and Hope" comprise some fine Christian lyrics; many of them familiar to us, such as this: —

I was a wandering sheep, I did not love the fold;
I did not love my shepherd's voice, I would not be controlled, &c.

Here are some less familiar, and of great beauty: —

    Beyond the smiling and the weeping I shall be soon:
        Beyond the waking and the sleeping,
        Beyond the sowing and the reaping,
            I shall be soon!

Love, rest, and home, — sweet hope!
Lord, tarry not, but come!

. . . .

Beyond the parting and the meeting I shall be soon:
Beyond the farewell and the greeting,
Beyond this pulse's fever-beating,
I shall be soon!
Love, rest, and home, — sweet hope!
Lord, tarry not, but come!

---

Cling to the Crucified! His death is life to thee,
Life for eternity!
His pains thy pardon seal; His stripes thy bruises heal;
His cross proclaims thy peace, bids every sorrow cease!
His blood is all to thee.
It purges thee from sin,
It sets thy spirit free,
It keeps thy conscience clean.
Cling to the Crucified!

---

Far down the ages now, her journey well-nigh done,
The pilgrim Church pursues her way, in haste to reach the crown.
The story of the past comes up before her view;
How well it seems to suit her still, old, and yet ever new,
'Tis the same story still of sin and weariness, —
Of grace and love still flowing down to pardon and to bless.
'Tis the old sorrow still, the brier and the thorn;
And 'tis the same old solace yet, the hope of coming morn.

---

'Tis not for man to trifle! Life is brief,
And sin is here.
Our age is but the falling of a leaf,
A dropping tear.
We have no time to sport away the hours,
All must be earnest in a world like ours.

Not many lives, but only one have we,
One, only one;
How sacred should that one life ever be,
That narrow span!

Day after day filled up with blessed toil,
Hour after hour still bringing in new spoil.
. . . . .
O life below! how brief and poor and sad!
One heavy sigh!
O life above! how long, how fair and glad!
An endless joy!
Oh, to be done with daily dying here!
Oh, to begin the living in yon sphere!

The following beautiful hymn for the Sabbath was written by one of England's greatest scholars, Dr. Wordsworth, Canon of Westminster Abbey. "I was with him in the library," says the correspondent who gave it to the press, when he put his arm in mine, saying, 'Come upstairs with me: the ladies are going to sing a hymn to encourage your labor for God's holy day.' We all then sang from manuscript the hymn. I was in raptures with it. It was some days after before I knew it was written by himself."

O day of rest and gladness, O day of joy and light,
O balm of care and sadness, most beautiful, most bright!
On thee the high and lowly, bending before the throne,
Sing, *Holy, Holy, Holy*, to the great *Three* in *One*.

On thee at the creation the light first had its birth;
On thee for our salvation Christ rose from depths of earth;
On thee our Lord victorious the Spirit sent from heaven,
And thus on thee most glorious a triple light was given.

Thou art a port protected from storms that round us rise;
A garden intersected with streams of Paradise;
Thou art a cooling fountain in life's dry, dreary sand;
From thee, like Pisgah's mountain, we view our promised land.

Thou art a holy ladder, where angels go and come,
Each Sunday finds us gladder, nearer to heaven, our home;
A day of sweet refection thou art, a day of love,
A day of resurrection from earth to things above.

"Going Out, and Coming In" is the title of an exquisite little lyric by Isabella Craig. It is too good to abridge a line of it.

In that home was joy and sorrow, where an infant first drew breath,
While an aged sire was drawing near unto the gate of death;
His feeble pulse was failing, and his eye was growing dim, —
He was standing on the threshold, when they brought the babe to him:
While to murmur forth a blessing on the little one he tried,
In his trembling arms he raised it, pressed it to his lips, and — died!
An awful darkness resteth on the path they both begin,
Who thus met upon the threshold, — going out, and coming in!
Going out unto the triumph, coming in unto the fight;
Coming in unto the darkness, going out unto the light!
Although the shadow deepened in the moment of eclipse,
When he passed through the dread portal, with the blessing on his lips;
And to him who bravely conquers, as he conquered in the strife,
Life is but the way of dying, death is but the gate of life!
Yet awful darkness resteth on the path we all begin,
When we meet upon the threshold, — going out, and coming in!

It has been beautifully said, " In our world there are two very interesting events of Christian history; the one is that of the young disciple entering the Church Militant, the other is that of the aged disciple passing away from earth to join the Church Triumphant."

This, Miss Isabella Craig has delicately and yet forcibly expressed in the above lines. She took the Crystal Palace prize offered for the best poem on Burns, in 1856. It was the beautiful thought of a recent English hymnist, that "two streams flowed from the threshold of Eden, — the river of life and the fountain of tears!"

Here is a striking poem, by Dr. B. H. Kennedy, who is rector of West Felton, England: —

Ask ye what great thing I know
That delights and stirs me so?
What the high reward I win?
Whose the name I glory in?
    Jesus Christ, the Crucified!

What is faith's foundation strong?
What awakes my lips to song?
He who bore my sinful load,
Purchased for me peace with God,
    Jesus Christ, the Crucified!

. . . . .

Who defeats my fiercest foes?
Who consoles my saddest woes?
Who revives my fainting heart,
Healing all its hidden smart?
    Jesus Christ, the Crucified!

Who is life in life to me?
Who the death of death will be?
Who will place me on His right?
With the countless hosts of light?
    Jesus Christ, the Crucified!

Mary Howitt's brilliant "Thoughts of Heaven" need no introduction to secure a welcome:—

They come as we gaze on the midnight sky,
When the star-gemmed vault looks dark and high,
And the soul, on the wings of thought sublime,
Soars from the dim world, and the bounds of time.
Till the mental eye becomes unsealed,
And the mystery of being in light revealed.
They rise in the Gothic chapel dim,
When slowly comes forth the holy hymn,
And the organ's rich tones swell full and high,
Till the roof peals back the melody.

Thoughts of heaven! from his joy beguiled,
They come to the bright-eyed, sinless child;
To the man of age in his dim decay,
Bringing hope that his youth had borne away;

To the woe-smit soul in its dark distress,
As flowers spring up in the wilderness;
And in silent chambers of the dead,
When the mourner goes with soundless tread;
For, as the day-beams freely fall,
Pure thoughts of heaven are sent to all.

This is a beautiful stanza, the closing one of William Howitt's poem on the Sabbath:—

O'er the wide world, blest day, thine influence flies!
Rest o'er the sufferer spreads her balmy wings;
Love wakes, joy dawns, praise fills the listening skies;
The expanding heart from earth's enchantment springs;
Heaven, for one day, withdraws its ancient ban,
Unbars its gates, and dwells once more with man!

Margaret Mercer is the author of the following admirable lines:—

Not on a prayerless bed, not on a prayerless bed,
 Compose thy weary limbs to rest;
 For they alone are blest
  With balmy sleep
  Whom angels keep;
Nor, though by care oppressed, or anxious sorrow,
Or thought in many a coil perplexed for coming morrow,
  Lay not thy head
  On prayerless bed.
. . . . . . . .
Arouse thee, weary soul, nor yield to slumber,
 Till, in communion blest,
 With the elect ye rest,
Those souls of countless number;
 And with them raise
 The note of praise,
Reaching from earth to heaven;
Chosen, redeemed, forgiven!
 So lay thy happy head,
 Prayer-crowned, on blessed bed.

How little faith we have in the efficacy of prayer! yet, however faithless we may become in its exercise, there is a reality in its power. Did we remember that in the ratio of our faith is its efficacy, we should cease to wonder that our prayers are sometimes unanswered. The heathen and the worldling do not so regard prayer, in times of extremity; when their ordinary resources fail them, they, too, resort to prayer. It is said that when the Saxon king, Ethelred, invaded Wales, he observed near the Britons a host of unarmed men. He inquired who they were, and was told that they were monks of Bangor, praying for the success of their countrymen. "Then they have begun the fight against us," he said: "attack them first."

All who are taught by the Spirit, know that what the air of heaven is to the body, what sunshine is to the eye, what spring is to flowers, herbs, and trees, prayer is to the believing soul. Without it, the soul would sicken and die.

Here is one of the late Dr. J. M. Neale's splendid poems: —

> The foe behind, the deep before,
> Our hosts have dared and passed the sea;
> And Pharaoh's warriors strew the shore,
> And Israel's ransomed tribes are free!
> Lift up, lift up your voices now,
> The whole wide world rejoices now!
> The Lord hath triumphed gloriously!
> The Lord shall reign victoriously!

Happy morrow, turning sorrow into peace and mirth;
Bondage ending, love descending o'er the earth;
Seals assuring, guards securing, watch His earthly prison;
Seals are shattered, guards are scattered, Christ hath risen!

> No longer must the mourners weep,
>   Nor call departed Christians dead;
> For death is hallowed into sleep,
>   And every grave becomes a bed.

Now once more Eden's door open stands to mortal eyes.
For Christ hath risen, and men shall rise.

. . . . . . . .

It is not exile, rest on high; it is not sadness, peace from strife;
To fall asleep is not to die, to dwell with Christ is better life.

Our kindred and friends, who have passed from the domain of Time to the great Eternity, we should tenderly remember. Because we have been obliged to bury their cherished forms in the darkness and silence of the tomb, we need not cease to enshrine, in our inmost hearts, the sweet memories of their kindly words and deeds, until we, by God's great bounty, rejoin them in the great festival of eternal life. "Very dear were they when with us; lovingly would we think of them, now they have left us."

The hymn so familiar to Sunday-school gatherings, "Jesus is mine," was composed by Henry Hope, of Dublin, and first printed in 1852, for private circulation, but has since been included in numerous collections.

Now I have found a friend, — Jesus is mine;
His love shall never end, — Jesus is mine.
Though earthly joys decrease,
Though earthly friendships cease,
Now I have lasting peace, Jesus is mine.

Here is another sweet song, engendered in a sick-room, by Jane Crewdson, of Manchester, England, who recently, during protracted illness, beguiled her seclusion by writing numerous beautiful effusions, like the following: —

I've found a joy in sorrow, a secret balm for pain,
A beautiful to-morrow, of sunshine after rain;
I've found a branch of healing near every bitter spring;
A whispered promise stealing o'er every broken string;

I've found a glad hosanna for every woe and wail,
A handful of sweet manna when grapes from Eshcol fail;
I've found a "Rock of Ages," when desert wells were dry,
And, after weary stages, I've found an Elim nigh, —
An Elim, with its coolness, its fountains, and its shade,
A blessing in its fulness, when buds of promise fade.
O'er tears of soft contrition I've seen a rainbow light, —
A glory and fruition, so near, yet out of sight.
My Saviour! Thee possessing, I have the joy, the balm,
The healing and the blessing, the sunshine and the psalm;
The promise for the fearful, the Elim for the faint,
The rainbow for the tearful, the glory for the saint.

Charlotte Brontё, the well-known authoress, wrote some remarkable lyrics. We select a stanza or two from her "Twilight Reveries:"—

The human heart has hidden treasures,
  In secret kept, in silence sealed:
The thoughts, the hopes, the dreams, the pleasures,
  Whose charms were broken, if revealed.

. . . . . .

And there are hours of lonely musing,
  Such as at twilight's silence come,
When, soft as birds, their pinions closing,
  The heart's best feelings gather home.
Then in our souls there seems to languish
  A tender grief that is not woe;
And thoughts that once wrung groans of anguish
  Now cause but some mild tears to flow.

. . . . . .

And it can dwell on moonlight glimmer,
  On evening shades and loneliness,
And, while the sky grows dim and dimmer,
  Feel no untold and sad distress:
Only a deeper impulse given
  By lonely hour and darkened room,
To solemn thoughts that soar to heaven,
  Seeking a life and world to come.

Emily, the sister of Charlotte Brontё, has, in her last poem, these striking lines: —

No coward soul is mine,
No trembler in the world's storm-troubled sphere;
　I see Heaven's glories shine,
And faith shines equal, arming me from fear.

. . . . . . .

　Naught wakens doubt in one
Holding so fast by Thine infinity;
　So surely anchored on
The steadfast rock of immortality!
　With wide-embracing love
Thy spirit animates eternal years,
　Pervades and broods above,
Changes, sustains, dissolves, creates, and rears.
　Though earth and man were gone,
And suns and universes ceased to be,
　And Thou wert left alone, —
Every existence would exist in Thee.

Like the clouded spirit of Cowper, did the other sister, Anne Brontë, seem to live; although her closing hours were cheered by light from Heaven. "Her belief to her then did not bring to her dread, as of a stern Judge, but hope, as in a Father and Saviour; and no faltering hope was it, but a sure and steadfast conviction, on which, in the rude passage from time to eternity, she threw the weight of her human weakness, and by which she was enabled to bear what was to be borne, patiently, serenely, victoriously." Very touching is her "Prayer:" —

My God, (oh, let me call Thee mine, — weak, wretched sinner though I be!)
My trembling soul would fain be Thine; my feeble faith still clings to Thee;
Not only for the past I grieve, — the future fills me with dismay;
Unless Thou hasten to relieve, Thy suppliant is a castaway!
I cannot say my faith is strong, I dare not hope my love is great, —
But strength and love to Thee belong; oh, do not leave me desolate!

I know I owe my all to Thee; oh, take the heart I cannot give;
Do Thou, my strength, my Saviour be, and *make* me to Thy glory live!

Her last song on earth ended with these beautiful, trustful words: —

If Thou shouldst bring me back to life, more humbled I should be;
More wise, more strengthened for the strife, more apt to lean on Thee;
Should death be standing at the gate, thus should I keep my vow;
But, Lord, whatever be my fate, oh, let me serve Thee *now!*

These lines written, the desk was closed, the pen laid aside for ever.

The Brontë family were remarkable for their strength of character and genius, as their writings sufficiently prove. These three gifted sisters followed each other, in rapid succession, to the grave. They were, however, sustained, under protracted physical suffering, by the consolations of the Christian faith, and died in peace.

The magic power of song is the same in all languages and among all peoples. Song is coeval with creation: "the morning stars sang together," and, when the present dispensation shall have ended, the "children of the Resurrection" shall "come to Zion with songs." Moses and Miriam and David and Solomon, with the ancient prophets, and the "most favored among women," with the angelic band, sang a Saviour born; and the Redeemer himself, at the paschal supper, with his disciples, sang an hymn. Sacred song has formed a constituent part of Christian worship, throughout the centuries, and will continue such to the end of time. It is also ever the sweet solace of the sick-chamber.

# TENTH EVENING.

## MODERN ENGLISH AND AMERICAN.

*(Continued.)*

# TENTH EVENING.

## MODERN ENGLISH AND AMERICAN.

*(Continued.)*

BY its association with some personal incident or event, how fondly do we sometimes cherish the memory of an old hymn! And how doubly dear to us does it become, when it is identified with the history of those we have "loved and lost"! But not as mementoes of the past, merely, do these devotional melodies charm us, as with talismanic power: they also tend to elevate and refine the heart, inspiring it with a noble ambition towards a happy, tuneful, Christian life,— a life of inward harmony, thankfulness, and peace.

"Stand up, stand up for Jesus!" a heart-stirring hymn, was written by Mr. George Duffield, a Presbyterian clergyman of Detroit. It was composed to be sung after a sermon on the death of the Rev. Dudley A. Tyng, whose dying counsel to his ministerial brethren was expressed in the above words.

The Christmas number of the "Household Words," for 1856, contains the "Wreck of the Golden Mary;" and, although you may not expect it, there you will find a beautiful Christian lyric, commencing, "Hear my prayer, O heavenly Father!" Both the story and the hymn are the production of Harriet Parr, better known to the reading public by her *nom de plume* of "Holme Lee;" and as the incident is germain to our purpose, we may as well give the reader the main points of it.

The story runs, that the ship "Golden Mary" struck on an iceberg, and the passengers and crew had to take to the boats, in which they remained, suffering great privations, for some days. To beguile the time, they told stories. This hymn was repeated by one Dick Tarrant, a youth who had given himself up to dissipation, on being disappointed in love. Having become a burden to his friends, they had sent him off in the "Golden Mary" to California, to get him out of the way. After telling, in touching terms, some of his experience, he continues, "What can it be that brings all these old things over my mind? There's a child's hymn I and Tom used to say at my mother's knee, when we were little ones, keeps running through my thoughts. It's the stars, maybe; there was a little window by my bed, that I used to watch them at, — a window in my room at home, in Cheshire; and if I was ever afraid, as boys will be after reading a good ghost story, I would keep on saying it till I fell asleep." — "That was a good mother of yours, Dick: could you say that hymn now, do you think? Some of us might like to hear it." — "It's as clear in my mind at this minute as if my mother was here listening to me," said Dick; and he repeated, "Hear my prayer, O heavenly Father!" &c. Well might George Herbert sing, —

> A verse may catch a wandering soul, that flies
> Profounder tracts, and, by a blest surprise,
> Convert delight into a sacrifice.

On the border of a little mountain stream, near the village of Munson, Mass., might have been seen, some few years since, a well-worn foot-path leading from an adjacent cottage down among the trees and alders that skirted a babbling brook; and there, beneath a shelving rock, might have been found a well-used Bible. If those trees had tongues, they might tell of many an heartfelt, earnest prayer, that went up from beneath that shady solitude into the ever-accessible ear of God. The pilgrim whose feet were wont so oft to seek that hallowed retreat, where none but God could hear, loved to linger there, not only to lift up the voice of prayer and praise, but also to consult the Sacred Oracles. A true lover of nature, with a soul alive to the beautiful, and susceptible of its benign and refining influences, she dearly loved this little sylvan sanctuary. One summer evening, when repairing thither, as she supposed, unnoticed by any human being, some one rudely and irreverently invaded the privacy of her devotions, insultingly reproaching her for her habit of making this spot an oratory for worship. Returning home, sorely grieved by the wickedness of the assault, she sought relief in prayer, and soon her mind became again composed: and, taking a pen, she wrote, as an impromptu answer to the assailant, that famous hymn, —

> I love to steal awhile away from every earthly care,
> And spend the hour of setting day, in humble, grateful prayer.

Would you know who this saintly one was? It was the beloved mother of Mr. S. R. Brown, of Auburn, N.Y., to whom (through the columns of the "Watchman and Reflector") we are indebted for these interesting particulars. We are told that she was self-taught as to human knowledge, but she was evidently no inapt scholar in the school of Christ. This beautiful lyric might never have been known to the world, had not Dr. Nettleton discovered its value, and placed it with his "Village Hymns." We shall sing this hymn hereafter, with increased interest, knowing the occasion which originated it; and the authoress will be endeared to us by her many prayers.

"Many prayers have gone up from that solitary place, not only for herself and her children, but for those that were afar off. Her heart was as broad as the world in its sympathies. Long before there was a foreign missionary organization in this country, she used to send the small sums she could earn or save to the early missionaries in India and South Africa, through a Christian merchant of Philadelphia, whose ships visited those regions. She gladly gave up her only son once to go to China, and again, in her old age, to go to Japan. When she parted with him, in 1859, as she took her seat in a railway carriage, to go a thousand miles west, to find her last home on earth, there was no tear in her eyes, and the only symptom of emotion observable was a slight quiver of her lip as she kissed him good-by. She died in 1861, aged seventy-eight years."

Faber's beautiful poem, "The Shadow of the Rock," commences with these fine stanzas: —

> The Shadow of the Rock! Stay, pilgrim, stay!
> Night treads upon the heels of day;
> There is no other resting-place this way.
>     The Rock is near,
>     The well is clear:
> Rest in the Shadow of the Rock!

The Shadow of the Rock! The desert wide
Lies round thee like a trackless tide,
In waves of sand forlornly multiplied.
    The sun is gone,
    Thou art alone:
Rest in the Shadow of the Rock!

The Shadow of the Rock! All come alone;
All, ever since the sun hath shone,
Who travelled by this road have come alone.
    Be of good cheer,
    A home is here:
Rest in the Shadow of the Rock!

The following noble numbers he entitles "The Heart's Home:"—

Hark, hark, my soul! angelic songs are swelling
    O'er earth's green fields, and ocean's wave-beat shore!
How sweet the truth, those blessed strains are telling,
    Of that new life when sin shall be no more!
Darker than night life's shadows fall around us,
    And, like benighted men, we miss our mark;
God hides Himself, and grace has scarcely found us,
    Ere death finds out his victims in the dark.
Onward we go, for still we hear them singing,
    "Come, weary souls, for Jesus bids you come;"
And through the dark, its echoes sweetly ringing,
    The music of the gospel leads us home.

Faber's hymns are, for the most part, impressively grand: that on the "Greatness of God" is an instance. We cite two stanzas of his hymn on the "Eternity of God:"—

Without an end, or bound, Thy life lies all outspread in light;
Our lives feel Thy life all around, making our weakness strong, our
    darkness bright;
    Yet is it neither wilderness nor sea,
    But the calm gladness of a full eternity!

Self-wearied, Lord, I come; for I have lived my life too fast;
Now that years bring me nearer home, grace must be slowly used
   to make it last;
  When my heart beats too quick, I think of Thee,
  And of the leisure of Thy long eternity!

Our extracts from Dr. Newman cannot fail of interest to the reader. The hymn was written off Sardinia.

Oh, say not thou art left of God, because His tokens in the sky
Thou canst not read; this earth He trod, to teach thee He was ever
 nigh.
He sees, beneath the fig-tree green, Nathaniel con His sacred lore;
Shouldst thou thy chamber seek, unseen He enters through the
 unopened door.
And when thou liest, slumber-bound, outwearied in the Christian
 fight,
In glory girt with saints around, He stands above thee through the
 night.

Here is another extract from the same source: —

  Oh, say! is it to die
To wear the Saviour's radiant form of brightness?
 To see Him as He is, with glory crowned?
To stand in robes of pure, unspotted whiteness,
 Joining the songs of happy saints above?
 . . . . . .
  No! no! we cannot die:
In Death's unrobing room, we strip from round us
 The garments of mortality and earth;
And breaking from the embryo state that bound us,
 Our day of dying is our day of birth!

How seldom are we accompanied with the consciousness of being heirs to an immortal existence, — an inextinguishable being, — a measureless succession of ages of unalloyed happiness! Thoughts tending thitherward are energizing and elevating as well as comforting: as when the eye, lingering over a beautiful landscape imparts to the mind a deeper and keener sense of the harmony and beauty of nature than a mere cursory glance could impart. It is good for us, occasionally at least, to indulge also a little introspection, so that we may ascertain how we stand with respect to the eternal world. Good thoughts are winged messengers of God to men, — the bread of life without the mortal leaven.

How many noble minds have been first illuminated with light from heaven, in the academies of the Scottish metropolis. Among the number was the devout Mr. Cheyne, a Christian minister of rare excellence and high mental endowments. He was a pupil of Dr. Chalmers's Divinity Class at the University, and an associate of Dr. H. Bonar. Preaching was his favorite engagement, and he was eminently successful in the pulpit. He was born in the year 1813, and died in 1843. We present a fragment from one of his hymns: —

>     When this passing world is done,
>     When has sunk yon glaring sun,
>     When we stand with Christ in glory,
>     Looking o'er life's finished story, —
>     Then, Lord, shall I fully know —
>     Not till then — how much I owe!
>
>     .   .   .   .   .
>
>     Even on earth, as through a glass
>     Darkly, let Thy glory pass,
>     Make forgiveness feel so sweet,
>     Make Thy Spirit's help so meet;
>     Even on earth, Lord, make me know
>     Something of how much I owe.

Another of his hymns is entitled "Jehovah Tsidkenu," ("The Lord our Righteousness," the watchword of the Reformers).

I once was a stranger to grace and to God,
I knew not my danger, I felt not my load;
Though friends spoke in rapture of Christ on the tree,
Jehovah Tsidkenu was nothing to me.

Macduff, the Scottish clergyman, and well-known author of the "Words of Jesus," and similar works, wrote this fine hymn:—

Christ is coming! let creation bid her groans and travail cease;
Let the glorious proclamation hope restore, and faith increase.
    Maranatha! Come, thou blessed Prince of Peace!
Earth can now but tell the story of Thy bitter cross and pain;
She shall yet behold Thy glory, when Thou comest back to reign.
    Maranatha! Let each heart repeat the strain!

. . . . . .

Long Thy exiles have been pining, far from rest and home and
    Thee;
But in heavenly vesture shining, soon they shall Thy glory see.
    Maranatha! Haste the joyous jubilee!
With that "blessed hope" before us, let no harp remain unstrung;
Let the mighty advent-chorus onward roll from tongue to tongue,
    Maranatha! Come, Lord Jesus, quickly come!

S. F. Smith, an eminent Baptist minister, of Newton, Mass., has contributed some excellent hymns, such as "Softly fades the twilight ray," "When thy mortal life is fled," "My country, 'tis of thee," &c.

We cull from "English Lyrics," by C. L. Ford; the following verses entitled "Marah:"—

    God sends us bitter, that the sweet,
      By absence known, may sweeter prove,
    As dark for light, as cold for heat,
      Brings greater love.

    God sends us bitter, as to show
      He can both sweet and bitter send;
    Thus both the might and love we know
      Of our great Friend.

> He sends us bitter, that Heaven's sweet,
>   Earth's bitter o'er, may sweeter taste,
> As Canaan's ground to Israel's feet
>   For that great waste.
>
> . . . . .
>
> And, lo! before us in the way
>   We view the fountains and the palms,
> And drink, and pitch our tents, and stay
>   Singing sweet psalms.

Mrs. J. Luke, of Clifton, Gloucestershire, who edited the "Missionary Repository" for several years, and wrote works for children, &c., is the author of the touching little poem, so familiar to our Sunday-school teachers and scholars: —

> I think, when I read that sweet story of old,
>   When Jesus was here among men,
> How He called little children, as lambs, to His fold,
>   I should like to have been with them then.
> I wish that His hands had been placed on my head,
>   That His arm had been thrown around me,
> And that I might have seen His kind look when He said,
>   "Let the little ones come unto me!"

The above was composed in the year 1841, in a stage-coach, for a village school, near Poundsford Park.

E. H. Sears, born in 1810, in Berkshire, Mass., has written several prose works, "Athanasia, or Foregleams of Immortality," &c.; also several glowing sacred lyrics, including those well-known hymns, "It came upon the midnight clear," and "Calm on the listening ear of night." We subjoin the opening stanzas of the first-named: —

> It came upon the midnight clear, that glorious song of old,
> From angels bending near the earth to touch their harps of gold:
> "Peace to the earth, good-will to man, from heaven's all-gracious
>   King;"
> The world in solemn stillness lay to hear the angels sing.

Still through the cloven skies they come, with peaceful wings un-
    furled;
And still their heavenly music floats o'er all the weary world;
Above its sad and lowly plains they bend on heavenly wing,
And ever o'er its Babel sounds the blessed angels sing!

Thomas Davis, one of the recent English poets, thus sings: —

> Why comes this fragrance on the summer breeze,
>     The blended tribute of ten thousand flowers,
> To me, a frequent wanderer 'mid the trees
>     That form these gay, yet solitary bowers?
> One answer is around, beneath, above:
> The echo of the voice, that God is love!
>
> Why bursts such melody from tree and bush,
>     The overflowing of each songster's heart:
> So filling mine, that it can scarcely hush
>     Awhile to listen, but would take its part?
> 'Tis but one song I hear where'er I rove,
> Though countless be the notes, that God is love!

Dr. Monsell, of Winchester, England, is too well known by his volumes of exquisite religious lyrics, to need further introduction: we present the first and last stanzas of his impressive hymn on Gethsemane: —

Wouldst thou learn the depth of sin, all its bitterness and pain?
What it cost thy God to win sinners to Himself again?
    Come, poor sinner, come with me, —
    Visit sad Gethsemane!

. . . . . .

Hate the sin that cost so dear; love the God that loved thee so;
Weep, if thou wilt, but likewise fear to bid that fountain freshly flow,
    That gushed so freely once for thee
    In sorrowful Gethsemane!

His hymn of Spring allegorized is replete with lyric grace and beauty: —

The spring-tide hour brings leaf and flower, with songs of life and love;
And many a lay wears out the day in many a leafy grove.
Bird, flower, and tree seem to agree their choicest gifts to bring;
But this poor heart bears not its part, in it there is no spring.
Dews fall apace — the dews of grace — upon this soul of sin;
And love divine delights to shine upon the waste within:
Yet, year by year, fruits, flowers, appear, and birds their praises sing:
But this poor heart bears not its part, its winter has no spring.
Lord, let thy love, fresh from above, soft as the south wind blow;
Call forth its bloom, wake its perfume, and bid its spices flow!

Bishop A. C. Coxe, of Western New York, has, in his "Christian Ballads," given to the religious world some of the choicest of sacred lyrics. We regret our restricted space forbids our citing more than the following brief extracts: —

### MATINS.

The lark is in the sky, and his morning note is pouring:
He hath a wing to fly, so he's soaring, Christian, soaring!
His nest is on the ground, but only in the night;
For he loves the matin-sound, and the highest heaven's height.
Hark, Christian, hark! at heaven-door he sings!
And be thou like the lark, with thy soaring spirit-wings!
. . . . . . . .
There is morning incense flung from the childlike lily flowers;
And their fragrant censer swung, make it ours, Christian, ours!
And hark! our Mother's hymn, and the organ-peals we love!
They sound like cherubim at their orisons above!
Pray, Christian, pray, at the bonny peep of dawn,
Ere the dew-drop and the spray that christen it are gone!

### THE CHIMES OF ENGLAND.

The chimes, the chimes of Motherland, of England green and old,
That out from fane and ivied tower a thousand years have tolled;
How glorious must their music be as breaks the hallowed day,
And calleth with a seraph's voice a nation up to pray!

Those chimes that tell a thousand tales, sweet tales of olden time;
And ring a thousand memories of vesper and at prime!
At bridal and at burial, for cottager and king;
Those chimes,—those glorious Christian chimes,—how blessedly
  they ring!

Mrs. Lowell's exquisite poem, "The Morning-Glory," is full of tenderness. Listen to some passages from it:—

We wreathed about our darling's head the morning-glory bright;
Her little face looked out beneath, so full of life and light,
So lit as with a sunrise, that we could only say,
"She is the morning-glory true, and her poor types are they."
    .     .     .     .     .     .     .     .
We used to think how she had come, even as comes the flower,
The last and perfect added gift to crown Love's morning hour;
And how in her was imaged forth the love we could not say,
As on the little dew-drops round shines back the heart of day.
    .     .     .     .     .     .     .     .
The morning-glory's blossoming will soon be coming round;
We see the rows of heart-shaped leaves upspringing from the
  ground;
The tender things that winter killed renew again their birth;
But the glory of our morning has passed away from earth!

In fitting companionship with the foregoing, we present some of the fine lines of James Russell Lowell:

> But all God's angels come to us disguised,—
> Sorrow and sickness, poverty and death,
> One after other lift their frowning masks,
> And we behold the seraph's face beneath,
> All radiant with the glory and the calm
> Of having looked upon the front of God.

---

God scatters love on every side freely among His children all,
And always hearts are lying open wide wherein some grains may
  fall.

There is no wind but soweth seeds of a more true and open life,
Which burst, unlooked for, into high-souled deeds, with wayside beauty rife.
We find within these souls of ours some wild germs of a higher birth,
Which in the poet's tropic heart bear flowers whose fragrance fills the earth.

Who is not familiar with Professor Longfellow's beautiful "Psalm of Life"? Its fame has, indeed, reached beyond the limits of the language in which it was composed; for it has been rendered into many others, and even the Chinese, by a Mandarin; a copy of which has been sent to the author.

Life is real! Life is earnest! And the grave is not its goal;
"Dust thou art, to dust returnest," was not spoken of the soul.

Art is long, and Time is fleeting; and our hearts, though stout and brave,
Still, like muffled drums, are beating funeral marches to the grave.

In the world's broad field of battle, in the bivouac of Life,
Be not like dumb, driven cattle! Be a hero in the strife!

Trust no Future, howe'er pleasant! Let the dead Past bury its dead!
Act,—act in the living present, heart within, and God o'erhead!

Lives of great men all remind us we can make our lives sublime,
And, departing, leave behind us footprints on the sands of time!

His "Ladder of St. Augustine" may be styled a homily set to music; while his "Resignation," "Hymn to Night," "Footsteps of Angels," and a few others, have become classic. So joyous and healthy a spirit inspires the Muse of Longfellow, that it is not surprising his works should be among the most popular of the age. Listen to some of his beautiful imagery:—

> Whene'er a noble deed is wrought,
> Whene'er is spoken a noble thought,
>> Our hearts in glad surprise
>> To higher levels rise.
> The tidal wave of deeper souls
> Into our inmost being rolls,
>> And lifts us unawares
>> Out of all meaner cares.

---

Let us be patient! these severe afflictions not from the ground arise;
But oftentimes celestial benedictions assume this dark disguise.
We see but dimly through the mists and vapors; amid these earthly lamps
What seem to us but sad funereal tapers may be heaven's distant lamps.

Longfellow's "Suspiria" is a rare and touching song for the "Christian sleeper:"—

Take them, O Death! and bear away whatever thou canst call thy own:
Thine image, stamped upon this clay, doth give thee that,—but that alone!
Take them, O Grave! and let them lie folded upon thy narrow shelves,
As garments by the soul laid by, and precious only to ourselves.
Take them, O great Eternity! our little life is but a gust,
That bends the branches of thy tree, and trails its blossoms in the dust!

"No English poet," writes a recent London reviewer,[*] "has equalled the tenderness and felicity of Longfellow, in his lyric and descriptive poems. Their popularity is marvellous. What can excel "The Psalm of Life"? It lives in all our memories like music, and is repeated in pulpit, platform, and parliament, with a frequency that does not attend the poetry of any other writer."

[*] Dr. Cumming.

One of the most remarkable poems of the age is that entitled "Yesterday, To-day, and Forever," by Rev. E. H. Bickersteth, of London. The object of the work, as stated by the author, seems to be to awaken deeper thought about things "unseen and eternal," by combining some of the pictorial teachings of the Divine Word. He says the design of this poem has been laid up in his heart for more than twenty years, while the execution of it has occupied him only about two years. Bold as is the essay to construct an epic, after Milton, and on his subject, he has, in it, according to the English critics, achieved a great success. We subjoin the closing passage: —

>Such are the many kingdoms of God's realm;
>And in these boundless provinces of light,
>We, who once suffered with a suffering Lord,
>Reign with Him, in His glory, unto each,
>According to his power and proven love,
>His rule assigned. But Zion is our home;
>Jerusalem, the City of our God!
>O happy home! O happy children here!
>O blissful mansions of our Father's house!
>O walks surpassing Eden for delight!
>Here are the harvests reaped, once sown in tears;
>Here is the rest by ministry enhanced;
>Here is the banquet of the wine of heaven;
>Riches of glory incorruptible;
>Crowns, amaranthine crowns of victory;
>The voice of harpers harping on their harps;
>The anthems of the holy cherubim;
>The crystal river of the spirit's joy;
>The Bridal palace of the Prince of Peace;
>The Holiest of Holies! God is here!

The following passage is equally beautiful: —

>Thus Heaven is gathering one by one, in its capacious breast,
>All that is pure and permanent, and beautiful and blest;
>The family is scattered yet, though of one home and heart,
>Part militant in earthly gloom, in heavenly glory part;

But who can tell the rapture, when the circle is complete,
And all the children, scattered now, before the Father meet?
One fold, one Shepherd, one employ, one universal home!
"Lo, I come quickly!" Even so, "Amen, Lord Jesus, come!"

One of the selectest and most perfect of our modern hymns, is that commencing, —

> My faith looks up to Thee,
> Thou Lamb of Calvary,
> Saviour Divine!

It is, as is well known, the production of Dr. Ray Palmer, of New York, who wrote it in 1830. It was not suggested by any particular incident; but, in the author's own words, "written because it was born in his heart, and demanded expression." He adds, "I gave form to what I felt, by writing, with little effort, the stanzas. I recollect I wrote them with very tender emotion, and ended the last lines with tears." Some ten years afterwards, the author met his friend, Dr. Lowell Mason, in Boston, who spoke of his projected new Hymn and Tune Book, and requested a hymn or two for his Collection. The author then gave him a copy of this hymn. Dr. Mason seems to have been gifted with prophetic vision, when he told Dr. Palmer, a few days after he received the hymn, that he would be best known to posterity as its author.

As originally written, the hymn consisted of six stanzas; the first two are omitted, four only being given in the Church Collections. It has been translated into Arabic, and much used at missionary stations in Turkey. It has not only been translated into Tamil, but into Tahitian, the Marratta, and will doubtless find its way wherever the Bible has penetrated.

There is a little incident connected with this hymn:

it is as follows. During the late insurrection in Syria, early one morning the students of the Protestant Seminary were assembled for worship. Reading the Scriptures and prayer had passed, and they were in the act of singing those lines of this hymn, —

> "When griefs around me spread,
> Be Thou my Guide,"

when they were disturbed by the sound of firing in the streets, and a number of the savage Druzes rushed into the chapel.

The following sacred lyric, written by Dr. Ray Palmer expressly for this work, will not fail to be read with great interest. It is entitled "The Rock of Ages."

> O Rock of Ages! since on Thee
> By grace my feet are planted,
> 'Tis mine, in tranquil faith, to see
> The rising storm, undaunted;
> When angry billows round me rave,
> And tempests fierce assail me,
> To thee I cling, the terrors brave,
> For Thou canst never fail me;
> Though rends the globe with earthquake shock,
> Unmoved Thou stand'st, Eternal Rock!
>
> Within Thy clefts I love to hide,
> When darkness o'er me closes;
> There peace and light serene abide,
> And my still heart reposes;
> My soul exults to dwell secure,
> Thy strong munitions round her;
> She dares to count her triumph sure,
> Nor fears lest hell confound her;
> Though tumults startle earth and sea,
> Thou changeless Rock, they shake not Thee!
>
> From Thee, O Rock once smitten! flow
> Life-giving streams for ever;
> And whoso doth their sweetness know,
> He henceforth thirsteth never;

My lips have touched the crystal tide,
    And feel no more returning
The fever, that so long I tried
    To cool, yet felt still burning;
Ah, wondrous Well-Spring! brimming o'er
With living waters evermore.

On that dread day when they that sleep
    Shall hear the trumpet sounding,
And wake to praise, or wake to weep,
    The judgment-throne surrounding;
When wrapt in all-devouring flame,
    The solid globe is wasting,
And what at first from nothing came
    Is back to nothing hasting;
E'en then, my soul shall calmly rest,
O Rock of Ages! on Thy breast.

It has been beautifully said, that "true religion always leads the graces in her train." It is, indeed, to the Christian's eye alone that intellectual beauty reveals herself without a veil and in all her charms. The worldling resembles the microscope, which magnifies little things, but cannot apprehend great ones; whereas the Christian, who lives by faith, may be compared to the telescope, bringing near things that to the eye of sense are unseen. Thus "the vision and faculty divine" reveals itself in such gushes of holy song as the following: —

Since o'er Thy footstool here below such radiant gems are strown,
Oh, what magnificence must glow, my God, about Thy throne!
So brilliant here these drops of light, — there the full ocean rolls,
    how bright!

If night's blue curtain of the sky, with thousand stars inwrought,
Hung like a royal canopy with glittering diamonds fraught,
Be, Lord, thy temple's outer veil, what splendor at the shrine must
    dwell!

These brilliant stanzas are doubtless at once recognized as from the glowing pen of Dr. Muhlenburg, of New York, whose untiring devotion to the Hospital of St. Luke has endeared his name to the many admirers of his Muse. His most popular hymn, "I would not live alway," was comprised in six eight-line stanzas: this last is not given in our church books: —

>That heavenly music! hark, sweet in the air
>The notes of the harpers, how clear ringing there!
>And see, soft unfolding those portals of gold,
>The King all arrayed in His beauty behold!
>Oh, give me, oh, give me the wings of a dove,
>To adore Him, be near Him, enwrapt with His love:
>I but wait for the summons, I list for the word,
>Alleluia, Amen, evermore with the Lord!

Mr. Bryant's poems are so familiar to us, that it is scarcely necessary to present extracts from them. We venture to give the opening passage of his fine "Forest Hymn:" —

>The groves were God's first temples. Ere man learned
>To hew the shaft, and lay the architrave,
>And spread the roof above them; ere he framed
>The lofty vault, to gather and roll back
>The sound of anthems; — in the darkling wood,
>Amid the cool and silence, he knelt down,
>And offered to the Mightiest solemn thanks
>And supplication. For his simple heart
>Might not resist the sacred influences
>Which, from the stilly twilight of the place,
>And from the gray old trunks that high in heaven
>Mingled their mossy boughs, and from the sound
>Of the invisible breath that swayed at once
>All their green tops, stole over him, and bowed
>His spirit with the thought of boundless power
>And inaccessible majesty. Ah, why
>Should we, in the world's riper years, neglect

God's ancient sanctuaries, and adore
Only among the crowd, and under roofs
That our frail hands have raised? Let me, at least,
Here, in the shadow of this aged wood,
Offer one hymn, — thrice happy, if it find
Acceptance in His ear.

———

So live, that when thy summons comes to join
The innumerable caravan, which moves
To that mysterious realm, where each shall take
His chamber in the silent halls of death,
Thou go not, like the quarry-slave at night,
Scourged to his dungeon, but, sustained and soothed
By an unfaltering trust, approach thy grave
Like one who draws the drapery of his couch
About him, and lies down to pleasant dreams.

Bryant's "Thanatopsis," one of his earliest and best productions, closes with the above solemn strain of stately verse. Washington Irving has the honor of having first introduced Bryant's poetry to the British public, with an appreciative estimate of its merit. We now subjoin, in response to this, the opinions of two eminent English critical authorities, of a recent date: —

"We have not a lyric poet superior to William Cullen Bryant: he is less known to the multitude, but is highly admired by appreciative minds. For terse, compact, and vigorous lines, rich in thought and reason, and in music, he has no living equal."

"There is no poet more essentially American, whose genius is more especially the product of native thought and culture than Bryant. He is the American Wordsworth; and his name has done for the rolling prairies and boundless savannahs of that great continent what Wordsworth did for his beloved lake country."

E. W. Townsend, a modern poet of England, gives this choice metrical homily: —

> Nothing in this world is dumb,
> Or silent, if we do but come
> The very inmost truth anear,
> And listen with awakened ear.
>
> Wisdom may we often learn
> From smallest things: a waving fern,
> Growing in a shady place,
> May be a minister of grace.
> . . . .
>
> In ourselves the music dwells;
> From ourselves the music swells;
> By ourselves our life is fed
> With sweet or bitter daily bread.

These fine stanzas are by the late N. P. Willis: —

> The perfect world by Adam trod
> Was the first temple built by God;
> His fiat laid the corner-stone,
> And heaved its pillars, one by one.
> He hung its starry roof on high, —
> The broad, illimitable sky;
> He spread its pavement, green and bright,
> And curtained it with morning light.
> The mountains in their places stood,
> The sea, the sky, and "all was good;"
> And when its first pure praises rang,
> The "morning stars together sang."

A happy union of beautiful sentiment with the music of verse is seen in this sweet lyric, by the Rev. C. W. Baird, of Rye, N.Y.: —

> In all the scenes of childhood's day
> That memory paints, as years recede,
> The beauty of a blessed deed
> Is last to fade away.
> . . . . . .

The guileless love that lasted long,
The zeal of piety unfeigned,
The courage of a heart unstained,
That only feared the wrong;
The lingering prayer put up at night,
Low bending by my mother's knee;
The tear of pity, and the glee
Of innocent delight, —
These are the memories that she brings,
Kind guardian of mine earlier days,
These are the nightly thoughts that raise
Mine eyes to holier things.

H. T. Tuckerman, our American poet and essayist, has given us some graceful and expressive stanzas on Palestine, that shrine of sacred story : —

Oh for a glance at those wild hills, that round Jerusalem arise!
And one sweet evening by the lake that gleams beneath Judea's skies!
How anthem-like the wind must sound in meadows of the Holy Land,
How musical the ripples break upon the Jordan's moonlit strand!
Behold the dew, like angels' tears, upon each thorn is gleaming now,
Blest emblem of the crown of love there woven for the Sufferer's brow!
Who does not sigh to enter Nain, or in Capernaum to dwell, —
Inhale the breeze from Galilee, and rest beside Samaria's well?
Who would not stand beneath the spot where Bethlehem's star its vigil kept,
List to the plash of Siloa's pool, and kiss the ground where Jesus wept?
Gethsemane who would not seek, and pluck a lily by the way?
Through Bethany devoutly walk, and on the Mount of Olives pray?
How dear were one repentant night where Mary's tears of love were shed!
How blest, beside the Saviour's tomb, one hour's communion with the dead!

What solemn joy to stand alone on Calvary's celestial height!
Or kneel upon the mountain-slope, once radiant with supernal light!
I cannot throw my staff aside, nor wholly quell the hope divine,
That one delight awaits me yet, — a pilgrimage to Palestine.

Gerald Massey, one of England's renowned self-made poets, who has, through severe difficulties, achieved for himself an honorable position in the literary profession, is known best by his glowing and touching poem of "Babe Christabel," a portion of which is annexed: —

> In this dim world of clouding cares,
> We rarely know, till wildered eyes
> See white wings lessening up the skies,
> The angels with us unawares.
>
> . . . . . .
>
> Our beautiful Bird of light hath fled:
> Awhile she sat with folded wings,
> Sang round us a few hoverings,
> Then straightway into glory sped:
> And white-winged angels nurture her,
> With heaven's white radiance robed and crowned;
> And all love's purple glory round
> She summers on the Hills of Myrrh.
>
> . . . . . .
>
> Strange glory streams through life's wild rents,
> And through the open door of death,
> We see the Heaven that beckoneth
> To the beloved, going hence.
> God's ichor fills the hearts that bleed;
> The best fruit loads the broken bough;
> And on the wounds our sufferings plough,
> Immortal Love sows sovereign seed.

Hugh Stowell, Canon of Chester, and Dean of Salford, near Manchester, is the author of several works, both in prose and poetry; and is especially commended to our present notice as the writer of that favorite hymn, —

> From every stormy wind that blows,
> From every swelling tide of woes,
> There is a calm, a sure retreat, —
> 'Tis found beneath the mercy-seat.

That favorite hymn, alike with young and old, "There is a happy land," was composed by Andrew Young, of Edinburgh, who for many years had occupied a high position as an instructor of youth.

The fine hymn, "All hail the power of Jesus' name," first appeared in 1780, and was written by the Rev. E. Perronet, of the English Episcopal Church. This hymn was altered by Mr. Duncan, to whom its authorship has been sometimes erroneously ascribed.

The subjoined extracts are from the graceful pen of Alice Cary, of New York, whose volumes of sketches, in prose and verse, have been so popular: —

> I cannot plainly see the way, so dark the grave is: but I know
> If I do truly work and pray, some good will brighten out of woe;
> For the same hand that doth unbind the winter winds sends sweetest showers,
> And the poor rustic laughs to find his April meadows full of flowers.
>
> . . . . . . . . .
>
> Why should I vainly seek to solve free-will, necessity, the fall?
> I feel, — I know, — that God is love, and, knowing this, I know it all.

---

> Bow, angels, from your glorious state, if e'er on earth you trod,
> And lead me, through the golden gate of prayer, unto my God.
> I long to gather from the Word the meaning full and clear,
> To build unto my gracious Lord a tabernacle here.
>
> . . . . . . . . .
>
> The angels said, God giveth you His love, what more is ours?
> Even as the cisterns of the dew o'erflow upon the flowers,
> His grace descends; and, as of old, He walks with men apart,
> Keeping the promise, as foretold, with all the pure in heart.

Phœbe Cary, of New York, sister of the above, is author of many beautiful sacred lyrics; this, for example: —

> One sweetly solemn thought comes to me o'er and o'er, —
> I'm nearer home to-day than I have ever been before:
> Nearer my Father's house, where the many mansions be;
> Nearer the great white throne, nearer the jasper sea;
> Nearer the bound of life, where we lay our burdens down;
> Nearer leaving the cross, nearer gaining the crown.

J. F. Clarke, a clergyman of Boston, was born in 1810; he wrote several popular works in prose and verse; amongst the latter, the following terse and vigorous stanzas: —

> Father, to us, Thy children, humbly kneeling,
> Conscious of weakness, ignorance, sin, and shame,
> Give such a force of holy thought and feeling,
> That we may live to glorify Thy holy name;
> That we may conquer base desire and passion,
> That we may rise from selfish thoughts and will,
> O'ercome the world's allurement, threat, and fashion,
> Walk humbly, gently, leaning on Thee still.

Sarah A. Miles, of Brattleboro', Vt., is the author of some hymns. One follows: it is entitled "A Foretaste of Heaven."

> When on devotion's seraph-wing the spirit soars above,
> And feels Thy presence, Father, Friend, God of eternal love!
> The joys of earth, how swift they fade before that living ray,
> Which gives to the rapt soul a glimpse of pure and perfect day!

One of the sages of the seventeenth century, Arthur Warwick, once said, "Life is but my walk, and heaven my home; so that, travelling towards so pleasant a destination, the shorter the journey, the sooner the rest." Vainly we essay, meanwhile, to peer into the unrevealed and unattained.

Not from the flowers of earth, not from the stars,
Not from the voicing sea may we
The secret wrest which bars our knowledge here
Of all we hope and all that we may fear — hereafter.

We watch beside our graves, yet meet no sign
Of where our dear ones dwell. Ah! well,
Even now, your dead and mine may long to speak
Of raptures it were wiser we should seek — hereafter.

O hearts we fondly love! O pallid lips,
That bore our farewell kiss from this
To yonder world's eclipse! Do ye, safe home,
Smile at your earthly doubts of what would come — hereafter?

Grand birthright of the soul, naught may despoil!
O precious, healing balm, to calm
Our lives in pain and toil! God's boon, that we
Or soon or late shall know what is to be — hereafter!

This fine lyric is by a young lawyer of New York, George Cooper, who beguiles his professional studies by such meditative musings as the foregoing.

Mrs. H. Beecher Stowe is the author of these beautiful stanzas, on the words "Abide in me:" —

That mystic word of Thine, O Sovereign Lord!
  Is all too pure, too high, too deep for me:
Weary of striving, and with longing faint,
  I breathe it back again in prayer to Thee!
Abide in me! o'ershadow by Thy love
  Each half-formed purpose and dark thought of sin;
Quench, ere it rise, each selfish, low desire,
  And keep my soul, as Thine, calm and divine.

As some rare perfume in a vase of clay
  Pervades it with a fragrance not its own, —
So, when Thou dwellest in a mortal soul,
  All Heaven's own sweetness seems around it thrown.
The soul alone, like a neglected harp,
  Grows out of tune, and needs Thy hand divine:
Dwell Thou within it, tune and touch its chords,
  Till every note and string shall answer Thine.

She has these fine lines in a poem entitled "The Other World:"—

It lies around us like a cloud,—a world we do not see;
Yet the sweet closing of an eye may bring us there to be.

. . . . . . . . .

Sweet hearts around us throb and beat, sweet helping hands are stirred,
And palpitates the veil between with breathings almost heard.

. . . . . . . .

And in the hush of rest they bring, 'tis easy now to see
How lovely, and how sweet a pass, the hour of death may be;—
To close the eye, and close the ear, wrapped in a trance of bliss,
And, gently drawn in loving arms, to swoon to that from this.

We next present some specimen stanzas of our Western Muse. The first extract is from a poem by J. H. Perkins; and the second, by Otway Curry:—

By earth hemmed in, by earth opprest, 'tis hard to labor, hard to pray;
And of the week, for prayer and rest, we've but one Sabbath day.
But purer spirits walk above, who worship alway; who are blest
With an upspringing might of love, that makes all labor rest.
Father! while here, I would arise in spirit to that realm; and there
Be every act a sacrifice, and every thought a prayer!

---

We strive with earthly imagings to reach and understand
The wondrous and the fearful things of an eternal land
We talk of amaranthine bowers and living groves of palm,
Of starry crowns and fadeless flowers and skies for ever calm.
We talk of wings and raiment white, and pillared thrones of gold,
And cities built with jewels bright, far in the heavens, of old.
Are these things more than fancy's play? are they, in very deed,
The free soul's guerdon, far away, its everlasting meed?
Or shall the spirit, in its flight beyond the stars sublime,
See nothing but the radiance white of never-ending time?
Shall things material change again, and wholly be forgot?
And round us only God remain, a universe of thought?

We know not well, — we cannot know: our reason's glimmering light
Can nothing but the darkness show of our surrounding night.
But soon the doubt and toil and strife of earth shall all be done,
And knowledge of our endless life be in a moment won.

Whittier, who has been pronounced by an English critic, "the most poetic of our American poets," has embodied some fine thoughts in the following beautiful lines, from a poem entitled "Our Master."

He cometh not a king to reign; the world's long hope is dim;
The weary centuries watch in vain the clouds of heaven for Him.
Death comes, life goes; the asking eye and ear are answerless;
The grave is dumb, the hollow sky is sad with silentness.
The letter fails, and systems fall, and every symbol wanes;
The Spirit over brooding all, Eternal Love, remains.
And not for signs in heaven above or earth below, they look,
Who know, with John, His smile of love, with Peter, His rebuke
In joy of inward peace, or sense of sorrow over sin,
He is His own best evidence, His witness is within.
No fable old, nor mythic lore, nor dream of bards and seers,
No dead fact stranded on the shore of the oblivious years;
But warm, sweet, tender, even yet a present help is He;
And faith has still its Olivet, and love its Galilee.
The healing of His seamless robe is by our beds of pain;
We touch Him, in life's throng and press, and we are whole again.
Through Him, the first fond prayers are said our lips of childhood frame,
The last low whispers of our dead are burdened with His name.

. . . . . . . .

O Love! O Life! our faith and sight Thy presence maketh one:
As through transfigured clouds of white we trace the noonday sun,
So, to our mortal eyes subdued, flesh-veiled, but not concealed,
We know in Thee the Fatherhood and Heart of God revealed!
We faintly hear, we dimly see, in differing phrase we pray;
But, dim or clear, we own in Thee the Light, the Truth, the Way!

. . . . . . . .

Alone, O Love ineffable! Thy saving name is given;
To turn aside from Thee is hell; to walk with Thee is heaven!

. . . . . . . .

Our Friend, our Brother, and our Lord, what may Thy service be?
Nor name, nor form, nor ritual word, but simply following Thee!

. . . . . . . .

Thy litanies, sweet offices of love and gratitude;
Thy sacramental liturgies, the joy of doing good:
In vain shall waves of incense drift the vaulted nave around,
In vain the minster-turret lift its brazen weights of sound:
The heart must ring the Christmas bells, the inward altars raise;
Its faith and hope thy canticles, and its obedience praise!

From a splendid poem, entitled "The Death of Jacob," by the Rev. William Alexander, M.A. (being the poem to which an "Accessit" was awarded by the judges of the best poem on a sacred subject, in the University of Oxford, June 1, 1857):—

> I saw the Syrian sunset's meteor-crown
>   Hang over Bethel for a little space;
> I saw a gentle wandering boy lie down,
>   With tears upon his face.
>
> Sheer up the fathomless, transparent blue,
>   Rose jasper-battlement and crystal wall:
> Rung all the night-air, pierced through and through
>   With harps angelical.
>
> And a great ladder was set up the while
>   From earth to heaven, with angels on each round:
> Barks, that bore precious freight to earth's far isle,
>   Or sailed back homeward bound.
>
> Ah! many a time we look on star-lit nights
>   Up to the sky, as Jacob did of old,
> Look longing up to the eternal lights,
>   To spell their lines of gold.
>
> But never more, as to the Hebrew boy,
>   Each on his way, the angels walk abroad;
> And never more we hear, with awful joy,
>   The audible voice of God.
>
> Yet to pure eyes the ladder still is set,
>   And angel visitants still come and go;
> Many bright messengers are moving yet
>   From the dark world below.

Thoughts that are red-crossed Faith's outspreading wings;
   Prayers of the Church aye keeping time and tryst;
Heart-wishes, making bee-like murmurings,
   Their flower the Eucharist;

Spirits elect, through suffering rendered meet
   For those high mansions; from the nursery door
Bright babes that climb up with their clay-cold feet,
   Unto the golden floor.

These are the messengers, for ever wending
   From earth to heaven, that Faith alone may scan;
These are the angels of our God, ascending
   Upon the Son of man.

## How beautiful are the following stanzas : —

Rests he now well, whose pilgrim staff and shoon
   Lie in his tent; for on the golden street
They walk, and stumble not, on roads star-strewn,
   With their unsandalled feet?

Rests he not well, who keepeth watch and ward,
   In sweet possession of the land loved most,
Till, marshalled by the angel of the Lord,
   Shall come the Heaven-sent host?

Who has not felt in some dear churchyard spot,
   When evening's pencil shades the pale-gold sky, —
Here at the closing of my life's calm lot,
   Here would I love to lie;

Here where the poet-thrush so often pours
   His requiem hidden in green aisles of lime,
And bloody-red along the sycamores
   Creepeth the summer time;

Where, through the ruined church's broken walls
   Glimmers all night the vast and solemn sea,
As through our broken hopes the brightness falls
   Of our eternity?

But, when we die, we rest far, far away,
   Not over us the lime-trees lift their bowers;
And the young sycamores their shadows sway
   O'er graves that are not ours.

> Yet he is happy, wheresoe'er he lie,
> Round whom the purple calms of Eden spread,
> Who sees his Saviour with the heart's pure eye,—
> He is the happy dead!

Sir Edward Denny, of England, is a writer on prophecy, and author of some excellent hymns on the subject of the Second Advent, and other sacred themes. Here are a few lines from his pen:—

> Sweet was the hour, O Lord! to Thee, at Sychar's lonely well,
> When a poor outcast heard Thee, there Thy great salvation tell!
>
> . . . . . . .
>
> There Jacob's erring daughter found those streams unknown before,
> The water-brooks of life, that made the weary thirst no more!

Anna Shipton, whose numerous hymns and devotional lyrics have been so widely esteemed, seems to be one of the divine order of suffering humanity, for her sweet music has had its birth in the chamber of sorrow. Listen to her melodious numbers:—

> I heard the wavelet kiss the shore, ere lost within the sea,
> And the ripple of the silvery tide seemed as a psalm to me:
> Contented with God's holy will, its feeble voice to raise,
> To hymn His glory, and be lost, nor thirst for human praise.
> Lord, make me, like the ocean's voice, obedient to Thy will:
> Thy purpose work as faithfully, and at Thy word be still.
>
> . . . . . . .
>
> I marked the soft dew silently descend o'er plain and hill,
> On each parched herb and drooping flower the heavenly cloud distil.
> As noiseless as the sun's first beams, it vanished with the day;
> But the waving fields told where it fell, when the dew had passed away.
> Lord, make me like the gentle dew, that other hearts may prove,
> E'en through Thy feeblest messenger, Thy ministry of love!

---

> I am waiting as the day wanes, waiting
> The light of the coming dawn to see;
> As the weary child lies watching for its mother,
> I am longing, O my Lord Christ, for Thee!

Down here, the shadow and the sadness,
  The conflict with the foe in fierce array;
Up there, the joy of sinless service,
  Never to pass away!
I am waiting in the noontide, waiting
  A gleam of the promised cloud to see,
That shall bring to us the brightness of Thy glory;
  I am longing, O my Lord Christ, for Thee!
Down here, the tempter still accusing,
  And wiles that unwary feet betray;
Up there, the smile of my Belovèd,
  Never to pass away!

---

Oh for my home of glory, that death's dark veil enshrouds,
It gleams in beauty o'er me, as day dawns from the clouds.
Bright are the hopes we borrow from joys that cannot wane;
To-day we weep, to-morrow brings sunshine after rain.
. . . . . . .
My soul is often weary, weary of self and sin;
Often the way seems dreary, oft sinking fears within.
But while on Jesus gazing, each fiery dart is vain;
My soul alike is praising for sunshine after rain.

The beautiful Christian lyrics of Miss A. L. Waring, of Neath, Wales, are characterized by pure and elevated sentiment and felicitous expression. Her hymns are universally admired for their spiritual beauty and earnest expression of Christian experience. We all remember that favorite hymn, "Father, I know that all my life," &c. Here are two other poems, less familiar: —

  Love shall teach us, while on Him we lean,
    That in the certainty of coming bliss,
  We may be yearning for a world unseen,
    Yet wear our beautiful array in this.
  Ours be a loyal love for service tried,
    To show, by deeds, and words, and looks that cheer,
  How He can bless the scene in which He died
    And fill His house with glory even here.

> Some, in their sorrow, may not know
>   How near their feet those waters glide, —
> How peaceful fruits for healing grow,
>   And flowers for beauty, by their side:
> They may not see, with weeping eyes
>   Upon the dreary desert bent,
> How glorious, straight before them, lies
>   The Eden of their soul's content.

"You will excuse me, if I ask you to look out for the sunlight the Lord sends into your days," said a deep thinker; and very needful is the precept. We are so apt to note the dark days, rather than those more common days of sunshine. And it is one of the distinguishing characteristics of a Christian, that he abounds in thanksgivings.

The beautiful hymn, "Jesus, I my cross have taken," the authorship of which has been erroneously attributed to Montgomery, and others, was written by Lyte, in 1833. The concluding stanzas are vigorous and terse: —

Take, my soul, thy full salvation! rise o'er sin and fear and care;
Joy to find in every station something still to do or bear.
Think what Spirit dwells within thee, what a Father's smile is thine,
What a Saviour died to win thee: child of heaven, shouldst thou repine?
Haste then on from grace to glory, armed by faith, and winged by prayer;
Heaven's eternal day's before thee, God's own hand shall guide thee there.
Soon shall close thy earthly mission, swift shall pass thy pilgrim days;
Hope soon change to full fruition, faith to sight, and prayer to praise!

Lyte, whose Christian lyrics have become familiar to most readers of sacred verse, was born at Kelso,

1793; and had to struggle hard for the benefit of a liberal education. While tending a dying-bed, his heart was quickened into spiritual life: although his arduous and self-denying labors for the sick and bereaved superinduced consumption in his own case. After travelling some time on the Continent in quest of health, he settled in the quiet little town of Marazion, on the shore of the beautiful bay of Mount St. Michael, in Cornwall. Here he married; and finally fixed his abode at the parish of Brixham, at which place he wrote most of his hymns, so remarkable for their pure Christian sentiment and simplicity of diction. Some of them were written "from under the cloud;" for example this, —

> My spirit on Thy care, Blest Saviour, I recline;
> Thou wilt not leave me to despair, for Thou art Love divine!"

The autumn of 1847 was approaching, and he must needs take his last journey to the genial south. "They tell me," says he, "that the sea is injurious to me. I hope not; for I know of no divorce I should more deprecate than from the lordly ocean. From childhood it has been my friend and playmate, and never have I been weary of gazing on its glorious face." He did go, never to return. Before he went, he wished to preach once more to his people. He preached on the "Holy Communion," and it was solemnly significant to hear him say, "O brethren! I can speak feelingly, experimentally, on this point; and I stand here among you seasonably to-day, as alive from the dead, if I may hope to impress it upon you, and induce you to prepare for that solemn hour which must come to all, by a timely acquaintance with, appreciation of, dependence on, the death of Christ!" This was his last appeal. And for the last time, he dispensed the sacred elements to his sorrowing flock; and then, exhausted with his effort, he retired with a soul in sweet repose on that Christ whom he had preached with his dying breath; and, as the evening drew on, he handed to a near and dear relative these undying verses, together with his own adapted music for the hymn, —

> Abide with me! Fast falls the eventide;
> The darkness deepens; Lord, with me abide!
> When other helpers fail, and comforts flee,
> Help of the helpless, oh, abide with me!
>
> Swift to its close ebbs out life's little day;
> Earth's joys grow dim; its glories pass away;
> Change and decay in all around, I see;
> O Thou who changest not, abide with me!

"This was his last hymn upon earth. He reached Nice, and there his spirit entered into rest. He pointed upwards in passing, and murmured softly, 'Peace, joy!' while his face brightened into smiles, as the shadow of his last cloud melted before the 'Light of Life!'" *

Few indeed, if any, of modern hymns have equalled that true song of the heart, by Sarah F. Adams, of Dorsetshire, England, commencing, "Nearer, my God, to Thee, — nearer to Thee." She was a person of "strong sensibility and deep religious earnestness." She died in 1849, after protracted illness; "almost her last breath," it is stated, "passed away in unconscious song." One of her hymns, less familiar to us, begins thus: —

* Christophers.

> He sendeth sun, He sendeth shower,
> Alike they're needful for the flower;
> And joys and tears alike are sent
> To give the soul fit nourishment.
> . As comes to me, or cloud or sun,
> Father, Thy will, not mine, be done!

One of the divinest of heart-utterances in song that modern times have bestowed upon us is that world-renowned hymnic prayer, —

> Just as I am, without one plea,
> But that Thy blood was shed for me,
> And that Thou bidst me come to Thee, —
> O Lamb of God, I come!

The cherished name of its author, Charlotte Elliott, will not easily be lost to the Church; for a sympathetic chord has been struck in this beautiful lyric, which must ever quicken into spiritual accord the heart of the Christian. The plaintive melody of the refrain cannot but awaken a responsive echo in every devout soul; as the sad notes of some lone bird are caught up and repeated amid the stillness of the sylvan solitude. This sweet singer is beautifully said to be "a lover of nature, a lover of souls, and a lover of Christ."

The hymn commencing, " My God, my Father, while I stray," was written in 1834. Another popular hymn of hers begins: —

My God, is any hour so sweet, from blush of morn to evening star,
As that which calls me to Thy feet, — the hour of prayer?
Blest is that tranquil hour of morn, and blest that hour of solemn eve,
When, on the wings of prayer upborne, the world I leave.

One more exquisite lyric from her pen we subjoin:

Thou glorious Sun of Righteousness,
    On this day risen to set no more;
Shine on me now to heal and bless,
    With milder beams than e'er before.
Shine on thy work of grace within,
    On each celestial blossom there;
Destroy each bitter root of sin,
    And make Thy garden fresh and fair.
Shine on Thy pure, eternal word,
    Its mysteries to my soul reveal;
And whether read, remembered, heard,
    Oh, let it quicken, strengthen, heal.
Shine on those unseen things displayed
    To faith's illuminated eye;
And let their splendor cast a shade
    On every earthly vanity.

As a fitting counterpart and companion to Miss Elliott's beautiful effusion is that written by Rev. R. S. Cook, of New York: it was sent by the author to Miss Elliott, and has since been incorporated into Sir R. Palmer's Collection.

Just as thou art, without one trace
Of love or joy or inward grace,
Or meetness for the heavenly place, —
    O guilty sinner, come!

. . . . .

Burdened with guilt, wouldst thou be blest?
Trust not the world, it gives no rest:
I bring relief to hearts oppressed, —
    O weary sinner, come!

Come, leave thy burden at the cross,
Count all thy gains but empty dross:
My grace repays all earthly loss, —
    O needy sinner, come!

Come, hither bring thy boding fears,
Thy aching heart, thy bursting tears,
'Tis mercy's voice salutes thine ears, —
    O trembling sinner, come!

There is a Wordsworthian simplicity and touching beauty about the following sweet lyric, that every one will admit on its perusal. The author is A. D. F. Randolph, of New York: —

A little child, six summers old, so thoughtful and so fair,
There seemed about her pleasant ways a more than childish air,
Was sitting one sweet summer eve beneath a spreading tree,
Intent upon an ancient book that lay upon her knee.
She turned each page with careful hand, and strained her sight to see,
Until the drowsy shadows slept upon the grassy lea;
Then closed the book, and upward looked, and straight began to sing
A simple verse of hopeful love, this very childish thing:
"While here below, how sweet to know His wondrous love and story;
And then, through grace, to see His face, and live with Him in glory!"
That little child, one dreary night of winter wind and storm,
Was tossing on a weary couch her weak and wasted form;
And in her pain, and in its pause, but clasped her hands in prayer
(Strange that we had no thoughts of heaven while hers were only there),
Until she said: "O mother dear, how sad you seem to be!
Have you forgotten that He said, 'Let children come to me'?
Dear mother, bring the blessed Book; come, mother, let us sing."
And then again, with faltering tongue, she sung that childish thing:
"While here below, how sweet to know His wondrous love and story;
And then, through grace, to see His face, and live with Him in glory!"
Underneath a spreading tree a narrow mound is seen,
Which first was covered by the snow, then blossomed into green:
Here first I heard that childish voice that sings on earth no more,
In heaven it hath a richer tone, and sweeter than before:
"For those who know His love below," so runs the wondrous story,
"In heaven, through grace, shall see His face, and dwell with Him in glory!"

J. H. Abrahall, one of the living English poets, is author of the following: —

### VIA, VERITAS, VITA.

Hast thou been lured by pleasure gay
From the straight heavenward path to stray?
Seek Christ! In Him thou find'st the *Way!*

Fain wouldst thou, in the pride of youth,
The heights of knowledge climb forsooth?
At Christ's feet sit thou! He is *Truth!*

Dost tremble at the soul's stern strife
'Mid world with deadly dangers rife?
Let Christ dwell in thee! He is *Life!*

In reflecting upon the multitudinous array of sacred lyrics that have passed under our review, and which do not afford even an approximate idea of their vast numerical extent, we are amazed at their prodigious numbers.* How much more should we wonder, could we know the yet greater number of those silent ones, the music of whose souls has remained all unsung, and died with them. Dr. O. Wendell Holmes has made this thought the subject of one of the most delicious lyrics in the language. So, gentle reader, if you have not met with it, you shall no longer be deprived of an intellectual pleasure; and if you have read it, it will bear repeating. Here it is: —

We count the broken lyres that rest, where the sweet wailing singers slumber,
But o'er their silent sister's breast the wild flowers who will stoop to number?
A few can touch the magic string, and noisy Fame is proud to win them:
Alas, for those that never sing, and die with all their music in them!

* Germany alone boasts of having nearly one hundred thousand hymns.

Nay, grieve not for the dead alone whose song has told their hearts'
  sad story, —
Weep for the voiceless who have known the cross, without the
  crown of glory!
Not where Leucadian breezes sweep o'er Sappho's memory-haunted
  billow,
But where the glistening night-dews weep on nameless sorrow's
  churchyard pillow.
O hearts that break and give no sign, save whitening lip and fading
  tresses,
Till death pours out his cordial wine, slow-dropped from misery's
  crushing presses, —
If singing breath or echoing chord to every hidden pang were
  given,
What endless melodies were poured, as sad as earth, as sweet as
  heaven!

Endless, indeed, have been those melodies which have made musical the saddened hours of the Past. Like the innumerable sermons and homilies, they prove the inexhaustibility of the Bible; for the essence of both homilies and hymns is derived therefrom. And, like "the non-inventibility of Christ," — to quote the expressive phrase of Lavater, — this indefeasible usufruct of the Sacred Oracles proves their Divinity.

Here our desultory gossip as well as our selections ought, and would terminate, were it not for the silent yet eloquent claim of sundry sweet waifs of beauty, whose appeal is irresistible. In our extended pleasure-excursions among the various flower-gardens of sacred poesy, we have met with many an unacknowledged, modest, wayside blossom, seemingly all too coy to court the society of the rich parterre. Some of these we have culled, and now group together. They are gossamer-like, fragile, but very fair, many-colored, of delicate hue, and of dainty perfume; and will, we think, form a fitting and fragrant bouquet of memory, with which to close our Collectanea.

>Yet, O Time! attend my prayer,
>Though thy cold hand blight my hair,
>Touch me softly,—spare, oh, spare
>  Life's best beauty, love and truth:
>Let the withering control
>Of thy years, as on they roll,
>Spare the freshness of my soul,—
>  Spare the fervor of my youth!

---

'Tis not the number of the lines on life's fast filling page,
'Tis not the pulse's added throbs, which constitute their age.
Some souls are serfs among the free, while others nobly thrive;
They stand just where their fathers stood,—dead, even while they live!
Others, all spirit, heart, and sense; theirs the mysterious power,
To live, in thrills of joy or woe, a twelvemonth in an hour!
Seize, then, the minutes as they pass: the woof of life is thought,
Warm up the colors, let them glow, by fire or fancy fraught.
Live to some purpose; make thy life a gift of use to thee!
A joy, a good, a golden hope, a heavenly argosy!

---

>Up above, the thoughts that know not anguish,
>  Tender care, sweet love for us below,
>Noble pity, free from anxious terror,
>  Larger love, without a touch of woe.
>
>Down below, a sad, mysterious music
>  Wailing through the woods and on the shore.
>Burdened with a grand, majestic secret
>  That keeps sweeping from us evermore.
>
>Up above, a music that entwineth
>  With eternal threads of golden sound
>The great poem of this strange existence,
>  All whose wondrous meaning hath been found.

Down below, the church, to whose poor window
    Glory by the autumnal trees is lent,
And a knot of worshippers in mourning,
    Missing some one at the sacrament.

Up above, the burst of Hallelujah,
    And (without the sacramental mist
Wrapped around us like a sunlit halo)
    The great vision of the face of Christ!

---

Oh, rapture too seraphic! Oh, bliss beyond compare!
When our Saviour and His chosen ones break through the glowing air,
When the groans of marred creation are changed for songs of praise,
And earth and heaven, in concert sweet, their loud hosannas raise!

---

    Full of vows and full of labor,
        All our days fresh duties bring;
    First to God, and then our neighbor,
        Christian life is an earnest thing.

    Onward, ever onward pressing,
        Yet untried as angel's wing,
    Believing, doing, blest and blessing,
        Christian life is an earnest thing.

---

Thank God, for other feet that be by ours in life's wayfaring;
For blessed Christian charity, believing, when she cannot see,
Suffering her friends' infirmity, enduring and forbearing.

---

Yes, I need thee, heavenly city, my low spirit to upbear;
Yes, I need thee, earth's enchantments so beguile me with their glare:
Let me see thee then these fetters break asunder, I am free.
Then this pomp no longer chains me, faith hath won the victory!
Heir of glory! that shall be for thee and me!

Soon where earthly beauty blinds not, no excess of brilliance palls,
Salem! city of the holy! we shall be within thy walls,
There beside yon crystal river, there, beneath life's wondrous
    tree, —
There, with nought to cloud or sever, ever with the Lamb to be!
Heir of glory! that shall be for thee and me!

---

    Pilgrim of earth! who art journeying to heaven,
        Heir of eternal life, child of the day!
    Cared for, watched over, beloved and forgiven, —
        Art thou discouraged because of the way?

. . . . . . . .

    Be trustful, be steadfast, whatever betide thee,
        Only one thing do thou ask of the Lord, —
    Grace to go forward wherever He guide thee,
        Simply believing the truth of His word.

    Still on thy spirit deep anguish is pressing,
        Not for the yoke that His wisdom bestows;
    A heavier burden thy soul is distressing,
        A heart that is slow in His love to repose.

    Earthliness, coldness, unthankful behavior, —
        Ah, thou mayst sorrow, but do not despair;
    Even this grief thou mayst bring to thy Saviour,
        Cast upon Him e'en this burden and care.

    Bring all thy hardness, His power can subdue it:
        How full is the promise! the blessing how free!
    "Whatsoever ye ask in My name, I will do it;"
    "Abide in My love, and be joyful in Me!"

---

Be prayerful; ask, and thou shalt have strength equal to thy day;
Prayer clasps the Hand that guides the world, — oh, make it then
    thy stay;
    Ask largely, and thy God will be
    A kingly giver unto thee.

---

    Not *now*, my child, — a little more rough tossing,
        A little longer on the billows' foam;
    A few more journeyings in the desert-darkness,
        And *then* the sunshine of thy Father's home!

Not *now*, — for I have wand'rers in the distance,
  And thou must call them in with patient love;
Not *now*, — for I have sheep upon the mountains,
  And thou must follow them where'er they rove.

Not *now*, — for I have loved ones sad and weary;
  Wilt thou not cheer them with a kindly smile?
Sick ones, who need thee in their lonely sorrow;
  Wilt thou not tend them yet a little while?

Not *now*, — for wounded hearts are sorely bleeding,
  And thou must teach those widowed hearts to sing;
Not *now*, — for orphans' tears are thickly falling;
  They must be gathered 'neath some sheltering wing.

. . . . . . . .

Go with the name of Jesus to the dying,
  And speak that name in all its living power;
Why should thy fainting heart grow chill and weary?
  Canst thou not watch with me one little hour?
One little hour! and then the glorious crowning,
  The golden harp-strings, and the victor's palm;
One little hour! and *then* the Hallelujah!
  Eternity's long, deep thanksgiving psalm!

C. P

---

Life's youngest tides, joy-brimming, flow
  For him who lives above all years,
Who all-immortal makes the now,
  And is not taken in Times's arrears:
His life's a hymn the seraphim
  Might hark to hear or help to sing:
And to his soul the boundless whole
  Its bounty all doth daily bring.

---

O Thou true Life of all that live,
  Who dost, unmoved, all motion sway,
Who dost the morn and evening give,
  And through its changes guide the day!
Thy light upon our evening pour,
  So may our souls no sunset see,
But death to us an open door
  To an eternal morning be!

"Why weepest thou? whom seekest thou? the living with the
  dead?"
Take young spring-flowers and deck thy brow, for life with joy is
  wed:
>   The grave is now the grave no more!
>   Why fear to pass that bridal-chamber door?

---

I look to Thee in every need, and never look in vain;
I feel thy strong and tender love, and all is well again:
>   The thought of Thee is mightier far
>   Than sin and pain and sorrow are.

Discouraged in the work of life, disheartened by its load,
Shamed by its failures or its fears, I sink beside the road:
>   But let me only think of Thee,
>   And then new heart springs up in me.

Thy calmness bends serene above, my restlessness to still;
Around me flows Thy quickening life, to nerve my faltering will:
>   Thy presence fills my solitude;
>   Thy providence turns all to good.

---

Have you never felt the pleasure of forgiving fraud or wrong,
Rippling through your soul like measure sweet of sweetest poet's
  song?
Have you never felt that beauty lies in pain for others borne?
That the sacredness of duty bids you offer love for scorn?
'Tis the Christian, not the Stoic, that best triumphs over pain.

---

From lips divine, like healing balm to hearts oppressed and torn,
The heavenly consolation fell, " Blessed are they that mourn."
Unto the hopes by sorrow crushed a noble faith succeeds;
And life, by trials furrowed, bears the fruit of loving deeds,
How rich, how sweet, how full of strength, our human spirits are,
Baptized into the sanctities of suffering and of prayer!

---

The flowers live by the tears that fall from the sad face of the skies,
And life would have no joys at all, were there no watery eyes.
Love thou thy sorrow, grief shall bring its own excuse in after
  years,
The rainbow! — see how fair a thing God hath built up from tears.

Give words, kind words, to those who err:
Remorse much needs a comforter.
Though in temptation's wiles they fall,
Condemn not: we are sinners all.
With the sweet charity of speech,
Give words that heal, and words that teach.

---

When we cannot see our way,
Let us trust, and still obey:
He who bids us forward go
Will not fail the way to show.

---

Rest, weary soul!
The penalty is borne, the ransom paid,
For all thy sins full satisfaction made;
Strive not to do thyself what Christ has done,
Claim the free gift, and make the joy thine own:
No more by pangs of guilt and fear distrest,
Rest, sweetly rest!

---

A solemn murmur in the soul tells of the world to be,
As travellers hear the billows roll, before they reach the sea.

---

Beyond these chilling winds and gloomy skies, beyond Death's gloomy portal,
There is a land where beauty never dies, and love becomes immortal.

. . . . . . . .

The city's shining towers we may not see, with our dim, earthly vision;
For Death, the silent warder, keeps the key that opes those gates elysian;
But sometimes, when adown the western sky the fiery sunset lingers,
Its golden gates swing inward noiselessly, unlocked by unseen fingers;
And while they stand a moment half-ajar, gleams from the inner glory
Stream brightly through the azure vault afar, and half reveal the story.

O land unknown! O land of love divine! Father all-wise, eternal,
Guide, guide these wandering, way-worn feet of mine into those pastures vernal!

---

See the rivers flowing downward to the sea,
Pouring all their treasures bountiful and free;
Yet, to help their giving, hidden springs arise;
Or, if need be, showers feed them from the skies.
Watch the princely flowers their rich fragrance spread,
Load the air with perfumes, from their beauty shed;
Yet their lavish spending leaves them not in dearth,
With fresh life replenished from their mother earth.
Give thy heart's best treasures: from fair nature learn;
Give thy love, and ask not, wait not a return.
And the more thou spendest from thy little store,
With a double bounty God will give thee more.

---

Voices so many haunt me on my road,
Oh, tell me, Angel, which the voice of God?
"'Tis that which most relieves thee of thy load."

Yet to me, Angel, oft it doth appear
As if His voice were terrible to hear.
"That is thy own defect, and sin-born fear."

And oft about me is a voice at eve,
That tells me that for ever I shall grieve.
"That *He* hath such a voice, do not believe."

Yet sometimes, too, at eve, ill voices die,
And comes a whisper of tranquillity.
"*His* voice is speaking in that evening sigh."

And sometimes round me sweetest murmurs ring,
"There is a happy end for every thing."
"That is heaven's chorus, earthward echoing." *

---

Why shouldst thou fear the beautiful angel, Death,
Who waits thee at the portals of the skies,
Ready to kiss away thy struggling breath,
Ready with gentle hand to close thine eyes?

* Household Words.

How many a tranquil soul has passed away,
Fled gladly from fierce pain and pleasures dim,
To the eternal splendors of the Day!
And many a troubled heart still calls for him.

---

I am weary, my Saviour, of grieving Thy love:
Oh, when shall I rest in Thy pleasure above?
I am weary; but oh, let me never repine
While Thy word and Thy love and Thy promise are mine.

---

How easy it is to keep sin-free,
How hard thy freedom to recall!
For 'tis the heavenly doom that we
Forget the heavens from which we fall.
What holy lives we all should live,
Might we remember joy and pain:
Alas, that memory, like a sieve,
Should hold the chaff and drop the grain!

---

Words are mighty, words are living,— serpents with their venomed stings,
Or bright angels, crowding round us, with heaven's light upon their wings:
Every word has its own spirit, true or false, that never dies;
Every word man's lips have uttered lives on record in the skies.

---

I slept, and dreamed that life was beauty;
I woke, and found that life was duty.
Was my dream, then, a shadowy lie?
Toil on, sad heart, courageously;
And thou shalt find thy dream shall be
A noon-day light and truth to thee.

---

Call them not *dead*,— the faithful, whom
    Green earth closed lately o'er,
Nor search within the silent tomb
    For those who "die no more."
The cold earth hides them from our love,
But not from His, who pleads above.

. . . . . .

> We saw the momentary cloud,
>   The pale eclipse of mind,
> From earthly sight, that came to shroud
>   The deathless ray behind;
> A moment more, the shade is gone, —
> The sun, the spirit, burneth on.
>
> To die: 'tis but to pass, all free,
>   From death's dominion here,
> To burst the bonds of earth, and flee
>   From every mortal fear;
> To plunge within that gulf untried,
> And stand beyond it, glorified.

Having thus completed our swift survey of the broad domain of sacred song, we now, gentle reader, offer a valedictory word at parting; and a kindly word it should be, inspired by the goodly company we have been sharing during this decade of pleasant evenings. Very delicious have been these manifold melodies of Christian faith and hope, coming to us athwart the centuries. Our ears have been feasted with their concord of sweet sounds; and our hearts, — have they not been stirred, and oft-times thrilled, with sympathetic emotion? Have we not felt our souls so refreshed and quickened by their celestial ministrations, — their gushes of holy song, — as to desire not only to enshrine their memory in our inmost hearts, but also — catching the sweet infection of their tuneful experience — to render our own a perpetual hymn of praise? To be in sympathetic harmony with these heaven-taught singers, we, too, should seek to rehearse the story of the Cross, in like persuasive eloquence of lip and life, that others, nay, that all, may become participants of "the unspeakable Gift." Then may we hope that the great matin-hymn of Christianity, ever fresh as from the lips of angels on the plain of Bethlehem, shall be echoed from every clime of earth, and ascend in one grand choral chant, as incense to the sanctuary of Heaven.

> "There angels fold, in love, their snowy wings,
>   There sainted lips chant in celestial measure,
> And spirit-fingers stray o'er heaven-wrought strings;
>   There loving eyes are to the portals straying,
> There arms extend, a wanderer to enfold;
>   There waits a dear, a holier One, arraying
> His *own* in spotless robes and crowns of gold."

But the rich Christian melodies which have been so long regaling our listening ear are now to cease; and in parting with the sweet companionship of these gifted sons of song, we linger fondly to catch the last echoing cadences of their delicious numbers; as we are wont to do over the farewell syllables of cherished friends. For have we not been privileged to share alike in their ecstatic raptures and their sorrowing refrains, their beautiful lessons of wisdom and their soul-exulting prophecies? Many-hued have been their bright creations, and many-voiced their melodious utterances; but the burden of their song is interpenetrated by one and the same great theme, — the Cross of Calvary, and the spiritual warfare which it inspires in every true human soul. This great central fact of our Christian faith has been, throughout the procession of the centuries, the grand altar-shrine around which the priesthood of sacred song have ever rendered the homage of their votive offerings. As we have seen, in the earliest ages, the Hebrews chanted, in solemn numbers, their anthems of adoration, by the inspired lips of their prophet-bards; and in the apostolic Church the same sublime chorus was taken up in the language of the polished Greek; while it was again re-echoed in the majestic cadences of the Latin, with some variations, throughout the lapse of the mediæval ages, down to the glorious epoch of the Reformation, when it found heroic utterance in the German; and lastly, in the rich combinations of our own glorious vernacular. Nor will the theme, so august and sublime, ever become trite, or lose aught of its soul-quickening energy, either with poet or peasant, so long as time shall last, or human hearts shall continue to be saddened by the sins and sorrows of earth, or soothed and solaced by the entrancing visions of the rapturous and saintly joys of Heaven. For never should it be forgotten, that, among the royalties and beatitudes of that world of light and life, evermore the voice of holy psalm and glad hosanna thrills the happy spirits of its redeemed and rejoicing multitudes, with an ecstasy of bliss altogether unknown to the denizens of this shadowy, sin-smitten world of ours. Would we, then, aspire to the true nobility of Christian life, — while we cherish chiefly the rich treasury of Divine Truth enshrined in the sacred Oracles, — let us not hold in small esteem their spiritual teachings, conveyed to us by these beautiful translations into song.

> "God sent His singers upon earth,
> With songs of sadness and of mirth,
> That they might touch the hearts of men,
> And bring them back to heaven again."

Then, even as a wayside sacrament will these persuasive measures prove to us, along our pilgrim-path, — brightening and beautifying our dark and shady places, — and, as by a divine alchemy, transmuting our bitterest sorrows into serenest joys. Let memory be but true to her trust, and, among the choicest of her spoils, as a celestial benison, will be the precious legacy thus bequeathed to us by the gifted and the good, — the priesthood of holy song. Like some saintly evangel will these sweet lyrics oft-times prove their potency, by urging our dull souls, full panoplied for the warfare, — with sandal-shoon and pilgrim-staff, — onward and upward in the divine life; till, leaving the discordant accompaniments of earth all forgotten, we attain to where —

> "No groans shall mingle with the songs
> Which warble from immortal tongues."

# INDEX OF NAMES.

|   | PAGE |
|---|---|
| ABNEY, Sir T. | 284 |
| Abrahall, J. H. | 477 |
| Adam of St. Victor | 58 |
| Adams, Mrs. S. F. | 473 |
| Addison, J. | 281 |
| Adolphus, Gustavus | 121, 125, 181 |
| Albert, Prince | 172 |
| Aldana, F. de | 206 |
| Alexander, Rev. W. | 467 |
| Allston, W. | 382 |
| Ambrosian hymnology | 32, 36 |
| Andrew of Crete | 27 |
| Anatolius of Constantinople | 27 |
| Angelo, Michel | 200 |
| Anselm of Lucca | 63 |
| Arndt, F. M. | 156 |
| ———, Frederick | 134 |
| Arnold, G. | 130, 135 |
| Apocalypse, the | 20 |
| Atterbury, Bishop | 293 |
| Augsburg Confession | 123 |
| Augustine, St. | 33, 291 |
| BACON, Lord | 225 |
| Baird, Rev. C. W. | 459 |
| Barbauld, Mrs. | 353 |
| Barrow, Dr. I. | 338 |
| Barton, Bernard | 421 |
| Baxter, Rev. R. | 275 |
| Beattie, J. | 347 |
| Bede, the "Venerable" | 49 |
| Beecher, Rev. H. W. | 14, 18, 272 |
| Beddome, B. | 326 |
| Bernard of Clairvaux | 51 |

|   | PAGE |
|---|---|
| Bernard of Cluny | 55 |
| Berridge, J. | 336 |
| Bethune, Rev. G. W. | 412 |
| Bickersteth, Rev. E. H. | 453 |
| Blair, R. | 289 |
| Blake, W. | 358 |
| Boehler, P. | 322 |
| Bogatzky, C. H. | 158 |
| Bohemia, Eliz., queen of | 211 |
| Bonar, Rev. H. | 426 |
| Bonnar, Rev. J. | 339 |
| Bossuet, Rev. J. B. | 196 |
| Bowring, Sir J. | 203, 422 |
| Boyse, J. | 304 |
| Brady and Tate | 275 |
| Bremer, Frederika | 389 |
| Breithaupt, J. | 132 |
| Brontë, Charlotte | 434 |
| Browne, Sir T. | 264 |
| ———, Mrs. Phœbe | 441 |
| Browning, Mrs. E. B. | 32, 414 |
| Bryant, W. C. | 458 |
| Bunyan, J. | 277 |
| Burnett, Bishop | 340 |
| Burns, Robert | 360 |
| Byrom, J. | 294 |
| Byron, Lord | 395 |
| CALVIN, J. | 188 |
| Campbell, T. | 289, 363 |
| Canada, mission to | 191 |
| Canitz, Baron von | 131 |
| Captives to the Indians | 357 |
| Carlyle on Luther | 92 |

## INDEX OF NAMES.

| | PAGE |
|---|---|
| Cary, Alice | 462 |
| ———, Phœbe | 463 |
| Catholic League, the | 122 |
| Cennick, J. | 326 |
| Chalmers, T. | 348 |
| Charles, Mrs. | 425 |
| Charlemagne | 46 |
| Christianity | 184 |
| Clarke, J. F. | 463 |
| Clement of Alexandria | 21 |
| Coleridge, S. T. | 99, 376 |
| ———, Hartley | 377 |
| Collier, A. | 258 |
| Colonna, V. | 201 |
| Congregational singing | 274 |
| Cook, Rev. R. S. | 475 |
| Cooper, G. | 464 |
| Cosmas | 27 |
| Council of Constance | 87 |
| ——— of Trent | 84 |
| Cowper, W. | 341, 346 |
| Coxe, Bishop A. C. | 449 |
| Crabbe, Rev. G. | 358 |
| Craig, Isabella | 429 |
| Craik, Mrs. | 423 |
| Crashaw, R. | 250 |
| Crewdson, Jane | 433 |
| Cross, idolatry of the | 49 |
| Crosswell, Rev. W. | 411 |
| Curry, Otway | 465 |
| | |
| DACH, Simon | 128, 150, 177 |
| Damascenus, J. | 29 |
| Damiani, Cardinal | 62 |
| Dante Alighieri | 199 |
| D'Aubigne, Merle | 85, 188 |
| David's Psalms | 13 |
| Davis, J. | 231 |
| ———, T. | 448 |
| Davies, S. | 327 |
| Day, Stephen | 309 |
| Denny, Sir E. | 469 |
| De Pontes, Madame | 153 |
| Derzhavin, G. R. | 206 |
| De Wette | 137 |
| Dies Iræ | 68, 70 |
| Dies Vitæ | 72 |
| Diet of Spires, the | 91 |
| Doane, Bishop, G. W. | 409 |
| Donne, Dr. John | 14, 230 |
| Dryden, J. | 265 |

| | PAGE |
|---|---|
| Drummond H. | 190, 233 |
| Dwight, Rev. Dr. | 356 |
| Duffield, Rev. G. | 439 |
| | |
| EARLY English hymns | 219 |
| Essay on Man | 292 |
| Elizabeth, Queen of Bohemia | 211 |
| Elliott, Charlotte | 474 |
| Ephræm Syrus | 23 |
| | |
| FABER, Rev. F. W. | 442 |
| Feltham, Owen | 419 |
| Fénelon, Archbishop | 196 |
| Fleming, Paul | 133 |
| Fletcher, Giles | 227 |
| Flatman, T. | 290 |
| Foolish Dick | 313 |
| Fortunatus, V. | 47 |
| Francke, A. H. | 150 |
| Franzin, Bishop | 182 |
| Fuller, Thomas | 227, 288 |
| | |
| GAUSSEN, M. | 19, 190 |
| Gerhardt, P. | 141, 146 |
| Gellert, C. F. | 154 |
| German Hymn-book | 140 |
| Germany, Reformation in | 87 |
| ———, Protestant feuds | 118, 123 |
| Gerson, J. | 65 |
| Gervinus on Luther | 92 |
| Geneva, city of | 187, 188 |
| Gill, Rev. W. | 272 |
| Gilfillan, Rev. R. | 11 |
| Gleim, J. W. L. | 152 |
| Gloria in excelsis | 23 |
| Goethe, J. W. von | 166 |
| Graham, J. | 361 |
| Grant, Sir R. | 390 |
| Gray's Elegy | 305 |
| Gray, D. | 406 |
| Greeley, Horace | 17 |
| Green, T. | 349 |
| Gregorian Chant, the | 45 |
| Gregory the Great | 44 |
| ——— of Nazianzum | 25 |
| Greenland, mission to | 180 |
| Gustavus Adolphus | 121, 125, 181 |
| Gutig, J. | 178 |
| Guyon, Madame | 187, 191 |
| | |
| HABAKKUK, book of | 13 |
| Habington, W. | 253 |

## INDEX OF NAMES.

| | PAGE |
|---|---|
| Haldane, R. | 188 |
| Hall, Rev. R. | 33, 349 |
| Hamilton, Rev. J. | 19, 299 |
| Handel's Tunes | 322 |
| Hart, J. | 296 |
| Heber, Bishop | 388 |
| Hebrew Lyrics | 12 |
| Heermann, J. | 129 |
| Hemans, Mrs. F. | 411 |
| Henrietta, Princess L. | 108 |
| Hensser-Schweizer, Mrs. M. | 168 |
| Herbert, George | 240 |
| Hermann, N. | 108 |
| Herrick, R. | 236 |
| Heylyn, P. | 232 |
| Hilary, St., of Arles | 35 |
| Hildebert of Tours | 64 |
| Hilten, J. | 87 |
| Hofel, J. | 111 |
| Holland | 185 |
| Holmes, O. W. | 477 |
| Hood, T. | 402 |
| Hope, H. | 433 |
| Houghton, Lord | 419 |
| Howitt, Mary | 430 |
| ——, William | 431 |
| Huntingdon, Lady | 334 |
| Huss, J. | 87, 100 |
| Hymnology of Europe | 197 |
| Hymns, English | 272 |
| ——, their influence | 126, 357 |
| IMMORTALITY, conscious | 445 |
| Indulgences | 85 |
| Irving, Rev. Edward | 14 |
| Isaiah, extract from | 13 |
| JEFFREY, Lord | 404 |
| Jerusalem, my happy home | 76 |
| Joseph, St., of the Studium | 28 |
| Jude, extract from | 19 |
| Judson, Rev. A. | 392 |
| KAMPHUYZEN, D. R. | 185, 203 |
| Keble, J. | 252, 399 |
| Ken, Bishop | 280 |
| Kennedy, B. H. | 429 |
| Khernvimij, M. | 210 |
| King, Bishop H. | 237 |
| Kingsley, Rev. C. | 417 |
| Klopstock, F. T. | 166 |

| | PAGE |
|---|---|
| Knox, W. | 404 |
| Körner, C. T. | 164 |
| LANGBECKER. | 111 |
| Lange, P. | 137 |
| Lindemann, J. | 139 |
| List, H. W. | 417 |
| Löwenstern, M. A. von | 135 |
| Lomonossov, M. V. | 210 |
| Longfellow, H. W. | 278, 451 |
| Lope de Vega | 204 |
| Louis, emperor | 186 |
| Lowell, Mrs. | 450 |
| ——, J. R. | 450 |
| Lucas, Archbishop | 102 |
| Luke, Mrs. J. | 447 |
| Luther, M. | 88, 92, 98, 104, 106 |
| Lützen, battle of | 124, 126 |
| Lyte, Rev. H. F. | 471 |
| Lyttleton, Lord | 375 |
| MACDONALD, Rev. G. | 236, 247, 255 |
| Macduff, Rev. Dr. | 446 |
| McCheyne, Rev. Mr. | 445 |
| Maerlant, J. van | 187 |
| Mahan, Rev. Dr. | 20 |
| Malan, Rev. C. | 190, 193 |
| Malt, Sermon on | 337 |
| Manrique, Don J. | 204 |
| Marpurger | 158 |
| Maria, Queen of Hungary | 214 |
| Marot, Clement | 195 |
| Mary, Queen of Scots | 193 |
| Marvell, A. | 264 |
| Mason, Rev. Dr. | 190, 276 |
| Massey, Gerald | 461 |
| Mediæval hymns | 43 |
| Melancthon, P. | 92 |
| Mentz Cathedral | 186 |
| Mercer, Margaret | 431 |
| Methodist minister | 308, 325 |
| —— conference | 335 |
| Michel Angelo | 200 |
| Miles, Mrs. S. A. | 463 |
| Miller, J. | 99, 290 |
| Milton, J. | 254 |
| Milman, Dean H. H. | 400 |
| Moir, D. M. | 402 |
| Monsell, Rev. Dr. | 448 |
| Montgomery, J. | 283, 351, 369 |
| Moore, T. | 383 |

# INDEX OF NAMES.

| | PAGE |
|---|---|
| More, Mrs. H. | 354 |
| Moravian Brethren | 102 |
| Mothers, influence of | 299 |
| Motherwell, W. | 407 |
| Muhlenburg, Rev. Dr. | 457 |
| NAVARRE, Queen of | 194 |
| Neale, Rev. J. M. | 432 |
| Neander, J. | 112 |
| ———, J. A. W. | 115, 117 |
| Neumark, G. | 178 |
| Newman, Rev. Dr. | 444 |
| Newton, Rev. J. | 341 |
| Nicene Creed, the | 25 |
| Nicolai, Dr. P. | 109 |
| Niebuhr, B. G. | 184 |
| Norris of Bermerton | 247 |
| Novalis, F. von | 169 |
| OLIVERS, T. | 328 |
| Olney Hymns, the | 341 |
| O mother dear, Jerusalem | 75 |
| Oscar, King of Sweden | 183 |
| Oxford, city of | 333 |
| PALMER, Rev. Ray | 454 |
| Parr, Harriet | 439 |
| Perkins, J. H. | 465 |
| Perronet, Rev. E. | 462 |
| Peter the Venerable | 64 |
| ——— the Hermit | 66 |
| Petrarch, F. | 197 |
| Petöfi, S. | 213 |
| Phile, M. | 32 |
| Poetry, birthplace of | 11 |
| Pollok, R. | 406, 408 |
| Pope, A. | 289 |
| Porter, Professor | 168, 171 |
| Power, P. B. | 272 |
| Proctor, A. A. | 418 |
| ———, B. W. | 416 |
| Praise, invocation to | 271 |
| Prayer, power of | 432 |
| Protestant union | 122 |
| ———, origin of name | 91 |
| Prudentius | 37 |
| Psalms, the | 14 |
| QUARLES, F. | 238 |
| RALEIGH, Sir W. | 223 |
| Rambach, J. J. | 164 |

| | PAGE |
|---|---|
| Randolph, T. | 231 |
| ———, A D. F. | 476 |
| Reed, Rev. A. | 389 |
| Reed, Professor | 395 |
| Reformation, the | 83 |
| Responsive chanting | 34 |
| Reynolds, Dr. | 105 |
| Ringwaldt | 107 |
| Rhyme-Bible | 187 |
| Robert II. of France | 61 |
| Robertson, Rev. Dr. | 363 |
| Robinson, Rev. Mr. | 349 |
| Rock of Ages | 352 |
| Romaine, Rev. W. | 335 |
| Rosegarten | 111 |
| Rosenkranz, Baron von | 178 |
| Rothe | 149 |
| Rückert, F. | 171 |
| Ryland, Rev. J. | 356 |
| SACHS, H. | 96, 100, 102 |
| Saint George and dragon | 46 |
| Sandwich-Islands hymn | 215 |
| Sandys, G. | 232 |
| Savonarola, J. | 87, 199 |
| Schaff, P. | 69, 109 |
| Schiller, J. C. F. | 157 |
| Schmolke, B. | 139 |
| Scott, Sir W. | 360 |
| Scottish Sabbath | 359 |
| Seagrave, R. | 293 |
| Sedgewick, D. | 273 |
| Selnecker, N. | 101 |
| Seidl | 151 |
| Sermon, Saxon | 67 |
| ———, long | 338 |
| Shakspeare, W. | 228 |
| Shepherd, Rev. J. | 396 |
| Shirley, Rev. W. | 305 |
| ———, J. | 253 |
| Shipton, Anna | 469 |
| Sleeping in church | 338 |
| Smart, C. | 303 |
| Smith, Horace | 386 |
| Song, magic of | 436 |
| Sidney, Sir P. | 225 |
| Southey, R. | 378 |
| ———, Mrs. | 379 |
| Southwell, R. | 224 |
| Spenser, E. | 221 |
| Speratus, P. | 102 |

## INDEX OF NAMES. 495

| | PAGE | | PAGE |
|---|---|---|---|
| Spitta | 169 | VAUGHAN, Henry | 277 |
| Stabat mater | 72 | Vega, C. Lope de | 204 |
| Staupitz, Dr. | 89 | Veni, Creator Spiritus | 46 |
| Steele, R. | 290 | Virgin, worship of the | 77 |
| ———, Anne | 340 | Vittoria Colonna | 202 |
| Stephen of St. Sabbas | 31 | Vondel, J. van den | 185 |
| Sternhold and Hopkins | 275 | | |
| Stoke Pogis Church | 307 | WALLENSTEIN | 123 |
| Stowe, Mrs. H. B. | 464 | Waller, E. | 248 |
| Stowell, H. | 461 | Walton, Izaak | 249 |
| Swedish hymns | 180 | Warburton, Bishop | 291 |
| Swift, Dean | 338 | Waring, Miss A. L. | 470 |
| Synesius of Cyrene | 26 | Watts, I. | 283, 286, 335 |
| | | Weiszel | 134 |
| TASSO, T. | 197 | Welthem, L. van | 185 |
| Tate and Brady | 275 | Wesley, C. and J. | 309, 313 |
| Taylor, Isaac | 11, 81 | ———, S. | 317 |
| ———, Jeremy | 251 | Wetzel, F. G. | 100 |
| Te Deum laudamus | 32 | White, H. K. | 387 |
| Temperance | 338 | ———, Rev. J. B. | 375 |
| Tennyson, Alfred | 420 | Whitefield, Rev. | 334, 338 |
| Tersanctus | 32 | Whittier, J. G. | 466 |
| Tersteegen | 159, 161 | Wickliffe, J. | 100 |
| Tetzel outwitted | 86 | Williams, W. | 326, 375 |
| Theoclistus | 29 | Willis, N. P. | 459 |
| Theodulph of Orleans | 187 | Willmott, Rev. R. A. | 222, 281 |
| Thirty years' war | 122, 127 | Wilson, Professor J. | 20, 361 |
| Thomas à Kempis | 65 | Winkworth, Miss C. | 98 |
| ——— of Celano | 68 | Wither, G. | 234 |
| Thomson, James | 294 | Wordsworth, W. | 363, 366 |
| Toplady, A. | 350 | ———, Rev. Dr. | 428 |
| Townsend, E. W. | 459 | Wotton, Sir H. | 231, 233 |
| Trench, Archbishop | 122, 141, 425 | Wreck of "Golden Mary" | 439 |
| Trotznou | 100 | Wulffer | 129 |
| Tuckerman, H. T. | 460 | | |
| Turner, D. | 336 | YOUNG, A. | 462 |
| | | ———, E. | 287 |
| UHLAND, L. | 162 | | |
| Ulrich, Duke | 136 | ZEHN, | 147 |
| Uniformity of convent life | 77 | Zinzendorf, Count | 100, 147 |
| Universal Prayer, by Pope | 292 | Zwingli | 94, 97 |

Cambridge: Press of John Wilson & Son.

www.ingramcontent.com/pod-product-compliance
Lightning Source LLC
Chambersburg PA
CBHW021424300426
44114CB00010B/638